Musical Works, Copyright, and Generative AI

Musical Works, Copyright, and Generative AI

Legal Perspectives on Originality and Authorship

Anton Ylikallio

Wolters Kluwer

Published by:
Kluwer Law International B.V.
PO Box 316
2400 AH Alphen aan den Rijn
The Netherlands
E-mail: lrs-sales@wolterskluwer.com
Website: www.wolterskluwer.com/en/solutions/kluwerlawinternational

Sold and distributed by:
Wolters Kluwer Legal & Regulatory U.S.
920 Links Avenue
Landisville, PA 17538
United States of America
E-mail: customer.service@wolterskluwer.com

ISBN 978-94-035-2669-0

e-Book: ISBN 978-94-035-2679-9
web-PDF: ISBN 978-94-035-2689-8

Table of Contents

Preface

This dissertation examines the copyright eligibility of AI-generated musical compositions, exploring whether such works can qualify for protection under copyright law and, if so, who may claim authorship. The dissertation adopts a *de lege lata* approach, assessing the existing legal framework rather than proposing reforms. Likewise, it does not seek to advocate for granting copyright protection to AI-generated compositions.

The study employs a doctrinal legal research method, interpreting and systematising the relevant legal framework while incorporating insights from musicological analysis. It presents a novel approach to understanding musical works by deconstructing the compositional process into three stages: the underlying work, the source material, and prospective reproductions. This framework enables a precise mapping of creative input within AI-assisted compositional processes and facilitates an evaluation of whether copyright protection should be granted to AI-generated music.

A key issue explored is the relationship between pre-generation creative contributions (e.g., training data selection, model fine-tuning, and prompt engineering) and the final output generated by the AI system. The dissertation develops a benchmark for assessing whether these pre-generation contributions meet the requirements for copyright protection, drawing on case law and analogies from traditional frameworks for assessing musical compositions in a copyright law context. The analysis suggests that copyright eligibility hinges on the specificity and precision of the instructions shaping the musical work, as well as how clearly they are reflected in the resulting composition.

The dissertation utilises interdisciplinary analysis, combining legal and musicological perspectives to assess the originality and authorship of AI-generated music. In addition to theoretical inquiry, the study incorporates so-called mock performances and template compositions to illustrate how different degrees of human involvement influence the final musical output. By systematically analysing these factors, the dissertation offers a structured approach to determining the role of human creativity in AI-assisted compositions. This study argues that while AI presents new challenges, existing copyright principles can be adapted to address these complexities, ensuring a balanced approach between innovation, authorship rights, and legal certainty. The findings indicate that while some AI-assisted compositions may qualify for protection under existing legal standards, many will fail to meet the originality threshold.

Acknowledgements

The beginning of my project was marked by balancing careers in both law and music. Typically, I would start the morning with legal research and spend the rest of the day in my capacity as a musician, playing concerts, teaching piano, or handling administrative tasks. In autumn 2023, I shifted to full-time legal research with the express intent of completing my book. This was made possible by grants from *Svensk-Österbottniska Samfundet* and *Olga ja Kaarle Oskari Laitisen säätiö*, to whom I extend my thanks for their generous support. I have now completed the transition from a career as both musician and lawyer to full-time legal scholar at the University of Helsinki Faculty of Law. Still, music occupies a special role in my life, and I believe it gives me a unique lens through which to approach both legal analysis and other matters.

Many people have been part of this project and deserve my gratitude, but I want to single out a few in particular. First, I want to thank my primary doctoral supervisor, Professor Marcus Norrgård, for providing support and encouragement as well as valuable scholarly advice. It is no exaggeration to say that my career in legal research – and this book – would never have happened without your guidance. Second, I want to thank my secondary doctoral supervisor, Professor Taina Pihlajarinne, for insightful and precise comments on various versions of the manuscript, which greatly helped in keeping the core legal issues in sharp focus. Professor Anette Alén and Doctor of Laws Martti Kivistö read a draft in the summer of 2024, and your feedback helped me develop what was at the time a somewhat sprawling manuscript into a more coherent work. My thanks also go to Docent Katariina Sorvari and Professor Torger Kielland for acting as pre-examiners, reading and commenting on the final draft before it went into print. Even though you entered the process at a late stage, your observations helped me refine several important details. I also wish to thank Professor Ansgar Ohly for agreeing to act as opponent at the public defence of my dissertation. To round out the academic acknowledgements, I want to thank the wonderful people at the University of Helsinki Faculty of Law's Vaasa Unit for your warm companionship throughout my journey from undergraduate to faculty colleague.

Lastly, the biggest thanks go to my wife Anni and our daughters, Saga, Lilja, and Edith. You bring me joy and encouragement in good times and bad, whether in professional or personal matters. Without you sharing this journey, any achievement would feel incomplete.

Introduction

The inspiration for this book came from an unexpected intersection of my interests in law and music. In late 2020, I saw a video by Twoset Violin, a popular YouTube duo consisting of two professional violinists. The video showed them taking on the challenge of telling apart music composed by humans from pieces generated by AI. Each pair of samples contained one human-composed and one AI-generated composition. In several cases, both samples displayed striking musical appeal, leaving the listener unable to tell which was human-made. Though presented in a playful style, without any intent to raise deeper questions about AI's role in music, the high quality of the AI-generated pieces piqued my interest in the copyright implications of machine-created compositions. If AI systems can already compose with such proficiency, surely it is time to re-evaluate questions of authorship and copyright from an AI-specific perspective? With professional training in both law and music, I felt particularly drawn to this question and began to investigate it in earnest in early 2021. By then, copyright law's treatment of authorship and protection in the context of generative AI had already been the subject of lively scholarly debate for several years. My initial plan was to write an article on the copyright protection of AI-generated music. However, new facets kept emerging throughout the project, and what began as an article gradually evolved into a full-length book on the topic.

The writing of the book coincided with an exceptional period in the history of generative AI, both in terms of its capabilities and public reception. Generative AI is certainly not a new phenomenon, and it has attracted increasingly intense coverage from many perspectives throughout the 2010s. Nonetheless, the implications of high-performance generative AI applications were discussed mainly among professionals and enthusiasts, with the general public only vaguely aware of the issue. This changed considerably in the early 2020s. The release of advanced text-to-image generators provided something of a prelude, while the November 2022 launch of ChatGPT catapulted generative AI into widespread public awareness. This shift in perception became apparent whenever I discussed my research with family, friends, and acquaintances. Throughout 2021 and 2022, most people I spoke with – apart from those already interested in the field – grasped my research aims only in broad terms. In contrast, conversations in the past two years have prompted immediate recognition of the issues at stake, even among my least tech-savvy contacts. On the whole, it seems the planets were fortuitously aligned in the way my choice of research subject coincided with the rapid development of generative AI. For this, I am deeply grateful, and I hope this book will make a meaningful contribution to the timely discussion of copyright protection for AI-generated music.

CHAPTER 1

Introduction, Research Premise, and Methodology

1.1 INTRODUCTION

Artificial Intelligence (AI), commonly characterised as a branch of computer science focused on developing machines and systems capable of performing tasks traditionally considered to require human intelligence,[1] has played an increasingly significant role in society for many decades. In recent years, advancements in performance have accelerated the deployment of AI across various fields, igniting considerable media interest and discussions about AI potentially holding the key to addressing many of humanity's pressing challenges. Although most AI applications relate to functional tasks, the use of AI-powered tools for producing creative content has also become an increasingly important aspect of modern society. Capable text-to-image generators, such as DALL-E and Midjourney, were among the first programmes to demonstrate the artistic viability of generative AI technology, gaining widespread use even beyond technology enthusiast circles. However, both public perception and usage of generative AI arguably entered a new era with the November 2022 release of OpenAI's chatbot ChatGPT, which brought sophisticated large language models into the mainstream through its remarkable popularity.

While AI-generated music has yet to reach the level of artistic viability seen in image and text generators, it has nonetheless experienced significant growth in both performance and adoption in recent years. For example, AI music generator Udio attracted 600,000 users within its first two weeks of release in April 2024 and was reportedly generating 864,000 music files per day within a month of becoming publicly

1. Russell and Norvig 2010, pp. 1-2, list several definitions of AI. The AI Act Article 3(1) defines an 'AI system' as 'a machine-based system designed to operate with varying levels of autonomy, that ... infers, from the input it receives, how to generate outputs such as predictions, content, recommendations, or decisions that can influence physical or virtual environments'.

available.[2] Given such public interest, coupled with anticipated advancements in the underlying technology, it seems only a matter of time before music generation attains a role similar to that of image and text generation in content creation.

The increasing utilisation of generative AI presents complex challenges related to copyright, with two questions in particular standing out: how to regulate the use of protected works as training data and how to address the possibility of copyright protection for AI-generated outputs. Both issues are highly relevant to the content creation industry and the rapidly expanding market for AI-powered products, linking them to significant economic interests.[3] In addition, the quality of today's AI-generated content – unimaginable a mere decade ago – also prompts cultural and philosophical questions about the future value and role of human creativity. While some foresee a gradual displacement of human authorship, others remain sceptical of the concept of a truly creative AI model. As usual, the reality likely lies somewhere between these extremes. In any case, regulating training data usage and determining the copyright eligibility of AI-generated outputs will require balancing perspectives drawn from both economic and societal considerations.

This dissertation will explore copyright eligibility of AI-generated outputs with a special focus on musical content. Current state-of-the-art AI models function largely in a similar manner regardless of whether they generate images, text, or music, and the issue of copyright protection will be resolved in fundamentally similar ways across all disciplines. However, a special focus on music generation is warranted for two reasons. First, my own background makes this choice particularly relevant. In addition to my legal training, I also hold a master's degree in musical performance and have worked in the music industry in various roles for several years. This experience allows me to incorporate a musician's perspective alongside a legal-doctrinal one, enabling the formulation of nuanced arguments and research methodologies that explore less frequently observed possibilities. Second, although the advent of high-performance generative AI models necessitates a re-evaluation of authorship and copyright protection across all fields of creativity, I find that the process of composing music possesses certain idiosyncratic characteristics that make musical works a particularly intriguing field of study.

On this basis, I will present a perspective on the process of composing musical works that views the requisite creative input as the issuance of instructions describing musical attributes. This approach is designed to enable a more accurate 'mapping' of the creative phases involved in composing music, particularly as it relates to key

2. https://www.musicbusinessworldwide.com/the-train-has-left-the-station-ai-music-platform-udio-is-already-spitting/, accessed 27 August 2024.
3. A CISAC report published in December 2024 predicts that the market for generative AI music and audiovisual content will grow from EUR 3 billion today to EUR 64 billion by 2028. Similarly, revenues from generative AI services in these sectors are expected to rise from EUR 0.3 billion to EUR 9 billion annually, with AI-generated music projected to make up 20% of streaming platform revenues and 60% of music library revenues. At the same time, human creators are projected to face a EUR 22 billion revenue loss, with 24% of music and 21% of audiovisual earnings at risk due to AI's substitutional impact. Report available at https://www.cisac.org/Newsroom/news-releases/global-economic-study-shows-human-creators-future-risk-generative-ai, accessed 29 May 2025.

copyright law concepts such as authorship, work, originality, and reproduction. Through this process, the dissertation aims to provide new insights into how one can address the issue of claiming copyright for AI-generated musical compositions.

1.2 RESEARCH PREMISE AND QUESTIONS

The core research objective of this dissertation is to examine the copyright eligibility of AI-generated creative content. It will not discuss the question of whether and under what conditions the use of protected works as training data falls within the author's exclusive right under copyright law.

The primary research task can be illustrated through a practical example involving an AI model designed to generate musical compositions. We suppose the model was created by a team of developers who made a series of creative decisions, including the selection of training data and the design of the model architecture. The AI model – hereinafter called 'Model A' – allows users to select the genre, style, mood, key signature, and duration of the composition, after which the option to generate a track becomes available. Through this process, the users can generate musical compositions of passable artistic worth in the form of audio recordings.

Let us suppose a user, whom we call User A, creates a composition using Model A. He selects orchestral music as the genre, twentieth-century cinematic as the style, dramatic as the mood, E-flat minor as the key signature, and a duration of 2 minutes and 30 seconds. Upon pressing the 'generate track' button, a composition based on these selections is generated, which will be referred to as Composition A. Based on this scenario, two central questions are presented, which will guide the research conducted throughout this dissertation:

(1) Can Composition A and similar AI-generated compositions constitute musical works under copyright law?
(2) If they can, which party or parties can claim an exclusive right to them and on what grounds?

To address these questions, a total of five sub-questions concerning various features of the overarching inquiry need to be formulated. In examining whether the AI-generated Composition A constitutes a musical work, the key lies in examining the creative process that brought the composition into being. While there is little doubt that the melodic, rhythmic, and harmonic elements of Composition A would meet the traditional criteria for copyright protection if they had been manually created by a human composer, the question of protecting it depends on the nature of its creative process. Since protection can only be granted if the creative process satisfies the criteria generally applied to any work, the question – which presupposes certain components of the copyright assessment that will be discussed later – becomes:

(3) What are the requirements on the creative process of Composition A for it to qualify as a protected musical work?

The challenge in addressing this question lies in the fact that the utilisation of AI-powered tools introduces a new kind of relationship between creative input and resulting output. In examining the creative process of Composition A, it may well turn out that both the developers and the user of Model A engaged in creative decision-making of the kind usually associated with authorship and copyright protection. Yet, the connection between these choices and the melodic, rhythmic, and harmonic elements of Composition A may not be strong enough to warrant copyright protection. This raises one of the more challenging questions associated with copyright claims for AI-generated content:

(4) How should one determine whether the relationship between pre-generation creative contributions and the post-generation end result is to be considered sufficient to make the latter into a copyright-protected work?

In addressing this question, we are looking for the human contributions that shape or influence the musical attributes of the AI-generated – or AI-assisted – end result.[4] Some overarching comments on the interaction between human contributors and AI models are necessary here. Essentially, one can divide the stages at which humans participate in the creative process into three groups: development of the model, prompting, and post-generation manual editing of the model's outputs. Among these three groups, the input given during the manual editing stage is the least affected by the influence of generative AI technology. From a copyright law perspective, it functions similarly to any situation where a subsequent human contributor makes changes to a pre-existing composition,[5] and the post-generation contributor would be considered the author of all original passages added through manual revision of the AI-generated composition.

By contrast, *prompting* presents a novel challenge to assessing authorship and copyright protection.[6] The notion of incorporating the prompting of AI models into the process of creating new content, even in the context of artistically ambitious projects, has become ever more feasible as the performance of generative AI systems continues to improve. The prospect of incorporating prompting and AI-generation into creative projects appears particularly plausible in the field of text and image creation, due to the high levels of prompt adherence exhibited by systems such as ChatGPT or Midjourney. An important element of this dynamic is the possibility of editing the AI-generated text or image by issuing multiple iterative requests with the aim of refining certain selected aspects of the output. This potentially grants the AI system user considerable creative control over the end result, even in a process characterised by limited manual editing. Consequently, it is not surprising that the notion of creating copyright-protected works through prompting AI models has been discussed in the scholarly literature, with

4. The requirements of human input and a human author – as opposed to a machine author – is discussed in greater detail in Chapter 4.
5. Arrangements and other types of derivative compositions provide well-known examples of this scenario.
6. Prompting, or prompt engineering, is defined by Hu et al. 2021, p. 9 as the 'art of composing and formatting the prompt to maximize a model's performance on a desired task'. *See* section 2.1.4.

several scholars adopting a relatively positive attitude to the notion of creating protected works through prompting.[7]

Compared to their text and image-generating peers, current state-of-the-art music generation systems offer the user much less room for shaping the model output through prompting. Even the most capable systems only respond to prompts on a broad level (such as genre, style, instrumentation, and duration), which severely restricts the link between the user's creative choices and the musical attributes of the end result. Consequently, the outlook of this dissertation is that, at least for now, the creation of copyright-protected musical works through mere prompting is not particularly realistic. Of course, it is certainly possible to produce a protected musical work by first generating a composition based on broadly formulated prompts and then subjecting it to extensive post-generation manual editing. However, since that scenario will largely be covered by traditional analytical methods, such as those applied to derivative compositions, post-generation manual editing will not be considered when examining the relationship between pre-generation creative inputs and AI-generated outputs.

Accordingly, this dissertation will explore the entire pre-generation creative process – both prompting and development of the AI model – that contributes to shaping the musical attributes of the AI-generated outputs, to investigate whether the totality of creative choices made throughout the creative process could justify protecting the outputs. In addressing research question (4), a two-phase analysis of the relationship between the creative process and the resulting output will be applied. In the case of Composition A, the analysis unfolds as follows. First, the creative process must be examined to identify all the free and creative choices made prior to the AI model's generation of the composition and assess their contribution to shaping the musical attributes of Composition A. Second, one needs to evaluate whether the relationship between the creative choices made by the developers and the user of Model A and the musical attributes of Composition A is sufficiently close to provide a justifiable copyright claim to the composition.

While this two-phase framework addresses the core components of the copyright assessment in the context of generative AI, it does not directly clarify the precise conditions under which the relationship between the creative process and the resulting output can be considered sufficient. Even if one were to uncover all phases of training data selection, model architecture design, fine-tuning, and prompt engineering that precede Model A's generation of Composition A, along with their impact on Composition A's musical attributes, a clear method for determining the sufficiency of the relationship between creative choices and the resulting output remains elusive. In other words, it is not entirely clear by what criteria one should determine whether a sequence of pre-generation creative choices – such as model fine-tuning or prompt engineering – is to be deemed sufficiently linked to the post-generation end result. To provide new insights on this issue, the dissertation will deconstruct the compositional

7. A particularly liberal view is proposed by Lee 2024, p. 1539. More cautiously positive approaches are suggested by Leistner and Jussen 2025, pp. 18, 50 and Hugenholtz 2024, p. 18. The scholarly discussion on authoring protected works through prompting will be treated in greater detail in Chapter 7.

process and the ontology of a musical work to better understand how the concept is to be applied in the context of AI-assisted compositional processes. Accordingly, the fifth and sixth research questions will examine the ontological nature of musical works both in general and within the context of AI:

(5) How does a musical work come into being and how should one define its contents?
(6) How can one define the component parts of a musical work and the compositional process in a way that accurately accounts for the utilisation of AI-powered creative tools?

Although this dissertation's primary task is to examine the copyright eligibility of AI-generated music, a relatively thorough treatment of the ontology and components of musical works is also needed to explore these questions in sufficient depth. The analysis does not only consider how musical works have traditionally been treated under copyright law but also seeks to enhance the robustness of the analysis by incorporating musicological findings. By adding historical and interdisciplinary perspectives, the dissertation aims to offer a clearer basis for addressing the copyright eligibility of AI-generated music not only today but also in light of the likely rapid development of AI systems' functionality and performance. Given that these advancements are poised to open up new ways for human composers to interact with AI, it becomes increasingly important to revisit the ontological and epistemic aspects of musical works as understood in traditional copyright doctrine. By examining how the traditional framework has treated musical works – both in its explicit doctrines and its underlying assumptions – this analysis seeks to help establish a foundation for addressing the novel challenges that may arise from emerging and increasingly complex forms of human-AI interaction during the compositional process.

On this basis, the treatment of research question 5 will present a three-stage ontology of musical works divided into underlying work, source material, and prospective reproductions. This deconstruction contains both conventional and novel elements. The first and third stages of the ontology are reasonably conventional and have been treated in the scholarly literature through concepts such as inner and outer work, or the immaterial work and its manifestation. The second stage, however, introduces a novel perspective by treating the work's source material as an independent entity. Here, 'source material' refers to the communicative medium through which the abstract underlying work is externalised into actual musical expression. Musical notation and audio recordings have traditionally been the most common means of accomplishing this, but they do not constitute the only means available. The three-stage deconstruction can be illustrated as follows. In the first ontological stage, the composer conceptualises the underlying work as an abstract sequence of musical attributes. In the second ontological stage, the composer externalises the conceptualised work by representing its characteristics through some outwardly perceivable means, such as a music sheet or an audio recording. This constitutes the work's source material. In the third ontological stage, various agents – including but not limited to the composer – consult the musical information contained in the source material to reproduce the underlying work.

In many cases, *performing artists* play a significant role in transferring the contents of the work from the second to the third ontological stage. Performing artists are protected by separate neighbouring rights protection, which may come into play in scenarios involving AI-generated music. Phonogram producers' neighbouring rights may likewise be relevant in this context.[8] However, in this dissertation, the protection of AI-generated music – in the form of performances or audio recordings – will not be considered from the perspective of neighbouring rights protection. Instead, the focus is only on questions of authorship or copyright proper.

The three-stage deconstruction of the musical work's ontology helps define the contents of a work in the context of AI-assisted creative processes outlined in question (6). Importantly, it suggests that the process of composing a musical work ultimately constitutes an act of *issuing instructions*, whose execution can bring the intended musical expression into existence.[9] By viewing all compositional processes as acts of constructing instruction sets describing musical attributes, one can analogise traditional and AI-assisted compositional processes: Since a traditional compositional process ultimately amounts to the compilation of an instruction set, could not a sequence of pre-generation creative choices – such as an AI developer's efforts in training data selection or model fine-tuning – be deemed an analogous instruction set capable of providing an equally justifiable copyright claim to the resulting musical composition? After all, as the compilation of, e.g., a traditional music sheet is routinely deemed to produce a copyright-protected work, should not the same logic apply to the instructions issued in the context of AI-generated compositions? These questions warrant some commentary, leading to the most significant seventh research question.

Standard copyright doctrine posits that, whether one examines traditional musical notation or an AI developer's pre-generation creative efforts, the question of copyright protection hinges on whether the musical attributes – such as melody, rhythm, and harmony – produced through the execution of instructions can be linked to the prospective author's creative choices with sufficient precision and objectivity. This assessment necessitates a comparison between the instructions and the resulting musical expression to determine how similar they are, with a higher degree of similarity increasing the likelihood of granting protection. To justify a copyright claim, the instructions issued by the prospective author must influence the final output with sufficient specificity and precision. In the context of traditional musical composition and performance, this relationship tends to be straightforward: if a composer externalises her compositional conception by producing a music sheet, and a performer executes it with reasonable precision, the connection between the music sheet and the

8. The neighbouring rights of performing artists and phonogram producers are regulated in sections 45 and 46 of the FCA.
9. A similar point has been made by Arewa 2014, p. 470, who has characterised the musical work as a set of instructions. In addition, she emphasises that 'music is a performance art in which oral and aural aspects are essential'.

performance is generally clear enough to justify the composer's copyright claim to the work without issue.

As indicated above, this dissertation's research task is premised on the idea that a compositional process involving AI-powered tools is fundamentally similar to traditional composition. Here, too, there is an underlying conception of a musical composition on the part of the developer or user of the AI system, which is externalised through a sequence of pre-generation instructions. When the AI system executes these instructions to produce a musical composition, the contributors' compositional intentions are brought to fruition in a manner that parallels traditional composition. The analogy between a traditional and AI-assisted compositional process is summarised in the table below:

Prospective Author	*Instruction Set*	*Executor/Performer*	*End Result*
Traditional composer	Musical notation, audio recording, etc.	Performer(s)	Musical performance, audio recording
AI developer or user	Model development, fine-tuning, prompting	AI system	Musical performance, audio recording

Needless to say, this analogy is not without challenges. While both traditional and AI-assisted creative processes may be characterised as acts of issuing instructions, AI-assisted processes are more likely to face difficulties in meeting the specificity and precision requirements. This is because the instructions – related to training data selection, fine-tuning, prompts, etc. – may not describe the musical attributes of the resulting composition precisely enough to establish a convincing link between the pre-generation instructions and the post-generation output. This raises the following research question, which essentially reformulates question (4) with greater refinement:

(7) Under what conditions can one consider a sequence of instructions describing musical attributes: (i) to be sufficiently specific and (ii) sufficiently precisely reflected in the resulting composition to warrant copyright protection?

The primary issue weakening copyright claims for Composition A and other AI-generated compositions lies in the broadly formulated nature of pre-generation instructions. The AI system's generation process creates a barrier of inscrutability between the pre-generation creative choices and the final output, which means that these choices typically do not impact the final musical attributes with a high degree of specificity. Consequently, pre-generation instructions are unlikely to be reflected in the resulting composition with the same precision as when a composer manually produces a musical score and has it performed by a musician. The key question, therefore, is whether a sequence of pre-generation instructions can justify copyright protection even if they are only imprecisely reflected in the final composition. One scenario in which this might be considered sufficient for obtaining copyright protection is when the number of pre-generation instructions is high, since the imprecision in the execution of individual instructions may be offset by the sheer volume of instructions provided.

This argument can be illustrated by a comparison to Jackson Pollock's paintings. Pollock often employed a technique in which he poured, dripped, or splashed paint onto a canvas placed on the floor, resulting in a painting made up of abstract colour patterns.[10] While he could not control all the details of the patterns as precisely as a painter using traditional brush techniques, his painting is still likely to meet the originality threshold. This is because the number of creative decisions involved in producing the paintings was sufficiently high to outweigh the lack of precision in each individual choice. By making numerous choices guided by the underlying artistic vision, Pollock imprinted his 'personal touch' on the final result, thereby satisfying the requirements for copyright protection.

The same reasoning could be applied to the relationship between pre-generation choices and the post-generation result in the case of Composition A. One might hypothesise that Composition A qualifies for protection if the pre-generation choices are numerous enough and have sufficiently impacted the musical attributes of the composition. Although this provides reasonably clear criteria for determining the question of copyright protection, it is far from obvious when one should consider them to have been met. This dissertation aims to contribute new insights to the discussion by constructing a benchmark for assessing the sufficiency of the relationship between the creative process and end result that is applicable to all musical compositions, regardless of whether they are produced through traditional means or with AI-powered tools. The analogy between traditional and AI-assisted creative processes seeks to clarify the point at which an AI-generated composition may merit copyright protection and to identify the factors influencing this assessment.

As outlined in research question (7), the assessment of copyright eligibility hinges on two key components: the precision of the instruction set and the accuracy with which these instructions are translated into actual musical expression. To establish a general benchmark for evaluating these aspects, several musical compositions will be selected, and increasingly less accurate versions of each will be constructed. By examining this series of progressively altered renditions, it becomes possible to identify the point at which the relationship between the instruction set and its execution becomes too tenuous to justify copyright protection. This method will also provide insights about which factors most significantly influence the perceived distance between the instructions and their execution. The developed benchmark can then be applied to AI-assisted creative processes, providing insights into whether the connection between pre-generation contributions and post-generation results is sufficiently close to merit copyright protection. Further details on the execution of this

10. Pollock's painting technique is often used as an illustrative example by legal scholars addressing the issue of AI outputs and copyright protection. *See, inter alia,* Burk 2020, p. 263; Rognstad 2022, p. 185; Leistner and Jussen 2025, pp. 15-16.

examination will be discussed in the subsequent section concerning specific methodological questions.

Before concluding the presentation of the research task and questions, it is also worth noting that the overall emphasis of this dissertation will be on examining the law as it is (*de lege lata*) rather than how it should be (*de lege ferenda*). Likewise, there is no overarching intention to advocate for granting copyright protection to AI-generated compositions. Instead, the aim is to analyse the relevant materials and issues with objectivity and analytical argumentation, while acknowledging that absolute objectivity – at least in the strict sense – should be understood as an aspirational goal rather than an attainable state.

1.3 METHOD

1.3.1 Practical and Theoretical Approaches

This dissertation uses a doctrinal research method, through which it aims to interpret and systematise the contents of the applicable provisions. The distinction between interpretation and systematisation is also referred to as practical and theoretical approaches, respectively.[11] Overall, a practical examination focuses on interpreting specific statutes and other legally relevant statements, thereby approaching the law from a surface-level perspective. A theoretical examination, by contrast, endeavours to systematise the relevant field of law by developing its general doctrines into a coherent whole. It seeks to investigate the deeper-lying structures of the law, such as its core concepts and principles, to provide a framework that underlies or enables a case-specific interpretation of the appropriate provisions. The research questions listed in the previous section will require an approach that incorporates both practical and theoretical methods. Although the two approaches often overlap and interact, a closer reflection on their relationship in the context of this dissertation will help clarify the central aims of the research and the method through which these are pursued.

The practical-interpretative aspects of the research method are evident from the formulation of the research question. Determining whether AI-generated compositions can constitute musical works will require interpretation of section 1 of the Finnish Copyright Act (FCA), whose interpretation, in turn, needs to align with the CJEU's case law on the prerequisites of copyright protection. The surface-level interpretation focuses on assessing whether the requisites of originality have been met by the musical attributes exhibited by the composition under examination. The exclusive right to dispose of the work set out in FCA section 2 will also require interpretation to satisfactorily address the first research question.

The core concepts and principles of copyright law also need to be examined to satisfactorily address the research questions. The copyright law framework is arguably undergirded by a principle of neutrality that guides how the concepts of author and work are understood. In essence, the principle holds that access to authorship and

11. Hirvonen 2011, p. 22, Aarnio 1997, pp. 36-37.

copyright should not be impacted by factors such as the aesthetic merit, domain, or style a creation exhibits, or the technological means through which it is realised.[12] The principle is made evident by the broad range of modes or forms of expression a copyright-protected work can take. Not only does the FCA provide an extensive list of eligible forms of expression, but the neutral outlook is also reinforced by the provision's open-ended formulation.

Given the dissertation's focus on reconciling developments in generative AI technology and traditional copyright notions, the principle of technological neutrality plays a particularly central role. In the Framework Directive 2002/21, the EU expressed this by emphasising the 'desirability of making regulation technologically neutral, that is to say that it neither imposes nor discriminates in favour of the use of a particular type of technology, does not preclude the taking of proportionate steps to promote certain specific services where this is justified'.[13] Technological neutrality shapes the argumentation in this dissertation by examining how musical information is created and communicated from a neutral perspective, irrespective of the technical means employed.

In addition, overarching principles of proportionality, reasonableness, and fairness arguably also provide additional lenses through which the objectives of copyright law are examined when assessing the appropriate extent of the author's exclusive right in specific cases. These principles will come into play when examining how different vested interests should be weighed against each other in the light of copyright law's underlying objectives. One legislative instrument that reflects these considerations is the so-called three-step test. This test is embedded in both international conventions and treaties, as well as several EU directives,[14] and concerns the application of exceptions and limitations to copyright. It states that exceptions 'shall only be applied in certain special cases which do not conflict with a normal exploitation of the work or other subject-matter and do not unreasonably prejudice the legitimate interests of the rightholder'.[15] Given its focus on limiting the scope of copyright protection, the three-step test does not directly intersect with the main focus of this dissertation, which is to determine whether AI-generated compositions qualify for copyright protection in the first place.

Furthermore, shifting from the specifics of the three-step test to the broader foundations of copyright protection, copyright law's policy objectives are also arguably guided by overarching principles. A widely held view is that incentivising the creation

12. Haarmann 2014, p. 47; van Gompel and Lavik 2013, p. 3. Notably, the protection of stylistic features has been frequently discussed in due to the advent of high-performance generative AI, especially with regard to unlicensed copying of protected works for training data purposes and AI outputs' potential infringing of the training data. *See*, *inter alia*, Sobel 2024, pp. 1, 69-70; Sag 2023, p. 342.
13. Directive 2002/21 on a common regulatory framework for electronic communications networks and services (Framework Directive) [2002] OJ L108/33, Recital 18.
14. Article 9(2) Berne Convention, Article 13 TRIPS, Article 10(2) WIPO, Article 6(3) 1991 Computer Program Directive, Article 10(3) Rental Directive, and Article 5(5) Infosoc Directive.
15. Infosoc Directive Article 5(5).

of new works lies at the core of copyright law's policy rationale.[16] In his historical analysis of the Finnish conception of copyright, Kivistö identifies four key principles that have shaped the understanding of copyright as an object of ownership: rewarding authors for their intellectual endeavours, expanding the author's exclusive right, facilitating the smooth exchange of creative works, and safeguarding collective cultural or intellectual objectives by imposing limitations on exclusive rights.[17]

1.3.2 An Analytical Examination of Concepts

Concept definitions typically play a central role when examining the law. They are essential for legal argumentation in that they define and identify legal challenges in a given field of law by enabling lawyers to distinguish legally relevant material from other aspects of the surrounding factual reality. It is also with the help of concepts that legal issues or problems are located for further analysis.[18] Chief among the copyright law concepts to be examined throughout the dissertation are those of 'work' and 'reproduction'. Both concepts have direct normative relevance in that the statutory provisions tie certain legal consequences to them. As such, one might consider an examination of these concepts to constitute instances of surface-level interpretation rather than a theoretical systematisation. Although this characterisation accurately describes much of the research conducted in this dissertation, an examination through an analytical approach to doctrinal research introduces theoretical dimensions to the analysis as well.

The aim of the analytical method is to describe legal rules as accurately as possible by identifying ambiguities and uncertainties related to the concepts in use. By deconstructing and analysing them, it aims to produce a clearer and more comprehensive understanding of legally relevant questions and phenomena, thereby enhancing the resolution of legal problems.[19] In a somewhat polemic vein, the analytical method has also been described as aiming to reorganise and reformulate the relevant concepts to create a theoretical framework that allows the interpretation of surface-level legal norms 'without distracting theoretical baggage'.[20] Essentially, this outlook endeavours to break up traditional concepts into their constituent parts to facilitate an examination of the actual circumstances surrounding the relevant issue. Accordingly, it aims to enable an interpretation of statutory provisions better equipped to accommodate or take into account the social reality and the practical needs that spring from it.[21]

In this dissertation, the analytical approach is implemented by comparing the legal concept of 'authoring a musical work' to the actual process of 'composing a piece of music', to identify the conditions under which the act of composing should lead to

16. *See, inter alia,* Haarmann 2014, p. 46; Geiger 2021, p. 7; Senftleben 2023, p. 1536; Mezei 2020, p. 11; Pihlajarinne 2013, p. 1219, with further references.
17. Kivistö 2017, p. 225.
18. This formulation largely paraphrases Tuori 2000, p. 193. Smits 2017, p. 214 also makes a similar point. Aarnio 1997, p. 44 refers to concepts as the lens through which the legal reality is viewed.
19. Hirvonen 2011, p. 46.
20. Aarnio 1997, p. 43.
21. Aarnio 1997, p. 44.

considering the resulting composition a work. At its core, this involves critically examining the conceptual framework of copyright law by assessing potential discrepancies between the practical reality of composing and the legally defined concept of authoring a musical work. On this point, it resembles other research endeavours that seek insights into the concept of a work by examining the creative process from the perspective of those actively engaged in it.[22] More specific aspects of the method related to examining the relevant concepts from a musical expert's external perspective on copyright law will be addressed below.

1.4 SOURCES

1.4.1 The Traditional Three-Tier Hierarchy of Legal Sources

The pursuit of interpreting and systematising the law is intimately linked to determining the sources that qualify as legally relevant. This is typically addressed by placing the sources in hierarchical order based on the degree of legal relevance they have derived from the institutional weight carried by the party that issued it.[23] In the Finnish literature, Peczenik and Aarnio's three-part division of legal sources into categories of strongly binding, weakly binding, and allowed sources has been the paradigmatic approach, especially throughout the 1980s and 1990s.[24] Under this view, the sources are evaluated based on the degree to which they bind the judge's decision-making in a given case. Statutory texts and fundamental rights constitute *binding sources*, which a judge must follow. The legislator's preparatory works and the Supreme Court's case law constitute *weakly binding so*urces. Judges are generally expected to abide by these, but may deviate from them if argumentatively justified. The *allowed sources* are those whose use has not been explicitly forbidden, such as scholarly literature, various soft law instruments, and comparisons to foreign jurisdictions.[25]

Despite its age, I find this approach to the hierarchical relationship between different legal sources, which resembles Merkl's and Kelsen's *Stufenbau* theories,[26] to

22. Other recent examples utilising this type of approach are Tuomas Mattila, *Yhteistyö tekijänoikeudessa*, 2022, Alén-Savikko et al. (eds), *Muuttuva tekijä*, 2020, and Härkönen 2025a.
23. Hirvonen 2011, p. 957 crystallises the function of the hierarchical ordering of legal sources into eight points: (1) It is part of the self-understanding of modern law by defining the criteria for legitimate use of power, (2) It provides the framework for the theoretical systematisation and pragmatic coordination of law, thereby describing valid grounds for decisions, (3) It defines binding legal sources and systematises their hierarchy, (4) It maps the factual and normative context in which legal knowledge production and decision-making take place, (5) It forms a general framework, theoretical and conceptual model that connects elements from different branches of law, (6) It records the usage instructions for legal sources, creating predictability, (7) It provides the basis for legal and legitimate legal argumentation, and (8) It integrates the fundamental structures of law, legal dogmatics, and judicial decision-making.
24. Tolonen 2003, p. 27.
25. Peczenik and Aarnio's three-part hierarchy of legal sources is presented by said authors in, *inter alia*, Aarnio 1987, pp. 89-93; Aarnio 2011, pp. 150-152; Peczenik 1995, pp. 214-218. Peczenik formulates the three-part division by distinguishing between sources that one must (*skall*), should (*bör*), and may (*får*) follow.
26. Siltala 2003, p. 285.

provide a sound starting point for this dissertation. However, a modern approach to the three-part division should, of course, address and incorporate the influence of EU law into the enumeration of relevant legal sources. Both Karhu and Siltala have suggested updated versions of such a hierarchy that include sources derived from EU law and the European Convention on Human Rights.[27] (Incidentally, Siltala uses slightly different names for the hierarchical tiers, characterising them as obligatory, guiding, and possible sources).[28] As expected, the EU's treaties, regulations, and directives along with the CJEU's interpretation thereof are placed on the highest tier among obligatory sources by both researchers.

In copyright law, the influence of EU-level legal development and its superiority to national legislation has mainly been felt through the harmonisation of the concept of 'work' into an autonomous concept of EU law, which must be interpreted and applied uniformly among the Member States. For all intents and purposes, this has put the power to formulate the requisites of copyright protection firmly into the hands of the CJEU. How are the sources relevant for this dissertation, then, to be arranged into hierarchical order? Since the EU has harmonised Member States' copyright law through directives rather than regulations, the EU legislation's influence has become incorporated into the national legislation. The appropriate sections of the Finnish Copyright Act, whose interpretation needs to comply with the copyright case law of the CJEU, constitute the strongly binding or obligatory sources. The weakly binding sources play a relatively small role in the context of this dissertation, not least because the case law of the Finnish Supreme Court concerning the requisites of copyright protection largely predate the CJEU's intensified harmonisation effort, thereby making their applicability somewhat uncertain. Nonetheless, domestic case law that interprets the copyright requisites still holds relevance in cases addressing specific subject matter in light of the criteria established by CJEU case law, and domestic case law undoubtedly needs to be considered when assessing the copyright requisites – such as the originality standard – in a Finnish context.

The preparatory works, while certainly not unimportant, mostly play an auxiliary role in the analysis. However, research question (2) will require an examination of joint authorship, which has not been harmonised by the EU. National legal sources, including preparatory works, will therefore play a more significant role in the assessment of this question.

1.4.2 Reconciling Schematic and Dynamic Approaches to Legal Sources

In transitioning to discuss allowed sources, which form a broad and heterogeneous group, one must point out the distinction between *authoritative* and *substantive* legal sources. This distinction highlights that a legal source's relevance may stem from the

27. Karhu 2020, p. 1023; Siltala 2003, pp. 778-780.
28. Siltala 2003, pp. 779-780.

institutional weight it has in society or the material persuasiveness it carries.[29] Most legal sources undoubtedly rely on a combination of both, but overall, substantive persuasiveness should play a proportionally more significant role among allowed legal sources. After all, it is only natural that the further down the institutional hierarchy the giver of a normative-interpretative statement is, the greater the need to justify its relevance will be.

The notion of legal sources needing to justify their relevance through substantive persuasiveness underscores the fact that a schematic and hierarchical ordering of legal sources such as the one given above only provides the starting point for determining the law's normative contents.[30] In reality, legal reasoning is complex and context-dependent, often requiring the balancing of multiple arguments rather than strict reliance on a single source, no matter how authoritative or clearly formulated it may be. Wilhelmsson observes that the weight of legal sources - such as case law, statutes, and scholarly opinions - varies based on factors like relevance, age, and authority. Similarly, practical considerations may sometimes take precedence over formal legal norms, even leading to *contra legem* decisions.[31] Under this view, legal argumentation is ultimately a dynamic process shaped by multiple interconnected arguments. This need for adaptability is further heightened by the dissertation's focus on reconciling two distinct areas: the rapidly evolving field of generative AI technology and the niche subject of music copyright law. Due to its specialised nature, music copyright law compels doctrinal analysis to adopt a more dynamic methodological approach, including consideration of traditionally less relevant sources, such as foreign case law and comparative legal perspectives.

Which allowed sources might be relevant for addressing the research task, and where do they derive their legal weight from? Within national sources, the scholarly literature constitutes a notable source. Yet, the issues most crucial for this dissertation are currently only addressed on a relatively broad level. In addition, the Finnish Copyright Council has issued several rulings relevant to this dissertation's research task. Although these rulings are not binding, they carry considerable authority due to the council's status as an expert body. It has also been observed that the importance of the Council's rulings is further emphasised by the fact that copyright cases are relatively rare in case law.[32] By extension, this is even more applicable to the sub-fields of copyright law, such as applying the idea/expression dichotomy within music

29. Aarnio 1987, pp. 92-93. In fact, Aarnio uses the term 'substantial' rather than 'substantive'. Nonetheless, I find that 'substantive' more accurately reflects my understanding of the distinction between the two types of legal sources under discussion and also algins with Aarnio's argument. At p. 93, Aarnio notes that '[c]ertain sources of law enter the justification background on the basis of their material (substantial) significance. For this reason, they can be called substantial reasons or, to use the terminology of sources of law, substantial sources of law ... a substantial reason can never have justificatory power other than on the basis of its content.'
30. Makkonen 1998, p. 77 suggests an extreme expression of this sentiment by noting that when one talks about a 'source of law', one imagines that there exists some kind of 'source' from which the law is drawn.
31. Wilhelmsson 2020, p. 1184.
32. Sorvari 2005, p. 20; Mattila 2022, p. 16 points out that the Council's rulings carry particular weight in issues where its statement practice has been consistent and allows for broader generalisations.

infringement cases. Among foreign sources, authoritative Nordic sources hold particular relevance, as Nordic copyright legislation was developed collaboratively and remains largely uniform across countries. For the same reason, Nordic scholarly literature is especially significant within this category.

Two types of less conventional sources will also be utilised. First, lower-tier case law and similar materials from foreign jurisdictions – such as the USA, China, and the Czech Republic – have addressed issues related to AI-generated content more extensively than any currently available Finnish or EU sources. While these foreign cases hold limited weight in applying copyright statutes within Finnish courts, they offer potentially valuable insights into how judges and legal practitioners have addressed the challenges posed by AI-generated content. The relevance of this foreign case law is likely to diminish once comparable Finnish or high-tier EU decisions emerge, but at present, it provides a useful perspective on some of the key issues covered by this dissertation.

Moreover, even if high-tier Finnish or EU judgments were to become available in the recent future, it may align with the relevant issues only in a broad sense, meaning that one also needs to consult lower-tier and foreign case law to get a more precise judicial perspective on the specific questions of interest. This, of course, is not unusual within intellectual property research, where a researcher studying novel technology-related topics may often need to tolerate a low availability of highly compatible case law.[33] Second, in the analytical comparison between the practical reality of composing and copyright law's interpretation of it, input beyond traditional legal sources is required. This includes not only understanding the functionality of generative AI technology but also examining the interaction between composers and various technical tools from a composer's perspective. The following section will address specific methodological questions related to these issues, with section 1.6.3 being devoted to the use of legal sources.

On a general note, all sources – legislation, case law, literature, etc. – have been considered up to 15 June 2025.

1.5 SPECIFIC METHODOLOGICAL QUESTIONS

1.5.1 The Internal and External Perspectives on Examining (Music) Copyright Law

When examining the doctrinal research methodology, a distinction between internal and external perspectives on the law is often made. This distinction emphasises the fact that a doctrinal method investigates the law from within. Accordingly, the law is not only the source of inquiry but also the framework that shapes its interpretation and application. In other words, doctrinal research treats law as a self-contained system, where legal rules, principles, and precedents are analysed based on their internal logic

33. Pihlajarinne 2012, pp. 548-549.

rather than external influences.[34] On this basis, it is sometimes held that the legal researcher's methodological approach is – or should be – identical to the judge's.[35] A milder take on this is that the legal scholar should approach the sources as if he were bound by the same legal framework as a judge.[36] However, the legal scholar is also a member of the scientific community, meaning that legal scholarship should allow for the results to meet scientific standards. Tuori has characterised this as the dual citizenship of the legal researcher, who resides both in the world of legal practice and science.[37]

Accordingly, the legal scholar may approach the research task through a broader scientific and societal perspective, suggesting that the legal scholar has the freedom to draw upon a wider range of sources and methods in examining the issues at hand. Moreover, provided the analysis satisfies the relevant scientific and doctrinal requirements, the examination can yield insights that challenge and enrich the judge's strictly internal perspective on the law. This also aligns with one important and unusual characteristic of legal scholarship: that it is susceptible to and often actively seeks to influence and shape its object of examination, i.e., how the law's normative content is interpreted and applied.[38] Herein lies the potential for utilising input from an external perspective – such as a musicological investigation of a composition and its creative process – to enrich the doctrinal analysis. At least in theory, one might think that a rigorous interdisciplinary analysis of when the originality threshold has been met or a composition has been reproduced can greatly contribute to putting the legal order's understanding of the musical work in sync with the practices of today's composers and the music industry at large, which might improve the copyright framework's ability to realise the underlying policy rationale.[39] Needless to say, the practical realities of interpreting and applying copyright law are considerably more nuanced than that, and the judge's supposedly strictly internal approach to music copyright law is not necessarily in any urgent need of rescue through scholarly input relying on combining doctrinal and musicological methods.

How might one, then, utilise an external perspective to enrich the doctrinal analysis of music copyright law? It has been argued that while an interdisciplinary method might in theory offer significant insights, the primacy of the internal approach is often considered so fundamental that it limits the extent to which external viewpoints can meaningfully contribute to the issue. Therefore, interdisciplinary discussion may often amount to little more than a form of polite indifference, where different fields fail to properly engage, challenge, or synthesise each other's perspectives on the

34. Smits 2017, p. 210.
35. Wilhelmsson 2019, p. 23. Wilhelmsson does not endorse such a view of the legal researcher's methodology.
36. Strömholm 1981, p. 68.
37. Tuori 2013, p. 24; Tuori 2000, pp. 161-162.
38. Tuori 2013, p. 24; Smits 2017, p. 218.
39. Personally, I find that Ed Sheeran's statement in response to winning a rather frivolous copyright infringement claim neatly crystallises the potential harm an insufficiently informed court can cause to the music industry. This issue is discussed in detail in Chapter 6, where Sheeran's statement is also reproduced.

subject matter.[40] Under this view, the external perspective is seen as a complementary tool rather than a methodological equal to doctrinal analysis, and the value of external perspectives is determined by their ability to support, refine, or substantiate the findings of the doctrinally focused legal method.[41]

The interdisciplinary aspects of this dissertation's method largely align with this perspective. After all, placing too much emphasis on a musicological understanding of the originality of a musical passage – or whether it has been reproduced in a given performance – cannot take precedence over copyright law's internal perspective on originality or infringement. Nonetheless, interdisciplinary analysis can provide considerable value. Incorporating musical expertise from a composer's standpoint can deepen the understanding of the compositional process in two important ways. First, it helps distinguish between original and non-original musical attributes, particularly when assessing whether a sequence of broadly formulated instructions qualifies as an original work. Second, it clarifies the role of technical tools in the issuance and execution of these instructions, whether through musical notation, audio recordings, DAWs, AI systems, or other technologies. This aspect is particularly significant, as one of the central research tasks of this dissertation is to deconstruct the compositional process in a way that remains neutral with respect to the technical tools employed. From this perspective, the issuance of instructions is considered the essential creative act in composition, whereas the technical means used to communicate or externalise these instructions play a secondary, largely functional role.

The present section will explore more specifically how musical expertise can be integrated into doctrinal analysis, examining what it means to adopt a methodology informed by musical knowledge and how this approach can illuminate key legal questions.

1.5.2 The Specificity and Generality of Compositional Input

1.5.2.1 The Relevance of a Specificity-Generality Distinction for This Dissertation

Among the central principles of copyright law is the idea/expression dichotomy, which states that only the individual expression contained in a creation can be protected, whereas the underlying ideas remain in the public domain.[42] In the context of music, this means that commonplace melodic, rhythmic, or harmonic patterns are considered non-protectable compositional techniques, while only their specific formulation into passages reflecting the composer's individuality may qualify as a protected work. The rationale underlying this principle is that awarding protection to the common building blocks used to create new compositions would, in addition to its manifest unjustness,

40. Minkkinen 2017, p. 920.
41. Minkkinen 2017, p. 920.
42. Harenko et al. 2024, pp. 22-23; Nordell 2017, p. 308; Lemley 2024, p. 195; TRIPS Article 9(2); WIPO Article 2, Vaver 2002, pp. 22-29.

have a detrimental effect on the functioning of the copyright industry as a whole. While the soundness of this outlook is unlikely to be contested, the point at which a musical passage is deemed to contain sufficient individuality to pass from a non-protected compositional technique into a protected work can occasionally become difficult to define. Overall, this is about distinguishing between the 'truly individual' expression contained in the passage from the underlying compositional building blocks it utilises to accomplish said expression.[43]

The distinction between specificity and generality is important for research question (7) and the evaluation of whether the relationship between pre-generation creative choices and post-generation results is sufficient. This becomes particularly relevant in the context of AI-assisted creative processes due to the inscrutability associated with the AI system's execution of the pre-generation instructions, as this tends to diminish the directness and specificity with which these instructions are reflected in the resulting composition. Consequently, the pre-generation contributor is likely to have limited influence on the specific melodic, rhythmic, and harmonic attributes of the compositions.

A key question for determining whether copyright protection is justified in such cases, as illustrated by Jackson Pollock's painting technique, is whether the number of pre-generation instructions can outweigh the lack of precision in the individual choices. Examining this question in a musical context involves investigating whether a substantial number of pre-generation instructions can establish a sufficient link between the pre-generation contributor and the resulting composition. In practice, this entails assessing whether the determination of the style, genre, melodic shapes, chord progressions, accompaniment patterns, and similar features of the composition can suffice to establish an adequate connection to the end result. To explore how this may be investigated in the context of AI-assisted creative processes, it is necessary to briefly consider how such matters have been addressed in the copyright assessment of traditionally produced compositions.

1.5.2.2 The Overarching Challenges of the Specificity-Generality Distinction in a Musical Context

The quintessential music copyright case involves the right holders of song A initiating proceedings against those of song B due to the perceived similarities between the two songs. In such cases, the plaintiff will often argue that the similarity between the songs provides evidence of unlawful copying, while the defendant contends that they are coincidental, arising from the use of common musical building blocks. Among other things, this requires distinguishing between original expression and commonplace ideas. Here, the assumption is that the greater the reliance on commonplace compositional tropes and techniques, the higher the likelihood that a finding of infringement is unwarranted. Accordingly, the originality of one fragment can be viewed as having

43. A very similar point is made by Rahmatian 2024, p. 29.

an inverse correlation with the probability of that fragment being created coincidentally. This aligns with the notion that broadly formulated contents or similarities – such as the overarching character traits of a given genre or style – are much less capable of sustaining an originality claim than a more specifically articulated sequence of musical attributes. Simply put, specificity points towards originality and infringement, whereas generality suggests the opposite. Consequently, the generality-specificity distinction is largely equivalent to that between ideas and expression.

To tackle this issue in the context of a traditional infringement case, one must first break down the compositional elements of the contested songs to understand how each component contributes to the overall impression of similarity. Next, it is necessary to establish a benchmark for assessing whether the similarities between the fragments fall into the realm of ideas or their expression and whether the allegedly infringing passage could have been created independently. A useful method for addressing this issue is to isolate the elements contributing to the impression of similarity and investigate how frequently the same or nearly identical elements appear in earlier compositions. If similar elements are found in multiple works that predate the claimant's composition, this suggests that the similarities result from either coincidental double creation or both compositions drawing from a common earlier source, rather than from unlawful copying. Conversely, the absence of similar features in pre-existing works suggests that the claimant's composition is original and may have been (unlawfully) copied.

The strength of this approach lies in its reliance on concrete musical samples to distinguish between commonplace ideas and original expression. Simply put, it is much easier to argue that a given passage constitutes a commonplace compositional technique rather than original expression if one can point out a high number of pre-existing works containing identical or nearly identical passages. Yet, the investigation of pre-existing repertoire does not fully resolve all the challenges inherent in music infringement claims. Since the examples of pre-existing works rarely match the contested fragments exactly, the court still needs to engage in a more abstract and subjective assessment of the contested compositions to determine whether the similarities fall within the realm of ideas or expression.

Such challenges are particularly likely to arise when a copyright claim relies on a series of vague similarities spread over longer passages. In these cases, the copyright claim typically rests on a two-part argument emphasising the cumulation of many small elements: while none of the vague or indirect similarities may individually meet the originality threshold, their combined effect can collectively suffice to establish infringement. This line of reasoning is particularly relevant for research question (7), as it reflects the very difficulties characteristic of assessing copyright claims related to AI-generated compositions. Accordingly, this scenario presents an opportunity to draw parallels between traditional and AI-assisted compositional processes in light of existing music copyright case law. That is, by establishing a benchmark for the degree of vagueness and imprecision that the link between creative choices and end result can withstand in traditional compositional processes, it becomes easier to address the relationship between pre-generation choices and post-generation in the context of AI-assisted compositions.

1.5.3 A Benchmark for Assessing the Precision and Specificity Required of a Musical Work

1.5.3.1 The Comparison Between Prospective Reproductions and Underlying Works

To better explain the analogy between traditional and AI-assisted compositional processes, the terminology introduced in the discussion of research questions (5)-(7) provides a foundation for presenting the approach with greater precision. The proposed deconstruction of the compositional process divides the ontology of a musical work into three phases: the *underlying work*, the *source material*, and the *prospective reproductions*. The underlying work refers to the contents of the composition in the abstract sense, independently of its physical manifestations.[44] The source material is the epistemic and evidentiary means by which one can determine the contents of the underlying work. In musical compositions, the source material is typically in the form of musical notation or audio recordings. Finally, prospective reproductions occur when a performing artist - or other suitable agent - consults the source material to communicate the contents of the underlying work.

Based on this approach to the musical work's ontology, the copyright assessment will largely revolve around comparing the underlying work and the prospective reproduction to determine whether they exhibit sufficient similarity to justify copyright protection. Here, the source material serves as a reference point for the comparison, providing a standard against which the similarity is measured. In other words, protection is warranted if the prospective reproduction exhibits sufficient similarity to the underlying work, as evaluated with reference to the source material.

For instance, to determine whether a given performance constitutes a reproduction of Dolly Parton's song 'I Will Always Love You', one needs to examine the musical attributes communicated by the performance to assess whether it exhibits sufficient similarities to the underlying work. Since the underlying work is an ultimately abstract entity, the comparison can only be made with reference to a concrete piece of source material that provides information about the underlying work's contents. The source material constitutes the epistemic - or evidentiary - means by which one can link the musical attributes conveyed by the prospective reproduction to the free and creative choices made by the underlying work's author during the creative process.

In the case of 'I Will Always Love You', the original recording released in 1974 is probably the most reliable source material available for assessing the connection between underlying work and prospective reproduction. Thus, when assessing whether Whitney Houston's well-known version of the song constitutes a reproduction of Parton's composition, one needs to compare the melodic, rhythmic, and harmonic attributes exhibited by Houston's performance to those present in Parton's recording. If the similarities are deemed sufficient, Houston's performance can be linked to the

44. The underlying work resembles Kohler's view of the work as an immaterial entity that exists separately from its physical manifestations. This will be discussed in greater detail in Chapter 5.

free and creative compositional choices made by Parton, thereby making it a protected reproduction of the underlying composition.

1.5.3.2 Different Types of Source Material

This dissertation places significant emphasis on examining the various means through which the contents of a musical work can be communicated. Among the most efficient and precise options are audio recordings of performances, musical notation, and MIDI files. However, in accordance with the previously noted principle of neutrality, the technical means of communication should not affect the copyright assessment. Provided that the chosen method can convey the work's contents with sufficient precision and objectivity, any *data collection* should, at least theoretically, be eligible for copyright protection.[45] Consequently, the composer's copyright claim to a prospective reproduction depends on the precision with which it communicates the underlying work's contents. A two-part example can demonstrate this. On the one hand, one might transcribe the musical attributes conveyed by Parton's original recording into musical notation or a MIDI file. If executed with sufficient accuracy, they would almost certainly qualify as protected reproductions of the underlying work. On the other hand, describing the work's contents through a broadly worded formulation is less likely to achieve the necessary level of precision. To illustrate, let us examine the following description:

> 'I Will Always Love You' is a gentle, country ballad with a more understated and intimate vocal delivery. The song is in A major, featuring a simple arrangement with soft acoustic guitar and light backing instrumentation that supports the heartfelt, lyrical expression. The melody is smooth and straightforward, with a focus on clarity and emotion, while the subtle harmonic progressions evoke a sense of bittersweet farewell.

While this verbal description undoubtedly accurately conveys several musical attributes of the song, it is much too broadly formulated to meet the level of precision required for it to be considered a reproduction of Parton's composition. (We are not considering whether the description is copyright eligible as a literary work in its own right.) Accordingly, the verbal description cannot be regarded as a musical work, as its lack of specificity renders it susceptible to collapsing into the underlying non-protectable idea. However, if one were to incrementally enhance the description's precision and specificity, one might eventually convey the musical attributes of Parton's composition with sufficient detail to qualify as a protected reproduction of the work. This holds true even if one were to rely on the unorthodox and inefficient method of conveying musical information through verbal descriptions.[46]

---

45. *See* section with essential terminological definitions below regarding the term 'data collection'.
46. In this case, one would most likely need to use terminology borrowed from symbolic notation, such as denoting the melodic, rhythmic, and harmonic attributes of each successive musical measure. As a result, the description would largely amount to a poorly optimised version of symbolic representation.

1.5.3.3 Applying the Three-Part Deconstruction to AI-Generated Compositions

The same idea applies when considering copyright claims to AI-generated compositions. For a composition to qualify for protection, it must be possible to link its musical attributes to the free and creative decisions made during its creation. The above-mentioned three-part deconstruction of the musical work facilitates this process by framing the copyright assessment as a comparison between the prospective reproduction and the underlying work, with the source material serving as the reference point. Applying this approach to Composition A discussed in section 1.2, the prospective reproduction is represented by the audio file containing the relevant musical expression. The original work comprises all the creative decisions involved in producing the composition, while the source material provides the evidentiary and epistemic foundation for assessing the connection between the pre-generation creative choices and the musical attributes of Composition A. Under this view, the copyright assessment proceeds through the following steps:

- Firstly, one examines the data collection laid copyright claim to, that is, the audio file containing Composition A. For protection to be possible, the data collection must display musical attributes of at least some complexity.
- Secondly, one must investigate the creative process to determine whether the musical attributes of the data collection were caused by – or can be sufficiently linked to – the free and creative choices made by the prospective author(s).
- Finally, to perform the assessment described in the second step, one needs to examine the source material produced during the creative process, since the source material provides the evidence enabling the legal order to link the musical attributes of the composition to the free and creative choices made by the prospective author(s). In the case of Composition A, these may include creative choices related to training data selection, model architecture design, fine-tuning, and prompt engineering.

In the case of Composition A, the cumulation of creative choices among many contributors clearly plays a crucial role. If one were to examine only the prompt engineering in isolation, the description of the composition's musical attributes would be much too broad to sustain a copyright claim. After all, the user prompt merely requests a dramatic orchestral composition in the style of twentieth-century cinema music. In contrast, the combined effect of all pre-generation creative choices might conceivably achieve a quantity and specificity that meets the requirements for protection. This logic parallels the situation with the verbal description of 'I Will Always Love You' or Jackson Pollock's only partially controlled technique of splashing paint onto the canvas: Although a limited number of choices is unlikely to fulfil the requirements, their successive cumulation can eventually reach a level where the relationship between creative choices and the end result is strong enough to support a copyright claim.

1.5.4 Developing the Benchmark by constructing Instruction Sets, Mock Performances, and Template Compositions

How, then, does one determine the point at which the number of creative choices becomes extensive and specific enough to offset the partial lack of control over the final result? The primary challenge in evaluating copyright claims to AI-generated compositions arises from the novelty of creating musical works through the development and instruction of AI models. Even if traditional and AI-assisted compositional processes were to be analogised by treating all creative choices as instructions describing musical attributes, there is no clear precedent for evaluating the similarity between pre-generation creative choices and the post-generation composition to determine its eligibility for protection. To provide new insights on this issue, the dissertation will develop a benchmark for assessing the relationship between instruction sets describing musical attributes and their transformation into 'actual' musical expression.

The benchmark is constructed by taking a number of compositions under examination. A series of variations on these will be produced, each exhibiting increasing levels of inaccuracy. By introducing gradual distortions to different musical elements such as melody, rhythm, harmony, or structure, one can assess the point at which the altered version is so different that it no longer qualifies as a protected reproduction of the original composition. For example, in taking 'I Will Always Love You' under this kind of review, one would examine a short fragment of it and introduce alterations to its musical attributes. A few altered notes or rhythmic adjustments might not affect the overall impression of similarity. However, as more differences are introduced, the connection to the original composition will weaken and eventually break. This exercise gives insight not only into how much deviation is possible before a data collection stops being a (protected) reproduction but also about which musical elements – or combinations of elements – are most critical for preserving the identity and individuality of the composition. By experimenting with different types of inaccuracy, one can also better distinguish between the original and commonplace aspects of the composition as well as gain overarching insights into the nature of originality in the context of musical expression.

One can also apply the same method the other way around, by starting with a simple idea or building block, and successively add more features to it to determine the point at which the originality threshold is met. To put this method into practice, so-called *manual template compositions* are constructed. The name 'template composition' refers to the fact that unlike a traditional composition where the intended melodic, rhythmic, and harmonic attributes are specified with a great degree of precision, a template composition only contains a sequence of broadly formulated instructions, whose conversion into a complete piece of musical expression requires a subsequent agent to fill in or specify the missing details. The moniker 'template composition' is inspired by the fact that a sequence of broadly formulated instructions, like a template, shapes the specific contents of the resulting musical expression without defining them with the usual degree of precision or exhaustiveness. The creation of musical expression through such a process will raise intriguing questions not only about the overall copyright eligibility of the resulting compositions but also about the allocation of co-authorship stakes if two or more prospective authors contributed to creating or completing the template composition.

The construction and analysis of template compositions constitutes the most unconventional research method utilised in the dissertation and warrants some discussion at this stage. To examine the issues of originality and authorship allocation in detail, two template compositions are constructed in Chapter 6. The first template composition is very short, based on combining a simple chord progression and a melodic fragment with a few instructions that steer the melodic fragment's development. To this template, seven alternative completions are provided, which are then examined from the perspective of copyright eligibility and authorship allocation.

To gain more useful insights regarding the analogy between AI-generated compositions and Jackson Pollock's painting technique,[47] the second template composition's proportions were significantly expanded. This allowed for a deeper exploration of more complex issues related to originality – such as the specificity-generality distinction – and authorship allocation in multi-contributor settings. Again, several different completions of the template are provided. However, to get more meaningful results, I did not complete all templates myself, but instead they were completed by acquaintances who kindly volunteered to participate. Accordingly, the creative process of the template composition and its completions can be described as follows: To produce the template composition and its alternative completions, I first constructed the template in the form of a two-page document consisting of bullet-point instructions and a pre-filled music sheet containing the chord progression-based accompaniment.[48] These two documents were then sent to the template fulfillers, who rendered the instructions into compositions.

The primary benefit of having others complete the template is that it gives a more realistic and practical perspective on the notion of composing a piece through successive contributions by different creators. The fact that there are many completions also gives a more nuanced perspective on the range of outcomes a given template can yield. Furthermore, this method may help indicate whether the creative input most important for shaping the expression and identity of the end result was provided by the template maker or the template fulfiller. For example, if all completions of a given template produce a very similar impression, it – at least tentatively – suggests the crucial components of the piece's expression and identity appear to reside in the template. Conversely, if the completions vary significantly, this indicates that the fulfillers' creative input played a more decisive role in shaping the final work.

If one accepts the utility of this method, the next questions concern how many completions one needs and who should provide them. On the one hand, copyright does not measure aesthetic merit, skill, or labour. This suggests that, in theory, anyone's completion should be just as valid in demonstrating the range of possible interpretations a given template composition can yield. On the other hand, one might point out that in practice, most compositions relevant to copyright law – those that are at least

47. *See* the discussion regarding research question (7) above.
48. *See* section 1.9 regarding supplementary materials. The documents mentioned are contained in the Appendix, items 16 and 17.

moderately successful either artistically or commercially – tend to contain at least some measure of both skill and individuality. Therefore, I find that insights into the range of possible completions are more useful in cases where the template fulfillers possess both musical knowledge and an intent to create an individualised and artistically viable end result.

While I see value in examining the different ways a template composition can be realised, I do not consider it necessary or legally relevant to conduct a rigorous empirical study on the compositional choices of a large and representative sample of template fulfillers. Therefore, I asked four acquaintances to provide completions. All of them are professional musicians, but none specialise in musical composition. Given their musical background, one can assume they were both interested in and capable of creating compositions that reflected their individual artistic voices within the given constraints. Moreover, their knowledge of music theory made it possible to keep the instructions relatively concise, as they could be expected to understand many core concepts of musical composition without extensive explanation. Admittedly, all participants were classically trained musicians, and a wider range of completions could likely have been achieved by involving musicians from diverse genres and stylistic backgrounds. Still, I do not believe that increasing the number of template fulfillers or broadening the selection of musical styles would have significantly enhanced the insights gained from analysing the completions and the range of musical expression and individuality they exhibit.

1.5.5 The Communicative Medium Employed and the Senses It Engages

Whether one applies the method starting with broad formulations that are successively specified or the other way around, the investigation ultimately amounts to a similarity comparison between two data collections: the musical expression laid copyright claim to and the source material by which said expression can be linked to the author's creative choices. This raises the question of the form or medium in which the relevant compositional content is conveyed and the type of sensory perception it engages. On one hand, it could be argued that any form of communication directed at any sense should be valid, provided it conveys the work's content with sufficient precision and objectivity. On the other hand, practical considerations suggest that aural perception constitutes the most critical aspect of the investigation.

The emphasis on aural perception stems from two key factors. First, musical expression is inherently directed towards it, as music is generally understood as an art form 'concerned with combining vocal or instrumental *sounds* for beauty of form or emotional expression, usually according to cultural standards of rhythm, melody, and … harmony'.[49] Second, while there are other media for storing or communicating

49. Professor Gordon Epperson gives this definition in his Encyclopaedia Britannica article on music https://www.britannica.com/art/music, accessed 9 August 2024. Italics added. Another definition, also emphasising the importance of sound, is given by Levinson 1990, p. 273, who defines music as 'sounds temporally organized by a person for the purpose of enriching or intensifying experience through active engagement (e.g., listening, dancing, performing) with

musical compositions, the most accurate assessment of their content occurs through aural perception. This is because the individuality of a composition often lies in the subtle interplay of various musical elements, such as pitch, rhythm, harmony, and structure. Although it is possible to communicate this interaction with great precision through musical notation or various digital formats, comparing the overall impressions produced by two very similar compositions would be exceedingly difficult without relying on aural perception.[50]

Consequently, this dissertation adopts a viewpoint that while a data collection in any form may be protected as a musical work, its degree of originality must ultimately be assessed based on the attributes it displays when rendered into an audible form. In other words, the true essence of a musical work can only be fully appreciated once it has been heard, whether through a human performance (live or recorded) or a machine-generated output, such as a MIDI file. The development of the benchmark must therefore focus on the overall aural impression created by the samples under review, making the analysis of audio samples an essential part of the examination. For this reason, the investigation conducted in Chapter 6 will start with presenting instruction sets utilising musical notation and verbal descriptions. These instructions will be rendered into so-called mock performances of successively greater inaccuracy. The performances' ability to support a copyright claim will be assessed by evaluating the overall impression of similarity between the visually rendered instructions and their aurally perceived counterparts. Through this method, the point at which a visually expressed instruction set acquires or forfeits the level of specificity required to uphold a copyright claim can be assessed with reference to the overall aural impression it produces. To enable this examination, audio samples will be attached to the dissertation.[51]

1.6 A BROADER USE OF LEGAL SOURCES

1.6.1 General Remarks on Utilising Musicological Expertise

The primary aim of the benchmark discussed above is to clarify the distinction between original expression and commonplace ideas in cases where clear criteria – such as direct similarities between the contested data collections – are unavailable. If the data

the sounds regarded primarily, or in significant measure, as sounds'. Also note Arewa 2014, p. 470, who emphasises that 'music is a *performance art in which oral and aural aspects are essential*'. My italics.

50. Rahmatian 2024, p. 29 presents a similar argument, noting that 'What ultimately matters, also in an identification of whether there has been copyright infringement, are the sounds one can hear in the performance, not what is written in the score. For the purpose of musical copyright, the score is not an artistic work: similarity of notation without similarity of the listening experience points away from infringement.' Score is a synonym for music sheet.
51. The use of supplementary materials, such as audio files, will be discussed in greater detail in section 1.9.

collections under examination display only indirect similarities, one must necessarily use some degree of discretion in deciding whether the collective effect of the similarities is enough to offset the differences. For instance, a copyright infringement case may require the adjudicator to decide whether the similarities in the shape of the melodic contents, accompaniment patterns, and rhythmic groove outweigh the dissimilarities in the precise selection of pitches and chord progressions. The purpose of constructing the aforementioned benchmark is to guide the adjudicator on the significance of different musical elements that need to be weighed against each other. When the legal assessment requires dissection of the fabric of the contested compositions, consultation with musical or musicological expertise can plausibly enlighten the analysis. Therefore, it is appropriate to discuss the finer details of how such an interdisciplinary method could be employed, both in the context of musical copyright assessments overall as well as in constructing the aforementioned benchmark.

There are essentially two types of musicological expert input one might utilise.[52] First, musicological research, and especially music theory, can provide insight into the building blocks of musical compositions. By systematising common scales, chords, rhythm patterns, phrase structures, and chord progressions used across different genres and styles, it offers a structured understanding of the elements that form building blocks of most musical works. Legal practitioners can utilise this information to gain a more precise grasp of the musical components contributing to the overall impression of similarity between the data collections under examination. Simply put, by consulting a musicological dissection of the musical elements contributing to the overall impression produced by the relevant data collections, the legal practitioner can make a more well-informed assessment of whether the perceived similarities are of a quantity and quality that justifies copyright protection.

A more ambitious use of musicological expertise would involve asking musicologists to weigh the similarities and dissimilarities between the two data collections and provide an opinion on whether they constitute instances of the same work.[53] On the one hand, this method can certainly enlighten the discussion. Especially when combined with references to concrete musical examples, a musicologist's analysis can provide valuable added insight into the degree of originality and similarity exhibited by the data collections under investigation. On the other hand, a potential challenge in

52. Musicology is a broad field of research encompassing study of the history and phenomena of music. As enumerated in the Encyclopedia Britannica, it includes '(1) form and notation, (2) the lives of composers and performers, (3) the development of musical instruments, (4) music theory (harmony, melody, rhythm, modes, scales, etc.), and (5) aesthetics, acoustics, and physiology of the voice, ear, and hand.' https://www.britannica.com/art/musicology, accessed 9 October 2024. The field of scholarly study most relevant for this discussion is that of music theory. Nonetheless, I will refer to expert input form this field of study as musicology, mainly for reasons of linguistic expedience.

53. To clarify, the copyright assessment relevant for this dissertation will revolve around comparing data collections, whether it is a comparison between two contested compositions as in a traditional copyright infringement case, or comparing pre-generation creative choices to post-generation outputs. The term data collection is defined in section 1.8 about essential terminological definitions.

relying on musicological experts is their ability to connect musicological analysis with the legal distinction between commonplace ideas and original expression when assessing whether a data collection – such as broadly formulated instructions – meets the originality threshold. While a musicological dissection of the data collections can enhance the precision of legal analysis, it may be challenging to present the findings in a manner that is accessible and persuasive to legal practitioners who ultimately decide the case. Musicological expert opinions are therefore most effective when tightly integrated with concrete musical samples. For instance, the likelihood of coincidental double creation is far easier to substantiate when referencing examples from existing musical compositions, rather than relying solely on theoretical explanations of compositional techniques and 'musical grammar'. Notably, by incorporating pre-existing musical compositions into the similarity analysis, the copyright analysis adopts features resembling the examination of prior art in patent law.[54]

1.6.2 Experimental Methods: Prior Art Research and Mock Performances

A brief examination of Artikal Sound System's infringement suit against Dua Lipa will illustrate the potential utility of an examination method resembling patent law's prior art search. Filed in March 2022 in a Los Angeles federal district court, the lawsuit alleged that *Levitating* copied the band's 2017 song *Live Your Life*.[55] The relevant songs contain five-second passages exhibiting similarities so striking that they, on initial review, seem difficult to put down to coincidence. Therefore, a purely theoretical investigation focused on pointing out the simplicity of the melodic movement and commonality of the chord progression and rhythmic patterns may not be convincing enough to displace the intuitive impression that the similarities cannot have emerged coincidentally, even if it would be both rigorous and comprehensive. However, if the theoretical analysis is supported by pointing out the very similar passages contained in DNCE's song 'Cake By The Ocean' and Outkast's song 'Rosa Parks', the argument for coincidental double creation due to the utilisation of similar musical building blocks becomes significantly more persuasive.[56] On a more general level, this aligns with the notion that coincidental similarities are more likely than one might intuitively assume,[57] which is ultimately due to the small degree of variation within which many genres of popular music typically operate.

54. Several American scholars have recently discussed the notion of utilising a prior art search in copyright infringement cases. *See* Lowe and Burroughs 2024, pp. 113, 118; Fishman and Garcia 2023, pp. 1160, 1168.
55. *Cope v. Warner Records*, Inc., Case 2:22-cv-01384 (C.D. Cal. 2022). Adrian Gonzalez Cerrillo and Sana Hakim's analysis of the case is available at https://www.iplawwatch.com/2022/03/21/levitating-lawsuits-understanding-dua-lipas-copyright-infringement-troubles/, accessed 5 March 2025.
56. An alternative possibility is that both the claimant's and defendant's compositions were copied from said earlier work. In either case, the convincingness of the claimant's argument is severely diminished.
57. Bennet 2023, p. 65 also points this out, calling it 'something of a truism that coincidental melodic similarity is much more common than many people believe'.

Overall, the use of musicological expertise is arguably most effective when combined with concrete examples of pre-existing compositions. However, a key limitation of relying on this method is that the availability of suitable examples imposes natural constraints on how extensively it can be used, since the method becomes challenging to apply if suitable prior art examples are not available. To address this issue, mock performances can be constructed. As explained above, these expand the range of concrete musical examples by producing a succession of increasingly more invasive alterations to the relevant composition. This can provide a more comprehensive understanding of the compositions under examination by revealing the (interaction of) musical elements most critical for their individuality, identity, and recognisability. By linking the theoretical analysis of compositional elements – such as pitch, rhythm, harmony, and form – with aurally perceivable mock performances, it becomes easier to argue on the issue without relying on highly theoretical language that may be difficult to grasp for legal practitioners.

This approach can improve how musicological expertise and legal analysis interact. Rather than requiring musicologists to present intricate arguments about why the interaction between pitch and rhythm is more crucial to a composition's originality than its phrase structure or chord progressions, mock performances illustrate how changes in these elements affect the perceived similarity between the original composition and its alteration. By translating musicological insights into mock performances that legal professionals can more readily understand, this method enables an effective application of interdisciplinary expertise without becoming overly technical or theoretical. The goal is to complement the examination by drawing upon a high level of musical proficiency while keeping the analysis accessible and clear to legal practitioners.

The discussion about the core research task and the methodological means of addressing it can be summarised as follows: The solution to research question (7) – which inquires whether the composer's instructions are specific enough and sufficiently precisely reflected in the resulting composition – will essentially revolve around comparing a visually expressed sequence of instructions to its rendition into aurally perceivable expression to determine whether these constitute instances of the same work. This will depend on examining whether the visually expressed instruction set is specific enough to be sufficiently reflected in the corresponding musical performance to justify a copyright claim.

To determine the specificity required of the instruction set, I develop a benchmark for assessing when the required degree of specificity is reached. This inquiry largely overlaps with making a distinction between commonplace ideas and original expression, in which musicological expertise is set to play a crucial role. A potential challenge of using musicological expertise lies in it sometimes being overly theoretical and abstract, which can limit its persuasiveness in a legal context. To leverage high-level musicological expertise in a way that aligns with the demands of legal analysis, mock performances will be constructed. These integrate musicological understanding into concrete musical samples to supply the analysis with new insights into the relationship between ideas and their expression.

1.6.3 Consulting Case Law and Literature from Foreign Jurisdictions

Even if one were to successfully utilise musicological expertise and thereby clarify the relationship between musical ideas and their expression, the determination of whether a sequence of instructions contains sufficient specificity to meet the originality threshold will ultimately be made based on a legal-doctrinal analysis. As noted above, research question (7) largely hinges on determining the lowest degree of specificity an instruction set can contain while still being capable of upholding the author's copyright claims. The obvious challenge when examining this issue from a legal perspective is the low availability (high-tier) case law discussing the minute details of the originality threshold in the context of musical expression. This raises the question of utilising foreign case law to gain added insight, which warrants some discussion.

When consulting foreign legal sources, an overarching distinction can be made between legal research that has a directly comparative focus and that in which the domestic legal system is the primary focus.[58] When opting for the latter alternative, as is done in this dissertation, no direct and rigorous comparison between foreign and domestic law is carried out. Instead, foreign legal sources serve in an auxiliary or supporting capacity to help clarify some points relevant for the domestic legal issue under examination. In practice, said auxiliary capacity may entail that foreign case law and legal literature contain concrete factual situations and conflicts likely to arise within the domestic legal system. Strömholm points out that in such instances, one does not, *strictu sensu*, utilise foreign law as such. Rather, one uses foreign *practical experience* of the legal issues under examination.[59]

If the practical experiences align closely with the relevant legal issues, even foreign legal sources that are very remote from Finnish and EU copyright law could, at least theoretically, provide meaningful additions to the discussion. Further arguments bolstering the relevance of such sources could be had by noting that the concept of originality is very similarly defined in most jurisdictions.[60] Accordingly, one might think that legal sources concerning the evaluation of originality could hold relatively high relevance even if they were to be from otherwise remote jurisdictions, especially if their substance is highly compatible with the issue at hand. At the same time, a too assertive stance towards utilising the apparent similarities between different jurisdictions' understanding of originality is fraught with the dangers stemming from the challenges typically associated with comparative legal research, such as the difficulty of grasping the finer contextual nuances particular to less familiar jurisdictions.[61]

---

58. Strömholm 1971, p. 251; Norrgård 2002, p. 29.
59. Strömholm 1971, pp. 257-258. My italics.
60. Gervais 2024, p. 1101 notes that the 'notion of originality is, in fact, a worldwide standard, even though it is not explicitly spelled out in international treaties'.
61. Van Hoecke 2002, pp. 3, 10-11 points out that legal rules and concepts cannot be understood in isolation. This is because legal concepts of different legal systems, even when using the same terminology, can have different meanings due to the underlying legal culture. Therefore, the legal concepts must be considered within their legal, procedural, constitutional, historical, and socio-economic contexts. Similarly, de Cruz, as explained by Husa 2023, p. 7, emphasises the importance of 'organising the sources so that they reflect the philosophy and ideology of each legal system under the comparative-law microscope'. Strömholm 1971, p. 262 also notes that in

How does one, then, utilise foreign case law, and how should the relative importance of various cases and jurisdictions be determined? I will assess the relevance of foreign case law on two different grounds. The first is derived from a combination of the similarities between the relevant jurisdictions – either concerning a given provision or the copyright law framework more broadly – and the rank of the foreign court will determine the relevance of the judgment and the argumentation presented therein. Under this view, Nordic and especially Swedish case law (and the associated literature) hold particular relevance in a Finnish context. The quintessential example of this is the Swedish Supreme Court's *Landslaget v. Drängarna* case,[62] a music infringement case largely focused on determining the originality of a short musical passage residing at the very juncture between ideas and expression. It seems that this case scores unusually highly on most markers, pointing towards a high relevance of foreign case law. Not only are the Finnish and Swedish copyright frameworks materially very similar, but it is also a Supreme Court judgment, increasing its authority-based relevance. Finally, the material circumstances of the case align rather accurately with this dissertation's research task.

Jurisdictions of other EU Member States represent the next tier in this type of analysis. While not as ideologically or substantially close as the Nordic legal systems, they still share a relatively similar copyright law framework due to EU harmonisation efforts. In this regard, a specific German Federal Court of Justice (BGH) case holds notable relevance to the analysis in Chapter 6, as it addresses the nuanced distinction between ideas and expression in music copyright and provides valuable viewpoints on the appropriate role of expert testimony in resolving such disputes.[63]

In contrast, US case law is far removed from the Finnish or European assessment of musical copyright. Nonetheless, due to its material similarity to the issues under examination, it can enlighten the analysis due to the practical experience it offers. In the US, the late 2010s saw several high-profile music copyright infringement cases featuring very short fragments of music, which largely centred on the issue of distinguishing between original expression and commonplace ideas. The most noteworthy among these was the much-publicised *Williams v. Gaye* case, in which a copyright infringement claim was granted based on vague and rather unsubstantial similarities between the contested compositions. The verdict, which was upheld on appeal, was heavily criticised for misapplying the idea/expression distinction and thereby granting the plaintiff an exclusive right to a musical style.[64] Moreover, in a relatively short space of time, other similarly dubious infringement claims were made, such as *Gray v. Perry* and *Skidmore v. Zeppelin*. Overall, these cases highlighted the

comparative law, even the best bibliographies and bibliographic knowledge fall short without a minimum level of practical know-how, which must be acquired through personal experience in the relevant field, professional contacts, and other informal channels.

62. *See* section 6.4 below.

63. In relation to utilising German legal sources, one might also note that Peczenik 1995, p. 268, in his analysis of utilising foreign case law in (Swedish) legal argumentation, expressly mentions German law and scholarly literature as constituting viable allowed sources within national law. One must, however, note that this statement is made on a very general level and not specifically aimed towards copyright law.

64. *See* section 6.3.2 below.

importance of striking a balance between maintaining a low originality threshold and preserving the building blocks of new musical works within the public domain.

Although these cases lack direct relevance in a European context due to the remoteness of US copyright law, several factors – best understood as reflecting practical experience in Strömholm's sense – give them the potential to enrich the discussion. First, they resemble a real-life experiment into the consequences of assessing the originality threshold or the similarity of two musical compositions on an excessively lenient standard. They also provide examples of how infringement claims have been argued in situations where the contested musical fragments have been at the very juncture between ideas and their expression. In addition, the high pecuniary stakes have justified a high outlay of financial and intellectual resources in arguing the cases, which should be reflected in a richer variety of argumentation having been produced. On the whole, an examination of these cases can provide added insight into how the legal order has coped with the distinction between ideas and expression – which is largely equivalent to the distinction between specificity and generality that lies at the heart of this dissertation – in borderline cases.

Second, whether due to the larger volume of high-value copyright infringement litigation or to some other extra-legal reasons, US case law on music copyright infringement has inspired a larger body of research – conducted by both legal and other professionals – inquiring into how the similarity assessment between two compositions or the idea/expression distinction should be executed in the context of musical works. The US is also home to a specific type of professional activity referred to as 'forensic musicology'. As explained by one provider of such services, forensic musicology is a field of study that applies musical expertise 'to illuminate the relevant truths in matters of civil law'.[65] In sum, while the research efforts into music copyright assessment by US-based legal scholars, forensic musicologists, and others are not directly applicable in an EU law context, they may still provide a perspective on the dissertation's core research tasks that enlightens the discussion.

1.7 THE IMPACT OF MY DUAL ROLE AS LEGAL RESEARCHER AND MUSICIAN

1.7.1 The Musician's External Perspective on the Legal Concept of a Musical Work

In this section, I examine how my background as a professional musician has shaped the research task and methods. This perspective has not only informed the analysis but also inspired some of the most distinctive treatment of the research questions. Reflecting on how my musical expertise influences the legal analysis conducted throughout the dissertation is therefore appropriate at this stage.

On the whole, I find that my explication of the compositional process through the concepts of instruction set and source material stands out as an extra-doctrinally

65. https://www.musicologize.com/forensic-musicology-services/, accessed 12 September 2024.

inspired approach to assessing the requisites of copyright protection. Both the distinction of source material as a separate ontological stage of a musical work and the characterisation of the compositional process as the issuance of instructions have been directly inspired by my own firsthand experience of how musical information is communicated between composers, performers, and audiences. The crucial aspect of the musician's or performing artist's viewpoint on this issue is a stronger emphasis on the fact that the musical work is not what is written on the page, but what it *can become* when combined with the performer's input.

In the performing arts, the performer is generally not viewed as a passive actor that merely executes a given sequence of notes or commands. Rather, performers study the works to discover the 'meaning behind the notes',[66] which they proceed to channel through their own artistic contributions. In this interpretative process, the performing artists do not necessarily aim to reproduce the composer's original conception with as much fidelity as possible. Instead, they may choose to deliberately depart from the composer's description of the work and produce their own reinterpreted version of it. Moreover, such reinterpretations may turn out to greatly surpass the artistic or commercial viability of the original composition and thereby change the public perception of its contents. Whitney Houston's previously mentioned reinterpretation of 'I Will Always Love You' is a good example of this. Through reinterpretation, Parton's plaintive country song was transformed into an expansive power ballad, revealing previously undiscovered features of the composition. Overall, such an approach to musical works suggests that there exists no definitive version or expression of any given composition.[67] Instead, the work constantly evolves through performance practice, where each successive (re)interpretation contributes to and shapes the collective understanding of the composition's contents and identity.

Another point that stands out in a musician's perspective on the relationship between the underlying work's contents and a performer's interpretation of them is that the crucial components of a composition's identity often reside in a complex interaction between several musical elements, such as pitch, rhythm, harmony, and form. Furthermore, the key to artistic and commercial success typically depends on a subtle manipulation of such elements. Even a minor change to one element – whether stemming from features of composition, arrangement, or performance – can significantly affect the overall impact of the work by changing the interplay among these elements. Importantly, the interaction and hierarchy between these elements vary from piece to piece, making it challenging to establish universal guidelines regarding the extent and type of changes a composition can undergo before it loses its original identity or individuality.

To summarise, my externally inspired view of a musical composition's ontology suggests two non-legal observations. First, there exists no definitive source material that can exactly and exhaustively define the contents of a given composition, not least since the perception of a composition's contents or identity may continuously evolve

66. Copland 1988, p. 2.
67. Possible exceptions to this are compositions designed to be performed electronically. These, however, constitute a rather small minority of all compositions.

through performers' reinterpretations of it. Second, the precise characteristics of a composition's individuality and identity will often reside in a subtle interaction between several musical elements, which further exacerbates the difficulty of exhaustively defining the precise contents of a given composition. This line of reasoning inevitably leads to questions about the ontological nature of musical works: What exactly constitutes a musical work, and how can its contents be defined with precision?[68] The question is not without philosophical connotations, some of which extend far beyond what is relevant for a legal assessment of musical works. Nonetheless, I find that a brief extra-legal discussion on the ontology of musical works along such lines will be helpful for understanding the relationship between my perspective – shaped by a background in music – and the standard doctrinal take on what it means to compose, document, or reproduce musical works.[69]

In his book on a humanistic philosophy of music, Lippman describes the musical work as 'a nonaudible entity that exists only as an *object of intention* and not even as the retracing or conception or projection of any particular experience of music past, present, or future'.[70] This formulates an entirely abstract notion of a composition, aligning with the description of its ontological nature I suggested above. Since the work exists independently of any particular experience, including the composer's own conception, it supports the view that the work's contents cannot be exhaustively captured in any piece of static documentation. Instead, all that is available for defining the work's contents are various instances of source material, each describing the underlying object of intention with differing degrees of precision and authority. For example, consider the song 'I Will Always Love You': no definitive source material exists – whether in the form of performance, musical notation, or other documentation – that can exhaustively delineate what the song contains or what it can become. Even the composer's original recording of it provides only one, albeit a highly authoritative, interpretation of the song's contents and expressive potential.

Lippman's definition does not directly account for the work's coming into being. This aspect of the work's ontology is addressed by Ingarden, who notes that the author's labour 'fashions something ... that previously did not exist but from the moment of its coming into being does somehow exist quite independently of whether anyone performs it, listens to it, or takes any interest in it whatever'.[71] This statement accurately captures how the author's actions bring the composition into existence, but once it has received an externally perceivable manifestation, it can take on a life of its own that is entirely separate from the author's intentions and actions. Overall, based on Lippman's and Ingarden's views, a musical composition can be characterised as an abstract collection of musical attributes that serve as the foundation for creating a

68. Composer and musicology professor Mikko Heiniö, in an article published in the Finnish legal journal *Lakimies* 2013, p. 1177, discusses the respective roles of the composer and performer in communicating a composition and emphasised the challenges of defining the ontology of a musical work. Notably, Heiniö also served on the board of the Finnish collective rights society Teosto from 1999 to 2014.
69. These will be covered in greater detail in Chapter 5.
70. Lippman 2006, p. 41. My italics.
71. Ingarden 1986, p. 2.

specific – yet openly defined – sequence of musical expression. In other words, a composition is a flexible and evolving abstraction that can never be fully represented in a single version. It is brought into existence by composers and reimagined through performances, yet it remains an independent, intangible entity with a core 'meaning' that is interpreted differently by each individual.

While such reflections on the ontological nature of musical works can be interesting in their own right, they are not directly relevant for the legal analysis. The legal order simply does not need to unlock the true ontological nature of musical compositions in a philosophical sense or examine how the perception of a given composition changes due to imaginative performing artists revealing previously undiscovered facets of the work. Instead, the copyright law framework only needs to determine a series of criteria that enable a satisfactory commodification of composers' creative efforts. In this vein, Rahmatian has fittingly described copyright law's task as that of transforming music 'into discernable and static entities, "musical works", to which legal rights can attach'.[72] Essentially, this is achieved by linking certain objectively and precisely perceivable sequences of musical expression to the free and creative choices of human authors. To accomplish this, one does not need to delve any deeper into whether the performance does justice to the meaning behind the notes or the purported intentions of its composer. For instance, it may well be that Whitney Houston's reinterpreted version of 'I Will Always Love You' introduces considerable changes to the style, mood, and musical fabric of Parton's underlying composition. Yet, with the exception of a few short passages, the discrepancies between the underlying composition and Houston's version are far from significant enough to displace Parton's copyright claim to the latter. Thus, while the changes caused by the reinterpretation may be an interesting subject of musicological analysis, they generally lack relevance for the copyright assessment.

1.7.2 Utilising the External Perspective in a Legal Context

Even if the musicological – or even philosophical – nuances of the musical work's ontology are not directly relevant for the copyright assessment, I find that certain analytical methods inspired by them can be utilised to provide meaningful insights into the question of copyright protection in the context of AI-assisted compositional processes. In many ways, this aligns with the aims of a Law in Context approach, which seeks to take into account how legal norms and institutions are conditioned by culture and social organisation.[73]

From this perspective, the deconstruction of the musical work's ontology by examining it as an act of issuing instructions encoded into various types of source material plays a particularly important role. Using this deconstruction, both the questions of copyright eligibility and authorship allocation ultimately hinge on the precision with which a given data collection can be traced back to the creative choices

72. Rahmatian 2015, p. 116. Rahmatian makes a similar point in 2024, p. 20.
73. Selznick 2003, p. 177; Snyder 2024, p. 1485; *see also* Weckström 2011, pp. 29-31.

of the prospective author. This precision is assessed by comparing the relevant data collection – such as a musical performance, audio recording, or PDF file – to the creative choices contained in the source material provided by the author. To apply this framework to AI-assisted compositional processes, both traditional and AI-assisted creations are treated as instruction sets with varying levels of precision and specificity. As noted above, this results in an analogy between traditional and AI-assisted compositions using a parallel process: the specificity of broadly formulated instruction sets is progressively increased, while that of highly detailed instruction sets is gradually reduced. This dual approach aims to identify the threshold at which one process attains copyright eligibility while the other forfeits it, which should give insight into whether pre-generation creative choices can give a justifiable copyright claim to post-generation outputs.

In addressing the potential rewards to be reaped by this extra-legally inspired approach, I find that it can bring a fresh perspective to an issue – the copyright eligibility of AI-generated content – that has already been extensively treated in a voluminous and continuously growing scholarly literature. However, the approach carries certain risks, including the possibility that my reconceptualisation of the work's ontology may force legal definitions of authorship, work, and reproduction into roles for which they are ultimately ill-suited. It may also risk introducing unnecessary conceptual complexity by adding the notions of instruction set and source material into copyright assessments. Furthermore, any innovative approach, by its very nature, risks being too far removed from conventional discourse to meaningfully contribute to it. Nonetheless, I believe that applying sound judgment to the method described in this chapter will ensure that its potential benefits outweigh these challenges.

Another component of my research methodology rooted in my musical expertise is the application of mock performances to enhance the analysis and the construction of template compositions. My background has also fostered a greater willingness to experiment with unconventional analytical methods, such as drawing inspiration from patent law's prior art search to evaluate the originality of a given passage of music. The potential dangers of these approaches are similar to those outlined above, but I remain confident that the potential rewards outweigh the risks, provided that the innovative methods are applied with careful judgment and a solid grounding in conventional doctrinal methodology.

1.8 ESSENTIAL TERMINOLOGICAL DEFINITIONS

To enhance clarity, definitions of certain terms that are frequently used throughout the dissertation need to be given. Large parts of this dissertation will focus on examining various manifestations of compositions to determine whether they can be considered protected works. Accordingly, a term is needed that is neutral both regarding copyright protection and the form in which the musical information is conveyed. As already mentioned above, the term *data collection* will be used for this purpose. It has two defining features. First, it covers all possible forms in which the contents of a (musical) work can be communicated, such as a paper or PDF file displaying musical notation, a live performance, an audio recording, a MIDI file, a textual instruction set, etc. Second, it is neutral as to whether copyright protection is warranted. All performances, music sheets, PDF files, or audio recordings may not necessarily be protected works, but all of them can nonetheless be characterised as data collections. This neutrality makes the term 'data collection' useful for indicating the subject examined when assessing the satisfaction of the prerequisites of protection. For instance, Composition A – an audio file generated by an AI system – is undoubtedly a data collection, but whether it also is a protected reproduction of a work will be decided by assessing the relevant requirements of authorship, work and originality.

Another term that will see reasonably frequent use is *seeming originality*. This term is related to the discussion surrounding research question (3) and the fact that the availability of highly capable AI-powered tools has increased the importance of examining the creative process that brought the composition into being. In the era of high-performance generative AI, the mere existence of a data collection exhibiting melodic, rhythmic, and harmonic attributes that would normally meet the originality threshold cannot be granted copyright protection without also inquiring into the creative process that brought it into existence. Therefore, it becomes necessary to distinguish between two different types of meeting the originality threshold. On the one hand, a composition can seemingly meet the originality requirements, meaning that it exhibits all outward hallmarks of an original work. For example, Composition A undoubtedly satisfies this requirement in the sense that it would easily meet the requirements for copyright protection if it had been composed manually through a traditional creative process. On the other hand, originality can also refer to meeting *both* the requirements placed on the externally perceivable – melodic, rhythmic, and harmonic – attributes of a composition, *and* those placed on the creative process. For Composition A to meet this 'actual' originality requirement, it needs to have been produced by the prospective author having made free and creative choices of sufficient substantiality to make the composition reflect his or her personality. To enhance clarity and brevity, the term 'seeming originality' will be used to describe a data collection that exhibits all outwardly perceivable characteristics of originality, without addressing whether the creative process justifies copyright protection.[74] Some scholars have formulated the distinction between these two as amounting to a requirement of *originality causation*. I will discuss this term and its use in greater detail at the end of Chapter 5.

1.9 SUPPLEMENTARY MATERIALS: SHEET MUSIC AND AUDIO SAMPLES

To enhance the clarity of the musical analysis conducted in Chapter 6, both sheet music and audio samples will be incorporated in Chapter 6. The most relevant sheet music

74. Currently, there appears to be no generally used term for this. The USCO, in its report on the copyrightability of AI-generated outputs, uses the phrase 'outputs that would be copyrightable if created by a human author' to communicate a similar idea, whereas Gervais 2024, p. 1097 uses the formulation 'content that looks like material protectable by copyright'.

excerpts are printed within the main text, while complete scores of key compositions relating to the analysis of manual template compositions (*see* section 6.5) are included in the Appendix. Audio samples referenced in the analysis have been uploaded to the University of Helsinki's Helda database and can be accessed via a dedicated URL. A link to this URL is provided in the footnotes on each page that refers to an audio sample. For readers of the printed version, a QR code linking to the same URL is also included:

1.10 STRUCTURE OF THE DISSERTATION

To conclude this introductory chapter, a brief outline of the dissertation's structure will be provided. Chapter 2 introduces the phenomenon of AI and its utilisation for composing music. In examining the technical functionality of generative AI systems, particular attention is given to how a human contributor may impact the outputs generated by the AI, as this is the most relevant aspect for the dissertation's research task. Overall, the technical functionality underlying generative AI technology is examined in relatively extensive detail, as a sufficiently comprehensive grasp of its core features is essential for accurately addressing the research questions. In addition, the chapter also presents notable instances of the current and past deployment of AI for musical composition. Chapter 3 focuses on the fundamental conditions for copyright protection under FCA section 1 as interpreted in the light of EU copyright law. Chapters 2 and 3 provide the factual groundwork underlying the two concepts - generative AI and copyright law's overarching originality requirements - whose combination lies at the heart of this dissertation's research task.

Chapter 4 investigates the requirements placed on the creative process. Addressing the fact that the advent of high-performance AI systems has made it necessary to examine the work's creative process, it assesses how precisely the prospective author needs to control the creative process and the specificity with which she must determine or influence the eventual end result to be granted copyright protection. Based on this examination, it introduces and defines the concept of originality causation, a key concept that will play a significant role in the analysis presented in the final chapters of the book. Chapter 5 explores the ontological nature of works, presenting a three-stage deconstruction of a work's existence. In the first half of the chapter, this deconstruction is examined on a more general level with reference to several different types of creative expression, whereas the latter half is devoted to deconstructing the concept of a musical work.

Chapters 6 and 7 are the longest in the book, and also contain its most ambitious analysis. Chapter 6 examines what it ultimately means to compose music, applying the previous chapter's three-stage deconstruction to the creation and communication of musical information. In essence, it approaches the compositional process as one of issuing instructions that describe a sequence of intended musical attributes. The degree of specificity required of an instruction set to establish and uphold the identity of the underlying composition is explored by introducing and examining several instruction sets and gradually altering their specificity. This produces a benchmark for how much specificity generally is required of an instruction set for it to be considered a musical work to whose performances or other external manifestations one can claim copyright. The chapter also contains a discussion about the concept of joint works and how authorship should be allocated in situations with multiple contributors to a creative project.

Chapter 7 examines the copyright eligibility of AI-generated compositions. Utilising the previous chapter's inquiries into the required specificity of instruction sets, it analyses the relationship between pre-generation creative choices and post-generation end results to determine whether the link between them is strong enough to justify copyright protection. It breaks down the creative process behind generative AI systems and the compositions they generate to investigate to what extent these warrant characterisation as instances of composing musical works of authorship to which the contributors can lay copyright claim. The brief Chapter 8 presents the conclusions and final reflections, summarising the book by providing answers to the research questions stated at the beginning of this chapter.

CHAPTER 2

Generative AI: Technical Details and History

2.1 THE CORE COMPONENTS OF GENERATIVE AI MODELS

2.1.1 Essential Terminological Definitions and Structure of the Chapter

While there is no universally accepted definition of what the term Artificial Intelligence (AI) encompasses, it is commonly characterised as a branch of computer science focused on developing machines and systems capable of performing tasks traditionally considered to require human intelligence, with minimal or no human intervention.[75] AI is best understood as a broad umbrella term encompassing various computational approaches. Within this broad category, *machine learning* refers to methods that allow computers to learn from data and improve performance over time without being explicitly programmed for each specific task.

Neural networks are a specific type of machine learning model inspired by the structure of the human brain. They consist of interconnected layers of nodes, or 'neurons', which process input data through weighted connections. When these networks contain multiple layers – allowing for the learning of increasingly complex representations – they are referred to as *deep learning* models. Deep learning has

75. The AI Act Article 3(1) defines an 'AI system' as 'a machine-based system designed to operate with varying levels of autonomy, that ... infers, from the input it receives, how to generate outputs such as predictions, content, recommendations, or decisions that can influence physical or virtual environments'. Lee, Cooper, and Grimmelman 2024, p. 4 aptly note that '["AI" or "generative AI"] is not just one product from one company. Instead, "generative AI" is a catch-all name for a massive ecosystem of loosely related technologies, including conversational text chatbots like ChatGPT, image generators like Midjourney and DALL•E, coding assistants like GitHub Copilot, and systems that compose music, create videos, and suggest molecules for new medical drugs. Generative-AI models have different technical architectures and are trained on different kinds and sources of data using different algorithms'.

proven especially powerful in domains such as image recognition and natural language processing. *Generative AI* refers to a subset of deep learning models designed not only to analyse data but also to produce new content, such as text, images, music, or code. In the context of this dissertation, generative AI is particularly relevant for its capacity to enable high-level, machine-assisted creative expression. The distinction between AI models and AI systems also needs to be clarified. An *AI model* denotes the trained algorithm that performs a specific task – for instance, generating text or classifying images – while an *AI system* refers to the broader operational infrastructure in which the model is embedded, including data pipelines, interfaces, and deployment mechanisms that support its real-world functioning.[76]

The purpose of this chapter is to explain the technical aspects of how generative AI models function, insofar as they are relevant to the legal questions at issue. The early sections explore the key components of AI models from a relatively broad perspective. This is followed by an examination of algorithmically generated music, both in terms of its historical origins and its role in the current hype surrounding AI-powered products. The chapter then turns to the functionality of current state-of-the-art music generation models. The primary aim of this section is to provide a foundation for assessing whether the hypothetical Composition A, discussed in connection with research question (1), could qualify as a copyright-protected work.

2.1.2 The Basic Functionality of AI Models and the Black Box Problem

A rudimentary understanding of how generative AI models function is crucial for exploring the legal implications of AI-generated creative expression. The functioning of an AI model utilising a neural network architecture can be illustrated by an idealised example of how a sentiment analysis model might execute its task of predicting whether a product review is positive, negative, or neutral.

76. Quintais 2025, p. 5 explains the distinction by an analogy where 'the model is the engine, whereas the system is the car one drives on the road'. The distinction between general-purpose AI models and AI systems is not without relevance for the copyright-related provisions of the AI Act. However, the distinction holds limited significance for assessing copyright claims to AI outputs.

Figure 2.1 Visual Rendition of a Fully Connected Neural Network. Input and Output Layers on Left and Right, Respectively, with Three Hidden Layers in the Middle. The Neurons Are Represented by Circles, and the (Weighted) Connections by Lines

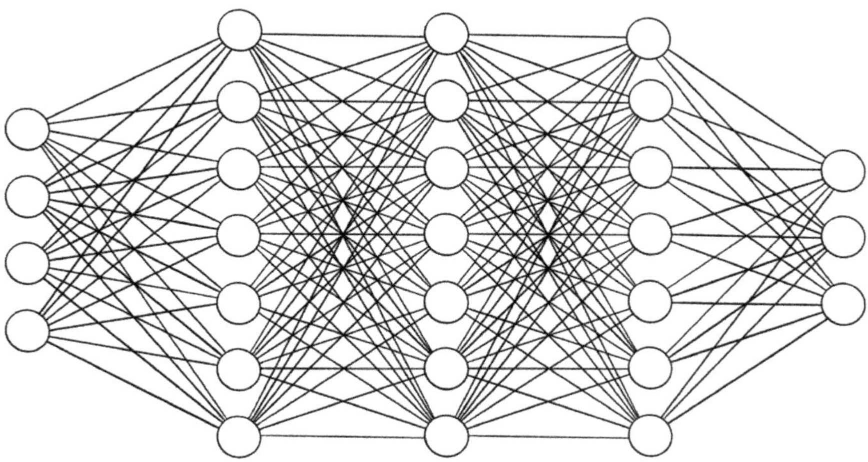

The *input layer* is where the network receives external data, in this case, a text. For the network to be able to process the text, it needs to be converted into numerical *tokens*. A token is a unit of text – such as a word, subword, or character – into which input data is segmented for processing by the model. Following this, the tokens undergo embedding, where the input tokens are converted into vectors by a word embedding algorithm.[77] These vector representations allow the network to capture semantic relationships between words. For example, the input might include sentences such as 'I love this product' or 'This is great'. The hidden layers then process these embeddings to identify patterns and dependencies between words. The goal is to progressively refine the data representation, capturing increasingly abstract features as the input moves through successive layers. Early hidden layers may learn that individual positive words, such as 'love' or 'great', contribute to an overall positive sentiment. Deeper layers begin to capture more complex interactions, such as the negating effect of words like 'not' appearing before otherwise positive words. These deeper layers – those further to the right in the figure – synthesise these features, integrating both individual word meanings and their contextual interplay. This enables the network to perform a more sophisticated analysis of the sentiment expressed in the text. Finally, in the output layer, each neuron's value represents the model's confidence in a particular sentiment classification, typically expressed as probability scores across the categories of positive, neutral, or negative.

Although this paints a very neat picture of neural networks, the 'division of labour' between the different neurons and layers is usually not as reminiscent of

77. Word2Vec and BERT are examples of word embedding algorithms.

human reasoning. This relates to the automated process by which the model improves its own performance. Because the model only focuses on the numerically determined accuracy of the end result, the process by which it is obtained is unlikely to follow a process that human reason can fathom, resulting in the oft-cited *black box problem*.[78] To get an accurate grasp of this issue, certain aspects of the neural networks' functionality need to be considered in more detail.

The performance of the model relies on optimising the connections between the neurons during training. Each neuron processes a weighted sum of its inputs and applies an activation function to produce an output. All neurons in adjacent layers are connected (*see* Figure 2.1), and the strength of each connection is determined by *weights* and *biases*, which serve as variable and constant in the activation function.[79] Essentially, the model's optimisation involves the successive adjustment of the weights and biases – collectively referred to as the network's *parameters* – based on a calculation of the model's performance. In the case of a sentiment prediction model, performance is measured by comparing the model's outputs to the reference labels provided in the training data.

The training process begins with the model's parameters initialised randomly. A *loss function* is used to evaluate the disparity between the predicted sentiment and the actual label of the input. The goal of training is to minimise this loss by iteratively adjusting the parameters through *backpropagation* and *gradient descent*. Backpropagation computes the gradient of the loss function with respect to each parameter, and gradient descent updates the parameters in a direction that reduces the loss.[80] Essentially, the training dataset provides examples with known target outputs, and the backpropagation algorithm, aided by gradient descent, adjusts the parameters to better match these target predictions until the loss stops decreasing. The purpose of this training process is to allow the model to generalise to unseen data, enabling it to predict the sentiment of sentences it has not encountered during training. This allows the model to output probabilities indicating whether the overall sentiment of a previously unseen input sentence is positive, negative, or neutral.

The aforementioned black box problem arises from the combination of initialising the parameters with random values and the automated process of minimising loss. The random initialisation gives the model a chaotic starting point without any logic in how the values of the neurons are related to each other. The performance is then improved iteratively through automatic adjustments – backpropagation with gradient descent – that *collectively* contribute to reducing loss.[81] As a result, the crucial

78. *See*, for instance, Bathaee 2018, pp. 901-902.
79. Weights and biases play distinct roles in the optimisation process. Weights govern the strength of connections between neurons, regulating the impact of input signals on the neurons. Biases contribute to determining the activation threshold of a neuron, influencing how readily it activates. Together, they enable the network to learn and effectively minimise loss during the training phase.
80. Gradients represent the rate of change of a function with respect to its parameters and are used in backpropagation to adjust the parameters during training.
81. Blazek aptly points out that such a training process 'forces neurons to compensate for the deficiencies of other neurons', https://towardsdatascience.com/why-we-will-never-open-deep-learnings-black-box-4c27cd335118, accessed 30 May 2025.

adjustments tend to become dispersed among multiple parameters, hindering individual neurons or modules from developing specialised functions akin to the step-by-step reasoning characteristic of the human brain's approach to pattern recognition or problem solving.[82] This can significantly diminish the transparency and explainability of the model's processes, leading to concerns ranging from debugging difficulties to ethical considerations and a reserved attitude to deploying deep networks for certain high-risk tasks.[83] Moreover, the lack of interpretability also tends to increase proportionally with the size or depth of neural networks, making the current trend of using ever-larger models especially vulnerable to the black box problem. The impact of the black box problem on the relationship between pre-generation creative inputs and post-generation outputs from the perspective of claiming copyright to the latter will be discussed further in section 7.3.2.

2.1.3 Autoregressive Generation, Foundation Models, and Fine-Tuning

Autoregressive transformer models, which underpin many of today's most proficient text and music generation systems,[84] leverage the same core principles of neural network training to compute probability distributions over possible outputs. Rather than classifying sentiment, these models are trained to predict the next token in a sequence based on the preceding context. During training, they are exposed to vast corpora of data – such as text or audio – and learn to model the statistical likelihood of a given token following a particular sequence of tokens.

At each step of generation, the model calculates a probability distribution over its entire vocabulary, ranking possible continuations by their learned likelihood. For instance, given the prompt 'The silence in the room was', the model might assign the highest probabilities to words such as 'deafening', 'palpable', or 'unsettling', based on patterns it has extracted from the training corpus.[85] It then samples or selects from this distribution to produce the next token, which is fed back into the model as input for the next prediction. This iterative mechanism continues until a complete output is formed.

An important aspect of developing a generative AI model lies in *fine-tuning*. Even if one were to produce a sophisticated text generation model, it will typically not provide particularly high-quality or prompt-sensitive outputs unless it undergoes substantial fine-tuning. This warrants a distinction between *foundation models* and *fine-tuned models*. A foundation model is a broadly capable system, trained on large and diverse datasets to develop general-purpose functionality. However, without further adaptation, such models often fail to deliver precise or task-specific outputs.

82. Nick Seaver 2019, p. 413 points out that today's widespread deep learning algorithms 'are often so complex that they pose interpretive challenges even to their makers'.
83. The AI Act's heavy emphasis on the risks of utilising AI systems is a case in point.
84. The models powering today's leading chatbots – such as GPT, Claude, and Gemini – are based on transformer architectures. The same applies to state-of-the-art music generation systems like MusicLM and MusicGen, which shall be discussed in greater detail below.
85. For ease of explanation, whole words are used here, though in practice tokens often consist of subword units.

Fine-tuned models are derived from foundation models through additional targeted training, with the goal of optimising their performance for specific tasks or use cases.

Fine-tuning is essentially about equipping a general-purpose model with specific capabilities to align its output with the intended use. A common example of this is refining the question-answering capabilities of a language model. If a model was trained on a text corpus indiscriminately scraped from the internet, it is unlikely to perform well on question-answer tasks. For example, a question about the capital of Finland may not always be followed by the correct answer; instead, it might be found in a quiz sheet, where it is followed by the next question. Consequently, the model may assign a relatively high probability of outputting an unrelated question rather than the correct answer. To address this issue, fine-tuning the model becomes necessary, and various methods exist for doing so. Full-parameter fine-tuning, wherein all the model's parameters are updated to better align with the desired output, is likely to yield optimal results. However, it comes with large computation requirements, making it feasible only for relatively small models. A more practical approach for fine-tuning larger models is to employ *parameter-efficient fine-tuning* (PEFT). Akin to fruit tree grafting, the idea is to introduce and train a small number of new parameters while retaining the parameters of the underlying general-purpose model.[86]

Two approaches warrant special mention. First, in a method known as *supervised fine-tuning*, the model is refined by providing it with a labelled dataset containing input-output pairs. For example, to enhance the model's performance in question-answer tasks, one might compile a carefully curated set of question-answer pairs to illustrate the desired output. While it may be highly effective for specific purposes, this method typically entails a substantial investment of human labour. Second, one may opt for *reinforcement learning with human feedback* (RLHF). Here, the idea is to generate multiple completions of a given prompt and have a human labeller rank the outputs from best to worst based on how well they align with the desired result. The ranked input-output pairs are then used as training data for constructing a *reward model* that gives a score to the outputs based on how well they correspond to the objective. In a process called *proximal policy optimisation* (PPO), the reward model is then used to fine-tune the general-purpose model to align with – or approximate – the policy indicated by the reward model. For example, OpenAI employed this technique to fine-tune GPT-3 to produce helpful, honest, and harmless results.[87]

While RLHF is often described as a form of fine-tuning, it is sometimes distinguished under the label of *alignment* rather than fine-tuning, as its primary aim is not merely to improve task performance but to adjust the model's behaviour to better reflect human values or preferences.[88] Overall, it must be emphasised that fine-tuning

86. The specific technique to use for this will vary depending on the model and training dataset. *Low-rank adaptation* (LoRA), the introduction of *adapter layers* and *prefix tuning* are common ways of accomplishing this.
87. Ouyang et al. 2022, p. 2. Needless to say, refining the underlying LLM to unlock the functionality of ChatGPT required enormous amounts of fine-tuning not only restricted to making it produce helpful, honest, and harmless outputs.
88. In the GenLaw Glossary, available at https://blog.genlaw.org/glossary.html, accessed 9 August 2025, alignment is defined as 'the process of taking a pre-trained model and further tuning it so

a model to generate outputs more attuned to the developers' artistic goals is potentially very significant for copyright eligibility of AI-generated musical compositions. Chapter 7 – and particularly sections 7.4.2 and 7.4.3 – will examine this issue in greater detail with reference to both real-world (MusicRL) and hypothetical (ExtraRL) examples.

Fine-tuning a model with specific and highly curated datasets poses a significant challenge in avoiding *overfitting*. Overfitting occurs when the model adapts too well to the training data, incorporating noise and irrelevant details. This can impair the model's ability to generalise to new, unseen examples, thereby reducing performance and undermining the intended benefits of fine-tuning.[89] Another risk when engaging in extensive fine-tuning is *catastrophic forgetting*, which refers to the tendency of a model to overwrite previously learned information when adapting to new data, resulting in a decline in performance on tasks it had previously handled effectively.[90] In other words, fine-tuning a foundation model too extensively may cause a significant decrease in overall performance. This can become relevant for the type of iterative fine-tuning of a music generation model discussed in section 7.4.3.

Another concern related to fine-tuning is *memorisation*, which refers to the model inadvertently retaining fragments of the training corpus within its internal parameters. This makes it liable to regenerate – or 'regurgitate' – near-exact copies of significant portions of the training data.[91] To counteract the possibility of overfitting, memorisation, and regurgitation, it is important to include a variety of examples in the training data that cover different aspects of the desired outcome. In our question-answer example, this would mean incorporating samples with a wide variety of question structures, answer formats, contextual scenarios, and ambiguity levels. Various technical measures can also be employed to mitigate the adverse effects associated with overfitting.[92] Furthermore, system-level measures, like filtering outputs and configuring model parameters to limit regurgitated responses, can reduce the risk of generating outputs that directly replicate memorised data.[93]

---

that its outputs are *aligned* with a policy set forth by the model developer ... While the goals of alignment are vast and pluralistic, current techniques for achieving better alignment are broadly applicable across goals. These techniques include reinforcement learning with human feedback and full model fine-tuning'. Italics in original.

89. Emanuilov and Margoni 2024, pp. 10-11; https://klu.ai/glossary/supervised-fine-tuning, accessed 2 February 2025.
90. Luo et al. 2023, pp. 2-3 and Liu et al. 2024, p. 3 explain this phenomenon at a broader level with reference to large language models.
91. Cooper and Grimmelman 2024, pp. 1, 18-20. Another term used for such unintended copying of training data is 'plagiaristic outputs'. *See* Rosati 2025, pp. 603, 606.
92. These include regularisation, dropout, early stopping, data augmentation, and batch normalization.
93. For instance, the company behind the popular Udio model (*see* Chapter 1), having been accused of copyright infringement, posted the following statement on X on 25 June 2024: 'The goal of model training is to develop an understanding of musical ideas – the basic building blocks of musical expression that are owned by no one. Our system is explicitly designed to create music reflecting new musical ideas. We are completely uninterested in reproducing content in our training set, and in fact, *have implemented and continue to refine state-of-the-art filters to ensure our model does not reproduce copyrighted works or artists' voices*.' My italics. Post available at https://x.com/udiomusic/status/1805694761891778783?s=46&t=R5LBnDmluUM1q9hD0liYVg&mx=2, accessed 2 February 2025.

2.1.4 Prompt Engineering

The most immediately apparent way of interacting with an AI model and influencing its outputs – and certainly the one most familiar to the average user – is through prompting the model to produce particular types of content. The growing importance of this interaction has given rise to the concept of prompt engineering, which has been defined as the 'art of composing and formatting the prompt to maximize a model's performance on a desired task'.[94]

In the example of Composition A, discussed in Chapter 1, the user prompted the model to generate dramatic orchestral music in E-flat minor, in a cinematic style, and with a duration of two minutes and thirty seconds. As previously noted, this creative input is unlikely to support a credible copyright claim to Composition A, since the relationship between the prompt's contents and the musical attributes of Composition A lacks the necessary specificity. However, even if the prompt used in the case of Composition A is insufficient to substantiate an authorship claim, this does not mean that prompt engineering could not under any circumstances be considered sufficient to justify copyright protection.

ChatGPT gives a good example of this. While having ChatGPT perform a mundane task such as document summation or suggested workout routines will not yield a particularly original result, there are numerous ways in which the prompt can be refined to increase the individuality of the model's output. With ChatGPT supporting prompts of several thousand characters, users have ample opportunity to shape the output in accordance with their creative aims. Among the most immediate ways to do so is by specifying the desired structure, format, or dimensions in the prompt. To further customise the output, one can add a few examples of target results, which are sometimes referred to as *few-shot prompting*.[95] Additional options include providing step-by-step instructions to exert greater control over the output. For instance, one might ask the model to generate a poem of 10 stanzas encompassing an introduction, call to adventure, character development, confrontation, climax, resolution, and epilogue, while also specifying the number of lines per stanza, rhyme scheme, and meter. To enhance control even further, one might generate successive drafts of the poem, providing specific instructions for each revision.[96] In this type of scenario, it is by no means implausible that the relationship between the user's creative contribution

94. Hu et al. 2021, p. 9.
95. *See*, for instance, https://www.promptingguide.ai/techniques/fewshot, accessed 2 February 2025. This is opposed to *zero-shot* prompting (*ibid.*), which refers to a model's ability to perform a task without having been given any examples of the desired output. In such cases, the successful execution of the task will be due to the model's capacity for generalisation or its having been fine-tuned. *One-shot prompting* indicates a successful completion of a task based on one example.
96. This is occasionally referred to as chain-of-thought prompting, *see* Maithili Badhan's article *Comprehensive Guide to Chain-of-Thought Prompting*, available at https://www.mercity.ai/blog-post/guide-to-chain-of-thought-prompting, accessed 2 February 2025.

– in the form of extensive iterative prompting – can be sufficiently reflected in the final output to warrant copyright protection.[97]

The precision and flexibility with which the generative model is able to adhere to the prompts has a dramatic effect on how closely the outputs reflect the intentions of the system user and how useful the generated outputs will be. Among the currently available systems, those specialised in text generation appear to excel in the degree of prompt adherence. Textual expression is very amenable to iterative refinement targeted at selected parts of the outputs, making it more plausible for a user to exert meaningful creative control on the end result. Text-to-image models, such as Midjourney or Dall-E, exhibit similarly impressive prompt adherence. Like text generation models, they also allow for iterative refinements to the image, where specific elements of the image can be adjusted while the remainder is kept largely intact.

This highlights a crucial disadvantage of music generation models: the degree of prompt adherence in such models, at least currently, tends to be significantly lower than that observed in text and image systems. For instance, Udio, one of the currently most proficient music generation models, mainly allows the user to control the outputs via tags representing broad categories such as genre, style, instrumentation, and duration.[98] One can also select the desired tone or voice by tags like 'emotional', 'scream', or 'cry', as well as specifying at which part of the song's structure – verse, pre-chorus, chorus, etc. – the lyrics are to appear. The system offers some possibilities to single out specific portions of the generated track for further (iterative) refinement, but the commands with which to steer the refinements remain limited to the aforementioned broadly formulated tags.

The inability to issue prompts more specific than tags related to genre, style, or instrumentation significantly reduces the likelihood of producing an original musical composition through mere prompting. For the user to obtain an original end result, the AI-generated track most likely needs to be exported and subjected to manual redaction. As noted in Chapter 1, this has pushed this dissertation to also explore other ways of interacting with music generation models and influence their outputs. The technical aspects of conditioning outputs in music generation will be discussed in greater detail in section 7.5, while section 2.3.3 addresses the technical foundations and common challenges of music generation more broadly.

2.2 AI-POWERED MUSIC GENERATION: A HISTORICAL PERSPECTIVE

2.2.1 Current Music Generation Models and a Few Historical Examples

In the realm of autonomous creative content generation, transformer-based text-to-text systems like ChatGPT and diffusion-based text-to-image systems such as DALL-E and

97. Similar arguments are made by Leistner and Jussen 2025, pp. 18, 50 and Hugenholtz 2024, p. 18. This issue will be discussed in greater detail in Chapter 7.
98. The Udio model can be accessed here: https://www.udio.com, accessed 15 June 2025.

Stable Diffusion have garnered significant attention compared to their music generation counterparts. Music generation models largely employ similar architectural solutions – which we shall explore in greater detail below – but their performance lags behind their text and image-generating peers. Still, various types of audio generation models are being developed at a dynamic pace, and 2023 was characterised by particularly promising improvements in the performance of AI-powered music generation, accompanied by an increasing excitement around it. This has led some to speculate that a 'ChatGPT moment' for music generation may be 'just around the corner'.[99]

Even with recent progress, significant weaknesses plague music models. Three distinct issues stand out as particularly noteworthy. First, music models often provide limited user impact on output and demonstrate only loose correlations between user input and the final result. Second, in examining the artistic viability of the outputs, maintaining contextual coherence over longer timespans is challenging. Third, applications that output raw audio often suffer from a lower sample rate, as well as producing less natural vocal and instrumental timbres. In the following section, we will examine possible technical solutions to addressing these issues and explore the current state-of-the-art models. But before delving into technical details, it is essential to provide a brief survey of AI-powered music generation's history to offer context.

The predecessors of today's (relatively) high-performance music generators are generally characterised by placing the creation of a composition – partially or entirely – outside the control of a human agent, relying on a combination of pre-determined rules and some degree of randomness. This approach to music generation has been termed *algorithmic composition*, although alternative concepts such as generative music, musical meta-creation, and musical computational creativity have also been proposed.[100] One notable precursor to modern algorithmic composition is various versions of a 'musical dice game', wherein precomposed musical fragments are rearranged by throwing dice.[101] A transition to computer-based applications occurred during the 1950s, often led by computer scientists, avant-garde composers, or collaborations between the two. One prominent early example is the *Illiac Suite for String Quartet* (1957), composed by a computer program developed by the composer Lejaren Hiller and the mathematician Leonard Isaacson.[102] In this work, the computer 'was programmed to generate random integers representing various musical elements, such as pitches, rhythms, and dynamics, which were subsequently screened through programmed rules of composition'.[103] Avant-garde composer Iannis Xenakis used

99. Ramponi 2023. Given the very impressive performance of models such as Suno and Udio, one might ask whether the 'ChatGPT moment' for music generation is not already upon us to at least some degree. Nonetheless, I would argue a more precise and flexible prompt adherence is required to fully unlock the potential of AI-generated music.
100. Pasquier et al. 2017, p. 1; Carnovalini 2022, p. 1.
101. Nierhaus 2009, p. 36.
102. Hiller 2025.
103. Hiller 2025.

stochastic algorithms in his creative process,[104] while his colleague John Cage experimented with various types of aleatoric music that incorporated randomly selected input to a considerable degree.[105]

Later experiments increasingly focused on having computer programs formulate the rules governing the composition's contents. One well-known example of this is David Cope's *Experiments in Musical Intelligence* (EMI), developed in 1992. EMI operates by analysing a set of musical compositions to derive an Augmented Transition Network (ATN) representing the style of the training corpus. It then uses pattern-matching algorithms to extract characteristic musical signatures, which are subsequently employed to generate new compositions that adhere to the inferred style specifications.[106] A reasonably handsome chorale in the style of J.S. Bach demonstrates the capabilities of the system.[107] It also fared well in an informal Turing test.[108]

The 2010s witnessed an increased emphasis on computer generation and the emergence of an increasing number of startups aiming to harness the rapidly improving technology. Notable among these startups are AIVA, Amper, and Jukedeck, which gained widespread recognition. Luxembourg-based AIVA (Artificial Intelligence Virtual Artist) was founded in 2016 with an intent to specialise in classical and symphonic music composition.[109] It has released several studio-recorded albums and became a registered member of Luxembourg's collective rights management organisation.[110] Notably, one of AIVA's compositions successfully passed as human-made cinematic music in a Turing test conducted by professional classical musicians on a popular YouTube channel.[111] However, the actual user experience with AIVA often falls short of the lofty expectations raised by its many accolades.

Similar to many other music generation programs, AIVA offers users a diverse range of genres to choose from, including ambient techno, modern R&B, traditional folk, strings & woodwinds, and epic orchestra. Outputs are generated in MIDI format, and users can edit the generated tracks directly within the app. The MIDI format of the outputs also allows high-fidelity reproduction if exported to a capable Digital Audio Workstation (DAW). The best tracks constitute reasonably competent background or 'space-filler' music,[112] but the overall compositional-artistic quality tends to be generic

104. Fernández and Vico 2013, p. 517. A *stochastic algorithm* is a computational method that incorporates randomness or probability to efficiently solve problems with uncertain or variable inputs. *See* Collet 2006, p. 3.
105. Cage's compositions *Music of Changes* and *Indeterminacy* provide well-known examples.
106. Fernández and Vico 2013, p. 526.
107. A (human) performance of the chorale is available at https://www.youtube.com/watch?v = PczDLl92vlc, accessed 2 February 2025.
108. *See* Johnson 1997.
109. Machuron 2016; Kalegasi 2017.
110. Bulayenko et al. 2022, p. 53 note that although AIVA has been marketed as 'world's first virtual artist recogni[s]ed by an author's rights society', this may give a slightly inaccurate representation of the relevant facts. As noted by the Advisory Committee of Rightholders of SACEM Luxembourg, the AI-model itself is not a member of SACEM. Moreover, '*a physical person*, a team member of AIVA Technologies, *is declaring works* under the pseudonym of "AIVA"'.
111. 'Can You Tell the Difference between AI and Human Composers?', https://www.youtube.com/watch?v = PmL31mVxOXA&t = 331s, accessed 2 February 2025.
112. Sobel 2021, p. 232.

and lacks long-term coherence. Amper and Jukedeck offer similar functionality and performance to AIVA. Both enable the user to manipulate certain features of the generated track, such as genre, mood, instrumentation, duration, and tempo.[113] Amper and Jukedeck were acquired, respectively, by TikTok in 2019 and Shutterstock in 2020, which certainly can be considered a testament to the promise their models contain.[114]

Towards the end of the 2010s, multiple AI music projects were launched by tech giants, including Google Magenta,[115] IBM's Watson Beat,[116] Sony's Flow Machines,[117] and Amazon's AWS DeepComposer.[118] The involvement of the big tech companies gave access to greater datasets and more computing power, which greatly expanded the possibilities of using more complex deep learning model architectures. Still, the outputs of the early big tech offerings remained relatively modest. Instead, the most significant avenue towards future development was provided by OpenAI's Jukebox, released in April 2020. Not only did Jukebox successfully combine music and vocals in its output but also the compositional-artistic quality and audio fidelity were impressive for its time.[119] From the vantage point of 2024, the audio-to-audio structure of Jukebox marked an important watershed, as it decreased the focus on symbolic representation of music (*see* below), showing the way towards the currently dominant trends within music generation: the use of raw audio input enabled by high compression of the training data, and a transformer architecture for generating the audio output.[120]

The 2020s have witnessed the emergence of numerous commercial apps focused on generating audio tracks with minimal user input. Examples include BeatOven, Boomy, Mubert, Riffusion, and Soundful. These apps typically allow users to specify the desired genre, mood, and duration of the track. However, while they produce passable background music in the desired genre, their audio fidelity and long-term compositional coherence remain too modest for inclusion in professional music production workflows. Overall, their outputs tend to occupy a middle ground between sounding like human-made compositions and the sample-based music templates that have been available in DAWs for decades.

Among these apps, Suno AI has stood out in my own testing. It offers users the option to generate lyrics for the song, which are then set to music according to the selected style. In catering to the prompts, Suno's model 'does not recognize artists'

113. A thorough presentation of the editing capabilities of Jukedeck is carried out in 'Jukedeck Demo – Create unique music for your videos in seconds', https://www.youtube.com/watch?v=jfs1k7krXt8&t=51s, accessed 2 February 2025. Since 15 December 2019, Jukedeck has been offline due to its acquisition by TokTok.
114. https://investor.shutterstock.com/news-releases/news-release-details/shutterstock-announces-acquisition-amper-music, https://www.musicbusinessworldwide.com/tiktok-parent-bytedance-buys-ai-music-company-jukedeck/, accessed 2 February 2025.
115. https://github.com/magenta/magenta, accessed 2 February 2025.
116. https://www.ibm.com/blogs/think/nl-en/2017/06/06/intro-watson-music/, accessed 2 February 2025.
117. https://www.flow-machines.com/, accessed 2 February .2025.
118. https://aws.amazon.com/deepcomposer/, accessed 2 February 2025.
119. Samples are available at https://openai.com/research/jukebox, accessed 2 February 2025.
120. Dhariwal et al. 2020, pp. 2-3.

names, but understand[s] genres and vibes'.[121] While the system occasionally struggles with providing suitable beginnings and endings to the songs generated, the audio outputs contain notably greater melodic inventiveness compared to most other generators discussed above. Thus, the outputs are clearly distinct from sample-based templates. Users have the choice to either randomly generate lyrics or supply their own. The quality of the output still varies, especially regarding the correlation between the prompts and the end result. Udio also exhibits a similarly impressive performance to that of Suno.[122] As already noted in section 2.1.4, Udio offers the user a number of tools for shaping the outputs, but creative control over the music generation is limited to choosing among a selection of broad tags, such as genre, style, and instrumentation.

2.2.2 Accounting for the Hype Associated with AI-Powered Products

The historical context of music and AI also needs to address the significant media attention AI-based products receive. The hype surrounding AI as the most significant disruptive technology of our time may often increase the attention and market value it commands, especially compared to a human-made creation of similar artistic quality. A striking illustration of this phenomenon comes from the art world, where *Edmond de Belamy*,[123] a painting generated by a Generative Adversarial Network (GAN) model, was auctioned for USD 432,500, far exceeding pre-auction estimates ranging from USD 7,000 to USD 10,000.[124] The painting is certainly not devoid of artistic merit, but it is not particularly controversial to suggest that the main allure of the piece lies in its mysterious and exciting algorithmic origins.

Another oft-cited example of AI-generated art is the Next Rembrandt. This project involved creating a 3D-printed painting based on data derived from Rembrandt's works. Utilising deep learning algorithms and facial recognition techniques, the research team analysed over 400 faces to determine the subject: a male figure aged 30 to 40, wearing black clothing, a hat, and facing right. The painting was produced using a custom-made 3D printer and specially formulated UV ink, resulting in a work that garnered global attention.[125] In terms of artistic merit, the painting is certainly not on par with an original Rembrandt,[126] but it still possesses considerable artistic quality. On the whole, it is difficult to see any clear potential for long-term commercial exploitation of the underlying technology. This is not least since the process of producing the painting evidently appears to have been exceptionally labour-intensive. Rather than

121. The Suno UI gives this explanation. The system is available at https://www.suno.ai/, accessed 2 February 2025.
122. Samples of Udio's outputs are available at https://www.udio.com/, accessed 2 February 2025.
123. https://www.christies.com/en/stories/a-collaboration-between-two-artists-one-human-one-a-machine-0cd01f4e232f4279a525a446d60d4cd1, accessed 2 February 2025.
124. https://www.christies.com/lot/lot-6166184/?sid = &intObjectID = 6166184&T = Lot&language = en, accessed 2 February 2025.
125. *See* Pickett-Groen 2018.
126. Guardian art journalist Jonathan Jones gave the painting a rather harsh critique, www.theguardian.com/artanddesign/jonathanjonesblog/2016/apr/06/digital-rembrandt-mock-art-fools? > https://www.theguardian.com/artanddesign/jonathanjonesblog/2016/apr/06/digital-rembrandt-mock-art-fools, accessed 2 February 2025.

constituting research and development aimed at producing straightforward return on investment through product sales, it seems more natural to view the project as a demonstration or experiment exploring the limits of what can be achieved with the technology available at the time.

Another category of AI-related projects that has captured public interest involves collaborations between human artists – whether contemporary or historical – and an AI-powered agent. In this category, a number of musical counterparts to the Next Rembrandt project warrant mention. DeepBach, unveiled in 2016, focused on generating chorale harmonisations in the style of J.S. Bach.[127] The model utilised a dependency network with shared parameters and a combination of two Recurrent Neural Networks (RNN) and a non-recurrent neural network to predict notes in each voice of a chorale, based on a database of J.S. Bach's chorale harmonisations.[128] The output performed well in a Turing test, as '1,600 listeners, of whom about a quarter were trained musicians, more than 50% thought examples of DeepBach's work were actually written by Johann Sebastian Bach'.[129] Although this achievement is notable, one must acknowledge that Bach's chorale harmonisations represent a particularly rule-dependent segment of his production, offering comparatively little room for compositional genius and individuality to manifest itself.[130] Consequently, both humans and machines may find it relatively easy to produce stylistically similar harmonisations.[131] Had four-part fugal passages of similar length been requested,[132] the machine-made creations would likely have fared much worse in a Turing test or in emulating the style of Bach in an artistically convincing manner. One sample of DeepBach's creations is available, a reharmonization of the hymn melody *Wer nur den lieben Gott läßt walten.*[133] While the harmonisation is not without artistic merit, certain passages are rather peculiar, and it is challenging to see notable potential for deploying the model beyond experimental purposes.

127. *See*, Hadjeres et al. 2017.
128. Hadjeres et al. 2017, pp. 4-5.
129. *See DeepBach Uses 'Deep Learning' To Create Music In The Style Of Bach*, available at https://www.synthtopia.com/content/2016/12/22/deepbach-uses-deep-learning-to-create-music-in-the-style-of-bach/, accessed 2 February 2025.
130. J.S. Bach is universally regarded as the pre-eminent composer in history by musicians spanning both classical and popular music traditions. (*See*, for instance, the video *The Bach Effect: What the GREATS Hear That You Don't*, where musician Rick Beato interviews many prominent current day musicians representing various genres about Bach's influence on their work and Bach's overall stature in music history, available at https://www.youtube.com/watch?v=UNgrH8u-IIc, accessed 2 February 2025.) However, Bach's chorale harmonisations, although greatly admired by most experts, arguably do not contribute to his overall legacy to any notable extent, as his greatest compositional achievements lie in a very large body of other works, such as his many concerti for different ensembles, the Well-Tempered Clavier, cello suites, sonatas and partitas for solo violin, his Cantatas, the two Passions, and the B Minor Mass. *See*, for instance, Wilson 2005.
131. This may also explain why this is the second time we encounter Turing tests performed with said highly specific body of work.
132. Fugal writing is equally rule-bound but leaves considerably greater creative space available to the composer. This makes it a better vehicle for demonstrating compositional ingenuity and individuality. *See* Chapter 6 for more details about the elements of musical composition.
133. https://www.youtube.com/watch?v=QiBM7-5hA6o, accessed 2 February 2025 embedded video at 1 min 27 sec.

Tech giant Huawei also ventured into AI-composed music in the late 2010s. They developed a smartphone application trained on the works of Franz Schubert with the aim of completing his famous *Unfinished Symphony.* The app only produced melodic output, leaving the completion of the symphony to rely on the assistance of composer Lucas Cantor not only for the entirety of the harmonisation and orchestration but also to 'draw out the good ideas from the AI, and *fill in the gaps* where necessary'.[134] The completion, which premiered with great fanfare in February of 2019, spans approximately 20 minutes of orchestral music. Apart from some vague references to the first movement of the original work, it bears little resemblance to Schubert's distinctive use of melody, harmonisation, instrumentation, and form.[135] Given the lack of clarity on which portions of the composition were generated by the AI model, it is challenging to assess the model's performance accurately. Ultimately, Huawei's project appears to have limited practical relevance in the field of AI composition, mainly serving as a means of generating publicity by merging the fashionable concept of AI with one of the great masterworks of classical music.[136]

The same seems to be the case with the Beethoven X project, in which Deutsche Telekom, to mark the 250th anniversary of Ludwig van Beethoven's birth, organised a team of international music and AI experts in spring 2019 with the aim of completing Beethoven's unfinished 10th Symphony 'with the help of [AI]'.[137] The completion is available on YouTube,[138] and the end result is much closer to Beethoven's style than Huawei's completion is to Schubert's. Had the entirety been composed by a generative AI model, the work would be very impressive indeed. However, details as to the model architecture and the extent of its compositional contribution to the completion are very scarce. Most likely, the completion was largely made by composer Walter Werzowa.[139]

In addition to the venerable masters of classical music, giants of popular music have also been invoked in recent AI projects. In 2016, Sony's Flow Machines AI software project, aimed at 'expanding the creativity of creators in music [through] research, development, and a social implementation',[140] released two tracks based on human-AI collaboration. The first, *Daddy's Car*, was inspired by The Beatles, whereas

134. https://www.classicfm.com/composers/schubert/unfinished-symphony-completed-by-ai/, accessed 2 February 2025. My italics.
135. In addition, I find it puzzling that the completion contains no reference whatsoever to the substantial sketches Schubert left of the uncompleted 3rd movement of the symphony.
136. The entirety of the work is available on YouTube, https://www.youtube.com/watch?v = _6O UGRsslJY. A far from flattering review of the premiere can be found here, https://theconversation.com/composers-are-under-no-threatfrom-ai-if-huaweis-finished-schubert-symphony-is-a-guide-111630, both links accessed 2 February 2025.
137. https://www.telekom.com/en/media/media-information/archive/beethoven-s-10th-symphony-completed-by-ai-633060, accessed 2 February 2025.
138. https://www.youtube.com/watch?v = Rvj3Oblscqw&t = 158s, accessed 2 February 2025.
139. This certainly is the impression left by the brief interviews with Werzowa and Ahmed Elgammal given in conjunction with the premiere of the completion. The latter is director of the Art and Artificial Intelligence Laboratory at Rutgers University, and 'led the AI side of the team' in the project. https://www.scientificamerican.com/podcast/episode/beethovens-unfinished-10th-symphony-brought-to-life-by-artificial-intelligence/, accessed 2 February 2025.
140. https://www.flow-machines.com/, accessed 2 February 2025.

the second, *Mr Shadow*, was created in the style of Irving Berlin, Duke Ellington, George Gershwin, and Cole Porter. Details as to the model architecture are again not readily available. According to the Flow Machine website, the software generated the composition, while Benoît Carré arranged and produced the tracks.[141] Rather vaguely, the Flow Machines team states that their software 'learns music styles from a huge database of songs. Then, exploiting unique combinations of style transfer, optimisation, and interaction techniques, it can compose in any style'.[142] Both tracks sound reasonably handsome and exhibit some broad similarities to their sources of inspiration. However, as in the case of the Schubert and Beethoven projects, it is difficult to assess the actual proficiency of the music generation software when the extent of the human input is unknown.

Yet another approach to human-AI collaborations was provided by American artist Taryn Southern, who released an album called I AM AI in 2017. One of the songs on the album, *Break Free*, has been touted as 'the first AI-composed pop song'.[143] From a quality perspective, the song does not differ from other pop songs in the same style, which might paint a rosy picture of the capabilities of the underlying AI technology. This impression becomes significantly tempered upon reading Southern's account of the creative process. Southern, who used the Amper program, explains that while Amper is 'really good' at instrumentation, it struggles with musical structure:

> [Amper] might give you a verse or the chorus and it's *up to me to stitch these pieces together* so that it sounds like something familiar you would hear on the radio. Once I'm happy with the song, then *I write the vocal melody and lyrics*.[144]

This description of the creative process gives the impression that Amper ultimately only supplied certain broad cues as to instrumentation and harmonisation, whereas Southern handled the – considerably more important – remaining parts of the creative work.

The skill, effort, and resources invested in the aforementioned projects are certainly worthy of both respect and admiration. However, they all seem to be characterised by significant caveats regarding the actual role played by the AI model. Based on the information made publicly available, the AI technology utilised does not present any clear cases of commercial exploitability outside of space-filling purposes. To my mind, the most artistically viable end results were obtained in the Rembrandt, Beethoven, and Southern projects. Yet, all three evidently involved proportionally significant amounts of human labour in producing the end result, and it seems highly

141. https://www.flow-machines.com/history/press/daddys-car-song-composed-artificial-intelligence-created-sound-like-beatles/, accessed 2 February 2025.
142. https://laughingsquid.com/daddys-car-a-song-composed-by-artificial-intelligence-created-to-sound-like-the-beatles/, retrieved accessed 2 February 2025.
143. *See* video *Break Free – The First AI-Composed Pop Song | Lyrics by Taryn Southern*, available at https://www.youtube.com/watch?v=XUs6CznN8pw, accessed 1 June 2025. One might, of course, point out that Daddy's Car was published before Southern's song, which raises the question whether the latter ought to be called the 'first AI-composed pop song'.
144. Plaugic 2017. My italics.

implausible that the AI technology used would scale well to deployment in commercial applications focused on autonomous content generation.[145] The next section will delve into the apps, publications, and technical solutions that have a more realistic chance of powering mainstream utilisation of algorithmic composition.

2.3 THE CURRENT STATE-OF-THE-ART AND THE TECHNICAL ASPECTS OF MUSIC GENERATION

2.3.1 Premise and Context of the Section

The purpose of this section is to examine the technical aspects of music generation in greater detail. This inquiry aligns with the broader premise that the creative process underlying a composition plays a crucial role in determining whether it qualifies as a copyright-protected work. As noted in Chapter 1, a *seemingly original* composition may fail to attract copyright protection because it does not sufficiently reflect the free and creative choices made by the author during the creative process.[146] In such cases, copyright eligibility will depend on the relationship between creative contributions made prior to generation and the characteristics of the resulting output. As previously discussed, this requires an evaluation of the free and creative choices made by both the user(s) and developer(s) prior to the model's generation of the work, and whether those choices shape the musical attributes of the resulting composition with sufficient precision and specificity. To facilitate this analysis, the present section explores the technical underpinnings of current state-of-the-art music generation systems, with a focus on identifying the types of creative decision-making involved in developing and using such models to generate music.

To gain a more concrete perspective on these issues, the AI music generation research projects undertaken by Google and Meta will be examined in detail. The reason for selecting these for closer examination is that they have been documented reasonably precisely in openly available publications. By contrast, the companies behind many of the currently available state-of-the-art music generation models have released very limited information regarding the design and training of their systems. Consequently, while Suno or Udio may currently produce more sophisticated outputs and functionality than Google's MusicLM or Meta's MusicGen, the latter offer significantly more insight into their underlying architecture and development process. This makes Google's and Meta's projects better suited to elucidating what types of pre-generation creative choices are involved in developing music generation models, and the extent to which those choices may be reflected in the musical attributes of the resulting outputs.

145. Of course, Amper's output can be used commercially other purposes, such as to provide Meta with training datasets for developing their MusicGen model. *See* Copet 2024, p. 5.
146. *See* section 1.9 about the concept of seeming originality.

2.3.2 Technical Aspects of Algorithmic Composition

In examining the technical aspects of algorithmic composition, the first notable challenge concerns the form in which music is represented. Unlike text or images, where standardised representations have been established around characters and pixels, music presents a more complex landscape for AI processing. There are various forms of representing music, with the most important divide being between symbolic and audio representation. The most well-known symbolic representation of music is traditional musical notation, but many other types of symbolic representation readable by computers exist, such as MIDI,[147] MusicXML,[148] and ABC Notation.[149] MusicXML, resembling traditional notation, is designed to encode music sheets with comprehensive notation symbols, including pitch, rhythms, dynamics, articulations, and more. MIDI is often preferred over MusicXML for exporting to DAWs for sound editing. This is because MIDI files contain performance data such as note events, velocities, and control changes, allowing for more flexible manipulation of sounds within the DAW environment.

Overall, symbolic representation excels in storing important musical information precisely and efficiently. Its main weakness lies in its inability to fully capture the richness of a musical performance, including aspects like interpretation, sound, and timbre.[150] Furthermore, only a small proportion of all existing musical works have been documented in symbolic representation, significantly limiting the available pool of training data for AI models. Despite this limitation, several models have been trained on datasets in MIDI format. For example, OpenAI's MuseNet used MIDI representations of music as training data for a music generation model based on their GPT-2 language model. MuseNet generates continuations to pre-existing compositions. The quality of its output varies, but the most impressive sample made available by OpenAI starts with the beginning of Chopin's Nocturne op. 27, no. 2, from which it gradually – and surprisingly convincingly – transitions into a piece in the style of Bon Jovi.[151]

As previously mentioned, OpenAI's Jukebox introduced a successful method of using raw audio signals as training data to output audio directly, bypassing the need for symbolic representation of music. Instead, it compresses the waveform audio input into a sequence of embeddings.[152] The primary advantage of using raw audio as input is the easy access to the majority of recorded music in existence for training data purposes. However, using raw audio as input data and training a model on it presents

147. Musical Instrument Digital Interface; a digital protocol that enables electronic musical instruments, computers, and other devices to communicate and synchronise with one another to control pitch, velocity, and duration of musical notes.
148. An XML-based file format for representing Western musical notation.
149. ABC Notation represents music in letter format. It is most commonly used in folk and traditional music communities, allowing musicians to share and transcribe tunes in a human-readable format.
150. The shortcomings of representing music symbolically will be examined in greater depth in Chapters 5 and 6.
151. https://openai.com/research/musenet, accessed 2 February 2025.
152. Dhariwal et al. 2020, p. 17.

several technical difficulties. Unlike text or images, audio is a continuous and multidimensional signal that evolves over time, making it challenging to model and generate accurately. To better understand this issue, it can be broken down into four distinct sub-components.

First, audio unfolds along a *temporal dimension*, as it encompasses changes in sound characteristics over time. Capturing and reproducing this temporal structure with sufficient precision is more intricate compared to dealing with the static information found in images or text. Second, the simultaneous interplay of pitch, rhythm, dynamics, and timbre makes an audio signal *multidimensional*.[153] This not only makes it more challenging to extract the most relevant features of the training data, but also makes it difficult to represent it in a way that avoids losing vital information while managing computational requirements. Third, the *inherent subjectivity* of the impressions evoked by an audio signal poses challenges to prompt adherence. Unlike text and images, which often have more concrete and universally understood representations, the perception of audio tends to be more subjective. Describing a musical passage accurately and satisfactorily can be challenging due to a lack of universally agreed-upon descriptors for certain sounds or musical elements,[154] impacting the model's responsiveness to prompts. Fourthly, there is much less availability of paired audio-text data.[155] This presents a challenge because the effectiveness of popular text-to-text and text-to-image generators relies heavily on large-scale training datasets that establish connections between input and target output.[156]

Many of the issues pointed out above can be significantly alleviated by high-quality *tokenisation* and *embedding*. As noted earlier, these represent different stages of the procedure by which input data – in this case musical expression – is translated into a form that the AI model can utilise. Tokenisation involves converting the audio signal into numerically expressed tokens, while embedding refers to representing these tokens as high-dimensional vectors. To further compress the representation and make it more efficient, the dimensionality of the vectors can be reduced by applying Residual Vector Quantisation (RVQ). In this process, similar vectors are grouped together, creating a *first codebook* with representative vectors from each group. Each original vector is then replaced by the *index* of the representative vector it most closely resembles.[157] The differences between the original vectors and their quantised counterparts, called *residuals*, are then quantised using a secondary codebook. This step captures the finer details of the data that may have been missed in the primary quantisation process. This cascading process is repeated multiple times, with each subsequent codebook providing a progressively finer approximation to the original vectors.

153. Pitch, rhythm, dynamics, timbre, and many other component parts of musical expression are examined in-depth in Chapter 6.
154. Agostinelli et al. 2023, p. 1, make a very similar argument by noting that 'it is not straightforward to unambiguously capture with just a few words the salient characteristics of [music]'.
155. Agostinelli et al. 2023, p. 1.
156. For instance, the internet is replete with images paired with descriptive captions.
157. Index refers to the position or identifier of the representative vector in the codebook that most closely resembles the original vector being quantised.

Overall, advancements in embedding techniques are poised to significantly enhance the capabilities of music generators. By capturing ever more refined semantic relationships and features in the input signal, improved embeddings can play a crucial role in training models to interpret user prompts accurately and generate music that aligns with desired styles and characteristics. Such enhancements would also reduce the amount of training data required to achieve high-quality output, making the training process more efficient and cost-effective. For its part, efficient compression with reduced loss enables the processing of larger datasets, facilitating smoother model training and faster generation of music.

Apart from embeddings and compression, the procurement and curation of a training dataset of sufficient size appears to be among the greatest current obstacles to producing high-performance music generation models.[158] A further challenge is that to make the model respond to textual prompts, it needs to be trained on a training corpus of music and text pairs. This contains two separate processes, as one must first acquire a set of paired audio-text samples and then design the model architecture to be able to process both audio and text tokens in parallel. One proposed solution to this challenge is provided by AudioLM. Endeavouring to enable self-supervised learning for audio generation purposes, it uses a transformer-based hybrid tokenisation scheme that combines semantic and acoustic tokens.[159] This allows it to train on speech inputs without an intermediate stage of transcribing or annotating the training corpus. As a result, the model can generate reasonably convincing continuations of audio files containing speech.[160]

2.3.3 Concrete Examples: Google's and Meta's AI Music Projects

The AudioLM model is part of a series of models developed by the Google research team, which have led to the release of music generation products at an increasing rate. In January 2023, Google released MusicLM, a model capable of producing 30-second music tracks based on text prompts.[161] In November 2023, Google released three new products, Lyria, Dream Track and Music AI Tools. Lyria represents their 'most advanced AI music generation model to date', whereas Dream Track is specialised for generating short music tracks for YouTube shorts videos.[162] AI Music Tools can transform a music input – whether singing, beatboxing or a MIDI file – into a new arrangement. Demonstrating the capabilities of this application, Google's promotional material shows a user humming a melody, which is promptly converted into an orchestral performance of the same melody. Finally, an improved version of MusicLM

158. Hilsdorf 2023.
159. Borsos et al. 2023, p.1.
160. Audio samples of the continuations made by AudioLM are available at https://google-research.github.io/seanet/audiolm/examples/, accessed 2 February 2025.
161. Audio samples produced by MusicLM are available at https://google-research.github.io/seanet/musiclm/examples/, accessed 2 February 2025.
162. *See* Google's publication *Transforming the future of music creation*, available at https://deepmind.google/discover/blog/transforming-the-future-of-music-creation/, accessed 2 February 2025.

called MusicRL was released in February 2024. The technology underlying these efforts has been presented in a handful of publications, which give insight into how the team at Google tackled the technical issues related to music generation. We shall examine these publications at some length, as they give insight into the crucial issues facing state-of-the-art music generation.

To address the challenge of embedding, the Google research team developed MuLan, a model capable of jointly embedding audio and natural language. To account for the two different modalities, audio and text, it has two separate embedding networks.[163] To get a suitable corpus of audio-text pairs to use for training, the team started with a collection of 50 million internet music videos. The text pairs came from the video titles, tags, descriptions, comments, and playlist titles. The text data contained considerable noise, since none of the text sources were 'guaranteed to be referring to the musical properties of the soundtrack'.[164] To improve the correlation between audio samples and their associated text data, they fine-tuned a pre-trained BERT model using a binary classification task on a curated set of 700 sentences manually labelled as music-descriptive or not.[165] Training on this dataset, the model learns to perform music tagging, music retrieval from text queries, and music classification.[166] On this basis, MuLan learns to create representations for both audio and text, since the vector embeddings contain information about both the audio signal and its associated textual information.

MusicLM builds upon the foundation laid by the AudioLM model. Instead of merely continuing an existing audio file as the earlier AudioLM model does, MusicLM can respond to complex prompts, such as 'enchanting jazz song with a memorable saxophone solo and a solo singer' or 'Berlin 90s techno with a low bass and strong kick',[167] by conditioning its output on descriptive text or an audio signal like a melody.[168] In the training process, three models collaborate to extract the necessary audio representations: a SoundStream model captures and compresses acoustic characteristics,[169] a masked language modelling (MLM) module represents semantic content, and the MuLan model provides a joint embedding space for both audio and text.[170] During inference, the text prompt is passed through the MuLan model to extract text tokens, which are given to the semantic model to get semantic representations. The combined semantic and text tokens are then fed to the acoustic model, whose output can be decoded and reconstructed using the SoundStream model to obtain the waveform output.[171] The juxtaposition of acoustic and semantic models stems from the

163. The publication refers to this as a 'two tower' structure (Huang et al. 2022, p. 1).
164. Huang et al. 2022, p. 4.
165. Huang et al. 2022, p. 4. BERT refers to a Bidirectional Encoder Transformer, a model architecture commonly used in natural language processing.
166. Huang et al. 2022, pp. 5-6.
167. Agostinelli et al. 2023, p. 3.
168. Agostinelli et al. 2023, p. 8. Humming, singing, whistling, or playing an instrument are mentioned as possible inputs.
169. SoundStream is a model that compresses raw audio into discrete tokens through RVQ, *see* Zeghidour et al. 2021, p. 2.
170. Agostinelli et al. 2023, p. 4.
171. Agostinelli et al. 2023, p. 5.

different roles they play in representing musical data. The acoustic model captures fine-grained acoustic details, whereas the semantic model enhances the long-term structural coherence as well as improves the prompt adherence.[172] Overall, as is evident from the description above, the MusicLM architecture is characterised by its complexity, and its employment of many different models for different tasks prompted one commentator to aptly compare the architecture to a Matryoshka doll.[173]

The model can also respond to audio prompts. In the promotional materials associated with the November 2023 release of Google's Music AI Tools, this functionality was demonstrated by transforming sung or hummed melodies into arrangements for various ensembles.[174] As indicated by the materials released by the research team, MusicLM's outputs seem rather promising.[175] Still, significant limitations remain: the sample length is capped at 30 seconds, the musical content is rather generic, the relationship between text prompts and end result does not appear particularly close, and the output sample rate remains relatively low at 24 kHz.[176] In addition, the long-term coherence of the 5-minute 'Long Generation' samples, whose mechanism was explained at length in the research paper,[177] is not convincing.

A second-generation successor to MusicLM, called MusicRL, was published in February 2024. As suggested by the samples released by the research team,[178] the output quality has been improved both regarding musical content and sound fidelity. As explained in the research paper published by the team, the main difference between the models lies in MusicRL having been fine-tuned using reinforcement learning from human feedback (RLHF).[179] The reward model was trained based on three criteria: adherence to the text prompt, audio quality, and user preference between the two tracks generated for each prompt. This reward model was then used to fine-tune the underlying model by adjusting the weights to maximise the reward score. The improved quality of the samples made available clearly shows that RLHF works well for improving the model. It remains to be seen how quickly the Google team manages to improve the performance of the model and related applications and whether the crucial steps unlocking further progress will pertain to scaling the training dataset, improving model architecture, RLHF-related tweaks or other types of fine-tuning.

172. Agostinelli et al. 2023, pp. 3, 7.
173. *See* Valerio Velardo's analysis of the research paper *MusicLM Generates Music From Text [Paper Breakdown]*, available at https://www.youtube.com/watch?v=eaqO5uT0G9Q&t=1209s, at 5 min 20 sec, accessed 2 February 2025.
174. The results, shown here https://www.youtube.com/watch?v=aeYU3_7IKCM&t=19s, accessed 2 February 2025, appear rather impressive at first glance, but one must remember that promotional materials typically do not represent the average output of a product.
175. The samples are available at https://google-research.github.io/seanet/musiclm/examples/, accessed 2 February 2025.
176. For comparison, the standard audio CD sample rate is 44,1 kHz.
177. To enhance long-term contextual coherence within the limits set by the 30-second context window, the output is divided into 15 second segments where each successive segment leverages the context provided by the previous segment. Agostinelli 2023, p. 8.
178. https://google-research.github.io/seanet/musiclm/rlhf/, accessed 2 February 2025.
179. Cideron et al. 2024, p. 1.

However, in light of the model's current performance and rate of improvement, it does not seem unthinkable that a 'ChatGPT moment' for text-to-music models trained on waveform datasets will occur in the coming years.

Another tech giant, Meta, has also made considerable efforts in music generation. In June 2023, it released MusicGen, a text-to-audio generator in many ways very similar to Google's MusicLM. Viewed from the user's perspective, both provide comparable outputs and functionality. It is of course easy to see a budding rivalry between the two internet behemoths' respective offerings, and the article published by the Meta research team directly invited comparison to MusicLM by pointing out how MusicGen outperformed Google's offering.[180] In examining the technical solutions underlying the model's performance, Meta's approach is different. Where Google opted for an elaborate architecture, Meta emphasised simplicity and a streamlined approach to data processing.

Overall, the main focus of MusicGen is on techniques for compressing the original (waveform) input signal, which allows them to use a higher sample rate than MusicLM: 32 kHz instead of 24 kHz. To accomplish this, the input signal is compressed in two stages. Their EnCodec model first uses a convolutional neural network to compress the raw audio into discrete tokens,[181] and these are further compressed through residual vector quantisation.[182] Together, these techniques allow the 32 kHz input signal to be compressed to 50 Hz, divided among four different codebooks. Further efficiency gains are obtained by having a transformer model process the quantised residuals in parallel through various interleaving patterns. Testing showed that a delay pattern gave the best balance between performance and computational efficiency.[183]

The output can be conditioned either by a text prompt or audio input, such as a melody. For text conditioning, three different pre-existing models were tried, which produced relatively similar results. The melody conditioning, which performed slightly less consistently,[184] was based on combining the chromagram of the raw audio and its text description.[185] In November 2023, Meta released a new version of MusicGen, which exhibited noticeable improvements in audio quality. The improvements are due to a process they call multi-band diffusion. This technique reduces the loss of fidelity

180. Copet 2024, p. 6.
181. Défossez et al. 2022, p. 3. As suggested by the name, *convolutional neural networks* ultilise the similarity between adjacent data points to compress the original input data.
182. *See* above for an explanation of RVQ. The quantisation is made several times in succession, and each quantiser encodes the quantisation error left by the previous quantiser, allowing for enhanced compression. This also makes the quantised codebooks interdependent, meaning that a compression error in the first codebook will accumulate through the series of quantisations. *See* Copet 2024, p. 3.
183. Copet 2024, p. 9. By contrast, MusicLM uses a hierarchical approach where the model alternates between acoustic and semantic tokens during inference. Google's approach results in greater computational cost.
184. Copet 2024, p. 6.
185. Copet 2024, p. 4. A *chromagram* is a form of representing sound visually based on classifying pre-determined pitches into colour-coded classes.

associated with the compression by processing different frequency bands independently, which mitigates the accumulation of errors in generating the audio.[186] However, the higher-quality output comes at a greater computational cost.[187] By increasing the architectural complexity and computational requirements, Meta's new model appears to have gone more towards the direction pursued by Google's team in seeking improvements.

The research teams of both Google and Meta formulated certain objective numerical metrics by which to measure their models' performance. Yet, one should beware of setting too much stock by such data, not least due to the inherent subjectivity associated with the perception of music and audio quality. The inherent subjectivity also underscores the importance of human evaluation as the primary benchmark for assessing the model's performance. Simply put, human subjective observation concerning the output's long-term compositional coherence or the 'naturalness' of the sound must necessarily remain the most appropriate metric for measuring model performance. In their current improved iterations, the models of both Google and Meta boast similar capabilities in both audio output and prompt adherence, although prompt adherence is difficult to reliably evaluate based on the samples made publicly available.[188]

2.4 CONCLUDING REFLECTIONS

2.4.1 The Technical Challenges of High-Performance Music Generation

What conclusions should one draw about the current state-of-the-art of algorithmic composition? Where are the greatest areas for improvement, and can they be achieved? On the one hand, applications such as Suno, Udio, MusicRL, and MusicGen clearly demonstrate that AI-generated outputs of reasonable quality are already a reality. The ongoing rate of improvement also suggests that progress towards higher-fidelity audio outputs with more convincing compositional content and long-term coherence is virtually inevitable. However, it is evident that existing state-of-the-art systems currently do not offer tools that can be seamlessly integrated into the workflow of professional music creators in a way that meaningfully impacts quality or efficiency. Despite the enticingly impressive promotional materials for Google's Music AI Tools,[189] the most probable scenario for deploying AI-powered tools among music professionals still involves performing routine tasks, such as generating stems and alternative

186. As explained in San Roman et al. 2023, pp. 5-6, the previous model started by generating the low frequencies and then moved to higher ones. Thus, any errors in generating the lower frequencies would accumulate and amplify throughout the generation process.
187. San Roman et al. 2023, pp. 10, 14.
188. One would need to get access to the models to properly formulate a viewpoint of the 'median prompt adherence'.
189. *See* above.

mixes.[190] Conversely, the availability of high-performance AI tools may reduce the need for musical expertise and labour input for amateur creators of musical content, particularly in the production of background music. Although machine-generated music already exists in this niche,[191] further advancements in the availability and quality of AI music outputs are likely to significantly increase the proportion of background music produced with the assistance of AI-powered tools.

In examining the potential bottlenecks in developing algorithmic composition and other AI-powered tools, the technical challenges can be divided into two distinct categories. The first challenge concerns data procurement and curation. When training models on raw waveform signals rather than symbolic representations, which has been the dominant approach in recent years, *source separation* plays a crucial role. For example, consider a waveform audio signal of a band performing a song; it typically contains merged input from vocals, guitar, bass, and drums, all combined into a single waveform file. While the original producer may possess the individual signals – or stems – in some cases, the component parts of a band's performance are often only available in combined files. This presents a significant challenge during the compilation and curation of training datasets, as the extent to which the individual stems can be separated will impact how accurately the embeddings represent the musically relevant content of the raw audio signal. In turn, this is likely to significantly influence the model's performance. Source separation systems, whether AI-powered or not, have been available for many years, and their continued development is likely to greatly enhance the procurement of high-quality training datasets.[192] In addition, it is worth noting that AI-powered source separation is a dynamic field of research in its own right.[193]

Second, the currently hegemonic transformer architecture exhibits certain inherent weaknesses that may pose challenges for achieving high-level long-term coherence and prompt adherence in music generation models. While transformers excel at capturing context in text generation, the increased data load associated with music generation critically shortens the context window, leading to lacklustre long-term coherence. A combination of using increased datasets, computing power, and fine-tuning, coupled with tweaks to the model architecture specifically tailored to the needs of music generation, may well come to significantly improve long-term coherence even in transformer-based models, but this is not certain to resolve all context-related challenges inherent to using transformers in music generation.

Another limitation of transformers is their lack of suitability for high-level prompt adherence. They rely on large amounts of data and computation, which unavoidably reduces control over and understanding of the model's workings, making it challenging

190. Professional musician Jesse Josefson also points this out in an interview on the role of AI in music production, https://www.youtube.com/watch?v=v4m_A8JxUZs&t=1895s, 8 min 40 sec, accessed 2 February 2025.
191. Ambian provides an example of a Finnish service providing machine-generated and (allegedly) royalty free background music. *See* https://www.ambian.fi/, accessed 5 December 2024.
192. One example is Demucs, a transformer-based music source separation model. *See* Rouard et al. 2022, p. 1.
193. *See*, for instance, Liu et al. 2023.

to condition the output with precision. This challenge is exacerbated by the subjective nature of music perception and the absence of universally accepted verbal representations for musical expression, in contrast to the relatively clearer frameworks found in text and images. As a result, it becomes much more difficult to produce embeddings that accurately capture the relationship between the waveform signal and its verbal-semantic counterpart. This difficulty may hinder or slow the adoption of autonomous music generation in professional creative tasks marked by a high artistic ambition. Some commentators have suggested that addressing the shortcomings of transformer models could involve incorporating features derived from rules based on music theory into the models.[194] If high-performance open-source transformer models with their associated datasets become publicly available,[195] this prospect is not entirely implausible, but only time will tell whether such approaches will come to play a substantial role in professional music creation.

2.4.2 Summary and Concluding Thoughts about AI and Its Deployment in General

This chapter has focused on two core issues. First, it aimed to describe the fundamental functionality of generative AI technology and its application in content creation. To achieve this, it provided an overview of deep learning and neural networks, outlining how they perform complex pattern recognition and leverage this to generate new content. To get a more precise insight into how music generation models function and what challenges are encountered in developing such models, Google's and Meta's research projects in the field were examined in detail.

The analysis indicated that the development of AI music models is typically characterised by two main pursuits. On the one hand, one needs to search for ways to reduce the number of computations required, either by finding ways of compressing the relevant training data into a smaller representation or by adjusting the model design to make it execute the relevant tasks more efficiently. On the other hand, various features – whether training datasets, layers, modules, or even separate models – can be added to enhance the model's outputs. This is likely to increase computational and labour costs, but it is often outweighed by the improved performance of the model. Often, the process of developing a model will include both pursuits in parallel, with various aspects of the model being tweaked iteratively on a trial-and-error basis. An interesting question, which in many ways is the most crucial one for the purposes of

194. For instance, Valerio Velardo speaks at some length about this possibility in his video *Transformers Explained Easily: Part 2 – Generative Music AI*, https://www.youtube.com/watch?v=ctbvMnbylsA&list=PL-wATfeyAMNqAPjwGT3ikEz3gMo23pl-D&index=18, at 57 mins, accessed 2 February 2025.
195. For instance, while the MusicGen code is openly available, the Meta teams relies 'on an *internal* dataset of 10K high-quality music tracks' during training. *See* Copet et al. 2024, p. 5, my italics. In other words, not all crucial components of making the model run well are openly available. Mezei 2025, p. 5 points out that Meta has a tendency towards 'open-washing', by which he means that big generative AI companies aim to make their practices and services seem more open than they are.

copyright protection, is to what degree the underlying human input is to be viewed as technical-functional or creative-authorial in nature. Needless to say, the development of large, high-performance models will contain substantial instances of both, and Chapter 7 will delve into this question in detail.

The second core issue covered by this chapter is to address the historical and definitional underpinnings of what is understood by the concept of AI and its central components. Although defining the concept of AI 'in a broad sense' will not have much significance for the legal questions to be discussed throughout this dissertation, its frequent invocation in a wide variety of scenarios makes it necessary to explain the role played by AI-powered systems in various endeavours touted as having incorporated AI technology. After all, whether it is a smartphone release or a completion of Beethoven's or Schubert's unfinished manuscripts, the considerable media attention commanded by the concept of AI incentivises promoters of various projects or products to emphasise the role played by AI.[196] Under these circumstances, it is prudent to closely examine the AI technology employed and its actual contribution to the project or product at issue, in order to avoid overestimating the creative and disruptive powers of current state-of-the-art AI models.

The same holds for other, non-generative deployments of AI technology. For instance, voice cloning is certainly a very important new development whose ramifications greatly transcend the music industry. The most distressing prospects relate to cloning or deep faking the semblance of influential people to pursue political or other vested interests. These concerns, of course, lie outside the scope of this dissertation. Within the music industry applications, cloning the voices of famous artists Drake and The Weeknd garnered considerable attention.[197] Hindsight may come to show that the hype and notoriety associated with that and other similar *causes célèbres* was somewhat exaggerated, but licensed voice cloning and other utilisation of the personal attributes of famous artists is nonetheless very likely to become a new way to (indirectly) monetise musicians' creative efforts.[198] Google's Dream Track, an application that creates songs in the style of famous singers, seems to give a good indication of this, as the voice of Charlie Puth and several other artists was licensed.[199] Of course, the actual impact on the music industry of the various AI applications will become easier to grasp as the technology continues to mature and the phase of gimmicky

196. A good illustration of the AI hype can be found in the marketing strategies of major smartphone manufacturers. Throughout 2024, virtually all leading brands highlighted AI as a key feature in their devices, showcasing its role in areas like photography, personalised user experiences, and performance optimisation. Based on Samsung's January 2025 release of their new phones, this year appears not much different, with the marketing heavily emphasising how the new devices unlock even more advanced AI capabilities, continuing the narrative of AI-driven innovation as a central selling point. *See*, *inter alia*, 'Samsung unveils new AI-powered smartphone in fight against Apple', available at https://www.ft.com/content/e8a403b0-0bdb-455b-b083-ef3ef50bc473, accessed 22 January 2025.
197. https://www.nytimes.com/2023/04/19/arts/music/ai-drake-the-weeknd-fake.html, accessed 2 February 2025.
198. This is also suggested by what Quintais 2025, p. 12 calls a 'tsunami of [licence] agreements between providers, rights holders and aggregators', which likely was caused by the copyright obligations placed on general-purpose AI model providers in Article 53 AI Act.
199. Veltman 2023.

publicity stunts utilising the notoriety of AI gradually subsides. In sum, while one should certainly not underestimate the potential of AI technology to greatly impact most aspects of the music industry and our lives at large, one does well to remember that the current media hype surrounding 'all things AI' may occasionally come to exaggerate the impact AI-powered systems can and will have.

CHAPTER 3

The Criteria for Determining Copyright Eligibility

3.1 PURPOSE, PREMISE, AND STRUCTURE OF THE CHAPTER

Research question (1) inquires whether the AI-generated Composition A could constitute a musical work. The traditional Finnish approach to interpreting this provision is to state that a work is an independent and original intellectual creation made by the author. However, the concept of a 'work' has been harmonised in the EU, which means that the EU's definition of the copyright requisites will ultimately determine the matter.[200] A key development in this area came with the Infopaq ruling of 2009.[201] Although harmonisation of Member States' copyright regimes had been pursued in the two decades prior to 2009, Infopaq ushered in a period of substantially greater harmonisation. Within the ten years following the Infopaq ruling, a number of further decisions clarified the EU-wide understanding of copyright eligibility. Collectively, these rulings have achieved what amounts to a prima facie total harmonisation of the prerequisites for copyright protection.[202]

The harmonisation was accomplished by declaring the concepts of 'work' and 'originality' autonomous concepts of EU law, whose interpretation is governed by the CJEU. To be regarded as a work, a creation must be 'original' in the sense of being the author's own intellectual creation. In turn, originality requires that the creation reflect the personality of its author as an expression of his free and creative choices.[203] Member State courts must grant copyright protection to all subject matter satisfying the

200. Cofemel, para. 29; Rosati 2023, p. 222; Schovsbo 2020, p. 4.
201. Infopaq, C-5/08, ECLI:EU:C:2009:465, henceforth 'Infopaq'.
202. Cofemel, para. 29, Rosati 2023, pp. 212-213.
203. Cofemel, ECLI:EU:C:2019:721, para. 30.

originality and work criteria as defined by the CJEU and deny protection to all subject matter that fails to do so.[204]

Sections 3.2 to 3.6 examine the process by which the copyright protection threshold was harmonised under these concepts and analyse their normative content. Section 3.7 proceeds to reflect on how to grasp the meaning of 'work' and 'originality' in practice, and how this relates to the type of technically and functionally dictated creative processes associated with developing high-performance generative AI systems.

3.2 A HISTORICAL PERSPECTIVE ON THE EU'S HARMONISATION OF THE COPYRIGHT REQUISITES

The CJEU was instrumental in harmonising EU copyright law under the concept of originality, but the concept of originality was not introduced into EU[205] law by the Court. It first appeared in the 1991 Computer Program Directive.[206] Its Article 1.3 states that:

> A computer program shall be protected if it is original in the sense that it is the author's own intellectual creation. No other criteria shall be applied to determine its eligibility for protection.

Several commentators have considered the directive's wording a compromise between the 'skill and labour' doctrine employed in the UK and the higher originality standard applied on the continent.[207] In particular, the provision's admonition that 'no other criteria shall be applied' seems to be aimed at the German treatment of computer works, which required creative input exceeding average programming skills to qualify for copyright protection.[208]

The 1993 Term Directive,[209] the EU legislature's next legislative statement on originality, is similarly focused on specific subject matter. In harmonising the term of protection of all types of works, the Directive needed to address the copyright treatment of photographs. Some Member States deployed a two-tier copyright regime

204. Funke Medien, ECLI:EU:C:2019:623, para. 24: 'It would then be incumbent on the national court to find that such reports were not "works" within the meaning of Article 2(a) and of Article 3(1) of Directive 2001/29'. *See also* Schovsbo 2020, p. 4.
205. It was called the European Communities at this time and until the formal establishment of the European Union in 1993. Henceforth, I will use 'EU' to refer collectively to the European Union and its predecessors.
206. Council Directive 91/250/EEC of 14 May 1991 on the legal protection of computer programs.
207. *Inter alia*, Stamatoudi 2017, p. 59; Mylly 2016, p. 913; Griffiths 2014, p. 1103, para. 20.09; van Eechoud et al. 2009, p. 41.
208. In stating its concerns about the obstacles to internal market, the 1988 *Green Paper on copyright and the challenge of technology*, p. 187 mentions both German and French judiciary practices as indicative of the 'significant differences' between the Member States' copyright regimes. In its Inkasso case, the German Supreme Court (BGH) stated that the creative achievement behind the development of a computer program must display creative input exceeding the average skills of a programmer to obtain copyright protection. According to Casas Vallés 2009, p. 120, this introduced 'a qualitative criterion to preserve the purity of the [German] system'.
209. Council Directive 93/98/EEC of 29 October 1993 harmonising the term of protection of copyright and certain related rights.

for photographs, one for original photographic works and another for non-original photographs covered by a related right.[210] As the distinction between different tiers of photographs was expressly determined by whether they were 'original', it was necessary to define the level of originality required of photographic works.[211] The following originality provision was provided by Article 6 of the Term Directive:

> Photographs which are original in the sense that they are the author's own intellectual creation shall be protected in accordance with Article 1. No other criteria shall be applied to determine their eligibility for protection.

This formulation is virtually identical to that given in the Computer Program Directive, suggesting conclusions of two kinds. On the one hand, an emphasis on assessing originality by the same criteria regardless of whether one examines computer programs or photographs implies an egalitarian attitude to all creative subject matter. In addition, one might consider it indicative of a system-building ambition on the part of the lawgiver.[212] On the other hand, one should beware of reading too much into the Directive provisions and their preparatory works. Similarly to the argumentation underlying the 1991 Computer Program Directive, the 1993 Term Directive did by no means expressly set out to prepare the ground for an acceleration of the Union's harmonisation effort and a 'one size fits all' requirements of originality.

As noted by one scholar analysing the 1993 Term Directive's place in the history of the originality criteria within EU copyright law, the harmonisation of the originality test was accidental, merely 'a side effect of the harmonization of the term of protection for all genres of copyright works'.[213] Furthermore, the directives' statements on originality differ in that the Term Directive states that a photographic work must reflect its author's personality in addition to being an intellectual creation. This requirement is absent from the Computer Program Directive, prompting some commentators to inquire whether the originality threshold for photographic works is higher than that of computer programs.[214] Adding to the ambiguity, the Term Directive cites the Berne Convention as the source of the requirement that the work reflects the author's personality.[215] The Berne Convention does not define originality, however, making the reference's practical significance somewhat unclear.

The criterion of originality was next addressed by the Database Directive of 1996. In Article 3, it states that:

> [D]atabases which, by reason of the selection or arrangement of their contents, constitute the author's own intellectual creation shall be protected as such by

210. van Gompel and Lavik 2013, p. 6.
211. Recital 17 of the old Term Directive (Council Directive 93/98/EEC).
212. This is borne out by the Term Directive's preparatory works, where the Council expressly pointed out that it considers the 'original in the sense of being the author's own intellectual creation' criterion formulated in the Computer Program Directive to be appropriate for this purpose'. Gompel and Lavik 2013, p. 7.
213. van Eechoud 2012, para. 14. Rahmatian 2016, p. 17 also considers the harmonisation of originality 'accidental'.
214. van Eechoud et al. 2009, p. 41.
215. 1993 Term Directive, Recital 17.

> copyright. No other criteria shall be applied to determine their eligibility for that protection.

Two indications of increased momentum in the development towards a generally applicable originality standard can be observed. First, both the 'intellectual creation' and the 'no other criteria' requirements were present from the beginning of the directive's preparation.[216] Second, the Commission expressly advocated for using the same formulation of the originality criteria as was given by the Computer Program Directive:

> Given the similarity in the creative processes involved and the fact that software is an essential component in database management, it seems appropriate to rationalise the definition of the criteria for eligibility for protection *into one and the same formulation*.[217]

This unambiguously establishes an identical standard of protection for computer programs and databases, with the Term Directive differing by containing the added criterion that a photographic work must reflect the author's personality.

How should one, then, evaluate the degree of harmonisation achieved by these three directives? A maximalist interpretation of the directives' harmonising effect is not entirely implausible. Although all three directives provided vertical harmonisation and worded their originality requirements in slightly different ways, the general tenor of the legislator's intentions was unmistakable. National copyright traditions differing from the originality standard formulated in the directives must give way to a uniform EU-wide standard. This possibility was not lost upon contemporary commentators, but the extent of the concrete interference with national copyright regimes was less evident.[218] The majority of scholarly commentary seems aligned towards considering the 1990s directives to have little significance for subject matter other than computer programs, photographs, and databases. Karnell suggested that the nascent EU originality standard – apart from disqualifying the German requirement of above-average programming expertise – amounted to little more than a 'play of words'. As long as national courts take care not to mention such 'ugly words' as quality or merit, they should be able to continue to apply their national traditions when assessing copyright eligibility.[219] Other commentators have deemed the directives' definitions of originality irrelevant for other categories of works than computer programs, photographs and databases because the directives were enacted 'without prejudice' to pre-existing

216. van Gompel and Lavik 2013, p. 8 cite the following preparatory documents: European Commission, Proposal for a Council Directive on the legal protection of databases, COM(92) 24 final, Brussels, 13 May 1992, pp. 60 (Recitals 14 and 15) and 67 (Article 2(3)); and European Commission, Amended proposal for a Council Directive on the legal protection of databases, COM(93) 464 final, Brussels, 4 October 1993, pp. 10 (Recitals 14 and 15) and 17 (Article 2(3)).
217. European Commission, Proposal for a Council Directive on the legal protection of databases, COM(92) 24 final – SYN 393, 13 May 1992, para. 2.3. p. 42. My italics.
218. Cohen Jehoram 2006, p. 631, commenting on a national Supreme Court decision in 2006, notes that an EU-wide understanding of originality is an 'unmistakable trend of several EU Directives'.
219. Karnell 1998, p. 80. Karnell also points out that he is not 'the first to express doubts about the attempts to define an originality standard for Europe-wide application' at p. 78.

regimes'.[220] The Commission Staff Working Paper of 2004 aligns with this assessment by stating that apart from computer programs, photographic works, and databases, Member States remain 'free to determine what level of originality a work must possess for granting it copyright protection'.[221]

3.3 THE INFOSOC DIRECTIVE AND ITS INTERPRETATION BY THE CJEU

The next directive relevant for the definition of an EU-wide originality standard was the Infosoc Directive. Similarly to the 1990s directives, Infosoc emphasises a functioning internal market and investment protection, but adds the purpose of enabling authors to receive 'an appropriate reward for the use of their works'.[222] This directive established exclusive rights to the reproduction, communication to the public and distribution of 'works', but did not define the concept. The degree of actual harmonisation achieved by the directive was not entirely clear at the time. The traditional view of the respective competences of Member States and EU law suggests that national jurisdictions are free to apply their own national characteristics concerning subject matter not regulated by the Union. Hence, divergent national standards as to what constitutes a work - apart from the explicitly harmonised categories of computer programs, photographic works, and databases - ought not to have been impacted by the Infosoc Directive. The 2004 Commission Staff Working Paper supports such a view, noting that the Member States remain free to determine the originality threshold within the domains not expressly covered by the 1990s trio of directives. Furthermore, the Working Paper did not consider the divergent originality requirements within the union to pose a noteworthy obstacle to trade within the internal market.[223]

The CJEU, however, did not share the views expressed by the Working Paper regarding the desired level and intensity of copyright harmonisation. This became evident in the Infopaq ruling, which gave the CJEU an opportunity to interpret the copyright threshold and the concept of originality in light of the existing body of directives. The case concerned an unauthorised reproduction of newspaper articles. The defendant, a media monitoring company, Infopaq, provided its customers with summaries of newspaper articles via email. The text of the articles was also made digitally searchable by scanning the articles and running them through text recognition software. To make it easier to find the searched word when reading the articles, the five words occurring before and after the word were displayed. Hence, 11-word fragments of the articles were made available to Infopaq's customers upon carrying out the digital

220. Griffiths 2014, para. 20.05.
221. Commission Staff Working Paper on the Review of the EC Legal Framework in the field of copyright SEC(2004)995, para. 3.1.
222. Infosoc recitals 4,7 and 10. In contrast to the Computer Program and Database directives, the Term Directive does not explicitly mention investment protection as a specific purpose.
223. Commission Staff Working Paper on the Review of the EC Legal Framework in the field of copyright SEC(2004)995, para. 3.1. 'In theory, divergent requirements for the level of originality by Member States have the potential of posing barriers to intra-Community trade. In practice, however, there seems to be no convincing evidence to support this.'

search. The articles' right holders argued that this practice infringed their exclusive rights, raising the question of whether displaying these 11-word extracts constitutes 'reproduction in part' under InfoSoc Article 2(a). Accordingly, the court needed to determine whether these brief fragments qualify for copyright protection.

Under the Infosoc Directive, authors have an exclusive right to the reproduction of their works, but the directive is silent on what constitutes a work. The CJEU could therefore have left the definition of the copyright threshold to the Member State courts by declaring the matter non-harmonised.[224] Instead, the Court decided to merge the 1990s directives' definition of 'originality' regarding computer programs, databases and photographs with the concept of 'work' as stipulated by the Infosoc Directive. According to the Court, both are based on the same principle of fostering creativity by maintaining a high level of protection for intellectual property,[225] and copyright protection will be granted to creations that are 'original in the sense that they are their author's own intellectual creation'.[226] The concept of originality as such was by no means new – it had been applied within national jurisdictions – but from now on, originality as formulated by the EU was to determine the copyright threshold of all categories of works.

The landmark outcome of Infopaq was to harmonise the standard for copyright eligibility under the concept of originality, placing its interpretation firmly in the hands of the CJEU. Inevitably, the Court received numerous referrals that allowed it to clarify various aspects of the unified EU-wide copyright standard left unspecified by Infopaq. As a result, the Court's jurisprudence now stands as the principal authority for defining 'originality' as an autonomous concept of EU law. The following section will therefore examine the additional precision provided by subsequent CJEU case law.

3.4 ORIGINALITY AS DEFINED BY THE CJEU'S POST-INFOPAQ CASE LAW

3.4.1 BSA Consolidates the Harmonisation of Originality

The next case to advance the harmonisation effort was the BSA case of 2010, which concerned the copyright eligibility of a graphic user interface (GUI). This decision provides added clarity not only about the originality criteria themselves but also about the Court's view of its own jurisdiction and the conflation of the 1990s directives' definition of originality with the horizontal harmonisation of 'works' given in Infosoc and Infopaq. The referring national court had inquired whether a GUI of a computer program is a form of expression of that program under the Computer Program Directive. Having examined these questions, the CJEU concluded that a GUI does not constitute an expression of a computer program and does not qualify for copyright protection under said directive. However, the Court then proceeded to state that a GUI

224. Rosati 2023, p. 219.
225. Infopaq, paras 35-36.
226. Synodinou 2012, p. 101 calls this the 'Infopaq European standard of originality', which describes the issue rather accurately.

can be protected 'by the ordinary law of copyright' under Infosoc, provided it satisfies the originality criteria laid down in said directive.[227] This expansive interpretative attitude drew some criticism in the scholarly literature. One commentator described the Court's actions as 'harmonization by stealth',[228] while another noted this practice might foster a sort of forum shopping by incentivising national courts and plaintiffs to design their arguments to show a clash between national provisions and the greatly expanded body of EU copyright law.[229] Overall, the BSA decision appears like a logical consolidation of the position taken in Infopaq, as it mandates the national courts to assess all copyright claims according to the concept of 'work' under Infosoc, regardless of whether the subject matter at hand aligns with the creative domains harmonised in the 1990s directives.

3.4.2 Limitations to Creative Freedom as Indicators of Non-originality

In addition to consolidating the harmonisation of the copyright threshold, the BSA ruling also introduced an additional (negative) criterion of originality. The originality requirements are not met by features of a graphic user interface 'differentiated only by their technical function' because the means of implementing the underlying idea 'are so limited that the idea and the expression become indissociable'.[230] The similarities to the US merger doctrine are obvious,[231] but the Court ties this requirement to the positive originality criteria formulated in Infopaq. That is, the indissociability of idea and expression rules out originality because the author would not be able 'to express his creativity in an original manner and achieve a result which is an intellectual creation'.[232]

The next relevant case, FAPL,[233] concerned the right to prohibit retransmission of football matches with reference to the exclusive right provided by copyright. Again, the positive originality criteria familiar from Infopaq and BSA were reiterated,[234] but the Court added an unambiguous rejection of the copyright eligibility of sporting events:

> [S]porting events cannot be regarded as intellectual creations classifiable as works within the meaning of the Copyright Directive. That applies in particular to football matches, which are subject to rules of the game, leaving no room for creative freedom for the purposes of copyright.[235]

227. BSA 44-46. The point is further emphasised in para. 51.
228. Rosati 2023, p. 220.
229. Alter 2000, p. 506.
230. BSA paras 48-49.
231. The similarities are also pointed out by the ECS 2024, pp. 10-11 in its Opinion on the MIO/konektra cases.
232. BSA para. 50.
233. Judgment of the Court (Grand Chamber) of 4 October 2011. *Football Association Premier League Ltd and Others v. QC Leisure and Others* (C-403/08) and *Karen Murphy v. Media Protection Services Ltd* (C-429/08). ECLI:EU:C:2011:631.
234. FAPL para. 97: 'To be [classified as a work], the subject-matter concerned would have to be original in the sense that it is its author's own intellectual creation'.
235. FAPL para. 98.

Another ruling that elucidated the copyright threshold by defining the negative definition of originality was the SAS case.[236] It concerned the copyright eligibility of a software programming language and the definition of what constitutes an expression of a computer program. Due to their connection to the originality of software programming, there is a clear link between the SAS and BSA cases. In BSA, the Court had already stated that the distinction between an idea and its expression is crucial for the originality assessment. Espousing a line of argument resembling the US merger doctrine, the Court stated that the methods of implementing an idea must not make the idea and its expression indissociable, as this does not 'permit the author to express his creativity in an original manner'.[237] The Court continued in a similar vein in the SAS ruling, providing more details on the reasoning behind disqualifying creative choices related to functionality. The main focus seems to be on avoiding undue restriction of the public domain, as granting copyright to the functionality of a computer program would make it 'possible to monopolise ideas, to the detriment of technological progress and industrial development'. Moreover, the Court emphasised that the copyright eligibility of a computer program must only extend to the individual expression of the work, so that it leaves 'other authors the desired latitude to create similar or even identical programs provided that they refrain from copying'.[238]

3.4.3 Painer: Originality Requires Free and Creative Choices Reflecting the Author's Personality

The importance attached to the availability of free and creative choices first suggested in FAPL became a more pronounced feature of the Court's originality evaluation in subsequent rulings. The Painer ruling of December 2011 was a particularly important milestone within this development. The dispute concerned the copyright protection and unauthorised publication of portrait photographs, and the case was instrumental in defining several aspects of the EU-wide originality threshold. Not only did it substantially enrich the understanding of the positive prerequisites of originality, but it also put to bed any doubts as to the relationship between the vertical harmonisation as mandated by the 1990s directives and the horizontal harmonisation provided by the Infosoc Directive.

The *Painer* case concerned the originality of a portrait photograph, which presented the Court with an opportunity to clear the ambiguity caused by the Term Directive's requirement that a work is to reflect its author's personality. As noted above, it had been unclear whether the Term Directive's requirement that a photographic work must reflect its author's personality imposes a higher originality threshold than that applied to computer programs and databases. Considering that the CJEU

236. Judgment of the Court (Grand Chamber), 2 May 2012 *SAS Institute Inc. v. World Programming Ltd*, C-406/10.

237. BSA paras 48-50. *See also* Sousa e Silva, Nuno, The Boundaries of EU Copyright Law: Cheese, Jeans and a Military Report in the Court of Justice, iii (1) M&CLR (April 2019), p. 139 https://doi.org/10.7559/mclawreview.2019.317, accessed 9 August 2025, and ECS in its Cofemel opinion, para. 14.

238. SAS para. 41.

had taken an active - or even activist[239] - attitude to connecting the 1990s vertical harmonisation with the horizontal harmonisation of the Infosoc Directive, it is not surprising that Painer marked a further step towards unifying the EU-wide concept of originality.

Not only did the Court reinforce many of its arguments by the precedent set by Infopaq, but it also emphasised that it 'has already decided' (in Infopaq) that originality is the only standard by which copyright eligibility is to be determined. Some commentators considered this to constitute a de facto merging of the concepts of 'work' and 'originality' as the key components of the copyright assessment.[240] The Court's formulation in paragraph 87 indeed gives this impression by directly referring to the Infopaq decision's definition of a 'work' to define the originality requirements as applied under the Term Directive.[241] The Court's argumentation also suggests all positive and negative definitions of copyright eligibility have been gathered into one unified originality standard that determines access to copyright protection in all cases.[242] The unified standard takes its cues both from the Term and Infosoc Directives to clarify the concept of EU originality.

Overall, the Court's argumentation on the originality criteria in the Painer ruling contains certain features that warrant mention. In paragraphs 87-89 of the judgment, the Court notes that 'an intellectual creation is an author's own *if it reflects the author's personality*'.[243] In turn, a work reflects its author's personality 'if the author was able to express his creative abilities in the production of the work by *making free and creative choices*'.[244] Paragraphs 90-93 clarify the issue further:

> As regards a portrait photograph, the photographer can make free and creative choices in several ways and at various points in its production.
>
> In the preparation phase, the photographer can choose the background, the subject's pose and the lighting. When taking a portrait photograph, he can choose the framing, the angle of view and the atmosphere created. Finally, when selecting the snapshot, the photographer may choose from a variety of developing techniques the one he wishes to adopt or, where appropriate, use computer software.
>
> By making those various choices, the author of a portrait photograph can stamp the work created with his 'personal touch'.[245]

239. Synodinou 2021, p. 53 notes the legality of CJEU's actions have been questioned, citing further sources.
240. Sganga (The notion of 'work'), p. 6: 'By ruling, in fact, that the level of protection granted cannot and should not depend on the degree of originality of the work,38 the Court ultimately sanctioned the merge of the notion of protected work with the concept of originality'. Rognstad 2022, p. 174. notes that 'It is believed that this [definition of originality] is a general consideration in EU copyright law, which also applies beyond the creation of portrait photographs'.
241. It reads 'the Court has already decided (in Infopaq) that copyright is liable to apply only in relation to a subject-matter, such as a photograph, which is original in the sense that it is its author's own intellectual creation.'
242. The statements in Painer, paras 94-95 significantly support such a conclusion. The same holds for para. 99 applying the Term Directive's provision after having cited the Infosoc Directive in the previous two paragraphs.
243. Painer, para. 88. My italics.
244. Painer, para. 89. Mt italics.
245. Painer, paras 90-93.

Here, three points are particularly noteworthy. First, the clear link between the conditions for obtaining protection and the decisions made during the multi-stage creative process. The Court did not only consider it sufficient to evaluate merely the final appearance of the photograph but also required an examination of the creation process and the choices made during it. Second, the CJEU noted the impact of the creative process's multi-stage nature on the resulting creation's originality. This suggests that the accumulation of creative choices made across several phases of the creative process can significantly influence both the perceived scope of the author's freedom to exercise their creative abilities and the level of originality attributed to the end result. Third, considering the relationship between original choices and technical constraints, one can point out that many of the creative choices mentioned by the CJEU as potentially relevant for conferring originality on the resulting photograph could be classified as technical in nature, such as lighting, framing, and camera angle. Accordingly, the ruling implies that even a technically geared choice can contribute to producing an 'original' end result, provided it allows the prospective author to express his creative abilities. This principle was further reinforced in the subsequent Brompton Bicycle judgment, which held that even decisions driven by technical considerations can satisfy the originality requirement, as long as they do not prevent the author from reflecting their individuality in the protected subject matter.[246]

3.4.4 Football Dataco and Conclusions on the First-Generation Post-Infopaq Case Law

The quick succession of cases concerning the originality standard had given the Court an opportunity to tie together the various statements on the conditions for obtaining copyright protection. A concise summation of the originality requirements defined up to that point was given in the Football Dataco ruling. Again, like in BSA and Painer, the subject matter at hand in the dispute had been harmonised in the 1990s, as the case concerned the copyright protection of databases. This provided the Court with an opportunity to connect the concept of originality as defined in the 1996 Database Directive with its own (post-Infopaq) case law. In setting out the requirements of copyright protection, the Court considers it apparent from recital 16 of the Database Directive that 'the notion of the author's own intellectual creation refers to the criterion of originality'.[247] The Court then proceeds to crystallise both the positive and negative definitions of originality provided by its previous rulings. First, citing Infopaq, BSA and Painer, it notes that originality requires the selection or arrangement of data allowing the author to express his or her creative ability 'in an original manner by making free and creative choices', which stamps the author's personal touch on the work.[248] Second, the negative definitions stated in BSA and FAPL are reiterated. That is, the conditions of originality are not met 'when the setting up of the database is dictated by

246. The Brompton Bicycle case will be discussed in greater detail in section 3.5.2 below.
247. Football Dataco, para. 37. My italics.
248. Football Dataco, para. 38.

technical considerations, rules or constraints which leave no room for creative freedom'.[249]

Overall, the key points of the post-Infopaq copyright case law can be summarised as follows. The copyright eligibility of all creative efforts is to be assessed by the same standard, the author's own intellectual creation requirement. It is met if the author can make free and creative choices reflecting his or her personality. Conversely, technical or functional constraints on the freedom to make creative choices are the chief indicators of a lack of originality. Granting protection to such creations would make it possible to monopolise ideas to the detriment of industrial and technological progress. Nevertheless, the mere presence of functional features or technical constraints cannot automatically rule out copyright eligibility. Even within functionally inclined creations, the presence of originality is the only factor that determines copyright eligibility. Therefore, as noted in the BSA and SAS rulings, one cannot rule out that partly functional or 'creatively constrained' subject matter would obtain protection, provided the author had enough creative freedom to stamp his or her personal touch on the work.

3.5 THE LATE 2010S CASE LAW

3.5.1 The Levola Case and the Problem of Defining the Protected Subject Matter

3.5.1.1 The Background and Main Arguments of the Levola Ruling

During the latter part of the 2010s, the CJEU was presented with three referrals, which gave it an opportunity to further flesh out the concept of a work and the criteria for copyright protection. First of these was the *Levola Hengelo* case about whether the taste of a spreadable cheese could be granted copyright protection. From a historical perspective, claiming copyright to a taste is a rather unorthodox venture. However, given that the copyright criteria had been formulated in rather open-ended terms in the Court's post-Infopaq case law, the notion of the taste of the cheese meeting the criteria did not appear entirely unreasonable. In addressing the issue, the CJEU noted that copyright eligibility requires the taste of a cheese to be classifiable as a 'work',[250] and this concept is to receive 'an autonomous and uniform interpretation throughout the European Union'.[251] In defining the applicable criteria, the originality requirements stated in the early 2010s copyright case law were reiterated, but the Court put even more emphasis on unifying all the criteria relevant for the copyright assessment. This was done by formulating a cumulative two-part test for copyright eligibility. First, citing the FAPL case, it noted that 'the subject matter concerned must be original in the

249. Football Dataco, para. 39. Later on, in its Cofemel and Brompton rulings, the Court refers to this but adds the word 'other'. That is, 'technical considerations, rules or *other* constraints'.
250. Levola, para. 34.
251. Levola, para. 33.

sense that it is the author's own intellectual creation'.[252] Second, 'only something which is the expression of the author's own intellectual creation may be classified as a "work" within the meaning of Directive 2001/29'.[253] Citing both the Berne Convention and its own SAS decision, the Court also pointed out that copyright protection may be granted only to expression, not to 'ideas, procedures, methods of operation or mathematical concepts as such'.[254]

Regarding the identification and delineation of the protected work, the Court noted that copyright eligible subject matter 'must be expressed in a manner which makes it *identifiable with sufficient precision and objectivity*, even though that expression is *not necessarily in permanent form*'.[255] This requirement was justified by the need for authorities and competitors to know clearly and precisely which features of a product are protected.[256] Furthermore, the determination of copyright protection must not rely on any element of subjectivity, as this would be detrimental to legal certainty. To clarify its stance, the Court compared the subjectivity and imprecision of a taste unfavourably to the objectivity and precision of more established creative domains such as literary, pictorial, cinematographic or musical works.[257]

3.5.1.2 Analysis of the Originality and Identification Criteria

The Levola ruling got a mixed reception in the literature. While few commentators took issue with the outcome,[258] the reasoning underlying the decision received less unanimous approval.[259] The Court's argumentation indeed includes some confusing features. First, the unfavourable comparison of gustatory expression to that of literary, pictorial, cinematographic or musical works. According to the Court, the identification of gustatory works depends on subjective taste sensations and experiences, whereas literary, pictorial, cinematographic and musical works are deemed precisely and objectively identifiable. Yet, this comparison seems to confuse the subjective appreciation and objective perception of works,[260] thereby holding gustatory expression to a different standard than other creative domains with a more established copyright pedigree, without any clear reason. After all, a reliance on subjective appreciation for identifying the core characteristics of a given creation can hardly be considered exclusive to gustatory works, as it plays a similarly crucial role within virtually all types of creativity.

Second, the Court argued against protecting gustatory works by noting that the *current* state of scientific development does not allow for a sufficiently precise and

252. Levola, para. 36.
253. Levola, para. 37.
254. Levola, para. 39.
255. Levola, para. 40. My italics.
256. Levola, para. 41.
257. Levola, para. 42.
258. Among others, the ECS argued against granting protection to a taste in paras 27-28 of its opinion on the case.
259. Sousa e Silva 2019, p. 145 calls its argumentation 'weak', whereas Rosati 2018 calls the two-part cumulative test 'headache-inducing'.
260. This is also pointed out by Rosati 2018.

objective identification of a taste. This implies that gustatory works were not declared permanently ineligible for protection, as allowance was made for a future discovery of the requisite scientific means that might unlock the possibility of granting copyright protection to tastes of food products. Such a scenario strikes me as incompatible with the core assumptions underlying the concept of authored expression. Simply put, if human sensory perception is not capable of detecting any differences between two creations 'of the same kind',[261] these creations should not be classified as works under any circumstances. Even if the range of tools, methods, and media through which works are created is constantly expanding, copyright has always been geared towards protecting the expression as observed through human perception. Accordingly, if human sensibilities cannot clearly distinguish between two similar creations - be these within the field of gustatory, literary, musical, or any other type of expression - then neither can reasonably be considered copyright eligible.[262] In my estimation, this holds regardless of how precisely the creation can be pinned down, measured, or delineated by technical or scientific means. Hence, the Court would have done well not to mention the potential impact of the state of scientific development, since it only adds confusion and ambiguity regarding the identification requirement attached to the copyright requisites.

3.5.2 Cofemel and Brompton: Consolidation of the Two-Part Test for Copyright Eligibility

The second entry into the trio of decisions clarifying the CJEU's stance on unusual copyright subject matter was Cofemel. The case concerned the copyright protection of clothing designs. The CJEU begins its analysis by reiterating the cumulative test formulated in Levola. To qualify as a 'work', there must 'exist an original subject matter', and 'classification as a work is reserved to the elements that are the expression of such creation'.[263] Emphasising the unification of the statements on originality accumulated throughout its case law, the Court notes that 'as follows from the Court's settled case-law ... it is *both necessary and sufficient* that the subject matter reflects the personality of its author, as an expression of his free and creative choices'.[264] Conversely, a subject matter is not original if it has been dictated by technical constraints to an extent, leaving no room for creative freedom. The Court reiterated the requirement of precise and objective definability.

While the criteria enumerated in the previous paragraph only reiterated those presented in previous case law, the Cofemel ruling made the noteworthy addition that the two-part test first introduced in Levola is 'both necessary and sufficient' to acquire protection. This seems to assert that the test addresses any form of creativity, even if

261. Levola, para. 43.
262. According to Cohen Jehoram 2006, p. 631, Verkade, AG to the Dutch Supreme Court, when addressing the copyright eligibility of a scent, noted two requirements of protection: 'originality and the rule that the *product to be protected is open to human perception*'. My italics.
263. Cofemel para. 29.
264. Cofemel, para. 30. My italics.

such creativity potentially overlaps with another type of IP protection. In this vein, the Court expressly notes that design and copyright protection are not mutually exclusive. However, it also adds that a cumulation of rights must not undermine 'the respective objectives and effectiveness of those two forms of protection',[265] meaning that 'concurrent protection can be envisaged *only in certain situations*'.[266] This indicates that the test's applicability across all categories of creations does not amount to a universal lowering of the copyright threshold. A design may be eligible for copyright protection, but only if it is the result of sufficient free and creative choices not dictated by its functional purpose.[267]

The Brompton Bicycle case completed the trio of cases on copyright claims to unusual subject matter. This case was about whether a foldable bicycle can receive copyright protection. The bicycle at issue had been patented by the bike company Brompton Bicycle. Upon the expiry of the patent, another company – Get2Get – started selling a similar bike, which led Brompton to sue Get2Get for copyright infringement. The CJEU once again referred to the formulations accumulated throughout its sizeable body of case law on originality. It reiterated the formulation of cumulative criteria first introduced in Levola,[268] along with the notion that 'it is both necessary and sufficient that the subject matter reflects the personality of its author, as an expression of his free and creative choices' as stated in Cofemel.[269]

The most noteworthy aspect of the Brompton regarding the formulation of an EU-wide originality standard, as already mentioned in discussing the Painer ruling, is its treatment of how technical and functional constraints impact the copyright assessment. On the one hand, the Court pointed out that creative choices differentiated only by their technical function cannot be deemed original, as protecting such creations by copyright 'would amount to making it possible to monopolise ideas, to the detriment, in particular, of technical progress and industrial development'.[270] On the other hand, if the choices were only partially dictated by their technical function, originality is possible. Accordingly, the Court's argumentation clearly indicates that the creative process having been dictated by technical or functional considerations does not automatically rule out the possibility of originality and protection.

Overall, this underscores that the making of free and creative choices lies at the centre of the originality assessment. If the prospective author makes a sufficient number of free and creative choices, then there should be no obstacles to obtaining

265. Cofemel, para. 51.
266. Cofemel, para. 52. My italics.
267. This aligns with the view expressed by the European Copyright Society in its analysis of the Cofemel case. At para. 13.1, it states that 'It is important to emphasise that the Court has already interpreted the originality concept in a manner which mitigates the risk of overprotection. Thus, for example, an author's work will only be protected where there is scope for creative freedom in its production. Creative freedom requires the making of "free and creative choices" ... It has also been established that the application of labour and skill, without the exercise of creative freedom, in the making of a utilitarian article is insufficient to demonstrate the originality required for copyright protection'. Citations and footnotes omitted.
268. Brompton, para. 22. Of course, the requirements themselves as crystallised in the two-part cumulative test of Levola built upon previous case law.
269. Brompton, para. 23.
270. Brompton, para. 27.

copyright protection, even if the creative choices are in part dictated by functional or technical constraints. In addition, one must point out that the Brompton ruling aligns with the argumentation given in Painer in suggesting that the creative process that brings the work into being, not just the end result, needs to be considered in deciding on the question of copyright protection.[271]

3.6 SUMMARISING REFLECTIONS ON THE HARMONISED ORIGINALITY STANDARD

In summarising the case law analysis conducted throughout the chapter, I find that the CJEU's harmonisation of the criteria that determine access to copyright protection certainly deserves some credit. The cumulative two-part test formulated in Cofemel crystallises the preceding decade's copyright case law into a rather compact and accessible two-part formulation: First, it is 'both necessary and sufficient that the subject matter reflects the personality of its author, as an expression of his free and creative choices'.[272] Second, the original subject matter must be 'identifiable with sufficient precision and objectivity'.[273] The *Brompton* case brought added clarity on another strand of the copyright case law – the relationship between functional constraints impact the possibility of granting copyright protection – by stating that technical or functional constraints do not rule out the possibility of protection, provided the prospective author had sufficient opportunity to make free and creative choices that reflect his personality.

Establishing the author's free and creative choices as the defining feature of creating a 'work' has the advantage of being equally applicable to all types of creative endeavours, whether functional or artistic in nature. However, the increased focus on the creative process, likely to be needed when addressing AI-assisted creations, is inevitably bound to raise ambiguities and questions. Some of these have been highlighted by two pending referrals to the CJEU, Mio et al. and USM Haller, both of which relate to creations of applied art, and were joined by the CJEU.[274]

The Mio case concerns an infringement claim involving a dinner table, while the USM Haller case deals with USM's modular furniture system, for which another company – Konektra GmbH – sold compatible parts, prompting USM to allege copyright infringement. The questions raised by the referring courts have the potential to further clarify several aspects of how originality and copyright infringement are to be approached. First, the referring court in Mio directly inquires into the precise meaning of the 'free and creative choices reflecting the author's personality' criterion and how the examination should be carried out. It also inquires into the respective significance of the creative process and the end result in satisfying the originality criterion, essentially asking to what extent the originality assessment should focus on factors surrounding the creative process and the 'author's explanation of the actual choices

271. Härkönen 2025a, p. 298.
272. Cofemel, para. 30.
273. Cofemel, para. 32.
274. Joined Cases C-580/23 and C-795/23.

that he or she made'.[275] The referring court in Haller/konektra adds further nuance by asking whether free and creative choices must be made knowingly in order to qualify as the kind required by established CJEU case law. The Swedish court's referral also raises questions about how the similarity assessment between two contested creations should be conducted and what degree of similarity is required between the contested creations. A further point concerns the distinction between ideas and expression in cases where the relevant creation incorporates pre-existing commonplace designs, which aligns with the discussion about the distinction between original expression and non-protected ideas.

The case is still pending, but the Advocate General Szpunar's opinion was given in May 2025. Three points raised in the opinion warrant brief discussion. First, Szpunar emphasised the importance of the end result. For him, it is 'not enough that the creator made free and creative choices: those must still be perceptible to third parties through the work itself'.[276] If proof of other factors present during the work's creation is available, this can be considered by the court hearing the case.[277] Nonetheless, the decisive weight clearly lies in the perceptible expression exhibited by the end result. One implication of Szpunar's position is that it does not seem to allow for a broad reading of the Painer ruling's suggestion that free and creative choices made during the creative process can contribute to the originality of the end result.[278] It remains to be seen how the CJEU will address this issue and the relative weight to be given to the creative process and the end result.

Second, on the question of conducting the infringement assessment, Szpunar made a connection to the Pelham I ruling on a phonogram producer's reproduction right,[279] noting that that the focus should lie on determining 'whether creative elements of the protected work have been reproduced in a recognisable manner in the allegedly infringing work'.[280] To my view, this should not be taken to suggest any change to the Infopaq-based infringement test.[281] Under this assumption, Szpunar's statement essentially reiterates what was already established through the emphasis on what is perceptible to third parties through the work itself.[282]

Third, on the idea/expression dichotomy in relation to pre-existing commonplace designs, Szpunar noted that a "work composed solely of available shapes may also be original, provided that the author has expressed his or her creative choices in the arrangement of those shapes". However, the creation will not be protected if the arrangement is conventional, since such choices would not be creative.[283] This appears to align rather well with previous CJEU case law on the distinction between ideas and

275. AG Szpunar's Opinion on *Mio/konektra*, para. 15.
276. AG Szpunar's Opinion on *Mio/konektra*, para. 45.
277. AG Szpunar's Opinion on *Mio/konektra*, para. 50.
278. Painer, para. 89. Härkönen also discusses this issue, *see* Härkönen 2025b.
279. Case C-476/17.
280. AG Szpunar's opinion on the joined cases C-580/23 (*Mio*) and C-795/23 (*konektra*), para. 67.
281. Infopaq, para. 51.
282. In her commentary, Derclaye gives Szpunar's introduction of the recognisability test a positive assessment, provided it is not taken to endorse a departure from the Infopaq test. *See* Derclaye 2025.
283. AG Szpunar's opinion on the joined cases C-580/23 (*Mio*) and C-795/23 (*konektra*), para. 54.

their expression, and should not result in any significant re-evaluation of how the question of originality is approached.

3.7 CAN A CONCRETE DEFINITION OF THE COPYRIGHT REQUISITES BE FOUND?

3.7.1 Outline of the Second Part of the Chapter

The second part of this chapter will examine what the phrase 'free and creative choices reflecting the author's personality' means and to what degree one can formulate a concrete definition of its contents. In other words, this section examines when a creative choice can be characterised as free, and whether there is a specific number of creative choices that is required to clear the originality threshold. This inquiry aligns with the dissertation's research task of finding the point at which an instruction set either gains enough specificity to clear the originality threshold or loses enough of it to forfeit the status of being a protected work.

Another aspect of the copyright requisites that potentially can be significant for the copyright eligibility of AI-generated compositions is whether the relevant criteria are universally applicable to all categories of creations or types of creative processes. On the one hand, the CJEU's case law has clearly established that copyright claims to all types of creative endeavours are to be assessed according to the same criteria: the standard of free and creative choices reflecting the author's personality. On the other hand, the Court's argumentation has occasionally – especially in the *FAPL* and *Levola* cases – seemed to be more concerned with obtaining a pragmatically desirable outcome rather than pursuing a mode of argumentation that would apply the underlying originality criteria in a systematically similar manner to all types of creations. This suggests that while a satisfaction of the originality criteria should in theory give access to copyright protection, certain types of creations may have greater difficulties in obtaining protection than others. It of course remains to be seen how the CJEU applies the originality criteria in the context of AI-generated outputs, but it does not seem far-fetched to think that AI-generated compositions at least initially might have difficulty in obtaining protection, even if both the creative process and end result appear to meet the criteria as set out in the Court's case law. In the following, the notion of creative choices dictated by functional and technical constraints shall be examined, as this will give greater depth to the discussion of what it means to compose a piece of music and how the novel methods unlocked by AI-powered tools impact the possibility of obtaining copyright protection.

3.7.2 Can a Quasi-Statistical Analysis of the Creative Process Enhance the Originality Assessment?

One possible approach to concretising the originality standard is to approximate the number of creative choices made by the author during the work's creation. Essentially, the idea is to assess a creation's level of originality by making a quasi-statistical analysis of the creation's intricacy and individuality. One legal device building upon this idea is the double-creation criterion, frequently referenced in Nordic law. It examines whether one can practically rule out 'that any other person could have made something closely alike'.[284] A similar concept of statistical uniqueness, originally attributed to Kummer,[285] has also been suggested. According to this view, the work is considered original 'if another author, under similar circumstances and with the same aim in mind, would not reasonably reach the same creative outcome'.[286]

In Finland, the double-creation criterion has frequently been used as an auxiliary criterion to concretise the degree of creativity required to clear the originality threshold. For instance, in 2005, the Finnish Supreme Court used it to determine the copyright eligibility of glossaries in primary school textbooks, stating that since the authors considered many factors – such as the students' successively improving ability to comprehend words of different difficulty levels – when selecting which words to include in the glossaries, it is evident that no one else undertaking a similar task would have arrived at the same result.[287] Some Finnish scholars have pointed out that the national tradition of using this criterion as a measure of a creation's copyright eligibility can be problematic.[288] Härkönen, for instance, has argued that the 'no one else would have arrived at the same result' argument differs from EU-law's originality concept by implying a more negative stance toward so-called double-creation scenarios, where two authors produce identical works independently of each other.[289]

Notwithstanding the criticism that has been voiced regarding the potential discrepancy between this criterion and the post-Infopaq EU law definition of the criteria for copyright eligibility, it was endorsed in the latest edition of the Finnish textbook on copyright law, published in 2024, where the criterion was directly equated with the concept of originality without discussing or problematising the issue further.[290] (Other potential discrepancies have also been discussed recently. The continued use of the 'work-threshold' concept and the separate requirement that the work is an independent creation of the author have sparked debate within the Finnish Copyright Council and scholarly literature, since this wording of the copyright requisites differ from those formulated by the EU.[291] While this discussion is certainly warranted, it ultimately focuses on the linguistic formulation of the criteria rather than their substantive assessment. Consequently, it holds little relevance for the research task of this dissertation.)

284. Dreier and Karnell 1992, p. 292. Also Nordell 1995, p. 633; van Gompel 2014, p. 128: '[courts] ask themselves the theoretical question whether it is conceivable that two or more authors, independently from each other, create exactly the same work'.
285. Kummer 1968, p. 30.
286. Stamatoudi 2017, p. 83.
287. KKO 2005:43, paras 6-7.
288. Mylly 2016, p. 908.
289. Härkönen 2024.
290. Harenko et al. 2024, p. 21. My translation of the relevant passage: 'The prerequisite for obtaining copyright protection is that the intellectual creation must be independent and original. This means it surpasses the work-threshold (*teoskynnys*). Originality indicates that no one other than the creator could reasonably be expected to arrive at a similar result if they were to independently engage in a comparable creative undertaking'.
291. TN 2024:3; TN 2024:4; Hoikka, 2024: Thesleff 2024.

An additional challenge to assessing the originality threshold through approximated statistical probability is that it is liable to overlook the creative process. Especially if applied too strictly or schematically, it might neglect the relationship between author and work or altogether eliminate the author from the originality evaluation.[292] In a similar vein, Nordell has noted that the double-creation test is liable to collapse into an examination of objective novelty, which will not contribute to answering the ultimately decisive question of whether the work is original in the sense of being the author's own intellectual creation.[293]

While these certainly constitute valid criticisms of the double-creation tests or other similar criteria for assessing the originality of a creation, I find that a quasi-statistical probability assessment can meaningfully enhance the analysis by providing a more precise standard of the degree of creativity required to justify protection. Its main benefit is that it can give a clearer idea about the number and nature of the choices that should be made for something to be considered an intellectual creation that reflects the author's personality. This can come into play in two distinct scenarios.

First, when technological advancements have unlocked a new type of subject matter to which copyright protection is claimed. This is an ever-present feature of copyright law, as it is only natural that authors will explore the possibilities afforded by new creative means and proceed to lay copyright claim to the results of their efforts. The legal order can struggle with the new types of creative subject matter, since it can be challenging to apply the originality standard to entirely unprecedented types of creations before any case law has accumulated. The history of copyright law also has a long history of scepticism towards new forms of creative expression.[294] Photographic art is a good example of this, as the legal order initially was sceptical about whether photographic art could be deemed equally worthy of protection as conventional art forms such as writing, painting, or music.[295] The sound sampling used in hip-hop music met with similar scepticism as to its status as a worthwhile form of creative expression.[296] It also faced the additional challenge of the unclear permissibility of its sound sampling practice. (Incidentally, this issue appears to remain unresolved to this day, considering the seemingly ever-continuing *Metall auf Metall* case, which was referred to the CJEU for a second time in 2023).[297] In these situations, the potential of the quasi-statistical approach to provide a more concrete formulation of the amount or degree of the creativity required by the generally applicable 'free and creative choices

292. Härkönen 2024; Van Gompel 2014, pp. 128-129.
293. Nordell 1995, p. 632.
294. This is also echoed in the practical circumstances surrounding the gradual expansion of the exemplificative list of eligible types of works in the Berne Convention. As noted by Aplin 2009, p. 3, with reference to Ricketson and Ginsburg, 'there has usually been a prolonged struggle which has preceded the admission of a new category of work to the list'.
295. Nordell 1997, p. 8. The clearest example of initial scepticism towards photographic copyright giving way is the U.S. Supreme Court case *Burrow-Giles Lithographic Co. v. Sarony*, which upheld photographer Napoleon Sarony's copyright claim to a portrait photograph of Oscar Wilde.
296. Falstrom 1994; Ylikallio 2021.
297. Case C-590/23, Pelham: Request for a preliminary ruling from the Bundesgerichtshof (Germany) lodged on 25 September 2023 – *CG and YN v. Pelham GmbH and Others*.

reflecting the author's personality' criteria can help the argumentation, as the greater concreteness can help determine whether granting protection is justified.[298] The greater concreteness can also make it easier to assess whether a ruling against protection would be indicative of healthy scepticism, downright prejudice, or an exercise in sound judicial reasoning.

The second scenario in which the greater concreteness provided by the double-creation evaluation can be useful is when the end result is conventional or unproblematic, but the creative process that produced it is not. This is the defining challenge in investigating copyright claims to AI-generated compositions, which also inspired the distinction between the *seeming* and *actual* originality of a composition: whatever reasons there may be not to consider it a 'work', these cannot be detected by examining the end result alone. As argued in Chapter 1, this ties the copyright assessment to the extent to which the author's creative choices are reflected in the musical attributes of the composition. Notably, this aligns with the Painer and Brompton rulings, which place greater emphasis on the creative process in evaluating copyright eligibility. This approach is poised for further clarification in the *Mio/konektra* case, as noted above.

To summarise the discussion on the double-creation standard, the main utility of an auxiliary criterion based on approximated statistical probability assessments can be considered to be that it gives more in the way of a concrete benchmark for determining whether a sequence of pre-generation creative choices and their relationship to the end result are sufficient to meet the requisite conditions and justify copyright protection. Simply put, this approach can counteract the vagueness of the 'free and creative choices reflecting the author's personality' standard.[299]

This can have both positive and negative effects. On the one hand, it appears much easier to produce a convincing argument as to whether a sequence of pre-generation creative choices – regarding training data selection, model architecture, fine-tuning, and prompt engineering – constitutes a creative process and end result that no one else would have arrived at if undertaking a comparable process, than it is to argue whether the pre-generation contribution and its impact on the resulting composition satisfies the vaguely formulated 'free and creative choices reflecting the author's personality' requirement. In this case, the hypothetical probability assessment clarifies the issue, with a low probability of double-creations suggesting originality, while a high probability suggests there is 'something missing on the subjective side, expressed in terms of personality-related concepts'.[300] On the other hand, a lack of vagueness can also tie the adjudicators' hands in a way that ultimately undermines the functioning of the copyright framework as a whole. As noted regarding the CJEU's position on the copyright eligibility of football matches and the taste of a spreadable cheese, the legal

298. Rosenmeier 2001, pp. 143-144, gives a positive evaluation of the double creation criterion on similar grounds after treating its pros and cons at length.

299. On similar grounds, Rosenmeier 2001, p. 143 considers the double-creation criterion, possibly supplemented by a theory of creative freedom, to be the best originality criterion available in copyright law. He calls it 'clearer, sharper, and more operational than traditional originality criteria, and it is the only solution if the application of the originality requirement in case law is to become clear and consistent'. My translation.

300. Dreier and Karnell 1992, pp. 291-292.

order may at times find it preferable to place some subject matter outside the realm of copyright-eligible creative expression on pragmatic grounds that do not necessarily uphold the open-ended definition of eligible subject matter with absolute logical consistency.[301]

On balance, a vaguely defined originality standard may ultimately be preferable, allowing courts greater flexibility to pursue pragmatic solutions to the interpretative problems that arise whenever technical - or other - developments unlock novel means for creators to express themselves. In this context, assessing the probability of double-creations can provide important insights as an auxiliary analytical tool to be utilised in specific situations, such as when the legal order is faced with unprecedented forms of creative expression. In such scenarios, the criterion is at its best when applied with discretion, to avoid potentially unintuitive outcomes based on a too rigorous or schematic application.

3.7.3 Originality and External Constraints on Creativity

Even if it may be deemed beneficial not to define the originality criteria binding the legal order's application of work and originality with too much precision, the concept of 'externally constrained' creative choices requires some discussion, since the distinction between creative choices dictated by technical or functional constraints and those considered 'authorial' - in the sense that they can confer originality on the resulting creation - is set to play an important role in the context of AI-assisted creativity. After all, creation of an AI-generated composition such as Composition A typically requires a considerable number of creative choices, but many of them may be characterised as almost exclusively geared towards various technical aspects of getting the AI system to work effectively.

An extreme viewpoint would be that all creative contributions related to designing the AI system and enabling its functionality - such as training data selection, model architecture design, fine-tuning, etc. - are solely dictated by technical-utilitarian constraints, whereby they cannot contribute to the originality of Composition A in any way. However, this is a much too simplistic take on the issue, as the choices made during the process of developing the AI system are typically made for a variety of purposes. While some, such as the choices related to data curation and compression, are clearly dictated by purely technical-functional concerns, other choices are based on a more nuanced rationale that also leaves room for individuality. Moreover, the CJEU's reasoning on the originality requirements in the Painer and Brompton rulings, as noted above, clearly suggests that the technical-functional nature of a creative choice does not automatically bar it from contributing to the originality of the end result.

301. In this context, one might note Sganga's viewpoint that the Painer ruling 'added to the picture an element, already implicitly advanced since Infopaq, which twisted the definition of protected work and opened the door to dangerous interpretative misunderstandings'. On Sganga's view, this was done by 'ruling, in fact, that the level of protection granted cannot and should not depend on the degree of originality of the work'. Sganga 2018, p. 6.

Compared to the subject matter at issue in the *Painer* and *Brompton* cases, the creative choices related to AI development face the additional challenge of only indirectly influencing the eventually resulting composition: Even if the developers of Model A were to make a considerable number of creative choices that cannot be deemed solely dictated by technical considerations, which also makes independent double-creations exceedingly unlikely, these choices must sufficiently shape the musical attributes of Composition A for copyright protection to be possible. Consequently, there appear to be significant obstacles to obtaining copyright protection based on creative choices related to AI system development. Yet, the possibility of protection cannot be ruled out, and to address this question in greater detail, an in-depth analysis of the pre-generation creative choices made during various phases of developing an AI system and their influence on the end result will be performed in Chapter 7.

CHAPTER 4

The Requirement of Authorial Intent

4.1 THE AUTHOR'S CREATIVE CHOICES AND THE REQUIREMENT OF AUTHORIAL AGENCY

4.1.1 The Concept of Authorial Intent

The previous chapter's analysis indicated that the prerequisite of a protected work is that it must reflect the personality of the author as an expression of his free and creative choices. This points towards the relationship between the creative process and the resulting work, holding the key to copyright protection.[302] There are many factors to this that warrant discussion, and the present chapter shall examine the notion that the creative choices that bring a work into being must be guided by a certain degree of *authorial agency* or *intent*.

The requirement of authorial agency - implied by the definition of a work as the author's own intellectual creation reflecting their personality through free and creative choices made during the creative process - can be broken down into three phases. First, there must be an *author*. It seems reasonably uncontroversial to claim that the author must be a human being.[303] Second, the author must engage in the act of

302. A very similar point is made by Hartmann et al. 2020, p. 75: 'In the end, the CJEU's focus on creative choice as the hallmark of intellectual creation suggests that it is the *process of creating* rather than the ensuing act of expression *that is truly decisive for copyright protection* provided there is an attributable connection between the creative process and the [resulting] expression'. My italics. Senftleben 2023, p. 1541 also presents a similar argument in Generative AI and Author Remuneration.

303. European Parliament Resolution 2020/2015(INI) of 20 October 2020, para. 15, which says 'works autonomously produced by artificial agents and robots might not be eligible for copyright protection, in order to observe the principle of originality, *which is linked to a natural person*, and since the concept of "intellectual creation" addresses the author's personality'. My italics. Many scholars have also argued that only natural persons, not machines, can be considered an author, such as Rognstad 2022, p. 174. Rosati 2017, p. 974; Ricketson 1991, p. 10 also emphasises the need for a human author.

authoring. That is, the author must make free and creative choices reflecting his personality. Third, while acknowledging that there is no express fixation requirement,[304] the author, for his work to gain practical relevance,[305] generally needs to undertake voluntary physical actions with the express intention of converting the mental conception into a physically discernible medium.[306] For instance, the author needs to transfer the mentally conceived sequence of words into a word processing document, whereby the work's contents become externally perceivable. This step completes the *external realisation* of the work.[307]

Undoubtedly, the phases of mental conception and external realisation often overlap, since authors typically update their conceptualisation of the pursued end result throughout the process of realising the work. Nonetheless, any physical action that contributes to externally realising the work must be preceded by some mental formulation of the intended end result. Otherwise, it cannot be considered a creative choice that reflects the author's personality. Simply put, the author must *intend* to create a work to claim copyright protection over it. Conversely, non-intended creations cannot receive protection.[308] The requirement of authorial intent has arguably always been present in copyright law, but until recently, there has been little need to address it in discussing the prerequisites of protection, since instances where artistically viable creations would have emerged with little to no authorial intent were very scarce prior to the advent of high-performance generative AI systems.[309]

The quintessential example to illustrate the concept of a non-intended creation is the scenario where a painting results from accidentally knocking over cans of paint, splashing onto a surface to form colour patterns resembling abstract art. While such patterns may be complex enough to meet the requirements of *seeming originality*,[310]

304. Haarmann 2014, p. 53.
305. Rahmatian 2024, p. 23 (with further references) points out that 'author's rights countries also require the work to be perceivable by the senses of third parties: the mere thoughts of the composer which have not been expressed to the outside world obtain no protection'. By 'author's right countries', Rahmatian refers to jurisdictions that do not impose an express fixation requirement, such as those under discussion in this dissertation.
306. This is also implied by the two-part cumulative conditions for copyright eligibility given in Levola, paras 36-37. Sganga 2019, p. 194, suggests an apposite formulation of this: 'Expression' entails a perceivable externalization of an idea, which communicates the author's creative (personal) touch in an original and distinguishable manner. In fact, *"expression" is the protected work* and, since it draws the boundaries of exclusivity against the public domain, it should be possible to describe it in clear, precise, intelligible and objective – or at least commonly shared – terms, as it is the case for every proprietary entitlement'. (My italics).
307. Ginsburg and Budiardjo 2019, p. 343 use the term 'execution of a work' to describe a very similar stage of the work's genesis.
308. AG Szpunar's opinion in *Mio/konektra* (para. 47) appears at first sight to contradict this, since he downplays the significance of the creator's subjective intentions. However, in the context of the referring court's question, this relates to a different kind of intention: whether the creator's own perception of his design choices as utilitarian or artistic should affect copyright eligibility. To my view, answering this in the negative does not impact the attitude towards the requirement of creative agency in the sense discussed here, i.e., that copyright presupposes creative choices that are more than accidental or unconscious.
309. Burk 2020, pp. 268-269 makes a similar point, although he frames it in terms of 'mental state of copyright authorship' as a distinction between 'causation of *fixation*' and 'causation of *expression*'. Emphasis in original.
310. The division into seeming and actual originality was introduced and defined in section 1.8.

the lack of authorial agency would invalidate any copyright claims to the painting. The table below illustrates the issue by enumerating the different phases of authorial agency in various types of creative expression:

Author	*Mental Formulation*	*Realisation*	*End Result*
Writer	Sequence of words	Type sequence into a word processing document	Text document, recitation
Composer	Sequence of musical attributes	Document the conception in musical notation or audio file	Music sheet, performance, audio recording
Painter	Sequence of colour patterns	Attach colour pigments to a surface	Painting

Overall, this indicates that the assessment of whether a creation should be granted copyright protection must investigate whether the creation is the result of free and creative choices reflecting the author's personality. As illustrated by the example of accidentally knocking over cans of paint to produce a painting, this indicates a further requirement of *authorial intent*, meaning that the contents of a creation must reflect the author's deliberate intentions in order to become protectable. The requirement of authorial intent essentially means that the creation cannot be too much of an accidental or fortuitous consequence of the author's actions, since this would not allow it to be characterised as having resulted from the author's creative choices. An alternative way of formulating this is to state that the author must sufficiently control the external realisation of the work, so that the underlying authorial conception aligns precisely enough with the creation's external realisation.

Although a certain degree of authorial intent or control over the end result is undoubtedly required to produce a protected work, it is equally clear that the author is not required to preconceive every aspect of the resulting creation with absolute precision before proceeding to externalise the work. Instead, the traditional view of a protected work allows for some discrepancy between the underlying mental conception and the end result,[311] meaning that the required level of creative control lies somewhere between pure chance and a flawlessly executed realisation of a fully pre-formed idea. The alignment between authorial intent and external realisation is particularly relevant when assessing copyright claims to Composition A and other AI-generated creations,[312] as AI systems typically place substantial portions of the

311. Hartman et al. 2020, p. 75 present a very similar argument at, stating that 'what is probably enough [for copyright protection] is *general authorial intent*. That is to say, it is sufficient that the author has a *general conception of the work before it is expressed, while leaving room for unintended expressive features*'. Emphasis in original. Similar points are made by Bulayenko et al. 2022, p. 43 and Ramalho 2021, pp. 71-72.
312. *See* section 1.2 about Composition A.

post-generation composition's musical attributes beyond the direct control of pre-generation contributors.

4.1.2 Authorial Intent and the Alignment Between Conception, Realisation, and End Result

To better grasp the relationship between authorial intent and end result discussed in the previous section, the genesis of a work can be described through the following steps:

- Formulating an authorial goal: The author establishes a creative purpose, such as 'I want to create an image of a monkey posing for a camera' or 'I want to compose dramatic orchestral music suitable for a cinematic adventure scene.'
- Mentally conceiving the work: The author envisions the artistic building blocks – such as a specific sequence of colour pigments, musical attributes – that will achieve the intended authorial goal.
- Externalising the mental conception: The author physically realises the mental conception by applying paint to a canvas, inserting notes into a music sheet or inserting sounds into an audio file.

For the end result to qualify as an 'intellectual creation reflecting the author's personality', there must be sufficient alignment between the author's mental preconception and the physical realisation of the work. In essence, the author needs to exercise sufficient creative control to make the end result meaningfully correspond to the underlying authorial goal and mental conception. To illustrate this issue with greater nuance, let us consider two paintings featuring abstract colour patterns of similar complexity and outward appearance. The first painting was the result of a long and painstaking session, where the author, who used a paint splattering technique akin to Jackson Pollock's, carefully considered which colour to select and where to aim each splatter. In contrast, the second painting was created when a person accidentally tripped over several cans of paint, which splashed onto an opportunely placed canvas.[313] The crucial difference between the two paintings lies in the alignment between authorial intent and external realisation. Although both paintings were *caused* by the actions of a human agent, the visual expression exhibited by the latter is not the result of the free and creative choices of the human agent, but of fortuitous circumstances outside the agent's control (tripping over cans of paint). Since the colour patterns of the latter painting came into being accidentally rather than as an expression of any underlying creative-authorial goals, they cannot be deemed reflections of the

313. It is, of course, highly improbable that accidentally tripping over cans of paint would bring about a painting that would even remotely approach the complexity of Pollock's paintings. It is equally improbable that the paint cans and canvas would happen to be placed in a way that allows this to take place. However, these facts ultimately lack significance for the point pursued.

human agent's will or personality, making it a non-authored creation that does not justify copyright protection.

Another example will illustrate how the author's mental state influences the alignment between authorial intent and external realisation. Let us suppose two compositions. Both are documented in the form of conventional musical notation, but neither makes use of traditional structures of musical expression, such as common scales, rhythmic patterns, chords, and form. Accordingly, the compositions are most accurately characterised as highly abstract musical sequences.[314] As in the previous example, we again suppose the former is created through painstaking effort in selecting which notes to insert into the music sheet, whereas the latter is made by inserting notes with utter indifference to the musical attributes of the end result. Consequently, the difference in creative control is very similar to that between the two paintings described above, suggesting that copyright protection should, at least in theory, be awarded only to the former composition. The reason for this warrants further discussion.

When examining the externally observable creative process, the physical actions behind either composition appear identical: in both cases, the authors press keys, which produce musical notation with the help of a sheet music application. However, the crucial difference lies in how the physical actions externalising the creation align with the underlying authorial intent. The first composer exercises deliberate creative control, ensuring the outcome reflects his vision with a high degree of accuracy. In contrast, the second composer is indifferent to the musical impact of his creative choices and exerts no meaningful control over the resulting composition. Without a guiding preconception, the external realisation cannot be deemed to reflect the second composer's personality or will. Accordingly, using the 'author's own intellectual creation' construction as reference, one might argue that such a composition is not an 'intellectual creation', but merely a 'physical creation', as the composer was not mentally engaged with the expressive qualities of the final result while producing the music sheet.

Based on the analysis above, authorial intent, creative control, and predictability can be deemed closely interconnected: An author who carefully preconceives a creation and exercises control over its realisation can precisely predict the outcome of the creative process at the moment of making the relevant creative choices. Conversely, where such guidance is lacking, the author is unlikely to be able to predict the end result with much accuracy. Consequently, the *predictability* of the end result at the moment of making the relevant creative choices appears to be an accurate measure of the degree of authorial intent guiding the creative process.

This predictability has a significant bearing on the question of laying claim to AI-generated compositions based on pre-generation creative choices. For the output to be considered a reflection of the author's creative choices, the author must be able to predict or foresee the expressive attributes of the end result with sufficient precision at the time of creative decision-making. Clearly, this is not the case with the example of Composition A given in Chapter 1, as the musical attributes of the composition only

314. Most listeners would probably characterise both pieces as musical gibberish.

align with the creative choices of User A in a very broad and imprecise manner. On a broader level, this issue has been discussed in early scholarly publications on AI outputs and copyright. Somewhat surprisingly, a case involving a Monkey Selfie has figured rather prominently in this discussion.[315] The case was about wildlife photographer David Slater setting up his photographic gear and 'borrowing' his camera to a macaque called Naruto, who took a selfie that went on to garner considerable attention. The case has been discussed rather actively in the scholarly literature on AI outputs, due to the inherent similarities to an AI model playing the part of the non-human creative agent.

Another analogy that has been frequently referenced by copyright scholars is Jackson Pollock's painting technique,[316] as it resembles AI-generated creations in that predictability and creative control are partially forfeited to fortuitous circumstances. Some cases involving actual AI-generated creations have already been decided, particularly in the US, and these will be discussed at greater length in Chapter 7. Despite the existence of these cases, I find that examining authorial intent through the lens of familiar modes of expression – painting and photography – will not only make the analogy between traditional and AI-assisted creative processes clearer but will also give an opportunity to engage with late 2010s and early 2020s scholarly discussion on the copyright eligibility of AI-generated outputs.

4.2 AUTHORIAL INTENT IN THE MONKEY SELFIE CASE

4.2.1 The Facts of the Case

There are different versions of how the Monkey Selfie photographs were created, but it seems uncontested that Slater set up the camera and a macaque called Naruto photographed itself using Slater's camera.[317] The case caught the public eye when People for the Ethical Treatment of Animals (PETA) filed a complaint for copyright infringement against Slater on behalf of the macaque. The pictures piqued the interest of copyright scholars due to the interesting questions they pose as to the respective creative contributions of Slater and Naruto. In their analysis, Ginsburg and Budiardjo present three hypothetical versions of the events that caused the photographs to come into being. In Version One, Naruto 'snatched Slater's camera away, and began snapping pictures, including the remarkably accomplished self-portrait that quickly garnered viral celebrity'. In Version Two, 'Slater had been studying the macaques in the reserve; realizing that the monkeys ... would not cooperate in a portrait-sitting,

315. The case has been discussed by, *inter alia*, Ginsburg and Budiardjo 2019, Guadamuz 2016, and Rognstad 2022.
316. *See*, for instance, Burk 2020, p. 263; Rognstad 2022, p. 185; Leistner and Jussen 2025, pp. 15-16.
317. The United States Court of Appeals for the Ninth Circuit. (2018). *Naruto v. David Slater, et al.* (No. 16-15469), p. 4: 'In 2011, a wildlife photographer, David Slater, left his camera unattended in the reserve. Naruto allegedly took several photographs of himself (the 'Monkey Selfies') with Slater's camera. Available at https://cdn.ca9.uscourts.gov/datastore/opinions/2018/04/23/16-15469.pdf, accessed 17 December 2024.

Slater positioned the camera to frame the shot, including setting lighting and perspective, and waited for a curious monkey to come along, stare at the camera, and push the button, which Naruto obligingly did.'[318] In Version Three, Slater sets up the camera as in the previous example and leaves the scene. However, the camera, set to take photographs at timed intervals, 'captures some other denizen of the wildlife preserve unexpectedly attacking and eating Naruto'.[319]

All versions provide slightly different perspectives on the question of authorial intent. It seems evident that the First Version does not feature any authorial intent on Slater's part. Version Two, for its part, equally plainly indicates that Slater intended to create a monkey selfie. The second version also bears many similarities to the Pollock painting technique's use of controlled randomness as a part of realising the work's expression. Accordingly, this version warrants a more thorough analysis of Slater's possible claim to the picture. The crucial question is whether Slater's mental conception and the actions undertaken to realise it align with sufficient precision to establish a valid authorship claim to the resulting photograph. As noted above, the Painer ruling plays a central role in determining the prerequisites for protection in an EU context. According to the CJEU, portrait photography provides the author with many opportunities to stamp the work with his personality:

> In the preparation phase, the photographer can choose the background, the subject's pose and the lighting. When taking a portrait photograph, he can choose the framing, the angle of view and the atmosphere created. Finally, when selecting the snapshot, the photographer may choose from a variety of developing techniques the one he wishes to adopt or, where appropriate, use computer software.[320]

In a conventional studio setting, the portrait photographer has well-nigh total sovereignty over the creative choices mentioned in the quotation. By contrast, the many unconventional features of the *Naruto* case raise the question whether circumstances outside Slater's control were significant enough to break the link between the mental conception and external realisation of the photograph's expression. Slater's own account of the creative process indicates he undertook actions both related to the aesthetic properties of the photographs as well as to coax the subjects to pose in the desired manner:

> I wanted to keep my newfound friends happy and with me. I now wanted to get right in their faces with a wide-angle lens, but that was proving too difficult as they were nervous of something – I could not tell what. So I put my camera on a tripod with a very wide-angle lens, settings configured such as predictive autofocus, motorwind, even a flashgun, to give me a chance of a facial close-up if they were to approach again for a play. I duly moved away and bingo, they moved in, fingering the toy, pressing the buttons and fingering the lens. I was then to witness

318. Ginsburg and Budiardjo 2019, p. 364.
319. Ginsburg and Budiardjo 2019, p. 373.
320. Painer, para. 91.

> one of the funniest things ever as they grinned, grimaced and bared teeth at themselves in the reflection of the large glassy lens.[321]

Later, Slater gave further descriptions of the actions undertaken to produce the photographs:

> [I had] angled the background to make sure the sun was behind the camera, not facing it. Then I set the camera so it made a funny, chk-chk-chk noise when you pressed the button, which the monkeys loved. I'd been working with these monkeys for two days, observing their behaviour, and knew they would eventually end up pressing the button. It still took a while, though.[322]

The photographing session 'lasted thirty minutes and produced hundreds of pictures, but only a few were in focus and usable, but three of them in particular were spectacular'.[323] As indicated by the quoted passages, the creative process behind the three successful pictures certainly lacks neither physical nor intellectual effort.[324] Yet, this may lack relevance for the originality assessment, since the *idea* of getting a monkey to take a selfie is not copyright eligible as such, and copyright protection will only attach to the selfie's photographic expression.[325]

Does the monkey selfie, then, contain sufficient photographic expression aligning with Slater's authorial intent? As in the previous example involving two different ways of splashing paint onto a canvas, one might link the relationship between authorial intent and resulting expression to the intensity of the author's engagement with the work's realisation. The author of a photographic work does not have to be the one pressing the shutter button, but the control exercised over the process of realising the mental conception must establish a strong enough link between the author's creative choices and the photographic attributes contained in the photograph.

On the one hand, all the camera settings were configured by Slater, meaning that many of his creative choices are directly reflected in the image. On the other hand, several of these choices – such as the use of a wide-angle lens, predictive autofocus, motorwind, and a flashgun – appear to have been dictated more by the practical need

321. Slater's website, http://www.djsphotography.co.uk/original_story.html, accessed 14 March 2025.
322. Rafaeli, J.S., 'I'm a Human Man Being Sued By a Monkey', https://www.vice.com/en/article/3knmnv/im-a-human-man-being-sued-by-a-monkey, accessed 17 December 2024.
323. Guadamuz, Andres, The Monkey Selfie: Copyright Lessons for Originality in Photographs and Internet Jurisdiction, 5(1) Internet Policy Rev. (2016), p. 2 https://doi.org/10.14763/2016.1.398, accessed 9 August 2025. Available at https://ssrn.com/abstract=2752461, accessed 17 December 2024.
324. Slater's description of the pictures' genesis paints a picture of the hard labour associated with tropical wildlife photography: 'I'd been hanging out with this troupe of monkeys for about 48-hours, never leaving their side, and gaining their trust. This is equatorial rainforest and I'm carrying about 50 lbs of gear, climbing over logs, through mud and cobwebs, watching for snakes and all that – but eventually they accepted me and started to groom me. I tried the camera on a self-timer to get a picture of that. I saw how the monkeys responded to the camera and that gave me the idea.' I'm a Human Man Being Sued By a Monkey, https://www.vice.com/en/article/3knmnv/im-a-human-man-being-sued-by-a-monkey, accessed 17 December 2024.
325. The skill and labour exhibited in the making of the photograph also lacks relevance for the originality assessment.

to capture the macaque within the frame as a properly focused image than by artistic intent. Other features, such as the macaque's pose and positioning in the frame, were completely independent of Slater's choices. On this basis, one might state that Slater's authorial intent was aimed at creating *a* monkey selfie, but due to the difficulty of communicating and cooperating with the subject, he failed to sufficiently control *what kind* of monkey selfie. Thus, Slater's endeavours executed the *idea* of a monkey selfie, but the expression of the idea came into being through predominantly fortuitous circumstances.

The macaque's inability to cooperate and obey instructions appears to be the decisive factor weakening the link between Slater's authorial intent and the photographic end result. This becomes more apparent if we suppose Slater took a selfie-style portrait photograph of a local guide who accompanied him to the jungle. The human subject would have been able to respond to instructions, giving Slater considerably greater control over the relevant creative parameters, even if the guide would be the one to press the shutter button. Moreover, Slater's enhanced control over framing, pose, settings and lighting would have enabled him to let the different creative parameters interact: Guided by his expertise and individuality, Slater could adjust the settings and lighting in relation to other parameters, such as the subject's pose and framing. This would allow him to form a more refined mental conception of the expressive result he was pursuing. As in the example of flinging paint at a canvas, the fact that the author's creative control is exercised over an extended period of time significantly strengthens the link between conception and realisation. While this, of course, is common to all creative processes, I find it particularly important for aligning the authorial preconception with the external realisation in creative processes that utilise partially uncontrolled input.

Based on the arguments pointed out above, I find Slater's copyright claim to be rather weak. However, other scholars have taken more favourable approaches to the originality of Slater's creative contribution. In their analysis, Ginsburg and Budiardjo note that 'although he left some elements to chance, many specifics of the grand design and most of its implementation remained Slater's'. Examining the case from an expressly EU-centred perspective, Guadamuz presents a similarly encouraging assessment of Slater's authorship claims. The choice of angle, focus and use of a tripod suggest a 'deliberate effort to try to get a picture that reflects the personality of the author'.[326] Furthermore, and more importantly, the ex-post selection among the hundreds of pictures taken by the macaque to determine the ones worthy of publication represented 'an intellectual exercise' worthy of making the resulting picture reflect Slater's personality. To substantiate his interpretation, Guadamuz cites the *Infopaq* case's emphasis on choice, sequence, and combination of words. However, this position can be criticised by noting that while the redaction of a photograph can certainly contribute to its originality, the mere ex-post selection of photographs does not confer originality on the end result. Granting authorship under these circumstances would amount to what is sometimes called 'authorship-by-adoption', in which the

326. Guadamuz 2016, pp. 8-9.

prospective author's sole creative contribution consists in the post-execution selection of an existing object that is put into a new context by declaring it a work of art.[327] This invites comparison to readymade art, such as Marcel Duchamp's pedestal-mounted urinal.[328] Yet, neither ex-post selection nor readymades can meet the originality criteria due to the requirement that the author engages in the work's creation.

4.2.2 Naruto Version Three: Realising the Photographer's Individual Perspective

The third version of the monkey selfie case provides an additional feature to the discussion about the relationship between conception and realisation. In Version Three, Slater set up his camera and other gear to capture a monkey selfie, but the camera recorded another animal unexpectedly attacking and eating Naruto. In this scenario, the relevant issue can be formulated in terms of the distinction between unprotected ideas and protected expression. Protection will only attach to the expressive features of his pictures. The idea-content, such as the overarching motif, subject, or informational value of the picture, cannot be protected. The interesting part of Version Three is that only the idea-content is changed by the unexpected appearance of the predator, whereas Slater's creative input remains essentially intact. Consequently, this scenario addresses the relationship between authorial intent, realisation, and end result in an interesting way.

In their analysis of Version Three, Ginsburg and Budiardjo take a positive view towards granting authorship to Slater. They suggest that nature photographers do not need to form a particularly accurate preconception of what the work should look like, instead considering it sufficient to form a conception that guides the execution of the work. Once a nature photographer completes the original plan by generating a photograph, the authorship requirements are fulfilled, even if unexpected events were to leave the photographer astonished by the contents of the resulting footage.[329]

Rognstad has also examined this hypothetical example, using it to illustrate a two-stage model for evaluating the relationship between intent, creative choices, and end result. The first stage considers whether the author made free and creative choices, and the second stage examines whether these choices are reflected in the end result. Under this view, intent is required at the first stage but is not relevant to the second. By making several deliberate choices, such as setting up the tripod and configuring the camera settings, Slater fulfilled the requirements of the first stage. Since these choices 'cover all features of the [resulting] image', Slater should be considered the author of it, even if many features of the photograph were completely unforeseen by him. For Rognstad, the crucial point is that 'no events other than the photographer's free and creative choices affected the taking of the photograph'. This is contrasted to the Second Version, where Slater handed over control of the taking of the photograph to the

327. Ginsburg and Budiardjo 2019, p. 367, Hugenholtz and Quintais 2021, p. 1204 also make similar points.
328. https://en.wikipedia.org/wiki/Fountain_(Duchamp), accessed 14 March 2025.
329. Ginsburg and Budiardjo 2019, pp. 375-376.

monkeys, making his copyright claim weaker, as 'originality is limited to traits covered by his free and creative choices, and does not include traits caused by the monkeys'.[330]

There is certainly merit to these interpretations of Version Three, but I find the great emphasis on the external realisation of the image's photographic expression difficult to reconcile with the idea of the (photographic) work as an intellectual creation that reflects the author's personality. This is because the alignment between authorial intent, realisation, and end result is insufficient, as the creative choices - such as the placement of the camera, choice of lens, and configuration of settings - were determined with regard to a completely different motif, a monkey selfie. Even if many of the resulting image's expressive features were directly caused by Slater's creative choices, the fact that the choices intended to express a completely different photographic motif precludes them from 'counting' as creative choices that reflect the author's personality. Under these circumstances, it does not seem intuitive to consider the photographic expression exhibited by the image a reflection of Slater's personality.

A possible exception to this would be if the creative choices made by Slater were so elaborate that they would meet the originality threshold regardless of the motif depicted by the image. However, it does not strike me as particularly likely that a series of photographic choices aimed at capturing a monkey selfie would be sufficiently elaborate to meet such a standard. Without being aimed at expressing a particular motif, I find it more plausible that Slater's creative choices would 'only' constitute an exercise in professional skill or expertise, and thereby fall short of the originality threshold. For the choices to lead to the creation of a photographic work, they would most likely need to accumulate with the precise selection of motif - whether this is a monkey selfie or predator attack - and other factors, such as the framing of the subject and moment of release.

This viewpoint is not unreasonable, considering the Finnish Copyright Council's originality assessment of photographs. The Council has not only ruled against originality in routine professional level photographs, such as a handsome image of Paavo Nurmi lighting the Olympic fire during the Olympic opening ceremony,[331] but it has also stated that a photograph can 'qualify for protection as a work if it reflects the photographer's original choices in such a way that the photographer's individual perspective on the subject is conveyed'. However, the originality threshold 'is not met if the photographic result is based solely on the photographer's technical skill and the skilful application of photographic techniques'.[332] Although this perhaps reads too much into the Council's argumentation, I find the emphasis on the photographer's individual perspective particularly noteworthy, since it suggests that the photographic choices - regarding the lens, settings, lighting, framing, etc. - need to be undertaken to express a preconceived photographic motif. Otherwise, they cannot be characterised as conveying the photographer's individual perspective on the subject, thereby breaking the alignment between the creative choices and the end result.

330. Rognstad 2022, pp. 186-188. *See also* Rognstad 2025, pp. 136-137.
331. TN 2003:6 (Paavo Nurmi sytyttää olympiatulen), TN 2016:4 (Ralliauton kuva).
332. TN 2016:4 (Ralliauton kuva), para. 15. My translation.

In conclusion, my objections to awarding protection in Version Three rest on the argument that meeting the originality threshold requires the choice of photographic attributes to be deliberately geared towards expressing the photographer's individual perspective of the subject. For the predator attack image to be a work attributable to Slater, the choice of lens, settings, and other features needs to be selected with this authorial goal in mind, so that it can convey his individual perspective on this subject.[333] On the whole, I find that this approach to the originality assessment conforms better with the notion that a work is an 'intellectual creation reflecting the author's personality'.

4.2.3 Naruto Version Four and the Progressive Accumulation of Creative Choices

The concept of the photographer's individual perspective and the effect this may have on the cumulation of creative choices through multiple stages of the creative process can be illustrated by introducing a Fourth Version of the monkey selfie case. In this scenario, the predator's attack was captured through an entirely conventional sequence of events. The creative process starts with Slater setting up the camera with the intention of creating a monkey selfie. Yet, while Slater was observing the scene with the photographic gear ready, a predator unexpectedly emerged and attacked Naruto. This sequence of events considerably enhances Slater's chances of making the image reflect his personality. Given that Slater was present when the predator emerged and fixed on Naruto, his professional and artistic acumen would have suggested how best to capture the scene developing in front of his eyes. Settings, framing and other aspects – as far as the speed of predator's actions allowed – would rapidly have been planned. The moment of capturing the predator's attack on Naruto would likewise have been guided by Slater's preconceived photographic narrative.

Regarding the alignment between authorial preconception, creative choices, and end result, this situation resembles Jackson Pollock's technique of flinging paint on the canvas. Since Pollock continuously observes the painting gradually taking shape before his eyes, his authorial intent inevitably influences the way each successive splash of paint is flung onto the canvas. Given that both authors are mentally and physically engaged with the creation throughout the process of external realisation, neither Slater nor Pollock can help let their physical actions reflect the underlying – albeit constantly evolving – authorial intent. This significantly strengthens the link between the authors' creative choices and the attributes of the end result, even if they exercise less than absolute creative control during the work's realisation.

The comparison between the Third and Fourth Versions highlights how the degree of alignment between authorial preconception and external realisation can influence the multi-stage build-up of creative choices, which, in turn, significantly impacts the originality of the final result. In the Fourth Version, Slater's ability to adjust

333. The exception would be if the choices are so elaborate that the originality standard will be met by any image that is captured with these settings.

the photographic settings at the moment of capture provides him with greater freedom to imprint his artistic vision on the image. This creative input continues into the editing stage, where adjustments to colours, lighting, and framing can further refine the image. Together, these choices build upon one another, allowing the photographic creation to take shape through a process that spans conception, execution, and post-production. As the choices are layered and refined across multiple stages of the creative process, they progressively enhance the opportunities for Slater to imprint his personality on the end result, even if the individual choices were to be subtle in nature. The cumulation of creative choices through several creative phases also bolsters the authorship claim in the light of the hypothetical double-creation standard discussed in Chapter 3, since the cumulation of choice is likely to cause an exponential increase in the number of possible outcomes. In the Third Version, by contrast, the cumulation of decision-making is much smaller. Since Slater intended to express a monkey selfie rather than the predator's attack, the choices were not made in pursuit of the artistic end eventually obtained. Moreover, unlike the Fourth Version, Slater did not have an opportunity to adjust his authorial (pre)conception prior to the capturing of the raw image. This decreases the alignment between preconception and realisation, undermining the multi-stage accumulation of creative choices.

This does not mean that the author, to produce a photographic work, must always lock in the motif before capturing the image. It is certainly possible for Slater to obtain an original result if he performs extensive ex-post editing on the fortuitously taken picture of the predator's attack. In this case, however, the creative choices related to editing would need to be of a more substantial nature. After all, the exclusive right would attach only to the editing itself, whereas any creative contribution that occurred before the taking of the picture – such as the pose of the subjects in the frame and the way these interact with the settings and lighting chosen by Slater – would not contribute to the originality of the end result. Moreover, due to the limited alignment between the pre- and post-capture creative contributions, the creative choices would not accumulate throughout several creative phases, diminishing the potential for an exponential increase in creative choices attributable to the author.

To summarise, in Version Three, Slater's creative choices were not allowed to build up throughout the different stages of creative input. The resulting lower number of creative choices means that the creativity supplied during the editing of the image would need to be of a more substantial character to achieve an original end result. Conversely, the progressive accumulation of creative choices in Version Four yields a much higher number of creative contributions, allowing Slater to obtain an original result even if his creative input is of a subtle nature.

4.3 SUMMARY AND CONCLUSIONS

As already stated in Chapter 1, the availability of high-performance generative AI has increased the need for examining the process through which a data collection – such as music, text, or images – was created. To qualify for protection, the creative expression exhibited by the data collection must be attributable to the creative choices made by the prospective author. To crystallise the components that impact this issue, the present chapter has divided the creative process into stages of authorial intent, external realisation, and end result, which need to be sufficiently aligned to produce an original work. Accidentally knocking over cans of paint to produce a painting was used as an illustrative example of a situation where a *seemingly original* creation lacks the necessary mental engagement during the creative process, suggesting that the painting should receive no protection. The other extreme in terms of how closely the authorial intent, external realisation, and end result can be aligned is demonstrated by painters like Leonardo da Vinci, who executed every part of their paintings with meticulously planned brushstrokes, often preceded by extensive preparatory studies. Most creative processes lie between these two extremes regarding the degree of authorial intent and engagement with the work during the creative process, but it seems safe to presume that higher degrees of engagement will correlate with a higher likelihood of obtaining protection.

The type of creative process most relevant for this dissertation is one where the author forfeits creative control over some – but not all – parts of the end result, as tends to be the case with AI-assisted creative processes where the prospective author interacts with an AI model by iteratively selecting targeted elements of the outputs for further refinement.[334] Consequently, this dissertation's research task focuses on determining *how much* creative control the author can forfeit and to what degree an engagement with the creative process can offset the lower degree of creative control. To lay the groundwork for this discussion and help draw an analogy between traditional and AI-assisted creative processes, this chapter investigated the alignment between authorial intent, external realisation, and end result in a number of traditional forms of expression: painting, musical composition, and nature photography. The central argument of this chapter is that, due to the requirement of authorial intent, only those creative choices or expressive features that sufficiently align with the author's underlying preconception can contribute to establishing a claim of authorship over the end result.

One consequence of the greater requirements placed on how a work – or data collection – was created is that evidence or documentation of the creative process may gain greater significance for the originality assessment. Before the advent of high-performance generative AI models, this requirement remained relatively hidden, since it was safe to assume that any creation exhibiting the outward hallmarks of originality also satisfied the requirements placed on the creative process. However, with generative AI models creating increasingly impressive outputs that are only *seemingly original*, the alignment between authorial intent, external realisation, and end result should gain a more concrete role in the copyright assessment. Consequently, copyright claimants may have to bear a higher burden of proof to show that the expressive elements contained in a work resulted from the author's creative choices rather than the AI system's autonomous generation. A possible implication of this is that a data collection will be presumed unauthored unless proven authored. This issue will be discussed in more detail in section 7.2.4.

334. This type of creative process was briefly discussed in Chapter 1 and will be examined in further detail in Chapter 7.

CHAPTER 5
The Three-Stage Ontology of a Work

5.1 PREMISE AND STRUCTURE OF THE CHAPTER

Having discussed the requirements for protection on a general level in the two preceding chapters, the present chapter transitions to apply the preceding analysis to formulate an approach to understanding the ontological nature of musical works, since this will have a bearing on how the concept of a musical work is understood in the context of AI-generated music.

As noted in the introduction in Chapter 1, one of the fundamental claims of this dissertation is that the process of composing music possesses certain idiosyncratic features that make musical works a particularly intriguing field of study in the context of utilising AI-powered tools during the creative process. Unlike a text or painting, composers typically externalise musical works in a form that requires further interpretation to fulfil the underlying authorial conception. This inspired the characterisation of the compositional process as one of issuing instructions that describe a given sequence of musical attributes. The purpose of this chapter is to add further nuance to the previous chapter's discussion on the creative process. The genesis of musical works will be traced through the stages of authorial intent, external realisation through issuing instructions, and the rendition of said instructions into 'actual' musical expression. The chapter is divided into three sections. The first section examines the relationship between mental conception and external realisation in the light of how the ontological nature of a 'work' has been addressed in the scholarly literature. The second section investigates various aspects of what it means to produce an instruction set containing musical information and the role of interpretation in producing the musical end result. The third section presents concluding remarks and analyses their significance in the context of this dissertation.

5.2 THE ONTOLOGICAL NATURE OF THE WORK

5.2.1 Historical Background

The work's ontological nature has been discussed extensively in the scholarly literature, with many authors addressing aspects that have direct relevance for the research task of this dissertation. Accordingly, a brief historical review is needed to place the dissertation's approach to the work concept into its historical context. In Chapter 1, the musical work was characterised as an abstract sequence of musical attributes that cannot be exhaustively defined. This invites comparison to Kohler's *Immaterialgütertheorie*, which views the work as an independent immaterial entity that exists separately from its physical manifestations.[335] Although criticised as being excessively abstract and metaphysical, Kohler's view was widely influential in Scandinavia until the mid-20th century, when Nordic scholars began distancing themselves from this theory.[336] One notable critic was Alf Ross, who formulated an experience theory in his 1945 article on the basic concepts of copyright law. Ross's article has been characterised as a milestone in the Nordic scholarly literature on copyright, and it also laid the groundwork for the so-called radical school.[337] Ross's innovation lay in viewing the work as a relative unity of the ideas shared across a series of experiences. Under this view, copyright does not grant control over the work itself, but over the material conditions necessary to experience the work, such as physical copies or performances.[338] Essentially, Ross's experience theory reframes the work as an abstraction tied to human experience, existing only as a conscious phenomenon in the minds of individuals.

Bergström built upon the groundwork of Ross's experience theory, introducing several concepts for addressing various facets of the work's ontological nature. For Bergström, the core distinction is between the inner and outer work. The inner work is a psychological reality, experienced actively by the artist and passively by the audience, whereas the outer work refers to the media through which the inner work is manifested and made accessible.[339] These media, whose defining feature is to convey the experience of the inner work,[340] were further divided into primary and secondary media. The *primary medium* is the first external manifestation of a work created by the author. It marks the point at which legal protection begins and acts as a reference point for determining which *secondary media* – such as copies or adaptations – belong to the same external work.[341]

Later scholars criticised these theories' reliance on the assumption that the experiences of the creator, the audience, and individual members of the audience are generally the same or similar. Three such viewpoints – those of Koktvedgaard,

335. Kohler 1892, p. 48.
336. Rosenmeier 2001, p. 27, with further references.
337. Strömholm 1970, pp. 21, 34.
338. Ross 1945, p. 345.
339. Bergström 1954, pp. 63-64.
340. Bergström 1954, p. 67.
341. Bergström 1954, pp. 65-66.

Strömholm, and Karnell – warrant mention here. Koktvedgaard is sceptical of using the term 'work' without giving it substantive meaning, warning that it risks inadvertently 'hypostasising' the concept (treating it as a real, independent entity).[342] He therefore emphasised the works' physical manifestations as holding the key to the issue, noting that the judges settling copyright disputes typically perceive the contested objects as individual things rather than parts of a general concept.[343] In his view, the work concept does not contribute anything to the legal analysis, but it may nonetheless have utility as a common linguistic tool in everyday language, provided one understands its limitations.[344]

Strömholm is sceptical of finding a universal, cohesive definition of a work, instead emphasising its multifaceted nature. He notes that the term 'work' can refer to both physical manifestations, such as copies, and broader abstract notions rooted in societal constructs of value and creativity. This inherent variability, he argues, allows the work concept to adapt and take on different meanings depending on the legal or contextual framework.[345] Accordingly, Strömholm sees the primary function of the work concept as that of a syntactic or adverbial modifier in legal language. Rather than being a tangible entity or object, the work operates as a unifying factor, linking diverse elements – such as copies, performances, and adaptations – within the overarching copyright framework.[346] This adverbial function highlights the work's role as a flexible, functional construct that facilitates legal interpretation and application without necessitating a rigid or metaphysical understanding of its essence.

Karnell also dismisses both the immaterialist theories of the 'work' and the Nordic experiential theories. His approach to the work concept highlights the process of comparing the contested creations in an infringement context. He introduces the idea of the 'attribute-work' (*egenskapsverk*), which refers to the shared complex of attributes between the original creation, or primary phenomenon (*primärföreteelse*), and a contested work, or secondary phenomenon (*sekundärföreteelse*). This attribute-work serves as the factual basis for assessing whether the secondary phenomenon is sufficiently similar to the primary one and thus infringes on the copyright protection afforded to it. For Karnell, the 'attribute-work' is the decisive element underpinning the author's claim to exclusive rights. He argues that copyright protection does not attach to the entire set of characteristics in the original work. Instead, it pertains only to those specific attributes relevant in the context of the comparison.[347] These attributes may differ depending on the nature of the infringement and the context of the evaluation.[348] Overall, Karnell's framework emphasises that copyright infringement assessments are fundamentally based on a similarity comparison. A secondary phenomenon is judged on its degree of similarity to the primary phenomenon, with the attribute-work

342. Koktvedgaard 1965, p. 113.
343. Koktvedgaard 1965, p. 115.
344. Koktvedgaard 1965, pp. 138-139.
345. Strömholm 1970, pp. 135-136.
346. Strömholm 1970, pp. 229-230.
347. Karnell 1970, p. 43.
348. Karnell 1968, p. 437, Karnell 1970, p. 43.

functioning as the evaluation's point of reference. By rooting his approach in observable, comparative criteria rather than abstract metaphysical constructs, Karnell positions his theory as both practical and aligned with the functional realities of copyright law.

5.2.2 The Three-Stage Division of the Work's Ontological Nature

As explained in Chapter 1, this dissertation approaches the ontological nature of a musical work through a three-stage division. In the first stage, the composer mentally conceives the *underlying work* as an abstract sequence of musical attributes. In the second stage, the mental conception is externalised by the composer through an outwardly perceivable medium, which serves as the work's *source material*. In the third stage, containing the *prospective reproductions*, various agents draw upon the musical information contained in the source material to duplicate or reinterpret the underlying work.

This three-stage definition of the work's ontology contains several clear points of alignment with the theories presented in the previous section. On the one hand, the first stage's abstract sequence of musical attributes is not unlike Kohler's metaphysical view of the work. The similarities become particularly evident when considering the suggestion, proffered in Chapter 1, that the work's contents cannot be exhaustively captured in any piece of static documentation, and that the only way of inquiring into the work's is by consulting various instances of source material which describe the underlying object of intention with differing degrees of precision and authority. On the other hand, the second and third stages are thoroughly pragmatic in nature. Here, the concept of work performs what Strömholm describes as an adverbial function, as it transforms neutral terms like composer, data collection, and duplication into their legal counterparts – author, work, and reproduction – within the framework of copyright law. Moreover, the emphasis on the source material as the epistemic or evidentiary means by which one can link the musical attributes conveyed by the prospective reproduction to the author's free and creative choices aligns with Koktvedgaard's and Karnell's focus on comparing the attributes exhibited by external manifestations. The use of terminology differs, of course, as I call the entities under comparison data collections, source material, and instruction set instead of manifestations or primary and secondary phenomena.

On this basis, one might consider this dissertation's take on the work's ontology to be primarily rooted in the pragmatic-linguistic tradition represented by Koktvedgaard, Strömholm, and Karnell. However, the great importance given to the indirect similarities between data collections contains elements pointing towards Ross's and Bergström's views of the work as a subjective experience. Namely, if two data collections exhibit only indirect similarities, the individual experience of the work will play an important role in determining whether the similarities in one group of attributes should outweigh the differences in another. The individual experience is further underscored by this dissertation's emphasis on how musical works are typically characterised by a subtle interplay between the musical attributes – such as their pitch, rhythm, harmony, and form – contained in the composition. Due to this subtlety, an overly objective-schematic analysis is likely to be too rigid a means of assessing the similarities and differences exhibited by two compositions, making it liable to produce unjustified judicial outcomes. Essentially, my viewpoint is that the greater the proportion of indirect similarities between the compositions under examination, the greater the need to consult the subjective experience of (listening to) the compositions rather than measuring similarity by some objective-schematic criteria, such as the number of duplicated pitches, rhythms, or harmonies. Consequently, the source material, such as a music sheet or audio recording, is not only construed as a Karnellian 'attribute-work' but also contains notable features of Bergström's medium capable of 'conveying the experience of the inner work'.

In the end, whether one construes the work's essence in Karnellian, Bergströmian, or even Kohlerian terms, the most important aspect of this dissertation's research task is to investigate how the author's creative contribution transfers from one ontological stage to another. In addressing this issue, the compositional process is viewed as an act of converting the underlying mental conception into a sequence of instructions, whose execution brings the intended musical expression into existence. Simply put, the act of composing, regardless of the technical tools utilised, amounts to issuing instructions that describe the musical attributes of the underlying work. There are several perspectives to the compositional process and its end result, which need to be taken into account, since they illuminate different aspects of the three-stage division of the work's ontology described at the beginning of this section.

First, the composer's perspective primarily emphasises the work's coming into being. As noted in the previous chapter, the creative process must start with the prospective author formulating an authorial goal, such as 'I want to compose a dramatic piece of orchestral music.' Guided by the authorial goal, the author proceeds to mentally conceive the desired combination of musical building blocks and attributes. Finally, the mental conception is documented into an externally perceivable form, such as a music sheet or audio recording. Upon externalisation, the composition has come into existence and requires no further actions on the composer's part. At this point, as suggested by Roman Ingarden, the composer has created something that previously did not exist but now exists 'independently of whether anyone performs it, listens to it, or takes any interest in it whatever'.[349]

Second, the performer's perspective. The performer's aim is to produce a musical performance, and the composition is the vehicle utilised for this purpose. The performer's interaction with the composition is therefore dominated by the pursuit of acquiring knowledge about its contents, which is done through the selection and interpretation of the available source material. This dissertation posits that the rendition of an instruction set into a musical performance generally requires considerable interpretative input.

Third, the legal order's perspective, which is similar to the performer's in its emphasis on making epistemic – or evidentiary – inquiries into the composition's

349. Ingarden 1986, p. 2.

contents. Especially when called upon to determine the relative weight of groups of indirect similarities and dissimilarities, the legal order's approach will also be characterised by interpretation, although the aim of the adjudicator's interpretative endeavours are different: the adjudicator seeks to establish whether the relevant data collections share enough attributes to be considered instances of the same work, whereas performers aim to learn the composition's contents in order to channel it through their own artistic skills and sensibilities when rendering it into a musical performance.

The different perspectives of the composer, performer, and adjudicator serve to illustrate the distinction between using the term instruction set or source material to denote data collections belonging to the second ontological stage that bridges the composer's mental conception and the prospective reproductions of a musical work. Both terms describe the same phenomenon and are largely interchangeable. However, the term *instruction set* appears more natural when examining the composer's viewpoint, whereas *source material* is more appropriate when the emphasis lies on epistemic or evidentiary inquiries into the composition's contents.

As noted above, the manner and precision with which the composer's creative contribution transfers between ontological stages lies at the core of the dissertation, as it holds the key to assessing the link between creative contribution and end result. Viewing the composer's contribution as an issuance of instructions will make it possible to draw an analogy between traditional and AI-assisted compositional processes, which, in turn, can give new insights into how the prerequisites of copyright protection can be assessed in the context of AI-assisted compositional processes. To lay the groundwork for this analogy, the present chapter will examine the creation of instruction sets in the context of a traditional compositional process in light of the three-stage deconstruction of the work's ontology.

5.3 CREATING AND COMMUNICATING MUSICAL INFORMATION

5.3.1 The Special Nature of Musical Expression

The characterisation of the compositional process as an act of issuing instructions stems from the fact that the external realisation of a musical composition generally requires two separate stages: documenting the underlying mental conception into an instruction set and rendering these instructions into a musical performance. To illustrate, the typical compositional process features a composer, who mentally conceptualises the composition based on the underlying authorial goal, such as 'I want to compose a dramatic piece of orchestral music.' To externalise the mental conception, the composer produces an instruction set describing the composition's musical attributes, usually in the form of musical notation. Provided the musical attributes exhibited by the music sheet are complex enough and have not been copied from elsewhere, the composition is likely to be considered a protected work under copyright law. However, to fulfil the purpose of undertaking the creative process, the instructions contained in the music sheet need to be rendered into a musical performance by a symphony orchestra, MIDI, or some other suitable means.

On this basis, the genesis of the dramatic orchestral composition can be divided into the following phases: formulating the authorial goal, selecting musical attributes, externalising these into an instruction set, and rendering the instruction set into aurally perceivable musical expression. Here, the instruction set, despite 'counting' as a protected work under copyright law, arguably represents a latent stage in the composition's genesis, since it does not fulfil the purpose of the compositional process. After all, music is an art form concerned with combining *sounds* 'for beauty of form or emotional expression'.[350] The most noteworthy aspect of distinguishing between a latent and 'actual' realisation of the composition is that the rendition of an instruction set – such as a music sheet – into a musical performance may often require considerable creative input from the performers.

Music is not the only art form that typically contains a distinct phase of compiling an instruction set. Architectural, choreographic, and dramatic works also have similar geneses, with dramatic works showing particularly notable similarities. Even if the playscript is likely to constitute a protected work in its own right, the purpose for writing the script will only come to fruition upon its dramatisation, which generally requires considerable creative input by directors, actors, stage designers, costume designers, and other personnel. Accordingly, one might characterise the playscript as a latent realisation of the creation and the dramatisation as its 'actual' realisation.

The discussion about the endpoint and underlying purpose of a creative process dovetails with a broader reflection on the ontological nature of a work and how it is distinguished from the various externalisations and experiences of the agents interacting with it. In the end, *any* creation is intended to elicit subjective experiences from the addressee upon exposure to it,[351] and one could argue that the fundamental purpose of creating a novel or oil painting is to inspire individual sensations such as beauty, shock, awe, or something else. Accordingly, the insertion of characters, words, and sentences into a text file or colour pigments onto a canvas could be considered a latent realisation of the creation, since the fundamental purpose will only be fulfilled when the novel or painting elicits the aforementioned subjective experiences from the addressee.

The crucial difference between creating a novel, an oil painting, and a music sheet – all of which 'count' as protected works – is that the music sheet is an instruction set that requires interpretative input from a performer before it can elicit the intended individual experiences from its addressees. On this basis, the following section will examine how musical information – such as the mental conception of musical attributes – can be externalised into an instruction set and what this instruction set tells about the underlying musical composition.

350. Epperson in Encyclopedia Britannica, available at https://www.britannica.com/art/music, accessed 15 March 2025.
351. There are, of course, some exceptions to this, such as computer programs, whose final addressee tends to be another machine or system intended to execute specific tasks or processes.

5.3.2 Visual Communication of Musical Information

A musical work can be documented in both visually and aurally perceivable forms, with the most common formats being sheet music, chord charts, or audio recordings.[352] *Sheet music* employs symbols to convey information about the intended pitches, rhythms, or chords (*see* picture). *Chord charts* outline the fundamental harmonic and rhythmic information relevant to a song or melody. Using chord symbols and rhythmic notations, they provide musicians with a simplified representation of a song's harmonic structure and rhythm. The condensed format allows musicians to quickly grasp the essential musical elements, but chord charts are unlikely to thoroughly capture the musical interpretation, style, or expressive nuances that musicians are expected to bring to a performance. A *lead sheet* provides both melody and chord symbols, and can be described as a hybrid between sheet music and a chord chart.

To better grasp the relationship between musical notation and its interpretation, let us examine musical notation more closely. The most important parameters indicated in a music sheet are those of *pitch* and *rhythm*. Pitch denotes the frequency – or 'height' – of a sound, while rhythm refers to the timing of the sounds. The desired pitch is indicated by inserting notes on linear staves. The higher the note is located, the higher the desired frequency of the sound. The rhythm or timing is indicated by the layout of the notes. White notes denote longer durations, while black notes, along with the addition of stems and beams connecting the notes into groups, indicate incrementally shorter durations. The passage of time is conveyed in a manner similar to the timeline in video editing software, where movement towards the right indicates elapsed time.

Using piano music as an example, the notated instructions described thus far will tell the pianist which keys to strike and what their temporal relation should be. In most cases, an execution of instructions on this level of detail – for instance, by having a MIDI render it into a musical performance – will make the composition recognisable. The resulting performance is also highly likely to duplicate the composition's musical attributes with enough substantiality and precision to make it a protected reproduction of a work.[353] However, a MIDI performance will probably not align very closely with the composer's mental conception of the intended musical expression, i.e., the underlying work or 'meaning behind the notes'.[354] Given that said meaning behind the notes and other creative contributions stemming from the interpreter rather than the composer provide a notable proportion of the musical expression conveyed by a typical musical performance, the nuances of how musical information transfers between the ontological need to be examined in greater detail, even if the discrepancy between the

352. Tabulatures, often referred to as tabs, are another common way of documenting music visually. They are a form of musical notation specifically designed for fretted instruments like guitars. Using numbers and lines, tabs represent the specific strings and frets used to play individual notes.
353. In the case of Chopin's Prelude shown on this page, the copyright term has expired, but that is beside the point.
354. Copland, 1988, p. 2.

underlying work and the MIDI performance is unlikely to impact the composer's copyright claim to it.

At its core, this is about the documentation, interpretation, and performative rendition of musical information. DeVlieger describes the role of interpretation by noting that:

> To a non-musician, the relationship between performer and score may appear relatively straightforward: all the performer needs to do is play what is written on the page. However, such a belief ignores the role of context in the interpretation of the score. This *contextual knowledge* is what allows a musician to determine what scores ... *are asking of the performer.*[355]

355. DeVlieger 2020, p. 30. 'Score' is a synonym for music sheet. My italics.

Prelude

'Suffocation'

Frederic Chopin (1810-1849)
Op.28, No.4

As shown by the many additional markings in the music sheet of Chopin's E minor prelude (*see* picture above),[356] composers may seek to convey a rather deep level of subtlety and finesse when externalising their mental conception into musical notation. Verbal and symbolic instructions as to the force of the indicated key strikes, use of sustain pedal, and minute subtleties of timing will contribute significantly to the performer's understanding of the composer's intentions.[357] Yet, despite all the ambition and effort, the music sheet must necessarily fail to exhaustively document the underlying composition. One reason for this lies in the interdependence of composers and performers and the importance of the relevant *performance tradition*. This is not likely to have a noteworthy impact on the legal assessment of the work's ontology. Nonetheless, I find that its examination deepens the understanding of how musical information transfers between different ontological stages, and the following section (5.3.3) will therefore pursue the matter in some detail. The contents of said section will be summarised at the start of section 5.4, providing readers the option to skip section 5.3.3 if they wish to proceed directly to the summary and subsequent analysis.

5.3.3 The Interpretation and Performance Tradition of Musical Compositions

Nicholas Cook has reflected on the importance of the performance tradition by having us imagine 'that Martian musicologists of ten thousand years hence are attempting to reconstruct an authentic performance of Chopin's E minor Prelude'.[358] Supposing the Martians manage to decipher the meaning of our notation system and execute the work with 'meticulous faithfulness to the score',[359] the resulting performance is unlikely to resonate with contemporary terrestrial audiences. '[I]ndeed, one would be inclined to think of someone who played Chopin's music in this manner, as being not so much unmusical as mentally deranged'.[360] Consequently, it seems that the Martians would have executed the instructions but failed to communicate the intended expression, highlighting an interesting aspect of the relationship between mental conception, documentation, and performance: While the performance should constitute a reproduction of Chopin's composition due to the accurate execution of the notes contained in the music sheet, it fails to impress contemporary terrestrial audiences because the instructions contained in the music sheet only come to life when interpreted with an understanding of the relevant aesthetic context.

356. https://wikisource.org/wiki/Prelude_in_E_minor,_Op._28,_No._4_%28Chopin%29, accessed 2 February 2025. The subtitle 'Suffocation' is not by the composer.
357. The interpretation of the hairpin markings alone is a subject of scholarly research in its own right. *See* Cheong 2019 and Kim 2012. An exhaustive analysis of the act of interpreting performance instructions with awareness of the performance tradition is given in Jackson 2005.
358. Cook 1992, p. 122.
359. Score is a colloquial synonym to the music sheet.
360. Cook 1992, p. 122. The use of the word 'deranged' sounds harsher than it was intended when taken out of its original context.

The relationship between musical compositions and their performance tradition has been the subject of much scholarly research,[361] and while it may elude objective definition, there certainly exists a notion of an 'aesthetically informed' interpretation of Chopin's Prelude. The public perception of the composition has been cultivated through the extensive history of performances of it, wherein the iterative interaction of performers and audiences has forged a shared understanding of the piece's essential artistic expression. How will the pianist's awareness of this tradition then manifest itself in a performance? Well, through the same actions, a music sheet aims to communicate: key strokes determined by the expressive interaction of pitch, timbre, and timing.[362] However, the interpretation is executed through intuitive rather than mechanical interplay between the performer's hands and ears, resulting in input variations so minute as not to be susceptible to visual representation.[363] Nicholas Cook illustrates this by describing an experiment where he performs the piece on an electric keyboard without hearing his own playing during the performance:

> I find on listening afterwards to the tape that I play either with an exaggerated and uncontrolled rubato, or else stiffly and correctly, with a military precision that results from counting 'one-two, one-two' as I play and slotting in each note at the appropriate point. To play in this mechanical manner is not to interpret the score *as it asks to be interpreted* in performance, but to execute it in the same way as a regimental sergeant-major expects his orders to be carried out: literally and unthinkingly; in short, *without imagination*.[364]

The notion of requiring interpretative imagination to discover how the piece 'asks to be interpreted' is particularly noteworthy. It demonstrates the difficulty of visually documenting or predetermining every aspect of a work's performance, arising from the fact that the work's essential artistic expression can only materialise upon the *combination* of the composer's and performer's respective creative contributions. Several other scholars have presented similar views. Jacobs, while emphasising that she 'do[es] not want to downplay the creative genius of the composer', nevertheless 'insist[s] on the *necessary creative function* of the performer'.[365] In a similar vein, Boorman notes that:

> [t]he relationship of the original musical text (the concept of the composer) to the notated text is the concern of the musicologist, rather than of the performer. The latter is expected to *move forward* from the notation, to *produce a new musical text, reflecting both ability and musicality*.[366]

361. *See, inter alia*, Ritchie 1984; Davies 1991; and Kivy 1988.
362. A scholarly analysis of the work's interpretation and performance tradition is given by Rink 2001, pp. 434-444. A light-hearted approach to describing the contents of the work is provided in Benjamin Zander's TED talk, available at https://www.youtube.com/watch?v=r9LCwI5iErE, accessed 2 February 2025.
363. An empirical analysis of timing when performing the relevant piece was made by Senn, Kilchenmann and Camp 2009. Palmer 1997, pp. 119-120 reflects on the relationship between interpretation and expressive timing patterns, noting the connection between greater expertise and increased use of expressive timing patterns.
364. Cook 1992, p. 128. My italics.
365. Jacobs 1990, pp. 77-78. My italics.
366. Boorman 2001, p. 414. My italics.

Another important aspect is highlighted by Bowen, who notes that the constantly evolving performance tradition will greatly shape the understanding of what the work's essential artistic expression consists of, noting the 'changing definition' of the work's contents and emphasising that the 'study of performance tradition of a musical work *is* the study of the musical work'.[367] Hence, to acquire the knowledge necessary to reproduce the essential artistic expression of the piece as understood by contemporary terrestrial listeners, the aforementioned Martians probably would need to examine several recorded performances of Chopin's composition along with reviews and scholarly analyses of them.[368]

Perhaps the most important takeaway from the discussion about the difficulty of precisely – let alone exhaustively – communicating a composition's contents through musical notation lies in realising that there is a significant difference between *intended* and *possible* interpretations of the source material. Even if one were to uncover and exactly reproduce how Chopin intended his composition to be performed, this would still not necessarily constitute the 'best' and certainly not the only way of interpreting the work effectively. Although not related to musical works and their interpretation, but to the staging of dramatic works, I find director Harold Clurman's analysis of the performer's role particularly illuminating. He notes that:

> It is all very well for the playwright to indicate that a speech be said 'angrily' or 'with a sob' or in a 'high querulous treble'. He will frequently find that if his directions are followed literally, the results will be ludicrous. The actor and the director generally take the playwright's instructions as a *clue to something the playwright is seeking to express*. They often find that to express most effectively what the playwright had in view they have to employ quite different means than those which the playwright has suggested.[369]

As Clurman aptly puts it, a performer can – or necessarily must – approach the author's instructions as a *clue* to what the author is seeking to express. The artistically most compelling performances are likely to be those where the combination of source material with the artistic personality and (re)interpretative flair of the performer is particularly well matched. It may well happen that a performer's deliberate deviation from the composer's instructions may reveal previously undiscovered facets of the composition at issue. The song 'I Will Always Love You' provides a good example of this. Despite the immediate and lasting success of the original version performed by the composer herself,[370] the song is best known today in the version made for the 1992 movie 'The Bodyguard' with vocals performed by Whitney Houston.[371] The latter

367. Bowen 2001, p. 430. Italics in original.
368. In the same vein, Lund 2012, p. 41 recommends that the jurors listen to several different recordings of the songs to account for the performer's creative input not to be evaluated in the copyright assessment.
369. Cole and Chinoy (eds) 1976, p. 276. My italics. Incidentally, Eidsvold-Tøien and Stenvik 2023, p. 755 argue that actors' performances 'in most cases fulfil the general requirements for copyright protection' due, *inter alia*, to the choices they make about how to express certain situations and relationships between the characters they portray.
370. Available at https://www.youtube.com/watch?v=IKsQR72HY0s, accessed 2 February 2025.
371. Available at https://www.youtube.com/watch?v=3JWTaaS7LdU&list=RD3JWTaaS7LdU&start_radio=1, accessed 2 February 2025.

version preserved most musical elements from Parton's source material, but rearranged it as a soul ballad, making notable changes to the instrumentation and structure of the song as well as its vocal execution.

Overall, the interdependence of compositional and performative appears to shape the performance tradition and public perception of a composition's contents in a way that draws comparison to the 'survival of the fittest' mechanism in evolutionary biology. Artistically compelling renditions of a composition are typically reproduced most frequently, making them more likely to influence subsequent performances of the work. This is because the greater exposure of successful renditions makes them contribute more to a work's performance tradition, which, in turn, functions as the foundation upon which the interpretative features of future performances are conceived. By contrast, artistically weaker interpretations are likely to garner less attention and fall into oblivion.

5.4 THE RELATIONSHIP BETWEEN UNDERLYING WORK, SOURCE MATERIAL, AND PERFORMANCE

5.4.1 Summary of the Previous Section

To summarise the analysis of the previous section, one can state that any piece of source material, even if it is a music sheet or audio recording made by the composer, provides only one perspective on the composition's contents. While a music sheet or audio recording made by the composer typically constitutes a very authoritative piece of source material, it cannot give an exhaustive account of the composition's contents. Therefore, an epistemic inquiry into the composition's contents – whether by a performer aiming to perform it or a judge assessing a copyright case – will revolve around consulting and interpreting one or more pieces of source material.

A distinctive feature of the interpretative process, especially when viewed from the performer's perspective, is that performers are expected to utilise their 'ability and musicality' to 'move forward' from the source to discover how it 'asks to be interpreted'.[372] This creates a dynamic performance tradition where interpretative features of a performance are conceived in interaction with previous performances and other source material. In turn, this means that the general perception of the characteristics of a given composition's individuality – how the composition 'asks to be interpreted' – will exist in a constant state of flux.

Although the quality of the interpretative input and its adherence to performance tradition can dramatically affect the perceived aesthetic worth of a given performance, as illustrated by the hypothetical example of the Martians' rendition of Chopin's Prelude, the legal distinction between this performance and that of today's celebrated concert pianists is negligible to non-existent. This is because the shortcomings of this performance stem from discrepancies that lack relevance for the legal evaluation, such

372. *See* citation of Boorman above.

as differences in timing and emotional expression. Incidentally, the legal impact of the performer's creative input is greater in Whitney Houston's version of 'I Will Always Love You' because it contains more apparent changes to the melodic, rhythmic, and harmonic fabric of the underlying composition.

5.4.2 The Challenges of Interpreting Source Material for Epistemic Purposes

Looking at determining the contents of a musical work in the broader context of copyright law, the feature that distinguishes musical works from most other types of creative expression is that musical compositions in most cases require an additional stage of interpretation for the author's mental conception to become fulfilled. The crucial difference compared to a novel or painting is that an agent acting entirely independently of the author – the performer interpreting the source material – needs to supply creative input to render the composition into the intended aurally perceivable form.[373]

While other forms of artistic expression, such as dramatic or choreographic works, also require an additional stage of interpretation, what sets musical expression apart is that assessing the defining characteristics of a musical work's identity in a copyright infringement claim is particularly likely to involve consulting the subjective experience of the composition. This is due to the complexity characterising the interaction between the musical attributes – pitch, rhythm, harmony, etc. – contained in the composition, and how even very small changes to one parameter of compositional input can have a profound effect on the perceived similarity between two data collections. Such considerations could perhaps also apply to many other types of expression, but music is further distinguished by the fact that minute details frequently come up for judicial review in the context of high-stakes infringement litigation: cases hinging on compositions exhibiting subtle or indirect similarities are not uncommon.

In examining the degree to which indirect similarities can contribute to making two data collections reproductions of the same work, the adjudicator must strike an appropriate balance in defining the *implied scope* of a work. The rationale for the notion that indirect similarities may lead to a finding of infringement is that introducing trivial changes to an existing work should not impact the author's right to it, as this would effectively allow copyright protection to be bypassed. Consequently, works – or original fragments thereof – are understood to have an implied scope that extends beyond their literal contents. A few altered notes or rhythmic adjustments might not affect the overall impression of similarity and are therefore considered within the

373. Bently 2009, p. 186, in discussing the concept of a musical work and allocation of authorship, notes that distinguishing between 'contributions to "music" and contributions to "performance" of the music' can occasionally become challenging. This is exemplified by the case *Hadley v. Kemp* (1999), in which members of the pop band Spandau Ballet asserted co-authorship of musical works initially credited only to the band's guitarist, keyboardist, and singer, Gary Kemp.

work's implied scope. However, as more differences are introduced, the connection to the original composition will weaken and eventually break.

This balance can be challenging to operationalise. Although the notion of a work's implied scope is not problematic as such, finding a schematic one-size-fits-all benchmark for its determination presents difficulties. For instance, tying the implied scope to a certain proportion of melodic, rhythmic, or harmonic similarity might provide a useful starting point, but this approach can occasionally produce counterintuitive outcomes. This is because the internal hierarchy and interaction among musical attributes can differ considerably between compositions. One composition may rely on commonplace harmonic patterns to support highly individual melodic content, whereas another might depend on an idiosyncratic use of harmony and texture. In other words, the pieces contain a different hierarchical relationship between the musical elements and their interaction. Assessing these compositions through a benchmark predominantly based on melodic similarity risks undervaluing the originality of the latter work. Therefore, while schematic-empirical benchmarks can be valuable tools, they should be complemented by an analysis informed by the (ultimately subjective) overall experience produced by the contested passages.

The challenges related to defining the musical work's contents for epistemic or evidentiary purposes can be crystallised through the following points. First, there exists no definitive piece of source material, since the full range of a composition's contents cannot be exhaustively delineated by a static data collection, such as a music sheet or audio recording. This is mostly due to the dynamic nature of musical compositions. More than most other types of creative expression – such as a novel or painting – musical compositions unfold through time and generally also require creative input from performers, which inevitably blurs the boundaries of the underlying composition. Second, the implied scope of the work is challenging to assess, which is due to the combination of two circumstances. Not only does the overall impact of a composition often stem from a subtle interaction of musical attributes, but the interaction and hierarchy between different musical elements also tend to be unique to each composition. Consequently, the implied scope of a composition should not be determined based solely on a rigid set of criteria, but needs to be complemented by consulting the subjective experiences it elicits.

On this basis, the ontology of a musical work can be formulated as follows: The process of authoring a musical work is ultimately about issuing instructions that set the parameters for a certain kind of individual experience. In turn, the object of copyright protection – the work – is the externally perceivable realisation of these instructions. To produce this instruction set, various technical-functional tools are available. Musical notation and audio recordings are the most common alternatives, but this dissertation aims to explore a technologically neutral approach to how the instructions setting the parameters of a certain individual experience are produced. More specifically, it aims to investigate the conditions under which the prospective author's interaction with AI-powered tools can be considered an analogous instance of issuing instructions to create a music sheet or audio recording.

5.4.3 Instruction Sets and the 'Originality Causation' Requirement

Whether the instructions are realised using musical notation, audio recording, or AI-powered tools, the decisive question is the degree of alignment between the authorial goal, its external realisation, and the musical attributes of the end result. In the three-stage division of a musical work's ontology, this is assessed by comparing the *prospective reproduction* to the underlying composition's *source material* to determine if they are sufficiently similar.

Two distinct factors need to be considered when making this assessment. First, the source material must show that the underlying composition contains enough complexity to meet all the outward hallmarks of an original work, which was referred to as 'seeming originality' in Chapter 1. In most cases, both the assessment and fulfilment of this requirement should be rather straightforward. Second, these attributes must have resulted from the free and creative choices made by the author. Other scholars have addressed the latter requirement in slightly different terms. Gervais talks about an 'originality causation test … [calling] for a determination of the cause of the creative choices that make a production seem copyrightable'.[374] Rognstad builds upon this idea, noting that the originality causation requirement 'may be synthesized as expressing that the free and creative choices of humans have *caused* the work to the extent that those choices *are reflected* in the expression of the work'.[375] Leistner and Jussen also argue that a requirement of causation has effectively been established in EU copyright law, since the creative decisions made by the author 'need to be *expressed* in a sufficiently *objective and clearly identifiable* manner in the ultimate result of the creative process'.[376]

On the whole, I find that all four formulations concerning the relationship between the creative choices and the end result lead to the same outcome, which can be referred to as the 'originality causation requirement'.[377] It also constitutes the primary obstacle to granting copyright claims to AI-generated compositions such as Composition A. To examine this issue in greater detail, the table summarising the analogy between a traditional and AI-assisted compositional process given in Chapter 1 is worth repeating:

374. Gervais 2020, pp. 2053, 2106. In a later article, Gervais 2024, pp. 1104, 1106 uses the concepts of a human 'proximate cause' of the work and the human input 'carrying over' to the machine output to address this challenge related to addressing copyright claims to AI-generated outputs.
375. Rognstad 2022, p. 182. Italics in original.
376. Leistner and Jussen 2025, p. 9. Italics in original.
377. Although using the concept of causation to describe the requirements place on the relationship between creative process and end result is both accurate and instructive, one should not make direct analogies with how the term 'causation' is used in tort law, as the term has a different scope and application in the two fields of law. A similar point is made by Leistner and Jussen 2025, p. 9.

Prospective Author	*Instruction Set*	*Executor/Performer*	*End Result*
Traditional composer	Musical notation, audio recording, etc.	Performer(s)	Musical performance, audio recording
AI developer or user	Model development, fine-tuning, prompting	AI system	Musical performance, audio recording

Composition A's issue with originality causation lies in the potential disconnect between the author's creative decisions during pre-generation phases – such as model development, fine-tuning, or prompting – and the musical attributes of the end result. While these pre-generation decisions may meet the standard of creativity and individuality usually required for copyright protection, the resulting composition's musical attributes might not sufficiently reflect the author's deliberate intent. This disconnect raises the key question: what degree of alignment is required between the author's intent, the external creation process, and the end result to be sufficient for copyright protection, and how should this alignment be assessed?

One approach to resolving this question is to evaluate the level of creative control exercised by the author. This involves analysing how precisely the author could predict the combination of attributes forming the resulting composition's musical expression at the moment of decision-making. This approach is particularly effective in addressing the element of randomness often present in AI-assisted creative processes. When considering the relationship between an instruction set and the resulting musical performance, one must examine both the precision of the instructions and the accuracy of their execution. Ultimately, this leads to research question (7), which in many ways is the most central inquiry of this dissertation: under what conditions can one consider a sequence of instructions describing musical attributes to be: (i) sufficiently specific and (ii) sufficiently precisely reflected in the resulting composition to warrant copyright protection?

To lay the foundation for explaining how these questions are applied to Composition A, let us first consider some of the other examples discussed throughout the book. The alignment between authorial intent, external realisation, and end result is particularly high in a typical performance of Chopin's Prelude. While Chopin could not exhaustively document every feature of his mental conception, his music sheet contains a high number of very precise instructions. Moreover, the performer executed these instructions with considerable precision. Consequently, the originality causation between Chopin's creative choices and the musical expression conveyed by the performance is clearly beyond doubt. Although Chopin could not predict every element of the musical expression conveyed in the performance, his instructions unquestionably ensured a sufficiently accurate realisation of his creative intent.

The 'second composer' described in Chapter 4, who was indifferent to the musical attributes of the resulting composition while producing the music sheet, exercises a different degree of creative control. On the one hand, his situation resembles Chopin's, as both, through deliberate physical actions, produced a music sheet that comfortably meets the requirements of seeming originality.[378] However, the key difference lies in the second composer's indifference to the musical expression obtained by rendering the instructions into a musical performance. As a result, even if a performer were to execute the music sheet with flawless precision, there would be next to no alignment between the second composer's authorial intent and the musical expression conveyed by the performance. By contrast, the 'first composer', introduced in Chapter 4 as the one who meticulously selected each note with deliberate intent to shape the musical outcome, would have a very similar claim to Chopin's whenever the music sheet is accurately executed. This is because he selected the combination of musical attributes with painstaking effort, likely leading to a high awareness of the musical attributes that would be conveyed by a performance of the composition.

A middle ground between these extremes is provided by a situation where the prospective author sets the parameters of the end result and guides the creative process based on the underlying authorial goal without exercising full control over the expression contained in the end result. Jackson Pollock's painting technique is the quintessential example of this scenario. A musical equivalent would be a contributor who formulates the overarching melodic, harmonic, and structural patterns of the composition and allows other contributors to supply the finer details. Essentially, this amounts to making a musical template, where subsequent contributors are invited to render it into a complete composition by filling in the blanks. If the template contains many instructions covering a substantial passage of music, the situation seems closely analogous to Pollock's creative process. Thus, it appears equally evident that the creation of the template meets the originality criteria and provides a claim to any composition produced in adherence to the template's instructions. For brevity and convenience, we shall henceforth call this the 'template composition' and its creator the 'template maker'. The table below shows the examples discussed on an ascending scale according to the degree of alignment between authorial intent and end result:

Creation	*Prospective Author*	*Authorial Goal*	*Realisation*	*Source Material*	*End Result*	*Originality Causation*
Accidental painting	bypasser	none	trip over paint cans	none[379]	painting	none
Second highly abstract sound sequence	second composer	produce a music sheet	insert notes into music sheet at random	music sheet	musical performance	none

378. The concept of seeming originality is defined in section 1.8.
379. Here, 'source material' refers to the means by which one documents or communicates a work's contents. One might argue that in the case of a painting, the source material and the end result are one and the same. However, I find it more appropriate to consider a painting as lacking source material in the sense that the concept applies to musical compositions.

Creation	*Prospective Author*	*Authorial Goal*	*Realisation*	*Source Material*	*End Result*	*Originality Causation*
Composition A	developers and user of Model A	compose music	Interaction with AI tools	source code, datasets, prompts	musical performance	tentatively negligible or at most average[380]
Template composition	template maker	compose music	compile instruction set	instruction set (template)	musical performance	average to high
First highly abstract sound sequence	first composer	compose music	compile instruction set	music sheet	musical performance	very high
Prelude in E minor	Frédéric Chopin	compose music	compile instruction set	music sheet	musical performance	very high

The table's evaluation of originality causation warrants some comments. To clarify, the premise of this examination is that originality causation is strongly correlated with the precision with which the prospective author can predict or foresee the expression ultimately contained in the end result.[381] The accidental painting and the second composer's creation contain no originality causation because there is no alignment between the authorial intent, their deliberate physical actions, and the expression contained in the end result. The originality causation of the template composition was higher than Composition A for two reasons. Not only is the template likely to have a greater impact on the end result achieved upon the completion of the template into a standard musical performance, but the template maker will also probably have a more accurate idea of how his creative choices will be reflected in the expression of said musical performance. By contrast, the pre-generation contributors to Composition A are not as likely to know, control, or foresee how their creative choices will be reflected in the end result at the moment of decision-making.

The argument for awarding protection to Composition A and other AI-generated compositions relies on their similarities to the template composition. In fact, one might consider AI-generated compositions to be a specific type or sub-category of template composition, since the pre-generation creative choices essentially amount to giving broadly framed instructions aimed at shaping the musical expression generated by the AI system. One might therefore speak of manual and AI-assisted template compositions when distinguishing between the two. Due to the lower foreseeability of the end result, AI-assisted template compositions typically have a lower degree of originality causation, which results in a weaker claim to the resulting compositions. Consequently, the

380. The analysis conducted in Chapter 7 will examine this issue in greater detail.
381. Gervais 2020, p. 2099 also ties access to copyright protection to the predictability of the outputs. A similar point was made by Samuelson as early as 1985, p. 1208. When discussing the copyright eligibility of computer-generated works, she noted that 'the programmer is no more able to *anticipate the output* than anyone else'. My italics.

central question becomes whether a larger number of creative choices during the making of the template can offset the lower degree of originality causation.

Arguments can be found both for and against granting protection. On the one hand, following the logic of the Pollock example, one might state that increasing the number of pre-generation creative choices must eventually reach a point where the link between the creative choices and the post-generation end result is strong enough to warrant copyright protection even if the average degree of originality causation for each individual choice is low. On the other hand, one could point out the fundamental differences between manual and AI-assisted template compositions and emphasise that a combination of the generality of the pre-generation instructions and the often minor impact of each choice on the musical-expressive attributes of the resulting composition falls below a sort of de minimis threshold: Even if the relevant pre-generation decisions were to be of a 'free and creative' character and expressly undertaken to produce a musical composition, their link to the resulting musical expression might still be too unconvincing to grant protection, no matter how many pre-generation decisions are made.

To find a balance between these alternative lines of argumentation, Chapter 6 shall examine how originality causation operates and its impact on authorship allocation in the context of a manual template composition. Following this, Chapter 7 will investigate the creative process of an AI-assisted template composition to determine what analogies can be drawn between the two and how this should be reflected in the copyright claims to the latter.

5.5 SUMMARY OF THE CHAPTER AND STRUCTURE OF THE NEXT TWO CHAPTERS

The core purpose of this chapter has been to present a three-stage understanding of a musical work's ontology into underlying composition, source material, and prospective reproductions. In this context, musical works have a special nature in two ways. First, the external realisation of the underlying composition often requires two distinct phases: a 'latent' phase where the author compiles an instruction set and another where a performer interprets the instructions to render them into 'actual' musical expression. Notably, the creative input provided by the performer in interpreting the instructions can have a significant influence on the musical expression contained in the performance. Second, the overall impression or experience elicited by aurally perceiving a musical performance relies in large part on a subtle interaction between several compositional elements, such as melody, rhythm, and harmony. Especially in comparisons involving indirect similarities between two data collections, this makes it difficult to pin down the defining characteristics of the underlying composition, whose sufficiently representative duplication will make a data collection into a protected reproduction.

The assessment of indirect similarities also requires the adjudicator to determine the *implied scope* of the work. This refers to the fact that a few altered notes or rhythmic adjustments may not impact the overall impression of similarity between two data collections, meaning that a data collection can be a protected reproduction even if it differs from the source material used as reference for the comparison. To determine the implied scope of the composition, one must take into account the hierarchical relationship of musical elements specific to the composition under examination. For instance, where one composition may be very original in its melodic content, another emphasises harmonic invention. This makes a one-sided reliance on literal or schematic benchmarks for assessing the originality of a given data collection liable to produce unintuitive or unjustifiable judicial outcomes, highlighting the importance of complementing a literal-empirical analysis with one based on the overall subjective experience elicited by aural perception. On this basis, the act of composing music is ultimately about issuing instructions that set the parameters for a certain kind of subjective experience upon rendition into a musical performance.

To determine whether the development or other interaction with AI-powered tools can fit this description and give a justifiable copyright claim to musical compositions, the compositional process needs to be assessed from the perspective of technological neutrality. The notion of originality causation becomes important here. This concept refers to the degree to which the prospective authors, at the time of decision-making, can predict or foresee the impact their instructions – i.e., creative choices – will have on the musical expression obtained by executing the instructions. A high level of foreseeability will generally indicate considerable alignment between authorial intent, external realisation, and end result, in turn justifying characterisation as an 'intellectual creation reflecting the author's personality'.

Composition through developing and interacting with an AI system lies in the middle between creating something through pure fortuity and with maximal alignment of authorial intent, external realisation, and end result. An analogy to traditional compositional methods was drawn by comparing AI-assisted compositional processes to manually compiling a musical template, where several musical elements – such as melody, rhythm, texture, and form – are defined in broad terms, and inviting subsequent contributors to supply the precise details. The analogy suggested one might divide template compositions into manual and AI-assisted template compilation. On this basis, the act of 'composing a musical work' can be formulated as making a series of creative choices that accomplish an instruction set or musical template, which can be rendered into a certain kind of musical expression. Whether the latter can sustain a copyright claim will depend on the degree of originality causation between the creative choices and the end result.

As implied in research question (7), the degree of originality causation will ultimately depend on how specific the instructions are and how precisely they have been executed in producing the resulting musical expression. Opposing arguments as to whether an AI-assisted process can sustain the degree of originality causation required to grant protection were already sketched at the conclusion of section 5.4. Aiming to provide further insight and nuance into this discussion, the following two chapters will examine the processes of both manual and AI-assisted template composition to analyse the degree of originality causation they provide. Chapter 6 will focus on manual template compositions, whereas Chapter 7 focuses on AI-assisted creative processes.

CHAPTER 6

Authorship of Manual Template Compositions

6.1 PREMISE AND STRUCTURE OF THE CHAPTER

The purpose of the present chapter is to examine the process of creating a template composition using traditional manual means. To lay the groundwork for this, the chapter begins by investigating what it means to compose a musical work. As noted in section 1.2, this analysis will be rather comprehensive, laying out the ontological and epistemic nature of musical works as it has been applied in traditional copyright law as well as enhancing the robustness of the analysis by incorporating musicological findings. The relative depth of the investigation – in terms of both scope and methodology – stems from the overarching purpose of the dissertation. In addition to laying the foundation for assessing whether AI-generated musical compositions can receive copyright protection, the dissertation also aims to place current compositional tools and techniques in their historical context, thereby helping to develop a technologically neutral understanding of musical works and their component parts in the era of high-performance generative AI.

The analysis starts by defining the concept of music and exploring the core elements of musical composition, including melody, rhythm, harmony, and form. Following this, the distinction between original expression and commonplace ideas will be examined using illustrative examples from existing music infringement case law, most notably the Swedish Supreme Court case *Landslaget v. Drängarna*.[382] The

382. Officially, the parties of the proceedings were EMI and Regatta, the respective music groups' record labels. Despite this, I will refer to the parties as Landslaget and Drängarna because the focus of the analysis will be on the compositional aspects of the contested compositions, which makes it more natural to refer to the actual composers of the passages.

purpose of this examination is to establish the minimum degree of input required to clear the originality threshold, as well as the means by which one might accurately determine this. Having examined the core musical building blocks and how they can be distinguished from protected musical expression, the analysis proceeds to investigate the questions of originality and authorship allocation in the context of template compositions. As explained in section 1.5.4, the idea is to start with a very rudimentary collection of musical building blocks – or an instruction set describing them – and gradually add more complexity to them to observe the point at which the template gains enough specificity and complexity to transition from a collection of commonplace ideas to a protected musical work. To complete the discussion, the chapter also includes a section discussing authorship allocation in multi-contributor scenarios, involving contributions from multiple individuals across different stages of the compositional process.

6.2 THE COMPONENTS OF A MUSICAL WORK

6.2.1 What Is Music?

Professor Gordon Epperson gives an inclusive yet accurate definition of the word 'music'. He describes it as an:

> art concerned with combining vocal or instrumental sounds for beauty of form or emotional expression, usually according to cultural standards of rhythm, melody, and, in most Western music, harmony. Both the simple folk song and the complex electronic composition belong to the same activity, music. Both are humanly engineered; both are conceptual and auditory, and these factors have been present in music of all styles and in all periods of history, throughout the world.[383]

Dictionaries offer similar definitions. The Cambridge dictionary characterises music as 'a pattern of sounds made by musical instruments, voices, or computers, or a combination of these, intended to give pleasure to people listening to it'.[384] Meanwhile, the Merriam Webster dictionary defines it as 'vocal, instrumental, or mechanical sounds having rhythm, melody, or harmony' that can be utilised through 'the science or art of ordering tones or sounds in succession, in combination, and in temporal relationships to produce a composition having unity and continuity'.[385] All the definitions above indicate certain core features. Music consists of sounds that have been deliberately manipulated to produce an expressive effect of some kind. Accordingly, one might suggest a polar dichotomy between music and noise, where former is designed to allow listeners to receive 'meaningful musical information in a distinct

383. Encyclopedia Britannica's article on music, available at https://www.britannica.com/art/music, accessed 4 January 2025. Another definition is given by Professor Jerrold Levinson 1990, p. 273, who defines music as 'sounds temporally organized by a person for the purpose of enriching or intensifying experience through active engagement (e.g., listening, dancing, performing) with the sounds regarded primarily, or in significant measure, as sounds'.
384. https://dictionary.cambridge.org/dictionary/english/music, accessed 4 January 2025.
385. https://www.merriam-webster.com/dictionary/music, accessed 4 January 2025.

way', while noise is largely uncontrolled.[386] A similar definition was suggested by Mummery LJ in the UK Appeals Court case *Sawkins v. Hyperion*, where he noted that:

> as indicated in the dictionaries, the essence of music is combining sounds for listening to. Music is not the same as mere noise. The sound of music is intended to produce effects of some kind on the listener's emotions and intellect.[387]

Many scholars representing a variety of scientific disciplines argue that the act of structuring sounds to construct music out of noise unlocks a very powerful form of communication. One scholar points out that '[m]ore so than any other artistic endeavo[u]rs, music possesses ethereal qualities that infiltrates and permeates multiple facets of our existence in a complex manner'.[388] Other researchers have noted that 'music affords biological benefits that elude common understanding ... [and the] neurological, physiological, and psychological responses that hearing music can generate are also well documented and remarkable'.[389] Not only do babies both born and unborn respond to music to an extent rivalling avid concert-goers,[390] but music is likewise used for various therapeutic ends due to its capability to evoke responses totally unrelated to the music itself. As explained by Keyes, 'music is a powerful communicative force, it also evokes a vast array of emotional responses from the recipients of it. It inspires, consoles, motivates, awakens, and energizes us'.[391]

Viewing music as a means of communicating meaning suggests many similarities with speech. In this vein, Richman notes that:

> the original process of fixing sequences into recognizable, repeatable, and significant definite somethings by entire communities was accomplished by speech and music making in exactly the same way and by the same means. In other words, in the beginning, speech and music making were one and the same: they were collective, real-time repetitions of formulaic sequences.[392]

This statement captures some key points about how music can acquire communicative meaning. Chiefly, the repetition of formulaic sequences enables the organisation of a group of sounds into a cohesive and harmonious whole. Repetition is indeed the mechanism through which disparate noises become coherent, and this perceived coherence subsequently allows them to acquire a deeper communicative – and artistic – meaning. As will be elaborated below in discussing the utilisation of *repetition schemes*, this process heavily relies on establishing a sense of structure through the repetition of various groups of sounds. Needless to say, what is considered pleasing or structurally coherent is highly contingent on cultural context, as aptly illustrated by an anecdote about a 19th-century Japanese concertgoer who preferred the cacophonic

386. Reybrouck, Podlipniak and Welch 2019, p. 2.
387. *Sawkins v. Hyperion* [2005] 1 WLR 3281, para. 53.
388. Keyes 2004, p. 421.
389. Craig and Laroche 2014, p. 47.
390. Keyes 2004, p. 421.
391. Keyes 2004, p. 422. He cites Anthony Storr's book Music and the Mind.
392. Richman 2000, p. 301.

sound of an orchestra warming up to the actual works subsequently performed during the concert.[393]

When these definitions and statements are considered with a view to defining music for the purposes of copyright law, certain observations need to be made. First, the open-ended approach to copyright eligibility indicates that the precise definition of the concept of music will not ultimately matter for the originality evaluation, since any creation – at least in theory – should be granted protection if it satisfies the general originality criteria. This means that in examining the originality of a musical composition, what matters is that the relevant aural stimuli stem from a conscious and deliberate manipulation of the underlying sonic building material.

Second, an important distinction between verbal and musical communication needs to be pointed out. As aptly described by Reybrouck, Podlipniak, and Welch, musical expression 'is mainly "experienced" rather than being solely "reasoned" and "interpreted"'.[394] Undoubtedly, musical expression may also utilise communicative structures that rely on the reasoned or interpreted meaning that a given musical structure – such as a scale, rhythm, or chord – has acquired within a certain social community or context.[395] In this sense, musical and verbal communication greatly resemble each other. However, compared to verbal communication, musical expression arguably makes greater use of input that is experienced rather than reasoned. As noted in the previous chapter, this suggests that defining the contents of a musical work can become more dependent on the listener's subjective impressions, which has obvious ramifications for the pursuit of defining a musical work with the objective precision usually associated with legal property entitlement.

6.2.2 The Constituent Parts of Musical Expression

In practice, the copyright analysis of music involves examining the structure of musical works to allocate exclusive rights to their various constituent parts. Essentially, this requires adopting the perspective of a composer to identify the musical building materials and their utilisation for creative purposes. How do composers, then, usually go about creating musical works? As already noted in the previous section, *any* collection of sounds can at least in theory acquire protection, which means that providing an exhaustive list of all potential creative parameters available to composers is challenging. However, the most commonly used parameters can be pinpointed and examined. This section will briefly outline them, setting the stage for analysing how creative choices are made within a musical context.

In most cases, pitch and timing stand out as the most fundamental parameters in shaping musical expression. Accordingly, most conventional musical expression can be understood as a function of pitch and timing, where the accurate execution of intended pitches in the correct temporal relation to each other generally renders the

393. Steel 2015, p. 69.
394. Reybrouck, Podlipniak and Welch 2019, p. 1.
395. *See* below, the section that discusses the possibility of assigning concrete extra-musical significance to musical expression.

underlying compositional input recognisable. Still, mere pitch and timing will seldom suffice to convey the full range of compositional nuance envisioned by the author. In fact, pitch is a subcomponent of what is referred to as a *tone*. As noted by Roederer, three primary sensations combine to produce the sensation of a musical tone: pitch, loudness, and timbre.[396] *Pitch* indicates the frequency or 'height' of the sound. *Dynamics* refer to volume, that is, the perceived loudness of the tone.[397] It is most frequently used as a performative device that establishes or emphasises the hierarchical relationship between the notes contained in the composition. Beyond pitch and timing, another potentially important factor influencing musical expression is *timbre*. It denotes the tone quality, allowing differentiation between sounds produced by various instruments, even if they share the same pitch and volume. Timbre can sometimes be a notable compositional feature in its own right. For instance, within electronic dance music, it is not uncommon for timbre to be the main focus of musical development, leaving pitch and rhythm in supporting roles.[398] Another notable use of timbre is in the two-second sample at issue in the long-running *Metall auf Metall* case,[399] where the sample's timbre is by far the most important compositional parameter featured in the sample.

Notwithstanding the occasionally considerable artistic impact of dynamics and timbre, the process of stringing together pitches often constitutes the most prominent part of the compositional input within most mainstream compositional styles. This process can be divided into several subcategories, where it is helpful to distinguish between horizontal and vertical arrangement of pitches.[400] Horizontal pitch arrangement often concerns the use of different *scales*. The major and minor scales are most frequently employed within mainstream pop music, while the pentatonic scale finds use in folk, blues, and rock music. In addition, modes, whole-tone, and synthetic scales are used in more niche genres within jazz, rock, and classical traditions. Vertical pitch arrangement, by contrast, indicates pitches that sound simultaneously and is often referred to as *harmony*. An instructive way of approaching harmony is by dividing groups of pitches into *chords*. Successions of chords are termed *chord progressions*, often relying on *harmonic function* for their artistic effect. Harmonic function refers to 'gravitational pull' between certain chords caused by the perceived – though culturally conditioned – predisposition of one chord to resolve into certain others. This perceived pull between chords provides composers with a convenient means of giving the musical narrative a sense of momentum and direction, making certain chord progressions occur rather frequently. Perhaps the most famous example of a commonly used

396. Roederer 2008, pp. 3-4.
397. *See* Rahmatian 2015, p. 93 addresses volume at greater length: 'What is called "volume" in music (indicated as "piano, forte" etc.) is a combination of acoustics (amplitude of the vibration), and the perception by the ear and processed by the brain (psychoacoustic phenomenon: intensity and loudness).'
398. Butler 2014, p. 46.
399. For a brief history of this case, *see* Bischoff 2023.
400. This terminology originates from musical notation, where melodies are written sequentially from left to right (horizontal), while harmonies appear as stacked notes on a vertical axis.

chord progression is the I-V-VI-IV progression,[401] whose ubiquity within mainstream pop music was parodied by The Axis of Awesome in their song *4 chords*.[402]

Scales, chords, and chord progressions are interconnected artistic devices that use similar means to build tension and drama within a musical narrative. Notably, both vertical and horizontal pitch arrangements often rely on juxtaposing *major* and *minor* modes as well as *consonances* and *dissonances*. A popular analogy to explain the difference between major and minor modes is happiness and sadness. Dissonance refers to the perceived harshness or unpleasantness of a group of pitches, whereas consonance indicates mellowness and harmoniousness. These contrasting qualities create tension and release, enabling the construction of dramatic arcs with varying proportions and intensity. Of course, the perceived harshness or mellowness of certain pitch combinations as sources of tension and resolution is a cultural construct that has evolved and continues to evolve over time.[403] Similar to many other creative endeavours, the merit and quality of pitch selection often lie in achieving a successful balance between the contrasting elements used.

Another approach to categorise compositional input is through the concepts of melody and rhythm. *Melody* refers to the combination of pitch and timing, while *rhythm* is an umbrella term for the timing of sounds. Thus, a melody is a linear selection of pitches whose temporal execution has been prescribed with some degree of precision. The melodic content may often be the most characteristic part of a composition's identity, but exceptions to this are possible, as has been pointed out in section 5.4.2.[404]

A number of less prominent terms warrant mention before concluding the analysis of the most common compositional building blocks. The *texture* of a passage refers to the interplay of tone, harmony and melody. The density and range of the simultaneously sounding musical lines also greatly influence the perceived texture of the piece. *Instrumentation* and *arrangement* likewise can influence the musical texture to great artistic effect.[405] These relate to the instruments selected to execute the musical material. *Form* is an important element of musical composition, describing the structure of a piece. The alternation between verse and refrain frequently used in songs provides a familiar example of using structural elements to enhance the artistic effect of the underlying material. The examination of form as an element displaying artistic proficiency also illustrates the process of composing rather poignantly. Form refers to

401. The functional relationship between chords is often indicated in Roman numerals.
402. Available at https://www.youtube.com/watch?v=oOlDewpCfZQ, accessed 5 January 2025.
403. *See* Lahdelma and Eerola 2020 for an empirical investigation into the relationship between dissonance and consonance. In addition, Arnold Schönberg'soft-quoted phrase 'the emancipation of dissonance', first mentioned in his 1911 book *Harmonielehre*, can also be seen as highlighting the cultural conditioning that determines what is perceived as consonant and dissonant. *See* Hinton 2010, pp. 568-570, 573.
404. In section 5.4.2, I noted that 'One composition may rely on commonplace harmonic patterns to support highly individual melodic content, whereas another might depend on an idiosyncratic use of harmony and texture.'
405. DeVlieger 2020, p. 249: 'The consideration of texture, timbre, and instrumentation is very important to the analysis of popular music for the purposes of copyright litigation, as *it is in these areas that musicians have the most room for creative expression*'. My italics.

the perceived structure of a piece as achieved through repetition of certain musical elements, which, in turn, are structures made of patterns of repetition. The contextual relevance of repetitions and *repetition schemes* will be addressed in greater detail below.

In sum, musical composition centres on combining sonic patterns in an artistically meaningful way. These meaning-conferring patterns can be divided into categories such as tone, arrangement, instrumentation, texture, rhythm, melody, harmony, chords, counterpoint, and form. These concepts are not mutually exclusive but rather tend to overlap. For example, whether a passage is better characterised as an instance of horizontal harmony or of counterpoint will often be determined not only by the properties of the piece at hand but also by personal preference. Despite occasional instances of subjectivity or conceptual overlap, the categorisation of the compositional elements – or musical building blocks – performs a valuable function in providing a means of verbalising certain inherently non-verbal workings of the musical narrative.

6.3 SEPARATING ORIGINAL EXPRESSION AND COMMONPLACE IDEAS

6.3.1 Calibrating the Originality Threshold

Having established the component parts or building blocks of musical compositions, the potentially very challenging matter of distinguishing between original expression and commonplace ideas remains.[406] This issue – which aligns with copyright law's overarching idea/expression dichotomy – surfaces in slightly different ways in copyright infringement cases involving compositions created through traditional means and the template compositions examined in this chapter. In a traditional copyright infringement case, the separation between expression and ideas tends to come to the fore in situations where two short fragments are very similar. Two questions emerge here: whether the plaintiff's fragment contains enough free and creative choices to distinguish it from the underlying building blocks, and whether the similarities between the contested fragments resulted from the defendant having copied original contents from the plaintiff's composition or because both passages utilise similar musical building blocks.

By contrast, when examining a template composition, the distinction between original expression and commonplace building blocks comes into play in determining whether the template contains enough specificity to distinguish it from the underlying building blocks to meet the originality threshold. To illustrate, an instruction set that only contains the phrase 'a dramatic piece of orchestral music' is much too generic to meet the originality threshold. However, the more elements one adds to the instruction set specifying *what kind* of orchestral composition one aims for – by indicating the type of melodic shapes, chord progressions, instrumental textures, or repetition schemes to be used – the closer it will come to meeting the originality criteria.

406. *See* Rahmatian 2024, pp. 29-31 for a thorough analysis of this issue.

Both the traditional infringement case and the template composition will ultimately centre on balancing the originality threshold in light of copyright law's underlying rationale of incentivising the creation of new works by rewarding the authors for their intellectual endeavours. If the originality threshold is set too high, the incentivising function suffers. Conversely, setting it too low is liable to give exclusive rights to common musical building blocks, which obviously works contrary to the law's purpose. Essentially, this balancing is about properly *calibrating* the originality threshold to align with copyright law's underlying rationale when performing the similarity comparison between the relevant data collections. (This applies regardless of whether two similar passages are examined in the context of a traditional infringement case, or a music template and its completion.)

6.3.2 Illustrative Examples of Applying a Low Threshold for Originality and Infringement

Two highly publicised American music infringement cases decided relatively recently will illustrate the difficulties and potential pitfalls involved in distinguishing between original expression and commonplace ideas. The first, the *Williams v. Gaye* case, concerns the aggregate effect of many indirect similarities resulting in a finding of infringement. The second, *Gray v. Perry*, is about whether a simple passage constitutes protected original expression or a non-protected musical building block. Both cases aptly demonstrate the dangers of calibrating the originality threshold to an excessively lenient standard.

The *Williams v. Gaye* case concerned the similarities between Robin Thicke and Pharrell Williams' song 'Blurred Lines' and Marvin Gaye's song 'Got To Give It Up.' The interesting feature of the case is that while the contested songs share many features of genre and style, they display very few literal similarities. This led Gaye's expert witness Judith Finell to state that upon a 'comprehensive view of "Blurred Lines" as a whole, there emerges a *virtual mosaic of elements* descending from [Gaye's song]', and that the 'link between the two works is undeniable – especially considering the *multitude of tiny creative details* that blend to form the completed works'.[407] In total, Finell lists around 10 such creative details and argues that this 'constellation of similarities' makes the songs sufficiently alike for Blurred Lines to infringe.

407. DeVlieger 2020, p. 197. My italics.

Figure 6.1 'Signature Phrases' of the Songs at Issue in Williams v. Gaye[408]

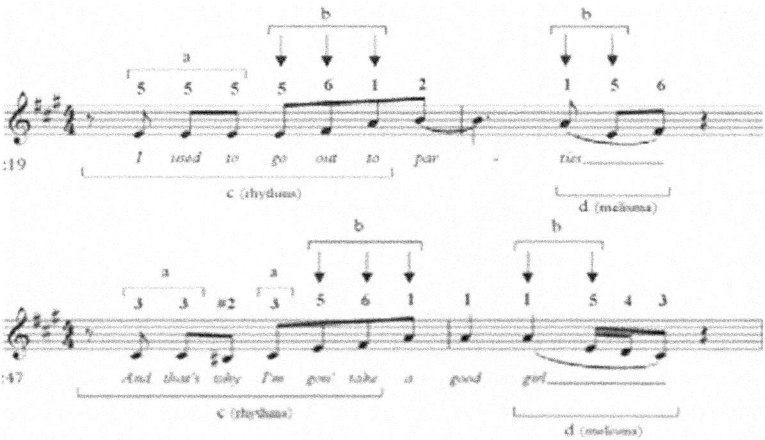

At first glance, this argument seems reasonably convincing, but the argument quickly unravels upon closer examination of the purported similarities listed. Among other things, Finell points to the alleged similarities between the songs' signature phrases (*see* Figure 6.1). However, neither an examination of the signature phrases' notation nor their execution in the recorded performances suggests any similarity apart from the odd duplicated note. The remainder of the alleged similarities are equally contrived and unconvincing, such as 'Theme X', off-beat hand clapping, and high-pitched exclamations featured in both songs (*see* pictures below). In addition, it is important to note that the fragments pointed out as similar are not only very short but also consist of exceedingly commonplace compositional input, making coincidental similarities particularly likely. Despite this, the fragments selected by Finell for comparison still exhibit notable dissimilarities. Under these circumstances, it seems difficult not to concur with dissenting Appeals Court judge Nguyen, who noted that Finell's analysis 'is the equivalent of finding substantial similarity between two pointillist paintings because both have a few flecks of similarly coloured paint':[409]

408. *Williams v. Gaye*, No. 15-56880 (9th Cir. 2018), p. 67.
409. *Williams v. Gaye*, No. 15-56880 (9th Cir. 2018).

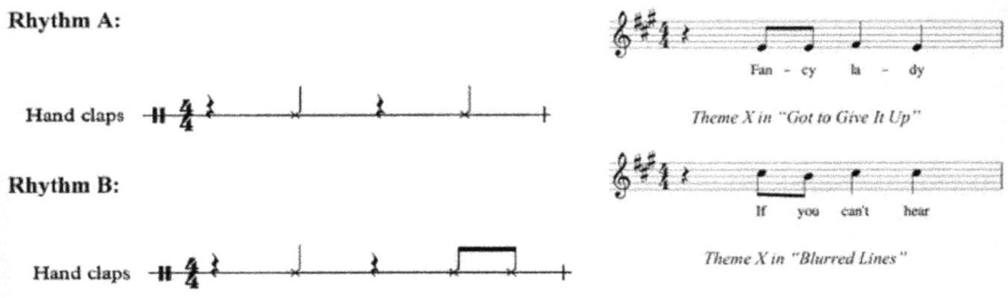

Source: *Williams v. Gaye*, No. 15-56880 (9th Cir. 2018), p. 75.

Notwithstanding the unconvincing evidence, both the trial jury and the Court of Appeals ruled in favour of Gaye. Understandably, the decisions faced criticism for effectively allowing Gaye to copyright a musical style and raised concerns about encouraging opportunistic infringement claims. The idea behind these concerns is that if the originality threshold is low enough to lead to infringement even if the similarities are confined to a few notes or commonplace stylistic features, the statistical probability of coincidental similarities between independently created compositions will grow considerably, creating ample opportunities for opportunistic infringement claims.

The puzzling part of the Blurred Lines ruling is that the contested songs did not even contain any direct similarities apart from some very broad features of style. In this sense, the *Gray v. Perry* case can be deemed a more traditional example of calibrating the originality threshold to both allow sufficient protection for compositional endeavours and keep common building blocks free for all composers to use. The contested similarities were the 4-bar synth riffs contained in Christian rapper Marcus Gray's song 'Joyful Noise' and pop singer Katy Perry's song 'Dark Horse'. The plaintiff argued that the synth riffs exhibit similar pitch, rhythm, timbre, phrase length, and texture.[410] The evidence presented convinced the trial jury, which awarded Gray 22.5% of the profits from Perry's song.[411]

This is a very peculiar outcome. While the similarities between the riffs indeed are considerable, one must arguably find that the similarities between the pieces are insufficient to sustain a justifiable finding of infringement. Similarities in pitch, rhythm, texture, pattern of repetition, and timbre, when examined as a whole, can undoubtedly be sufficient to establish infringement, even in passages as short as the ones at issue in the *Gray v. Perry* case. However, the problem in this case is that the similarities in rhythm cannot be given much independent significance, since they consist in a sequence of 16 consecutive semiquaver notes. This constitutes the simplest possible selection of rhythm, calling into question whether the choice of rhythm can be

410. Amici brief, p. 4, available at https://www.digitalmusicnews.com/wp-content/uploads/2020/01/Katy_Perry_Flame_514_Amici_Brief_Filed.pdf, accessed 9 August 2025; *Gray v. Perry*, No. 20-55401 (9th Cir. 10 March 2022). United States Court of Appeals for the Ninth Circuit, pp. 18-20.
411. *Marcus Gray et al. v. Katy Perry et al.*, No. 2:15-cv-05642-CAS-JC (C.D. Cal. filed 24 July 2015); Bosher (Music copyright infringement cases in US and UK), p. 283.

given much independent value in assessing the degree of originality contained in the plaintiff's riff.[412]

Figure 6.2 The Riffs at Issue in Gray v. Perry

The melodic shapes are likewise practically as commonplace as can be, using a descending minor scale pattern found in innumerable other compositions.[413] In addition, the similarities between timbres are essentially confined to the fact that they are synthetic keyboard sounds, which is much too generic to influence the tally of duplicated original attributes. As noted by jazz musician Adam Neely in his analysis, the plaintiff's riff is articulated with a sawtooth waveform paired with a very distinct glide between pitches, whereas the defendant's riff has a much airier quality and no glides.[414] To summarise, the impression of similarity accomplished through many small similarities dispersed among several musical elements – such as the mentioned pitch, rhythm, texture, pattern of repetition, and timbre – can certainly be enough to justify granting an infringement claim. However, in this instance, the similarities between the contested passages are too reliant on commonplace ideas to warrant a finding of infringement. Consequently, one might arguably consider this jury verdict to have erred in its calibration of the originality threshold.

A reversal of course was provided by the *Skidmore v. Led Zeppelin* case, which concerned the similarities between Led Zeppelin's 'Stairway to Heaven' infringed upon Spirit's 'Taurus.'[415] The similarity between the songs stemmed from their use of the same chord progression, built on a chromatically descending bass line, *see* Figure 6.3 below.[416] The Ninth Circuit Court of Appeals determined that the similarities between the two songs only involved common musical elements that are not subject to copyright protection.[417]

---

412. This riff will be discussed in greater detail in section 6.3.4.
413. Perry's expert witness also pointed this out, illustrating the point by listing more than 30 songs composed before Joyful noise that shared a similar ostinato. Intellectual Property Forum Issue 123 March 2021, p. 12, available at https://www.wilmerhale.com/-/media/files/shared_content/editorial/publications/documents/20210316-ipsanz-intellectual-property-forum-issue-123-march-2021.pdf, accessed 7 January 2025.
414. Neely, Why the Katy Perry/Flame Lawsuit Makes No Sense, https://www.youtube.com/watch?v=0ytoUuO-qvg, at approximately 2 min 30 sec to 3 min 10 sec, accessed 7 January 2025.
415. *Skidmore v. Zeppelin*, No. 16-56057 (9th Cir. 2020).
416. *Skidmore v. Zeppelin*, No. 16-56057, p. 27.
417. *Skidmore v. Zeppelin*, No. 16-56057, p. 7.

Figure 6.3 The Contested Passages of 'Taurus' and 'Stairway to Heaven'

This ruling also contributed to vacating the jury verdict in *Gray v. Perry* as a matter of law by the Ninth Circuit US Court of Appeals.[418] A commentator memorably likened this to a lifting of the Blurred lines curse,[419] and it also coincided with a ruling in favour of popular artist Ed Sheeran in a similarly frivolous infringement claim on the other side of the Atlantic.[420] Overall, the Blurred Lines ruling can be viewed as a real-life experiment of what happens when the originality threshold and its application to copyright infringement cases are improperly calibrated. The amicus brief in support of Williams and Thicke, signed by 212 musicians, gives a good indication of the Blurred Lines verdict's ramifications. Among other things, the brief poignantly notes that '[b]y eliminating any meaningful standard for drawing the line between permissible inspiration and unlawful copying, the judgment is certain to stifle creativity and impede the creative process'.[421] A similar sentiment was echoed by Ed Sheeran following his victory in the UK High Court:

> It's really damaging to the songwriting industry. There's only so many notes, and very few chords used in pop music. Coincidences are bound to happen [with so many songs being written every day] ... and I hope that this ruling means in the future baseless claims like this can be avoided ... Hopefully we can all get back to writing songs, rather than having to prove that we can write them.[422]

418. *Gray v. Hudson*, No. 20-55401 (9th Cir. 2022).
419. The statement was by Perry's lawyer Christine Lepera, available at https://www.nytimes.com/2020/03/24/arts/music/blurred-lines-led-zeppelin-copyright.html, accessed 7 January 2025.
420. *Sheeran & Ors v. Chokri & Ors* [2022] EWHC 827 (Ch) (6 April 2022).
421. Minsker, 'Blurred Lines' Appeal Gets Support From More Than 200 Musicians, available at https://pitchfork.com/news/67932-blurred-lines-appeal-gets-support-from-more-than-200-musicians/, accessed 12 February 2025.
422. Ed Sheeran Statement in Response to His Victory in the UK High Court, https://www.instagram.com/p/CcANzfhjaHL/, accessed 7 January 2025.

6.3.3 Utilising Expert Witness Reports

Having examined some examples of courts misjudging the calibration of the originality threshold, the core question is how one should determine the distinction between original expression and commonplace ideas, and what information the determination should be based on. The obvious inference is that the court tasked with deciding the matter can consult expert opinions. Depending on the jurisdiction, the expert opinions can come in the form of expert witnesses employed by the parties or a court-appointed expert. An interesting illustrative example of the role of expert opinion comes from the German Federal Court of Justice's (BGH) *Goldrapper* case.[423] The rapper Bushido had sampled an approximately 13-second sequence from the song 'Les Memoires Blessées' by the French gothic band Dark Sanctuary, which led to the latter suing for infringement. Therefore, the court, among other things, needed to determine whether the sampled passage meets the originality threshold. The contested sample, while it is relatively long and distinctive, relies heavily on existing melodic and harmonic patterns; *see* Figure 6.4 below.[424] Accordingly, it resides at the very junction between expression and idea, making it particularly relevant for the present discussion.

Figure 6.4 The Passage Sampled from Les Memoires Blessées

Both parties submitted expert opinions favourable to their respective sides of the argument. The regional and appellate courts had found that the passage was original and that the defendant's sampling of the passage therefore constituted copyright infringement. In making this assessment, the appellate court held that it could determine whether the passage was sufficiently distinct from the underlying compositional techniques without obtaining a judicial expert opinion. It claimed to possess the necessary expertise based partly on personal musical practice but primarily due to its extensive experience with music in the context of copyright infringement as members of a court specialising in copyright law.[425] The BGH did not agree with this assessment.

423. 16/4/2015, I ZR 225/12, p. 61(2), available at https://juris.bundesgerichtshof.de/cgi-bin/rechtsprechung/document.py?Gericht = bgh&Art = en&nr = 72506&pos = 0&anz = 1, accessed 7 January 2025.
424. Sheet music from https://blogs.law.gwu.edu/mcir/case/dark-sanctuary-v-bushido/, Dark Sanctuary's audio recording of the song is available at https://www.youtube.com/watch?v = O8lo9S55wSI. Both accessed 7 January 2025.
425. 16/4/2015, I ZR 225/12, p. 61(2).

It considered expert assistance indispensable for the evaluation, particularly in cases where the small change (*kleine Münze*) of copyright protection is considered.[426] In such cases, the BGH deemed merely listening to a sound recording by the trial judge to be insufficient.[427]

This ties in with more overarching problems when the expert opinions consulted are those submitted by the parties. Here, the court is almost invariably going to receive two conflicting reports: The claimant's expert dissects the songs emphasising their similarities and concludes that B reproduces A, whereas the defendant's expert reviews the same material to the opposite effect. What conclusions can one draw in such a situation? As pointed out by many scholars and commentators, it is not unthinkable that the respective experts are prone to formulating their opinions in a way sympathetic to the party who hired them, which may influence the objective validity of their testimony.[428] Even if the objectivity was not to be compromised, a distinctly possible consequence of the 'duelling' expert opinions is that they cancel each other out, leaving the adjudicators scarcely better off than prior to the reception of the expert testimony.[429] An empirical study into the matter by Lee and Moshirnia largely confirmed this hypothesis, as it found the effect of experts 'muted or diminished when presented as a battle of duelling experts with opposing views'.[430] Indeed, it seems far from implausible to think that a detailed and jargon-heavy altercation between opposing experts will be difficult for the court to interpret, which may obscure rather than illuminate the court's similarity analysis. One danger inherent to this situation is that the duelling expert testimony may cancel each other out even in unfounded cases. Even if the claim would be frivolous, the expert opinion arguing for infringement may be difficult to convincingly rebut, since the only practical way of doing so is through the battling experts scenario.

The utilisation of a court-appointed neutral expert, such as was advocated by the BGH, provides one way of guarding against such problems in calibrating the originality threshold. However, even if one were to mandate that all music copyright cases are to utilise a court-appointed expert – which, of course, is a thoroughly unrealistic prospect – there still remains the question of the criteria by which the distinction between commonplace ideas and original expression should be drawn. To investigate this issue, it is necessary to delve into how the utilisation of expert testimony can inform the issue, both from a traditional and a more experimental approach.

426. In German law, small change (*kleine Münze*) refers to a doctrine whereby creations with minimal originality and practical use can receive protection despite having little individual creativity. This includes commonplace creations, such as telephone directories, recipe books, catalogues, reproductions of artworks, and compilations. *See* Rahmatian 2013, p. 19, with further references.
427. 16/4/2015, I ZR 225/12, para. 64.
428. Bennet 2023, p. 61; Lee and Moshirnia 2022, p. 725; DeVlieger 2022, p. 92. DeVlieger suggests confirmation bias is a likely cause of the partisan outcome advocated for in expert opinions.
429. Lee and Moshirnia 2022, p. 712.
430. Lee and Moshirnia 2022, p. 786.

6.3.4 Different Uses of Expert Input and Experimental Methodological Approaches

As noted in Chapter 1, expert input, especially in the field of music theory, can provide insight into the building blocks of musical compositions. By systematising common scales, chords, rhythm patterns, phrase structures, and chord progressions used across different genres and styles, it offers a structured understanding of the elements from which compositions are made. There are several ways in which this can improve the court's grasp of musical works. The systematisation makes it easier to make connections between compositions. For instance, if certain chord progressions or melodic patterns have been identified in the musicological literature, it becomes easier to assess the degree to which a composition utilising such pre-existing patterns distinguishes itself from the underlying commonplace idea. In addition, a systematisation of musical elements should give insights into how many elements were utilised by a composer and how these elements interact. This can help in gauging the composition's degree of originality by suggesting a quasi-statistical model of the composition's – or passage's – originality. Essentially, such a model can approximate the number of musical outcomes among which the particular sequence of attributes was selected.

To illustrate what is meant by a statistical model of a passage's originality, we can examine the synth riff in 'Joyful Noise', which was at issue in the *Gray v. Perry* case. The riff contains 16 notes. In a traditional Western musical context, there are 12 available pitches, suggesting that, at least from a purely statistical perspective, the pitches of the riff were selected from among 12^{16} different possible combinations. In addition, the timing of each pitch could theoretically be chosen from up to 10 distinct note values, further compounding the exponential growth in the number of possible combinations. Based on this analysis, there should be little doubt as to the statistical uniqueness of Gray's synth riff, which, under a Kummerian approach,[431] might be sufficient to establish originality. However, this line of reasoning is far from persuasive in evaluating the riff's originality, as it overlooks the significant constraining effects of pre-existing compositional techniques and the established structures of 'musical grammar'. How, then, can one approximate the 'true' number of possible outcomes?

First, one might point out that the riff's use of only one note value eliminates the timing of the pitches from being considered when calculating the approximate number of outcomes. Second, existing harmonic structures further limit the number of possible outcomes. The riff utilises a diatonic minor scale, which limits the available pitches from 12 to at least 8. Third, the riff is built upon a very common melodic pattern that utilises the 3rd, 2nd, and 1st degree of the scale in descending order. Moreover, the many repeated pitches arguably limit the number of outcomes. Fourth, the riff utilises a repetition scheme divided into two subsections of 8 notes each, where the latter half duplicates the first half with only small changes, which, of course, considerably curtails the approximated number of outcomes. Based on such arguments, one might state that commonplace compositional techniques influenced or dictated the riff's

431. *See* Chapter 3.

contents to such a degree that, while one cannot state that the riff would contain no individual input at all, its individual input is not sufficiently distinct from the underlying musical building blocks to meet the threshold. By contrast, a 16-note riff utilising a wide variety of pitches and note values with little to no repetition is much more likely to be original.

This type of analysis may be persuasive in the context of an infringement claim. However, it may also suffer from the challenges inherent to conflicting expert testimony, as explained above. Furthermore, it may be difficult to present the musicological findings in a manner that is accessible and persuasive to legal practitioners who ultimately decide the case. Theoretical expert analysis may therefore be most effective when referencing specific and well-known examples of existing musical compositions, rather than relying solely on theoretical explanations that describe overarching features of certain compositional techniques or musical building blocks. As illustrated by the example of Artikal Sound System's infringement suit against Dua Lipa, discussed in Chapter 1, argumentation about a passage's genericity or the likelihood of its independent double-creation becomes significantly more convincing when coupled with examples of pre-existing compositions containing similar or even identical passages.

Inspired by the potential of combining theoretical analysis of compositional elements – such as pitch, rhythm, harmony, and form – with listening to audio samples in determining the distinction between original expression and commonplace ideas, I will utilise a method of constructing and analysing mock performances of compositions. The idea is to produce a succession of renditions of a composition, each of which introduces increasingly invasive alterations to various elements of the work. By listening to several mock performances that distort different parameters of compositional input, one can gain added insight into the defining characteristics of the composition's individuality and originality, which serve to distinguish it from underlying musical building blocks.

The purpose of this method is to combine systematic analytical techniques with the subjective experience elicited by hearing the relevant musical passage performed. This approach aims to leverage high-level expertise in music theory while avoiding the pitfalls of overly technical or jargon-heavy explanations. At the same time, by incorporating an extensive analysis of the relevant composition through the construction and examination of the mock performances, it also seeks to mitigate the subjectivity and lack of transparency associated with relying on the subjective impression of listening to a composition as the main reference for determining whether it should receive protection.

6.4 SIMILARITIES BETWEEN SIMPLE COMPOSITIONS AND MUSICAL TEMPLATES

6.4.1 *The Swedish Supreme Court's Landslaget v. Drängarna Infringement* Case

A deeper understanding of how the questions of originality should be assessed in the context of template compositions can be had by comparing them to very simple compositions that have been assessed in the context of a traditional infringement case. Such infringement cases typically actualise two key questions that are relevant for our discussion: whether passage A can be considered original despite being short and highly reliant on commonplace compositional techniques, and whether passage B duplicates enough of passage A's original contents to infringe on it. In the following, we shall investigate these questions more closely by examining the Swedish Supreme Court *Landslaget v. Drängarna* judgment NJA 2002 section 178.[432] It features two violin riffs, one by Landslaget and another by Drängarna. What makes this case particularly appropriate for the present discussion is that it features a comparison characterised by challenges very similar to those relevant for assessing template compositions. First, the plaintiff's riff was simple and highly reliant on commonplace compositional techniques, raising questions about whether it distinguished itself sufficiently from the underlying ideas to be an original work. Second, although the contested riffs were very similar, they did contain a few differences. This raised the question whether the overall impression of the riffs, notwithstanding the differences between them, could be deemed instances of the same work and thereby warrant a finding of infringement. In the following, we shall examine the case in greater detail to lay the foundations for drawing an analogy to the copyright assessment of template compositions.

The plaintiff's song *Tala om vart du ska resa* was composed in 1973[433] and contains the following violin riff, which appears in the intro and at various points throughout the song.

Figure 6.5 Tala om vart du ska resa (Landslaget)

The defendant's song, *Om du vill bli min fru,*[434] was released in 1995. It also contains a violin riff, which performs a very similar function within the song. Both as examined through listening and in the form of musical notation, there are considerable similarities between the two riffs.

Figure 6.6 Om du vill bli min fru (Drängana)

The defendants disputed both the originality of Landslaget's riff and having created their own riff by copying it, arguing that Landslaget's riff failed to meet the

432. Available at https://lagen.nu/dom/nja/2002s178, accessed 9 January 2025.
433. Available at https://www.youtube.com/watch?v = 8XS1Fb0wPLI, accessed 9 January 2025.
434. Available at https://www.youtube.com/watch?v = OTZxtUxdoSc, accessed 9 January 2025.

originality threshold as it is a simple and repetitive figure highly reliant on non-protected commonplace elements. They also claimed that their riff had not been copied, but had been independently created by drawing inspiration from 'Oxdansen', a traditional Swedish folk tune, which the composer had learned during his violin training in the 1970s. The Swedish Supreme Court rejected the defendants' claim of independent creation, noting that Landslaget's riff met the threshold for originality despite its simplicity, as its distinctive pentatonic phrasing and melodic structure set it apart from common musical conventions. The court found the similarities between the riffs so striking that they could not be attributed to coincidence or shared musical building blocks. These similarities were deemed so pronounced in their overall impression on the listener that they outweighed the minor differences in tempo, harmony, or phrasing, reinforcing the finding that the defendants' riff was not independently created but had been derived from Landslaget's riff. In the court's view, the defendants' argument that 'Oxdansen' inspired their melody was weakened by the court's finding of limited resemblance between 'Oxdansen' and either riff. Furthermore, the widespread popularity of Landslaget's riff made it unlikely that the defendants had not encountered it before composing their own. Accordingly, the court determined that the striking similarities between the riffs created a strong presumption of copying, which the defendants failed to rebut, leading to a finding of infringement.

Figure 6.7 The Main Motif of Landslaget's Riff

Although the judgment appears well-reasoned in both its argumentation and practical outcome, certain aspects of its assessment of the originality of and similarity between the riffs merit closer examination. I find it particularly relevant to discuss how one might distinguish between commonplace ideas and original expression with regard to the contested riffs. In the following, we shall examine Landslaget's riff in greater detail. Breaking down the riff into its constituent parts reveals the initial 11-note motif as its most important melodic material; *see* Figure 6.7. It is built out of two motivic cells: an ascending flourish using the pentatonic scale (notes 1-5), and the turning figure contained in notes 5-11. This main motif is repeated three times, producing most of the riff's bulk (notes 1-33). To complete the riff, a contrasting concluding passage was inserted (notes 34-43). How should one go about determining whether this is enough to meet the originality threshold? The above-mentioned quasi-statistical approximation of the riff's originality can serve as a good starting point. However, as noted when examining the 'Joyful Noise' synth riff, a purely statistical calculation of the number of possible outcomes will not give much information about the degree of originality unless one filters out the choices dictated by pre-existing compositional techniques and established structures of musical grammar from the evaluation.

The impact of repetition plays a key role in the assessment. On the one hand, it is intuitive to think that repeating a passage should not impact a passage's originality in any way. On the other hand, the repetition of various contents plays a crucial role in imparting structure and meaning to musical passages. The utilisation of repetition schemes concerning different elements of the compositional material generally plays a crucial role in the compositional process. To illustrate this and its impact on how Landslaget's riff and the possibility of Drängarna having independently double-created similar features, let us retrace the steps required to compose Landslaget's riff. This necessitates a small detour into music analysis, since the use of *cadences* will have a significant impact on the use of repetition schemes, both in Landslaget's riff and in the template compositions to be discussed below.

A notable feature of the riff's main motif is that when examined in isolation, it does not formulate a full musical sentence, as demonstrated by Audio sample 1,[435] wherein only the main motif is played. Using an analogy from textual expression, it halts midway through an idea, as if ending with a comma rather than a period. In music theory, the delineation of musical passages has been explained through several different means,[436] but the dominating one, which is also the most appropriate considering the attributes of the present riffs, subdivides musical narratives based on their use of cadences.[437] Cadences relate to the 'gravitational pull' between different harmonies, according to which certain chords have a predisposition to resolve into some chords and an antipathy towards others.[438] In music analysis, this is explained in terms of the chords' *tonal function*, often expressed in Roman numerals. By moving from the 1st degree to the 4th, the main motif sets up an expectation of ending the phrase on the 1st degree. This expectation is fulfilled by the concluding motif. Audio sample 2 shows how the combination of the main motif and concluding motifs accomplishes a satisfying whole.[439]

Despite constituting a satisfying and coherent passage on its own, Landslaget chose to add two verbatim repetitions of the main motif to complete the riff. This raises an intriguing question about the impact of these verbatim repetitions on the riff's originality. On the one hand, one might think that mere copying should not and cannot have any impact on the riff's originality, just as the verbatim repetition of any textual passage does not make it any more original. On the other hand, the two-time repetition of the main motif clearly influences the subjective experience elicited by listening to the riff. Apart from adding length to the riff, it also alters the perceived relationship between the motifs: by repeating the main motif three times, thereby producing an

435. Audio samples are available here: http://hdl.handle.net/10138/596102.
436. The Sibelius Academy's teaching materials on music analysis lists four different ways of demarcating and subdividing musical phrases: It might be based on the number of beats, natural breath units (a unit that feels natural to sing or play in a single breath), melodic curves (a musical phrase with a clear beginning and ending, forming a cohesive idea), or cadences. Available at https://web.uniarts.fi/aleatori/indexcc6d.html?id = 302&la = fi, accessed 10 January 2025.
437. Other scholars have also pointed out the potential relevance of cadences in leading copyright law's similarity analysis astray. *See* Craig and Laroche 2014, p. 60.
438. *See* section 6.2.2.
439. Audio sample 2 available at http://hdl.handle.net/10138/596102.

AAAB phrase structure, the expectation of a harmonically compatible concluding motif becomes much stronger. Consequently, its fulfilment is likely to produce a greater sense of satisfaction in the listener.

Overall, the choice of repetition scheme – which defines the phrase structure – has a significant influence on the perceived artistic flair of the riff. For example, Audio sample 3 plays the main and concluding motifs in an ABAB structure, which, at least according to my subjective experience, gives the riff a more repetitive and jarring character, noticeably diminishing its artistic merit.[440] Therefore, while it appears intuitive to think that verbatim copying of passages cannot as such increase the originality of any composition, this type of copying, when employed to achieve a particular repetition scheme, is unquestionably a meaningful aspect of the compositional process. The potential effects of repetition on the originality of a passage will be explored in greater depth below.

6.4.2 Arguments Against the Originality and Infringement of Landslaget's Riff

In its judgment, the Swedish Supreme Court observed that while the riff is simple and relies on conventional elements, the overall aural impression it produces suffices to meet the originality threshold. The lower courts and the Evaluation Committee of the Swedish Performing Rights Society had likewise considered the riff original. Despite such broad consensus,[441] which seems entirely reasonable when one listens to the riff, I find that there are arguments to be made against the riff's originality and Drängarna's alleged infringement. These arguments rest on a detailed examination of Landslaget's riff to identify which particular attributes contribute to this overall impression of originality and an analysis of these elements in light of the distinction between ideas and expression. On the whole, it is highly relevant to discuss the components contributing to the overall impression of the contested passages, particularly because the Swedish Supreme Court's judgment placed significant emphasis on the overall impression in assessing both the fulfilment of originality requirements and the similarity necessary for determining infringement. This emphasis had a substantial impact on the likelihood of granting infringement claims by effectively reversing the burden of proof. Instead of the plaintiff being required to prove that the contested similarities arose from copying, the defendants were obligated to demonstrate independent double creation – a burden they, in the court's estimation, failed to meet with sufficiently compelling evidence.

440. Audio sample 3 http://hdl.handle.net/10138/596102.
441. Available at https://lagen.nu/dom/nja/2002s178, accessed 9 January 2025. Lenemark, in his commentary on the case (2022, pp. 590-592), does not challenge the assessment that the riff is original.

Figure 6.8 Oxdansen (beginning)

In the following, we shall examine the factors influencing the overall impression of originality and similarity in greater detail. For this purpose, we must revisit the main motif and analyse it from the perspective of the creative process. First, one must examine the degree to which the motif distinguishes itself from underlying musical building materials. As noted above, the motif consists of two motivic cells: an ascending pentatonic flourish (notes 1-5) and a turning passage (notes 5-10). The defendants had pointed out the similarities to the Swedish traditional tune 'Oxdansen.' This observation is unquestionably valid, as 7 of the motif's 10 notes are identical in both pitch and rhythm to those in 'Oxdansen'; *see* Figure 6.8. In fact, the only additions Landslaget made to the pre-existing material were to add two notes at the start, which create a pentatonic flourish leading into the next bar, and the note B, which replaces the E from 'Oxdansen.' During the proceedings, the plaintiffs testified that they were not aware of the 'Oxdansen' tune when composing the riff. They described their creative process as an improvisatory session of experimenting with various ideas on the violin, from which the riff gradually developed. Even if one accepts this claim and assumes that the plaintiffs were neither consciously nor subconsciously aware of 'Oxdansen', the remarkable similarity between the two tunes highlights the main motif's limited originality. After all, the double-creation standard by its very definition ties the degree of originality to the likelihood of independently creating similar passages.[442] Accordingly, the main motif (notes 1-10), when examined in isolation, arguably does not sufficiently distinguish itself from the underlying building blocks to be considered original.

The next issue is to examine how the concluding motif adds to the riff's originality. What we are essentially asking is whether the combination of the main and concluding motif contains sufficient individuality to clear the originality threshold. Two contrasting dynamics come into play in this assessment. On the one hand, the cumulative effect of the melodic material contained in the motifs causes an exponential increase in the statistically possible number of outcomes, significantly increasing the likelihood of an original end result. On the other hand, both the stylistic baseline established by the main motif and the rules of musical grammar significantly limit the range of artistically viable compositional choices. What this means is that the combination of the stylistic context and preceding contents of the riff (the main motif and its repetitions) in effect functions as a musical template that steers the composer towards a relatively narrow range of choices. To explain what this template consists of, we can

442. *See* Chapter 3.

distinguish certain melodic, harmonic, and structural expectations, which the composer needs to take into account when selecting the attributes of the concluding motif.

The most significant factor limiting the range of creative choice stems from repeating the main motif three times and the very strong expectation that the riff will form an 8-bar phrase. Indeed, both the song's style and overall musical convention can be thought to produce a rather demanding syntactic requirement for a 2-bar concluding motif to round out the riff into a normal 8-bar phrase. Of course, nothing hindered Landslaget from using a 7- or 9-bar phrase structure, but it would produce a jarring effect that ruins the flow of the music. In essence, one might state that the three-time repetition of the 2-bar main motif raises a very strong expectation of an AAAB repetition structure. The unity and coherence of the riff is increased by having the concluding motif duplicate the main motif's rhythm. This is a common compositional technique, suggesting that whatever additional originality attributable to Landslaget is contained in the concluding motif must reside in the selection of pitch, as the choice of rhythm was entirely dictated by commonplace compositional techniques.

For its part, the choice of pitch is also limited by certain factors. Most importantly, the song's utilisation of tonal functionality creates a strong expectation of ending the riff on the tonic harmony.[443] There are three harmonically compatible options for end note – the 1st, 3rd, and 5th scale degrees – of which the 1st scale degree is by far the most commonly used. Landslaget's choice of ending the riff on the 1st scale degree can therefore be deemed more or less entirely dictated by musical grammar. Moreover, the means of getting to the final note is also rather standardised by compositional convention, with arriving at the last note through stepwise ascending or descending movement being the most common means. In composing the concluding motif, Landslaget chose a very straightforward 3-2-1 movement for arriving at the end note. While one cannot say it is totally devoid of creativity, it is nigh-on completely dictated by existing compositional tradition.

In addition to the strict expectations regarding the pitch choices in the concluding motif, several subtler musical structures further limit Landslaget's creative freedom. First, convention dictates a preference for small intervals and a relatively balanced distribution between ascending and descending movement. Given that the three preceding sections of the riff feature an ascending flourish, this steers the concluding passage toward a descending movement. Second, the main motif is heavily rooted in the pentatonic scale, and by repeating it three times, notes 1-33 create a tonal landscape strongly defined by the pentatonic scale. This establishes an expectation that the concluding motif's pitches will also adhere to the pentatonic scale. Taken together, these softer constraints have a significant influence on shaping the pitch choices for the concluding motif.

443. Carig and Laroche 2014, p. 60 and Steel 2015, p. 71 also point out that this is a common feature of most compositions that potentially may lead the legal similarity assessment astray.

6.4.3 How Persuasive Is the Argument Against Considering Landslaget's Riff Original?

To evaluate whether one can persuasively challenge the originality of Landslaget's riff based on the analysis presented in the previous section, let us recap the building blocks from which the riff was constructed by distilling them into three points. First, the riff's main motif consists of two motivic cells: an ascending pentatonic flourish and a turning figure reminiscent of the traditional 'Oxdansen' tune. Second, it follows an AAAB structure reinforced by the repetition of the same rhythm throughout all stages of the phrase. Lastly, the concluding motif is constructed by ending on the tonic harmony on the 1st scale degree, arriving there through a descending 3-2-1 movement and prioritising small intervals in its pitch selection.

Figure 6.9 The Main Motif and Its Repetitions in Landslaget's Riff

To facilitate an explication of the argument's core point, Figure 6.9 illustrates the structure of the violin riff. I have already suggested that the main motif, when examined in isolation, does not contain enough individuality to meet the originality threshold. On similar grounds of brevity and simplicity, it appears equally evident that the concluding motif as such does not meet the originality threshold. Moreover, the three-time repetition of the main motif arguably does not contribute meaningfully to the originality of the riff. Consequently, as both motifs individually fail to meet the originality standard, the riff's claim on originality must depend on the cumulative combination of the two. This means that the riff's originality – and, by extension, the defendants' alleged infringement – necessarily hinges on the concluding motif providing enough added creativity and individuality to the cumulative whole to meet the originality threshold.

On this basis, an argument against the originality of the riff could be built on the idea that notes 1-33 of the riff (the main motif and its repetitions) so strongly dictate the contents of the concluding motif that it fails to add enough creativity to the cumulative whole to make it meet the originality threshold. To wit, even if one considers the cumulative effect of the main motif, the repetition scheme, and the concluding motif, this argument would state that the limiting influence of commonplace compositional structures is strong enough to rule out originality. Yet, can such an argument be considered persuasive? Can one plausibly claim that the creative freedom exercised by Landslaget in composing the concluding motif was so severely restricted by the expectations raised by notes 1-33?

The previous section provided a detailed theoretical analysis of compositional techniques that constrained the range of outcomes. To provide a more practical addition to evaluating the impact of these constraints, I have constructed four mock performances, available in audio samples 4-7,[444] which offer alternative conclusions to the riff that adhere to the expectations set by the first 33 notes of Landslaget's riff. The purpose of these mock performances is to test whether substituting different concluding motifs significantly alters the overall impression of the riff. If the mock performances create a similar overall impression, it suggests that the creative freedom available to Landslaget in crafting the conclusion of their riff was notably constrained by the earlier notes. This, in turn, weakens the claim that the concluding motif contributes sufficient originality to make the entire riff original.

Figure 6.10 Alternative Concluding Motifs Played in Audio Samples 4-7

Comparing the four mock performances to Landslaget's original riff, available in a texturally comparable performance in audio sample 8,[445] the overall impression is very similar. Two different conclusions can be made based on this. On the one hand, one might view the similarity of the overall impressions as demonstrating that all the mock performances constitute instances of the same work, making them reproductions of Landslaget's riff. On the other hand, one could argue that considering the mock performances reproductions of Landslaget's riff requires that they duplicate the *original elements* of it. Here, one can emphasise that the duplication is confined to notes 1-33 of the performance, which is a non-original portion of the riff. Furthermore, while Landslaget's riff may be thought to meet the originality threshold when the concluding motif (notes 34-43) is added, one might contend that it only narrowly satisfies this threshold. As a result, the riff would be afforded only minimal copyright protection, insufficient to withstand the pitch changes introduced in the mock performances. Consequently, these performances could not be regarded as reproductions of Landslaget's riff.

On the whole, an important observation upon listening to the mock performances in audio samples 4-7 is that the overall impression varies so minimally despite the alternative conclusions containing numerous differences compared to Landslaget's riff. Audio sample 6 is particularly interesting in this sense, since it only duplicates Landslaget's concluding motif through the exceedingly commonplace descending 3-2-1 movement at the very end of the riff. This raises the question whether one can reasonably consider these similarities sufficient to make this audio sample a (potentially infringing) reproduction of Landslaget's riff. To my mind, the problem lies in that the duplication carried out through notes 1-33 constitutes such a large portion of the entire riff that it skews the overall impression of similarity in favour of considering it a reproduction. A seeming contradiction emerges: although neither the main motif nor its three-time repetition can be considered original individually, their proportional

444. Samples available at http://hdl.handle.net/10138/596102.
445. Audio sample 8 available at http://hdl.handle.net/10138/596102.

dominance over the riff as a whole (resulting from the AAAB repetition structure) creates a subjective listening experience liable to make the riffs intuitively seem like instances of the same work. In other words, the experience of listening to the riffs appears to yield a different originality assessment than one derived from the theoretical analysis of the riff's component parts made in the previous section.

In any case, I find that the defendants' strongest argument is to assert that even if Landslaget's riff were to be considered original, the protection afforded would be so narrow as to exclude the slightly modified version found in the defendants' song.[446] As expressed in the terminology presented in the previous chapter, the differences in the defendants' riff would fall outside the *implied scope* of Landslaget's riff. Although the Supreme Court's judgment is by no means faulty or ill-advised, I find its weakest aspect to be the grounds on which it deemed the riffs' similarities striking enough to presume copying and effectively reverse the parties' burdens of proof, since the impression of similarity largely arose from the duplication of sequences whose originality was, at best, debatable.

6.4.4 Conclusions about the *Landslaget v. Drängarna* Case

The analysis of the originality and infringement evaluation in the *Landslaget v. Drängarna* case aligns with the dissertation's research task in three respects. First, it has endeavoured to provide a more detailed analysis of how one distinguishes between commonplace musical building blocks and original expression when analysing musical compositions. Second, it has introduced the notion of using mock performances to make a theoretical analysis of the relevant musical passages and the overarching limitations of the composer's creative freedom more apparent. Third, it has endeavoured to demonstrate certain problems inherent in determining the originality and infringement of a musical passage based on the overall impression elicited by listening to the passage. Most notably, the overall impression may primarily be shaped by non-original attributes of the passage, which – at least theoretically – should not influence the outcome of either the originality or infringement analysis.

The relevance of this analysis for the assessment of template compositions lies in the parallels to be found between Landslaget's riff and a template composition. After all, the riff consists of a relatively small number of rather commonplace musical building blocks, much like a template composition. Given these similarities, the value of investigating how the questions of originality and infringement were – or could be – assessed in the context of a traditional music infringement case context is that it can be used as a foundation from which to draw analogies to assessing questions of originality and infringement in template composition, whether these are manual and AI-assisted.

446. Presenting a very similar argument regarding the underlying logic, Gervais and Judge 2009, p. 404 – albeit assessing the originality standard in an American context – have suggested that even 'borderline cases are likely to be found original, but the scope of protection is thin and another work will have to copy it almost exactly to infringe'. The European Copyright Society, in its Opinion on the *Mio* and *konektra* case 2024, p. 19, made a very similar point, also using the analogy of thin versus thick protection.

6.5 CONSTRUCTING MANUAL TEMPLATE COMPOSITIONS

6.5.1 Preliminary Remarks

Building upon the previous analysis, this section will investigate how the questions of originality and infringement can be assessed in the context of manual template compositions. To set up the discussion, it is necessary to clarify the positioning and significance of manual template compositions for the research task. The idea of a template composition is that the creative choices that accomplish the ultimately resulting musical expression is divided between two distinct phases executed by multiple contributors: The first-phase contributors formulate a template that determines the overarching melodic, harmonic, and structural patterns of the composition, whereas the second-phase contributors supply the specific details – filling in the blanks – to turn the template into complete standard composition.

Examining the issue from a copyright law perspective, this will in most cases result in seemingly original musical expression. The next issue is to determine whether the creative process satisfies the requirements of copyright protection, which are that the musical expression must have resulted from the free and creative choices of the contributors, so that it warrants characterisation as an intellectual creation reflecting the authors' personalities. At its core, this is about investigating how the authorial agency required by copyright law is to be applied to template compositions. It will be particularly relevant to assess how authorship is to be allocated between the different contributors. The relationship between template maker and end result will lie at the investigation's core, since it is most relevant for research question (7) and the examination of AI-assisted template compositions to be conducted in Chapter 7. In fact, research question (7) can be reformulated through the following pair of questions using the template terminology:

- Under what conditions is the creation of a musical template – specifying, *inter alia,* melodic shapes, rhythm patterns, chord progressions, and repetition schemes – specific enough to be considered an authored work?
- When the template is rendered into a piece of music by a subsequent contributor filling in the missing musical attributes, how precisely must the instructions contained in the template be reflected in the resulting composition for the template maker(s) to have a copyright claim to the resulting composition? In other words, can the resulting piece of music be considered a protected reproduction of the template maker's work described in the previous bullet point?

To investigate these questions, we shall construct a very simple musical template by taking a few commonplace building blocks, to which we will successively add more specifications. The increasingly complex templates will then be rendered into mock performances, and the questions of copyright protection and authorship allocation between the different creative contributors will be discussed based on a theoretical analysis of the relevant musical attributes and the subjective experience elicited by listening to the mock performances.

6.5.2 Compiling and Analysing a Simple Template Composition

For the first building block of our example template, I find the chord progression at issue in the *Skidmore v. Zeppelin* case to be a good choice. The inherent characteristics of the chord progression impart a natural momentum and a wistful character to the piece. However, creative choices are required to transform the abstracted chord progression into an actual musical narrative. There are small differences between Taurus' and Led Zeppelin's use of the progression, particularly regarding the end of the 4-bar loop, and we will choose the former for our composition due to two distinct advantages. Not only is it compatible with a wider range of melodic input, but the avoidance of the first harmonic degree at the end of each 4-bar section facilitates a smoother transition. We will duplicate the first two bars of the loop from *Taurus* and make a few small adjustments the bars 3 and 4 (*see* Figure 6.11).

Figure 6.11 A Minimum-Input Rendition of the Chord Progression at Issue in the Skidmore v. Zeppelin Case

As shown by audio sample 9, containing the passage in Figure 6.11,[447] this will already constitute a passable sequence of background music as is. However, the addition of even the simplest melodic motif will significantly enhance the artistic effect of the composition. To achieve this, we will incorporate the so-called Theme X discussed in relation to the Blurred Lines case (*see* above), and to indicate the ancestry of the emerging musical template, the project shall be called *Stairway to X 1.0*. Since the combination of the 4-bar loop and Theme X alone will not form a satisfactory musical narrative, we will need to issue further instructions on the development of the theme. There are many common techniques of musical composition that will accomplish this. We will use an 8-bar structure consisting of two iterations of the chord progression, followed by a return to the tonic (bar 9). To enhance the perceived unity and coherence of the melodic material, we shall utilise the same compositional technique as Landslaget and repeat the rhythm of Theme X in each bar.

This technique can make the musical narrative jarringly repetitive, and to avoid this, at least one input parameter needs to contain some variation. Selecting the pitch as the parameter for variation, two alternatives are particularly promising. First, one might alter the melodic pitches in bars 3-4 to establish a two-part structure indicative of a question-answer dynamic. Alternatively, one could vary bars 2 and 4. Both

447. Audio sample 9 available at http://hdl.handle.net/10138/596102.

alternatives allow Theme X to dominate the melodic content without making the music debilitatingly repetitive. In either case, introducing small variations in bars 5-8 will invigorate the musical narrative. An easy option is to slightly modify the pitches of the melody, as virtually any variation in pitch selection will work. This is because the chord progression provides momentum, while the repeated melodic rhythm and the structural similarity between the two halves (bars 1-4 and 5-8, respectively) ensure cohesiveness. On the whole, these instruction sets offer two distinct creative templates likely to yield a reasonably passable piece of music. For ease of identification, we can refer to the instruction sets as Stairway to X, versions 1.1 and 1.2.

Let us render these templates into music and analyse the impressions they produce. Compositions 1-3 follow the template of version 1.1,[448] while Compositions 4-6 follow that of version 1.2.[449] We suppose different people created the template and rendered it into a complete piece. For clarity and brevity, these are referred to as the 'template maker' and 'template fulfiller'. Overall, there are three issues one needs to examine. First, one must determine whether the composition, based on listening to the audio samples, is to be considered original works. Although neither substantial nor complex, each composition probably contains enough musical elements to meet the threshold of originality. Second, if we assume the compositions 'count' as original works, one must allocate authorship between the template maker and fulfiller. An approximately even split between the two may not be unreasonable. However, one interesting question actualised by the compositions' very low level of originality is whether the template maker's and fulfiller's creative contributions meet the originality threshold when viewed in isolation, and whether this should have an impact on the copyright eligibility of the compositions. This issue will be discussed in greater detail below in section 6.6. Third, one might inquire how broad the implied scope of the composition is. In other words, how many changes can the composition withstand before the authors forfeit their copyright claim on it? To assess this, we can examine the composition by constructing and analysing mock performances. As explained in Chapter 1, the idea is to introduce alterations to the compositions and analyse how this impacts the impression of similarity between original and altered versions, which should give insights into the decisive characteristics of the compositions' identities.

Let us explore the *implied scope* of Composition 1 using two mock performances in greater detail, by which we mean whether the composition can withstand alterations without the author losing their claim on the work. The first mock performance, available in audio sample 16, changes two notes, one at the start of bar 4 and another at the start of bar 5.[450] Upon consecutive listening to Composition 1 and its first mock performance, I find that these two changes do not sufficiently alter the overall

448. Performances of Compositions 1-3 are available in audio samples 10-12, available at http://hdl.handle.net/10138/596102, accessed 9 August 2025. Sheet music available in the Appendix, items 1-3.
449. Performances of Compositions 4-6 are contained in audio samples 13-15, available at http://hdl.handle.net/10138/596102, accessed 9 August 2025. Sheet music available in the Appendix, items 4-6.
450. Sheet music of mock performance 1 and 2 is available in Appendix, items 8 and 9.

impression of similarity between the two performances. Accordingly, akin to how the Swedish Supreme Court ruled in the *Landslaget v. Drängarna* case, they should be considered reproductions of the same underlying work. The second mock performance, available in audio sample 17, retains the variations already present in its predecessor and introduces two further changes by altering the first notes in bars 1 and 7. After these changes, enough distance may perhaps have been put between the original composition and the second mock performance for Composition 1's authors to lose their authorship claim to it. This conclusion suggests that the copyright protection afforded to Composition 1 is rather narrow: while it can withstand some variation, altering more than two melodic notes is liable to sever the link to the authors. The composition's low tolerance of variations is due to the generic and unremarkable nature of its melodic choices, as shown by examining the more distinctive Composition 7 and a mock performance thereof, available in audio sample 18.[451] This composition features larger intervals and a prominent use of the melodic minor scale, giving it a more distinct melodic contour, which helps it withstand the five variations contained in the mock performance without forfeiting the authorial link.

The greater the number of mock performances one constructs and observes, the deeper the understanding of a composition's creative essence or implied scope will become. In theory, one could map the perceived internal hierarchy and interaction of all the musical elements contained in the composition by constructing and observing an individual mock performance for each. However, this would probably be an unnecessarily thorough approach to examining the defining features of a composition's – or fragment's – identity. In most cases, a reasonably low number of mock performances can give a measure of a composition's distinctiveness or the internal hierarchy of its melodic, rhythmic, or harmonic attributes.

Overall, the construction and analysis of *Stairway to X versions 1.1 and 1.2* have illustrated the core aspects of what is meant by manual template compositions and what legal issues they may actualise. However, the problem with these template compositions lies in their lack of substance and distinctiveness, which makes the template maker's claim to the end result vulnerable even to small additions or alterations made by subsequent contributors. In turn, this makes them less relevant for an analogy to AI-assisted template compositions, where the authorship claims of the template maker – that is, the pre-generation contributors – must necessarily rely on a very high number of creative choices, since the template maker's input needs to withstand the often considerable additions made by the AI system. In other words, the assumption is that adding a high number of broadly formulated instructions to the template might give it sufficient robustness to 'shine through' the additions or alterations made by subsequent contributors without forfeiting the authorship claim. To acquire insights more relevant for this type of situation, it is necessary to construct an expanded version of the Stairway to X template.

451. Available at http://hdl.handle.net/10138/596102, accessed 9 August 2025. Sheet music available in Appendix, item 10.

6.5.3 Compiling a Complex Template Composition

6.5.3.1 Instruction Set for Stairway to X 2.0

This section presents an expanded version of the Stairway to X template composition, referred to as Stairway to X 2.0. The new version significantly increases the number of instructions, extending the template from 9 bars to 41. These instructions define the overall structure and direction of the composition, while leaving many specific details open for interpretation by subsequent contributors. This approach relies heavily on familiar compositional techniques and stylistic tropes, and the template has been designed to yield a musically coherent and aesthetically pleasing result regardless of how the blanks are filled. The analysis of this section occasionally adopts a technical tone, particularly in its treatment of how specific techniques are employed and what their effects are. Its purpose is to deepen the broader discussion about how to distinguish original expression from commonplace ideas in compositions that depend heavily on the latter. Readers with some familiarity with music theory may find this section more accessible, though a detailed understanding of the compositional techniques discussed is not essential to following the overarching argument regarding musical templates and their copyright eligibility.

The first template (Stairway to X 1.0) contained two alternative options for developing Theme X, but the instructions for Stairway to X version 2.0 will only use the first alternative. The familiar chord progression will continue as the backbone of the accompaniment and harmony. The melodic content of the initial 8-bar section will be constructed through the following three steps. First, Theme X is presented in bar 1 and repeated verbatim in bar 2. While the starting pitch of Theme X can be chosen freely, the rules of harmonic compatibility narrow the range of artistically viable options. The most likely starting pitches are C and E, due to their easy harmonic compatibility with the accompaniment, but more adventurous options are possible.[452] Second, bars 3 and 4 are to duplicate the rhythm of Theme X but need to introduce new choices of pitch lest the narrative become jarringly repetitive. This melodic 'slot' is rather flexible, allowing for a wide range of choices, provided the standard expectations raised by the chord progression, 8-bar structure, and the previous two bars are met. In practice, these expectations amount to using the diatonic scale and small intervals coupled with a relatively even distribution between ascending and descending movement. Third, the contents of bars 1-4 are to be repeated through bars 5-8. To give the musical narrative more momentum, some minor changes or variations can be introduced. Yet, to preserve coherence, neither the rhythm nor the first three pitches of bars 5 and 6 are to be changed.

When expanding the dimensions of the composition beyond the modest 8-bar scope of the first version, new motivic material needs to be added. Two types of structure-based compositional techniques will be useful for this purpose. First, we aim for an overarching ABA form for the entirety of the piece, as this is a straightforward

452. For instance, Composition X4 starts with D, which yields a surprisingly fresh result. *See* below.

way of producing a satisfying musical whole. The A-section will be dominated by Theme X and a repetition of its rhythm. The B-section will need to provide a sufficient contrast to enliven the narrative, but at the same time, it must also contain some motivic references to the A-section. This is because the intended 41-bar structure is unlikely to withstand the strain caused by an entirely unrelated middle section without losing its narrative coherence. (One can of course not rule out the possibility of producing an artistically sound 32-bar ABA structure by using totally different material between the contrasting sections, but this will require a higher level of skill and understanding in the choice of surface-level compositional input, which is likely to reduce the qualitative uniformity of the resulting compositions.) To achieve a smooth ABA structure with a high likelihood of accommodating surface-level variations while maintaining musical quality, we will modulate to the parallel key for the B-section and return to the tonic key for the recapitulation of the A-section.

Second, the A-section needs to be expanded beyond its current 8-bar scope to make the composition more substantial. The current 8-bar structure consists of two virtually identical 4-bar units, which allow for expansion through further repetition. Employing a compositional technique not unlike that used by Landslaget in composing their violin riff, the initial 4-bar unit can be expanded into a 16-bar structure through an AABA repetition scheme. This involves keeping the initial eight bars as is, adding four bars of new material, and concluding the A-section with a slightly altered restatement of the initial 4-bar unit. The new 4-bar unit to be inserted in bars 9-12 needs to strike a balance between two factors. Too little variation risks coming off as repetitive or monotonous. However, too much variation will not only disrupt the flow of the musical narrative but will also lessen the artistic impact of the transition to the B-section. Thus, bars 9-12 need to be only slightly different from the preceding eight bars so that the B-section can bring a noticeably greater contrast.

There are several parameters of compositional input available to accomplish this. One can vary the pitch, rhythm, accompaniment or register of the melodic notes, the interplay of which presents a virtually endless number of options. Given that the surrounding repetitions of the initial 4-bar unit use the Taurus chord progression, the option most likely to maximise the artistic room for error is to use the same progression. As a result, the 4-bar chord loop is used throughout bars 1-16. To provide contrast, both the pitch and rhythm of the melodic material should be varied. Theme X is busy and rhythmic in character, so the 'sweeping' or expansive effect suggested by longer note values, larger intervals and one-direction melodic movement is likely to provide the contrast needed. To steer subsequent contributors towards the desired contrast, bars 9-12 are to use the melodic rhythm displayed below (Figure 6.12) over the familiar chord progression. Preferably, the melodic shape of bars 9-10 and bars 11-12 respectively are to resemble each other for maximal likelihood of artistic viability, but other options can certainly be found by musically proficient (human) assistants. Bars 13-16 have a two-part task. In addition to repeating the initial material to conclude the A-section, they also need to make the transition into the B-section. The least invasive option is to repeat the first 3 bars verbatim and use the remaining bar 16 to modulate from A minor to C major. The obvious choice is to use a II-V-I chord progression to accomplish this. Thus, to complete A-section, bar 16 will feature D minor and G major chords combined with compatible pitches in the melody.

Figure 6.12 The Melodic Rhythm for Bars 9-12 Prescribed in Pursuit of a 'Sweeping' Musical Expression

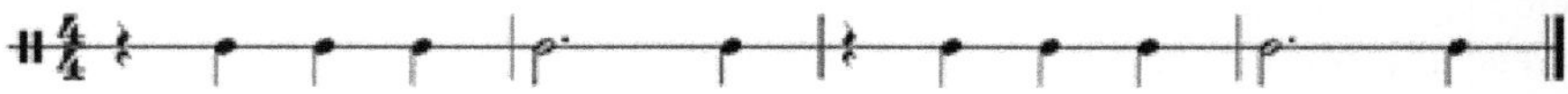

To construct the B-section, its overall structure must first be selected. A 16-bar structure consisting of 4-bar units is a convenient option. To avoid duplicating all structural features of the A-section, we shall use an ABAB repetition scheme for the B-section's 4-bar units. Following this, the 4-bar units need to be filled with melodic input. As noted above, the B-section needs to combine contrasting and novel input tempered with some familiar elements. One option is to introduce entirely new melodic material. This approach is not particularly well-suited for our purposes, as it is more labour-intensive and is likely to lessen the uniformity among different completions.

Another option is to recycle melodic material from the A-section to construct the B-section as well. Several factors make this a better option for this template. The modulation into a new key will provide an automatic contrast without bothering to create new material, as the familiar motifs will acquire a different effect when presented in a major key. At the same time, the use of similar – or even identical – melodic shapes is likely to enhance the coherence of the musical narrative. Just as in the A-section, the momentum of the narrative can be enhanced by introducing small melodic variations during the second half of the B-section. That is, bars 25-32 do not have to duplicate bars 17-24 verbatim, but it is allowed or even advisable to change the odd note here and there. The accompaniment will require some changes because the Taurus progression is less effective in the major keys. Moreover, a change in the heretofore static harmonic rhythm – locked at two beats for each chord – will provide some welcome variation. On these grounds, we will decelerate the harmonic rhythm to one chord change each bar. A particularly 'safe bet' is to build the harmony out of a diatonically descending bass line, as this gives the narrative a natural momentum. To balance the novelty of this material, the chord tones will be chosen to mimic the voice leading of the A-section's accompaniment. This 8-bar passage can be repeated verbatim to produce the needed 16-bar accompaniment.

The concluding section of the composition, a recapitulation of the initial A-section, is in many ways the easiest section to create. Usually, the preceding music produces numerous expectations regarding the concluding section's contents, meaning that one has little more to do than to meet the expectations through a sequence of rather simple creative choices. Of course, there is the option of ending the piece with a mechanical repeat of the initial A-section. However, this is not beneficial for our composition, as the similarity of the melodic material throughout bars 1-32 would cause a verbatim repetition of the entire A-section to produce a repetitive and rather tedious effect. A better idea is to repeat the A-section in a truncated and slightly modified form. Rather than a 16-bar structure, we will use a pair of 4-bar units, followed by a final bar bringing the piece to a close.

Certain universal narration techniques help narrow down the choice of compositional input for the recapitulation section (bars 33-41). First, the modulation from major to minor suggests a turn towards wistfulness or melancholy. Second, the intensity of the narrative tends to slow down towards the end, as if preparing the audience for the piece's impending conclusion. Both requirements - or expectations - are satisfied by reducing the degree of melodic activity. Presenting only fragments of the relevant melodic material will accomplish this. The impression of an impending conclusion can be enhanced by using fragments of motifs from various parts of the composition in a heretofore unprecedented order, which may suggest remembrance or reflection to the listener. Slower and more intermittent movement in the accompaniment will also enhance the effect pursued.

6.5.3.2 Analysing the Completions of the Template

Having compiled an instruction set for a substantial composition in the previous section, this section examines how the questions of originality and authorship allocation are assessed when the instruction set is rendered into musical expression by subsequent contributors. Compositions X1-X5, available in audio samples 19-23, provide five alternative renditions of the instructions described in the previous section.[453] The first composition contains my own rendition of the instructions. In the latter four, the instructions were rendered by acquaintances of mine who kindly volunteered to participate. To produce the compositions, the guidelines of the previous section were condensed into a two-page collection of instructions expressed in bullet point form and a music sheet into which the chord progression-based accompaniment had been pre-filled.[454] These two documents were sent to the template fulfillers, who produced compositions X2-X5 by supplying the missing melodic specifics.

From a copyright law perspective, Composition X1 is by far the least interesting. Its creative process shows no meaningful differences from any traditional creative process. Essentially, it constitutes a piano piece composed by me and will be treated accordingly under copyright law. By contrast, Compositions X2-X5 present a more complex scenario. Without doubt, each 41-bar and two-minute piece contains sufficient compositional input to meet the originality threshold. A more interesting question will therefore be on the allocation of authorship between the maker and fulfiller of the template.

Let us first examine the template maker's copyright claim to Compositions X2-X5.[455] To be considered a (co-)author of the compositions, the musical attributes contained in them need to result from the template maker's free and creative choices. To decide this question, one needs to compare the melodic, rhythmic, and harmonic

453. Audio samples available at http://hdl.handle.net/10138/596102. Sheet music of the same compositions is available in the Appendix, items 11-15.
454. *See* Appendix, items 16 and 17.
455. *See* Appendix, items 12-15.

attributes of the compositions to the template to determine whether they are similar enough to be considered instances of the same work. Couched in the terminology presented in Chapter 5, which we shall use in the examination below, one must compare the following two *data collections* to decide whether they are sufficiently similar: the *prospective reproduction* (Compositions X2-X5) to the *source material* (the template).

In making this comparison, only the duplication of original attributes found in the source material can contribute towards the template maker's authorship claim. In examining the potentially original elements of the source material, four separate features can be distinguished. First, the accompaniment contained in the lower staff of the music sheet. In bars 1-15 and 33-40, this is based on the Taurus chord progression, and in bars 16-32 on an equally commonplace progression based on a descending bass line. The extreme reliance on commonplace tropes means that the originality of this accompaniment, when viewed in isolation, is very low. Nonetheless, it might be enough to yield a very narrow copyright protection, meaning that a verbatim or near-verbatim duplication of the accompaniment through bars 1-41 could well be within the template maker's exclusive right. Second, the melodic rhythm, largely derived from the Blurred Lines song's Theme X. To my mind, this relies on commonplace elements to a degree that rules out originality and protection when examined individually, even if the entirety of the melodic rhythm through bars 1-41 were to be duplicated. Third, the instructions about pitch selection that steer the surface-level melodic development, such as the specifications contained in sections 3 and 5 of the two-page textual instruction set.[456] Lastly, the instructions that more broadly shape the repetition schemes and overall structure of the composition. When considering the cumulative effect of all these four categories of creative input, it is clear that the template not only easily meets the originality threshold but also that it should be able to withstand a reasonably substantial number of changes without the template maker forfeiting his authorship claim on the altered rendition.

The template fulfiller's claims to authorship lie in having selected the specific pitches to be included in the composition. Despite being considerably limited both by the pre-determined accompaniment and the many instructions mentioned in the previous paragraph, the creative contributions of the template fulfillers should have no trouble meeting the originality threshold and give them a co-authorship claim to the compositions. What remains to be decided is the authorship stakes allotted to each contributor. The template maker exercised a stronger overall influence on the composition, whereas the template fulfillers provided the most distinctive portions of the composition's expression. Accordingly, a 50-50 split of authorship does not appear altogether unreasonable. In Compositions X2-X5, the assessment of authorship allocation is made easier by the fact that the contributions of both co-authors could be identified based on direct similarities between the creative choices and the end result.

However, the assessment becomes considerably more challenging if part or all of the creative choices based on which the authorship is made are only indirectly

456. *See* Appendix, item 16.

perceivable in the compositions. The difficulty with assessing indirect similarities is that it inevitably tends to necessitate a more subjective examination of the composition's musical attributes. For example, if a subsequent contributor abides by the template maker's instructions only partially, authorship allocation becomes more challenging, as one needs to assess the hierarchical importance of the alterations. As noted above, the defining characteristics of a composition's identity tend to lie in a subtle interaction between several musical elements, and the hierarchical weight of a given sequence of notes does not necessarily have a linear relationship to the statistical proportion of a composition it represents.

As shown above by examining Composition 7, where the use of large intervals and less schematic choices of pitch yielded a much more distinctive end result with the same number of creative choices, the same number of pitch choices can have a very different impact on the distinctiveness of a given passage, which, in turn, should notably influence the passage's degree of originality. The distinctiveness of a given choice will depend on the interaction of several compositional elements and the musical context in which it plays out. Here, context is understood both in a micro sense, referring to the interplay between melodic shapes, rhythmic patterns, and harmonic functions, as well as in a macro sense focused on the broader stylistic contentions relevant for the musical passage at issue. On the whole, this points towards one of the dissertation's central claims: the degree to which a sequence of choices influences the distinctiveness - and originality - of a passage should not be determined by a purely theoretical analysis, but one where a theoretical analysis is complemented by an examination of the subjective experiences elicited by the passage.

For these reasons, an accurate assessment of each contributors' authorship claim can become particularly challenging in multi-contributor situations, where the composition is gradually shaped by several contributors independently of each other. The following section will delve into the multi-contributor scenario in greater detail.

6.5.3.3 *The Role of Contextual and Evolutionary Influence in Multi-contributor Compositions*

To get a more precise understanding of authorship allocation in multi-contributor situations, we will take Composition X2 under closer inspection, and examine a number of hypothetical situations where subsequent contributors make additional alterations to it independently of either the initial template maker or the fulfiller. Overall, Composition X2 distinguishes itself from the other completions by the wide melodic leaps inserted by the template fulfiller into bars 9, 11, 17, 19, and other analogous places.[457] We suppose a new composition, Composition X6, available in audio sample 24, whose process of creation went as follows:[458] A performer - we will call him the 'first improviser' - obtained the music sheet for Composition X2, intending

457. A performance of Composition X2 is available in audio sample 20, with sheet music in the Appendix, item 12.
458. A performance of Composition X6 is available in audio sample 24. A colour-coded music sheet is also included. Both are available at http://hdl.handle.net/10138/596102.

to record a performance of it. However, once recording started, his artistic acumen inspired him to improvise during certain parts of the performance. Most prominently, he filled in the wide melodic leaps characteristic of Composition X2 with connecting passagework. Compared to Composition X2, the resulting composition X6 contains differences in pitch and rhythm in bars 9-12, 14-15, 17-20 and 25-28. As is immediately obvious upon listening to the two compositions, the improviser's additions are not of a particularly drastic character, and the core characteristics of the composition remain thoroughly recognisable. Essentially, the improviser has added small embellishments to the pre-existing melodic contour without notably changing the overall impression of the piece.

Although there is nothing particularly remarkable about this sequence of events, it complicates the authorship allocation compared to Composition X2. To investigate the respective authorship claims to composition X6 by template maker, template fulfiller, and improviser, a colour-coded music sheet of Composition X6 will be helpful.[459] It shows the template maker's contributions in red, the template fulfiller's in blue, and the improviser's in green. Before proceeding to assess the respective contributions, two points need to be highlighted. First, the insufficiency of relying too schematically on examining the statistical proportions of literally duplicated notes. For instance, while the colour-coded music sheet shows many red note heads attributable to the template maker, particularly on the lower staff, these do not contribute much to the originality of the composition, since the lower-staff content – whether red or green – is exceedingly reliant on commonplace tropes. Second, in a scenario where multiple contributors add to the underlying composition one after another, one must take into account that the creative freedom of the later contributors is significantly reduced by the structural, harmonic, and contextual attributes already present in the underlying composition, since these may greatly reduce the range of actually viable options available to downstream contributors.

How are the template maker's and fulfiller's claims, then, impacted by the improviser's additions, and are the upstream contributors' creative choices sufficiently reflected in Composition X6 to give them an authorship claim to it? Let us examine the template maker's claims first. As is apparent from the colour-coded music sheet, the melodic features attributable to the template maker are either too fragmentary or too reliant on commonplace figurations to be deemed original. The directly perceivable features of Composition X6 that reflect the template maker's creative choices can be crystallised into four separate features:

- The Taurus chord progression is combined with Theme X to produce a piano piece, with the chord progression placed in the left hand and the melody derived from Theme X in the right.
- The chord progression is repeated four times through bars 1-16, with Theme X initially presented in the melody and making small variations to the melodic

459. The colour-coded music sheet of Composition X6 is available at http://hdl.handle.net/10138/596102.

pitches. The rhythm of Theme X is frequently repeated throughout the composition to enhance melodic coherence.
- The B-section begins with a modulation to the relative major key, featuring harmony based on a diatonically descending bass line with chord changes at each bar line. Its melodic content is derived from the A-section.
- The ABA structure is completed by inserting a condensed nine-bar recapitulation section, built from fragmentary allusions to the beginning, with increasing use of rests or longer note values to prepare the piece's conclusion.

Clearly, none of the four points, when examined individually, contains enough specificity to avoid characterisation as a commonplace idea rather than original expression. Accordingly, they would not be protected if examined in isolation. However, the cumulative combination of all four points may just hold enough specificity to meet the originality threshold, although a reasonably plausible argument against finding the four-point sequence original could certainly be made. In addition to the directly perceivable reflections of the template maker's choices, one must also take into account the contextual and evolutionary influence his choices wielded over both the template fulfiller's and the improviser's creative choices. To get a comprehensive understanding of this in the context of Composition X6, it is necessary to proceed to examine the template fulfiller's claims to said composition.

The core difficulty regarding the template fulfiller's copyright claim becomes immediately clear upon looking at the colour-coded music sheet: the small proportion of blue notes – those directly attributable to the template fulfiller's creative choices – is not only very small, but they appear in small fragments containing rather commonplace figuration. Accordingly, one might consider the template fulfiller's authorship claim weak to non-existent. However, the contextual and evolutionary impact of the template fulfiller's choices may change this situation. This becomes apparent when comparing the template fulfiller's contributions in bars 9-12 to those supplied by the first improviser. (The same also applies to bars 17-20 and 25-28, but bars 9-12 will be used as an illustrative example.)

The similar contours of the template fulfiller's and improviser's melodic input are clearly apparent, and since we know that the improviser supplied his melodic input by improvising on Composition X2, it is evident that the improviser's melodic contribution should not be seen as an independent creation but rather as an embellishment of the melodic content of Composition X2. An evolutionary relationship between the respective creative contributions to these bars becomes evident, where the input of upstream contributors influenced the end result by shaping the range of creative choices available to downstream contributors. The template maker first provided the accompaniment and prescribed a sweeping melodic movement. The template fulfiller then expanded upon this by formulating a melodic curve characterised by wide leaps, whose contents were greatly influenced by the melodic rhythm prescribed by the template maker. The pre-determined accompaniment and the stylistic and structural context provided by the piece as a whole further narrowed the range of viable pitches available to the template fulfiller. Finally, the improviser embellished the template fulfiller's input by filling in the melodic curve with compatible notes, as shown in Figure 6.13.

Figure 6.13 The Template Fulfiller's Input Is Circled to Illustrate the Evolutionary Relationship Between the Respective Melodic Inputs of the Template Fulfiller and the Improviser

Based on this iterative form of collaboration, how should one allocate authorship to the passage in bars 9-12 among the three contributors? Of course, the outlook should be to allocate authorship stakes based on the degree to which each co-creator contributed to – or caused – the original expression contained in the passage. While this may be a relatively straightforward assessment in most cases, the factual circumstances of the relevant passage's genesis complicate the evaluation. The chief problem is that only examining who selected the notes contained in the music sheet without also inquiring into the circumstances that led to or influenced their selection can produce intuitively unjustified outcomes. To avoid this, one must strike an appropriate balance between two different approaches.

On the one hand, one might focus on determining who directly caused the musical expression contained in bars 9-12. This approach is likely to give the improviser a strong claim, as he supplied all the melodic content, which arguably constitutes the central characteristics of the passage's identity. By comparison, the upstream contributors' claims might appear weak or even non-existent. The template maker's contribution, confined to the lower-staff accompaniment, is much too reliant on commonplace chord progressions and standard figurations to influence authorship allocation. Awarding the template maker a co-authorship stake in bars 9-12 would not be much different from claiming Bob Marely should have a co-authorship stake in Elton John's 'Can You Feel The Love Tonight' due to this song utilising the same I-V-VI-IV chord progression that also appears in 'No Woman, No Cry.' The template fulfiller's claim is even weaker, as the passage does not contain a single note attributable to him. Under this approach, the improviser would likely be deemed the sole author of bars 9-12.

On the other hand, one might seek to take into account the context and circumstances in which the improviser made his creative contribution. This approach seeks to acknowledge the evolutionary relationship between the template maker's, template fulfiller's, and improviser's respective contributions. From this perspective, attributing all the original expression in bars 9-12 to the improviser seems unjustified, as his creative choices were significantly shaped by the contextual framework established by the template maker and fulfiller. Consequently, this alternative view suggests that both upstream contributors should receive some portion of the authorship, even though the improviser's share would probably remain the largest.

This same dichotomy – between prioritising literal contributions versus contextual or evolutionary influences – extends to the entire composition. From a practical standpoint, one must recognise that overemphasising the analysis of factual circumstances and creative context could lead to evidentiary difficulties. Nevertheless, as far as it is practically feasible, contextual or evolutionary influences should arguably be considered when assessing authorship in multi-contributor creations. Moreover, evidentiary challenges may not always be insurmountable. For example, the present case of Composition X6 presents no issues with evidence, and similar processes in multi-contributor AI system development are also unlikely to pose significant difficulties in investigating the factual and contextual circumstances of creative contributions.[460]

In conclusion, allocating authorship among the three contributors based on an overall assessment that balances the two approaches described above, I find that a 40-30-30 split of authorship with the template maker receiving the largest share could be an equitable solution.

6.5.3.4 Authorship Allocation in a Multi-Contributor Scenario

To put further strain on the link between upstream contributors and end result, let us suppose a second improviser hears Composition X6 and makes her own version of it. We shall call this improvisation Composition X7, available in audio sample 25.[461] The most notable feature of Composition X7 is that its use of shorter note values gives it a more hectic character. As is evident upon listening to the piece, the similarities between the 'hectic' Composition X7 and its predecessors among all compositional elements – melody, harmony, structure, style, mood, etc. – are considerable. Yet, it is equally apparent that the direct duplication between Composition X7 and its predecessors has been drastically reduced. Some direct duplication nonetheless remains. As indicated by a colour-coded version of the music sheet,[462] the harmonic structure of bars 1-20, 25-28, and 33-41 corresponds to the template maker's initial instruction, marked in red notes. In addition, as indicated by the green notes, the melodic patterns of bars 17-20 and 25-27 duplicate the first improviser's additions. This pattern also appears in bars 9-11 of Composition X7. The notes provided by the second improviser are in black.

How should one assess the upstream contributors' claims to Composition X7 and the authorship allocation between all contributors? As already noted above, the template maker's authorship claim mostly relied on the combination of the harmonic structure and the overall design of the melodic rhythm and repetition schemes. In Composition X7, the second improviser's additions alter the melodic content of the composition, which considerably reduces the link between the template maker's instructions and Composition X7. While the composition mostly adheres to the harmonic structure of the initial template, the second improviser uses different chords

460. In AI development processes, interim versions are likely to be stored in the system's change log or version control system, enabling the retracing of the creative process.
461. Audio sample available at http://hdl.handle.net/10138/596102.
462. Colour-coded music sheet available at http://hdl.handle.net/10138/596102.

in bars 21-24 and 29-32, which noticeably break up the harmonic flow designed by the template maker. Due to these changes, I find that the link between the initial instruction set and Composition X7 has become too vague to sustain the template maker's authorship claim to it.

The green notes, indicating first improviser's melodic patterns, while quantitatively less remarkable than the template maker's red notes, carry a greater authorial weight. These melodic patterns raise two interesting questions related to copyright protection and authorship allocation. The first question is rather straightforward: are the patterns distinct enough to be considered original, whereby they would make the reproduction and communication of Composition X7 dependent on consent from the authors of Composition X6? On the one hand, one might highlight the shortness of the duplicated passages and their heavy reliance on commonplace melodic patterns, which might point towards the relevant passages being non-protected ideas rather than protected original expression; *see* Figure 6.14. However, as discussed regarding the *Landslaget v. Drängarna* case, simplicity, a short duration, and reliance on commonplace tropes do not necessarily rule out originality. To my mind, the relevant passage is very close to the juncture point between ideas and expression. Yet I find that its combination of two slightly different melodic arcs might just meet the originality threshold by the thinnest of margins. Moreover, since the passage is duplicated verbatim between Compositions X6 and X7, the authors of said passage would acquire a co-authorship stake in Composition X7.

Figure 6.14 The Melodic Passage Duplicated Between Compositions X6 and X7

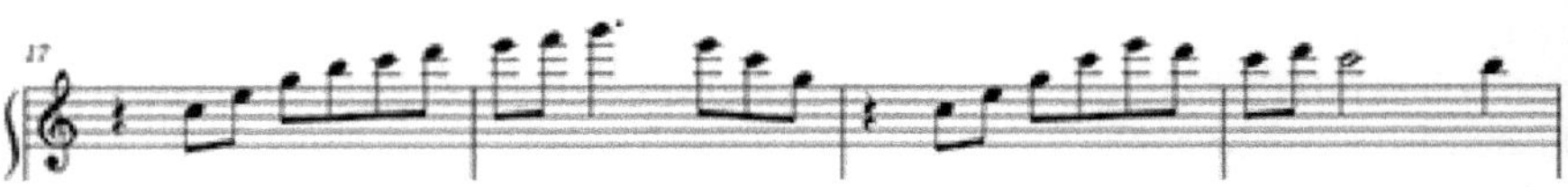

This leads to the second question: who are the authors of the passage exhibited in Figure 6.14? A straightforward alternative would be to attribute it solely to the first improviser, given that he introduced the passage when creating Composition X6. Thereby, Composition X7 would be a musical work co-authored by the first and second improviser, with the latter holding a substantially higher authorship stake. This is largely how things would pan out on a standard view. However, to perform a sufficiently nuanced analysis, one should also consider the creative process and how the creative choices of upstream contributors influenced the precise formulation of Composition X7's contents by either limiting the range of available creative choices or having an evolutionary impact on the relevant melodic and other patterns. As noted above, when the first improviser was transforming Composition X2 into Composition X6, the stylistic, micro- and macrostructural, and harmonic context provided by the underlying Composition X2 notably limited the range of viable options. Furthermore, there is arguably an evolutionary resemblance between bars 17-20 in Composition X6 and the corresponding passage in Composition X2, as illustrated by Figure 6.14 above. Should these factors impact the allocation of (co-)authorship?

Let us suppose it should. What are the options? One alternative is to suggest that the evolutionary influence exerted by the template fulfiller's melodic choices and the contextual attributes of the template maker's initial instruction set both give a 25% stake in the relevant passage (bars 17-20, displayed in Figure 6.14 above). Thus, authorship of this passage would be divided 50-25-25 among the first improviser, template maker and template fulfiller. Next, one needs to determine how large the co-authorship stake of Composition X7 should be based on the passage at hand. A 16% stake might perhaps be deemed justifiable. Consequently, the co-authorship of Composition X7 would be divided so that the second improviser holds 84%, the first improviser 8%, and the template maker and fulfiller 4% each.

This could perhaps be deemed an equitable solution to the question of authorship allocation, but it raises some questions. One might challenge the notion of the template fulfiller receiving a 4% stake through the evolutionary influence it exerted on bars 17-20, as this would constitute an unusually tenuous and indirect ground for granting authorship. From a broader perspective, the template maker's and fulfiller's respective claims to Composition X7 also highlight a potential challenge that is particularly likely to arise in multi-contributor scenarios: the notion that one co-creator's contribution could be small enough that, while clearly both noticeable and instrumental in shaping the musical expression of the end result, it is not substantial enough to provide an authorship claim.

One might illustrate this issue by imagining an alternative creative process for the hectic Composition X7. We suppose the underlying Composition X6 was subjected to a dozen further alterations, each by a different contributor independently of each other. We also suppose each alteration was small enough not to individually meet the originality threshold. The resulting alternative version of Composition X7 – which we shall call Composition X8 – has the following peculiarity: while it satisfies all the prerequisites of copyright protection both regarding the creative process and end result, the creative contributions of its 15 co-creators have been spread out so evenly over the entire composition that none of the individual contributions meet the originality threshold.

How should one, then, handle authorship allocation in this scenario? On the one hand, one might consider all 15 contributors co-authors of Composition X8 since each had a non-negligible contribution to the end result. The equitable division of the co-author stakes in proportion to the size and relative importance of each contribution can be challenging for several reasons, such as the potentially non-linear relationship between the quantity and quality of the different contributions when assessing their impact on the end result. After all, the artistic or authorial significance of changing a few notes can vary considerably depending on whether they, for instance, alter the arc of a pivotal melodic turn or introduce a few trivial changes to an accompaniment pattern. Moreover, the evolutionary influence of upstream contributions can influence the end result without being directly perceivable in it, further complicating the analysis. The high number and relative insubstantiality of each individual contribution also make it more difficult to place them in hierarchical order based on their contributions to the originality and identity of the composition. Consequently, the most practical – though probably not the most accurate – solution would be to divide co-authorship into 15 stakes of equal size among the contributors.

However, there is an alternative way of addressing the issue. Since the creative contributions that led to Composition X8's coming into existence were spread so thinly among its 15 co-creators as to render none of them individually original, one might argue that the composition lacks an author and therefore fails to qualify for copyright protection. A potential solution is to view the composition as a *joint work* under Section 6 of the Finnish Copyright Act. Applying the regulation on joint works to this type of multi-collaborator situation is not entirely straightforward, however, which warrants some elaboration.

6.6 TEMPLATE COMPOSITIONS AND MULTI-CONTRIBUTOR CREATIVE PROCESSES

6.6.1 The Concept of Joint Authorship

The concept of a joint work, which has not been harmonised within the EU, refers to the unification of several contributions into an integrated whole, where the co-creator's individual contributions have merged beyond the point of being distinguishable from each other. Section 6 of the Finnish Copyright Act states that if 'two or more persons have jointly created a work without their contributions constituting independent works, copyright shall belong to them jointly'. While this wording appears to apply seamlessly to AI-generated compositions and their creation processes, certain issues merit closer examination.

First, the statutory text does not clearly specify the criteria for determining whether a person involved in the creative process can be considered a joint author. Nor does the legislative history offer much clarity. The relevant preparatory document notes that joint authorship belongs to those who have 'assisted in the creation of the work', without further defining what this entails.[463] Legal literature generally assumes that a person must contribute by making creative decisions, meaning that mere technical assistance does not qualify an individual as a joint author. However, the extent of the creative contribution required for joint authorship is unclear.

A particularly strict interpretation is given by the Finnish Copyright Council's opinion 2003:15, concerning an arranger's copyright claims to a musical composition, where the Council held that a person can only be considered a joint author if her creative contribution exceeds the originality threshold.[464] Similarly, the Danish textbook on intellectual property law notes that protection should only be granted if an individual's contribution independently meets the originality requirement.[465] In the

463. Komiteamietintö 1953:5, p. 51.
464. TN 2003:15, p. 11.
465. Schovsbo et al. 2024, p. 119.

Finnish literature, Mattila has recently addressed this issue. He presents a different view, arguing that if the collaboration involves making free and creative choices in pursuit of a creative purpose, there is no reason to rule out the copyright eligibility of such an undertaking merely because the individual contributions may not necessarily meet the originality threshold.[466] In my view, this interpretation is better aligned both with the wording of the statute and with the principle that only technical or otherwise non-creative contributions should be excluded from joint authorship. The Swedish textbook does not directly weigh in on whether the individual contributions need to meet the originality threshold, but could be seen as leaning in this direction, since it emphasises the requirement of making artistic decisions as a condition for joint authorship.[467]

Second, it is unclear whether the 'joint creation' mentioned in the statutory text should be assessed by examining the creative process itself – that is, the collaboration and interaction between the co-creators – or the resulting creation. If section 6 of the FCA were to be understood as requiring not only seamless integration of individual contributions into a unified whole but also active collaboration and interaction among the participants during the creative process, it could lead to a conclusion where the result of a template-based multi-contributor compositional process such as Composition X8 will not be considered a joint work.

On the whole, the arguments supporting protection, even when individual contributions do not meet the originality threshold and the collaborators did not actively interact during the creative process, appear more intuitively justifiable. This holds true as long as the end result is original and each collaborator provided input through free and creative choices that reflect their respective personalities. However, an interpretation that completely does away with both the requirements that co-authorship is tied to the originality of each individual contribution and the requirement of active interaction between the collaborators will lead to equally peculiar outcomes.

If taken to its logical extreme, it suggests that a 200-word text, to which 200 different contributors have supplied one word each, could have as many credited authors, provided the creative process was 'of authorial nature' as opposed to mere technical assistance. Clearly, this interpretation would significantly impact the chance of obtaining copyright protection for AI-assisted compositions. The main drawback of this approach to joint authorship is the practical difficulty of managing copyrights shared by a potentially very large number of contributors. Determining a reasonable middle ground between the strict and lenient interpretations is far from straightforward. Central to this challenge is defining the collaborative nature of the creative process and distinguishing individual contributions in a way that avoids arbitrary distinctions. As the following section will demonstrate, finding an intuitively justifiable way to differentiate between co-authorship and acts like independent arrangements or alterations can be difficult.

466. Mattila 2022, p. 249.
467. Levin 2023, p. 132.

6.6.2 Could Composition X8 Be Deemed a Joint Work?

To examine whether multi-collaborator projects could be considered joint works, we shall look more closely at Composition X8. As previously noted, the composition was created by 15 different contributors, none of whose contributions meet the originality threshold. The crucial question is whether Composition X7 and the 200-author 200-word text are disqualified from being considered joint works due to the lack of individually original contributions.

This issue becomes particularly significant when viewed through the lens of its potential application to AI-generated compositions. The root of the problem seems to lie in technological advancements unlocking new forms of collaboration that either were not foreseen or were previously irrelevant to the legal framework. On the one hand, one might consider it intuitively unjustifiable to deny protection to both Composition X8 and the 200-author text due to the lack of an author, thereby consigning them to the public domain. As illustrated by the example of Composition X8, it would mean that an initially copyright-protected composition – namely, the underlying Composition X6 – would forfeit its copyright eligibility due to the alterations of the subsequent contributors. Not only is this a rather incongruous outcome, but it also seems at odds with copyright law's rationale of fostering creative efforts. After all, why should successive refinements to a composition result in the loss of copyright eligibility, to the detriment of all those who contributed to its creation? This apparent oversight likely reflects the legal system's limited exposure to such scenarios, as these anomalies have remained obscure enough not to cause any practical problems: While the examples of Composition X8 and the 200-author text could theoretically occur, they are unlikely to do so in real life.

By contrast, the prospect of using AI-powered tools to create artistically and commercially viable compositions through multi-collaborator efforts presents a far more pressing and realistic reason to address this issue with greater specificity. In my view, the most effective approach is to assess the alignment between authorial intent, externalisation, and the end result to strike the right balance between overly strict and overly lenient approaches to joint works. Although one could technically argue that most AI-generated compositions qualify as joint works under section 6 FCA, the lack of a sufficiently substantial or plausible connection between author and work remains a significant obstacle. Even if it were theoretically possible to grant co-authorship based on contributions that individually fall below the originality threshold, it would still be necessary to establish a minimum standard of personality reflection that such contributions must exhibit. To my mind, this would require a de minimis standard for the degree of alignment between the author's intent, the act of externalisation, and the resulting work.

As suggested when discussing the concept of *originality causation* in Chapter 5, this amounts to a requirement that the prospective co-author would need to sufficiently foresee the impact his creative choices will have on the end result at the moment of decision-making. We shall explore how this could apply to AI-assisted creative processes in Chapter 7.

6.7 SUMMARY AND CONCLUDING REMARKS

The main focus of this chapter has been to bring greater clarity to the distinction between original expression and commonplace ideas in the context of musical compositions. The underlying purpose is to determine when a series of broadly formulated instructions can meet the originality threshold, as this is a crucial factor in assessing whether AI-generated compositions can receive copyright protection.

To establish a foundation for this analysis, the chapter began by defining the concept of music and exploring the central elements of compositional input, such as pitch, rhythm, harmony, and form. It then examined how the distinction between ideas and expression is made in music copyright cases. This was referred to as the calibration of the originality threshold, wherein a balance needs to be struck between two conflicting interests: On the one hand, the originality threshold must be low enough for copyright law to properly serve its incentivising function. On the other hand, setting it too low risks removing common musical building blocks from the public domain, which would run counter to the law's purpose. To illustrate the challenges of performing this calibration, two highly publicised US cases – *Williams v. Gaye* and *Gray v. Perry* – were examined. It was argued that both verdicts set the bar too low in determining the degree of compositional creativity required to meet the originality threshold.[468]

This led to posing the question of how a successful calibration of the originality threshold is to be achieved. The consultation of expert reports was pointed out as likely to be a core component of performing a successful calibration. Two areas in particular were noted where expert input could significantly aid the process. First, by offering a structured understanding of how compositions are constructed, including the systematisation of common scales, chords, rhythmic patterns, phrase structures, and chord progressions used across different genres and styles. Second, by helping to assess the extent to which pre-existing compositional techniques and established structures of musical grammar influence or constrain the relevant compositional choices. In addition to these, to provide further insight into the distinction between commonplace musical ideas and original expression, a more experimental approach was suggested: constructing and analysing mock performances, where the contents of the relevant compositions are altered.

A related point that significantly influences how successfully the originality threshold is calibrated is the assessment of a composition's *implied scope*. This follows from the fact that minor discrepancies between two data collections – such as the two compositions relevant to a given copyright infringement case – will not displace the fact that they constitute instances of the same work. The chapter argued that the implied scope needs to be determined individually for each composition rather than through a schematic one-size-fits-all method, since each composition tends to utilise the relevant musical elements in a slightly different way. For instance, the core components of one

468. The latter, of course, was later overturned on appeal, *see* above.

composition's identity may lie in its melodic contents, while another's may primarily rely on rhythmic or harmonic characteristics.

To gain a more precise understanding of how the originality threshold is calibrated and how the implied scope is assessed, the Swedish Supreme Court case *Landslaget v. Drängarna* was examined. By breaking down and analysing the contested riffs, it was argued that the court's finding of infringement, while perfectly reasonable and supported by a broad consensus, ultimately relied on an overall impression of similarity largely derived from repeating the riff's non-original main motif. Overall, the examination of *Landslaget v. Drängarna* demonstrated how the process of distinguishing between commonplace musical building blocks and original expression, as well as determining a composition's implied scope, can be applied. In addition, due to the contested riffs' heavy reliance on commonplace compositional techniques, analysing the case also offers a useful analogy between traditional and AI-generated compositions.

Taking this analogy further, the chapter proceeded to construct two template compositions, Stairway to X first and second versions, for which several different completions were provided. The purpose of this was to examine under what conditions the creation of a musical template – indicating, *inter alia*, melodic shapes, rhythm patterns, chord progressions, and repetition schemes – can be deemed specific enough to constitute an authored work. The first version of Stairway to X, based on the chord progression from *Taurus* and a melodic fragment from *Blurred Lines*, was short and simple. To get more useful insights, the proportions of the template were expanded to produce a considerably more intricate second version. This instruction set was given several alternative completions, resulting in Compositions X1-X5. One of the completions, Composition X2, was subjected to further redaction, producing Compositions X6 and X7. This gave an opportunity to address finer details related to originality and authorship allocation in a multi-contributor creative process, which, in turn, potentially can hold significant relevance in assessing the creative processes of AI-generated compositions.

The outlook of authorship allocation in multi-contributor compositions is that the authorship stakes – either to the entire composition or a fragment thereof – are divided based on the degree to which each co-creator contributed to the composition's directly perceivable original expression. To illustrate this issue, bars 9-12, 17-20, and 25-28 of Composition X6 were examined in detail. In these passages, all the original expression arguably resides in the melodic content, as the harmonic accompaniment is commonplace enough not to contain any originality at all. Accordingly, since the first improviser had provided all the melodic content of said passages, one might reasonably consider him to be the only contributor with an authorship claim to them. However, this would not be justifiable considering the great degree to which his selection of melodic notes was influenced by the upstream contributors' – i.e., the template maker and fulfiller – contributions. In reality, the original expression of bars 9-12, 17-20, and 25-28 was obtained by the first improviser embellishing the underlying composition. Given that the template maker's and fulfiller's contributions greatly impacted which melodic notes the first improviser chose to insert into the relevant passages, this should influence how authorship is allocated between the three parties. Consequently, the template maker's and fulfiller's contributions were deemed to have exercised an *evolutionary and contextual influence* over the end result, which can give an authorship stake even if no directly perceivable reflections of the template maker's and fulfiller's creative choices are present in the melodic contents (the original expression) of the relevant passages.

To examine the notion of evolutionary and contextual influence in greater detail, the example of Composition X7 was introduced. Here, a second improviser made further additions to Composition X6, significantly increasing the distance between the template maker's and fulfiller's creative choices and the end result. Two different solutions for authorship allocation were discussed. On the one hand, one might consider the template maker and fulfiller to have forfeited their (co-)authorship claims, whereby Composition X7 would be considered co-authored by the first and second improvisers. On the other hand, one could adopt a generous attitude towards the contextual and evolutionary influence, giving both the template maker and fulfiller minor co-authorship stakes.

To gain deeper insight into the issue of authorship allocation, another example, Composition X8, was introduced. Its musical contents are identical to those of Composition X7, but the creative contributions involved in its creation are distributed among a much larger number of co-creators. Therefore, while Composition X8 satisfies all the prerequisites of copyright protection, both regarding the creative process and end result, the creative contributions of its 15 co-creators have been spread so evenly across the entire composition that none of the individual contributions meet the originality threshold.

More broadly, this example raises the question of whether co-authorship always requires the contribution to meet the originality threshold, or whether a smaller contribution can justify a co-authorship stake when considered a part of the originality of the work as a whole. Historically, this has not been a particularly pressing issue, as instances where large numbers of creative contributions each fall below the originality threshold have been relatively rare. However, this issue has gained greater relevance with the advent of highly capable generative AI systems, where the creative choices required to produce an AI-generated composition may often be divided among a large number of prospective co-authors. It was concluded that co-authorship theoretically could be granted to creative contributions falling below the originality threshold, but that there would still need to be some kind of minimum standard of personality reflection that such contributions must exhibit.

CHAPTER 7

AI-Assisted Template Compositions

7.1 THE CONTEXT, PREMISE, AND STRUCTURE OF THE CHAPTER

7.1.1 Bringing Together the Findings and Argumentation of the Preceding Chapters

The purpose of this chapter is to synthesise the strands of argumentation presented throughout the dissertation. It does so by examining whether an AI-assisted template composition could be granted copyright protection and how authorship would be allocated in that situation. To start the analysis, it is appropriate to clarify how the findings and arguments of the previous chapters are brought together to benefit the examination of copyright claims to AI-generated compositions.

As has been pointed out above, the seeming originality of the end result will not suffice to grant protection. Only if the creative process satisfies the criteria placed on it can protection be awarded. The idea pursued throughout this chapter is to examine whether the pre-generation creative choices needed to bring an AI-generated composition into existence and explore various arguments about whether these creative choices could meet the relevant criteria.

Looking at the pre-generation choices, there are two – occasionally overlapping – features that need to be considered. First, one needs to assess to what degree the choices are dictated by technical concerns, since this would make them unable to contribute towards the originality of the end result. This is a very valid concern in the case of AI development, since many of the creative choices involved in AI model development are of a predominantly technical nature. Second, there needs to be sufficient alignment between the authorial goal, its external realisation, and the end result, which was referred to as the degree of *originality causation*.

In Chapter 5, the originality causation requirement was described as meaning that a prospective author needs to foresee the musical attributes of the end result with sufficient precision at the moment of decision-making. For example, a user – such as

User A discussed in Chapter 1 – issuing prompts may well make many creative choices that significantly contribute to shaping the musical attributes of the compositions generated by an AI model. However, the user's creative contribution may fall short of satisfying the originality causation requirement if, at the time of issuing the prompts, he cannot foresee with sufficient precision how his creative choices will affect the musical attributes of the AI-generated end result.

On this basis, one might arrange the different compositional processes discussed throughout the dissertation into three tiers according to the degree of creative control exercised by the prospective author. The highest tier can be illustrated by a traditional creative process where the authorial conception is externalised by writing a music sheet, such as Chopin's writing of a detailed music sheet to externalise his Prelude in E minor.[469] When selecting which notes to insert into the sheet, Chopin could accurately foresee the musical attributes that would be conveyed by a performance of them. Therefore, there is a high degree of authorial causation between his choices and the musical expression contained in the performance. The middle tier of originality causation is represented by a manual template composition, such as the Stairway to X templates discussed in the previous chapter. Due to the broad formulation of the instructions, the template maker of Stairway to X 2.0 could not foresee the precise melodic attributes of Composition X2, let alone those of Composition X6. Instead, he only exercised vague control over them through the selection of the Theme X motif, repetition schemes, rhythmic patterns, and harmonic structure. While these choices did not determine the musical attributes of Compositions X2 or X6 with the same precision as Chopin exercised over a performance of his Prelude, the number of instructions – creative choices – made by the template maker was substantial enough to give him a co-authorship claim to the composition. In other words, the lack of precision characterising the instructions and their relationship to the end result was sufficiently offset by the quantity of choices contained in the instructions.

At the lowest tier of originality causation are the AI-generated compositions, since the pre-generation contributors – such as the aforementioned AI model developer in charge of training data selection – generally have considerably less creative control over the end result. After all, and returning to the illustrative example used in Chapter 1, it would be a rather bold claim to think that the developer of Model A at the moment of selecting training data could foresee the musical attributes of Composition A with the same precision as the template maker could predict the contents of Composition X2 when compiling the instructions for Stairway to X 2.0. However, even if the pre-generation creative choices that brought Composition A into existence have a significantly lower originality causation than Composition X2, one might still argue that the same logic as applied in granting the template maker copyright protection remains viable: Could not the sheer number of pre-generation choices collectively offset the low degree of originality causation characterising the relationship between each individual choice and the end result?

469. The division into tiers implies a value judgment. It is to be noted that the value judgment only concerns the degree of creative control, but does not weigh in on the worthwhileness or merit of the compositions representing each tier.

At least in theory, this argument can be deemed reasonably sound. If the creative process contains a very high number of pre-generation 'free and creative choices' whose express purpose is to shape the contents of the AI model's output,[470] one might consider the situation largely analogous to the template makers in Stairway to X and Composition X2. The problem, however, lies in the potential minimum threshold of originality causation suggested in the previous chapters. This stems from the intuitive implausibility of seeing a sufficient authorial link between many of the pre-generation creative contributions and the end result: While the selection of training datasets or the fine-tuning measures may constitute creative choices that contributed to shaping the musical attributes of the end result, the distance between the creative contributions and the end result is to be considered too great to form the basis of a copyright claim. The research task of this chapter is to investigate the various types of pre-generation creative choices, explaining their nature and the degree to which they influence the resulting AI-generated compositions. The core questions the chapter seeks to address can therefore be summarised as follows: how greatly did the choice contribute to shaping the musical attributes of the end result, and how precisely could the prospective author foresee the end result's musical attributes at the time of decision-making?

7.1.2 The Focus on Comparing Data Collections and the Implied Scope of a Composition

To assess originality causation - and whether the relationship between the creative choices and end result is close enough - we need a benchmark that evaluates all compositional processes on the same footing, regardless of the technical tools used to produce them. An overarching theme of this dissertation has therefore been to view all compositional processes as acts of issuing instructions describing a given sequence of musical attributes. By this token, it is intuitive to look at the copyright assessment as amounting to a comparison between two data collections: the musical attributes conveyed by the relevant audio file or musical performance, and the instruction set issued by the prospective author. In this comparison, the audio file functions as the prospective reproduction, whereas the instruction set is the evidentiary means by which the question of protection can be determined, as it provides a way of tying the attributes conveyed by the musical performance to the author's creative choices. Essentially, the comparison centres on determining whether there is sufficient similarity between these two data collections to make the musical performance into a reproduction of the underlying work. If the duplicated musical attributes - such as pitch, rhythm, harmony, and form - meet the originality threshold, the audio file will be protected.

Two challenges concerning this comparison stand out, both related to determining the *implied scope* of the underlying composition. First, insubstantial alterations to a composition do not necessarily displace the overall impression of similarity. This, of

470. The choices are free and creative in the sense of not being dictated by technical considerations or other constraints.

course, overlaps with the broader principle that one cannot circumvent copyright protection by making trivial alterations to a composition and thereby avoid infringing on the original work. Second, and more challengingly, a schematic one-size-fits-all method for assessing the amount of duplication between two data collections is liable to yield unintuitive outcomes in certain cases. The problem is that the interaction and hierarchy between different musical elements may vary considerably among compositions: One composition's most individual attributes may lie in the pitch selection, while another primarily focuses on harmonic and rhythmic patterns. Two different means of accounting for this have been suggested. One might dissect the relevant passages to better grasp which elements contribute to the impression of similarity between the data collections and whether these are to be characterised as original expression or commonplace ideas. In addition, one can complement the findings of the dissection-based analysis by examining the subjective impressions elicited by listening to the relevant passages.

Throughout the dissertation, it has been argued that the utilisation of a combined method of both dissection-based analysis and subjective experiences is particularly likely to be required in cases where the similarities between the data collections – prospective reproduction and source material – are predominantly indirect. This is particularly relevant in the context of AI-assisted creative processes, since the similarities between pre-generation creative choices and post-generation end result are typically – if not exclusively – indirect.

7.1.3 Structure

The chapter is divided into three parts as follows. To set the stage for the discussion, section 7.2 will present and discuss currently available case law on copyright protection of AI-generated outputs. Sections 7.3-7.5 then examine the technical aspects of the interaction between the human contributor and the AI model. This aims to set up a more precise discussion about how the concepts of work and reproduction should be approached in a generative AI context. Here, as well as in other parts of the chapter, the creative process of producing the MusicRL system will be used as an illustrative example. As noted in section 2.3.3, MusicRL is a music generation model developed by Google. The choice of MusicRL as an illustrative example is due to the relative complexity of its architecture and its detailed coverage in research publications, which makes it a suitable example for examining the stages during which human input could potentially be incorporated into the model's outputs.[471] It must be emphasised that the frequent references to MusicRL are made for practical purposes only, and do not imply that it is considered the most prominent or significant representative of state-of-the-art music generation. To provide more concrete insight into the potential situations in which pre-generation creative choices could justify authorship claims over post-generation outputs, the development process of a hypothetical music generation model

471. That is, training data selection, model architecture design, fine-tuning, iterative refinement, and prompting.

- ExtraRL - will be explored. Having examined both existing and hypothetical creative processes through sections 7.3-7.5, section 7.6 builds upon the preceding analysis to investigate whether - and under what circumstances - the requirement of originality causation could be fulfilled by pre-generation contributions.

At this stage, it is also appropriate to reiterate that the question of copyright eligibility will be approached from a *de lege lata* perspective, focusing on how existing legal frameworks apply to AI-generated compositions.

7.2 CURRENT CASE LAW ON COPYRIGHT AND AI-GENERATED CONTENT

7.2.1 The US Copyright Office's Approach

In laying down the groundwork for the discussion, an examination of court rulings on AI-generated content offers useful insights, even if these rulings do not represent jurisdictions relevant for EU copyright law or judicial tiers typically considered instrumental in shaping the law's normative contents. Current case law predominantly features outputs from text-to-image generators, as these were among the first generative AI models to see widespread use for content creation. Two cases decided by the US Copyright Office (USCO) warrant mention not only due to their notoriety but also because they were argued at relative length. The first one, Zarya of the Dawn,[472] concerned a comic book, whose illustrations had been created by prompting the generative text-to-image system Midjourney. The text as well as the selection and arrangement of images and text were deemed protectable, but the interesting parts of the case concerned the individual images. To address this question, the USCO first observed that Midjourney allows the user to issue text prompts, to which it responds by producing four alternative images. It is emphasised that Midjourney 'does not interpret prompts as specific instructions to create a particular expressive result ... [since it] does not understand grammar, sentence structure, or words like humans'. Instead, it converts the textual expression into tokens that 'can be compared to its training data and then used to generate an image'.[473]

In assessing whether the claimant Katarina Kashtanova had sufficiently influenced the images to warrant copyright protection, the USCO notes the iterative trial-and-error nature of the creative process, wherein she issued 'hundreds or thousands of descriptive prompts' until the 'hundreds of iterations [created] as perfect a rendition of her vision as possible'.[474] At first sight, this might seem largely analogous to most traditional processes of creating visual art with the help of various tools, but the USCO points out that 'Midjourney generates images *in an unpredictable way*.'[475] Therefore, users of the system are not authors in the sense required for copyright

472. U.S. Copyright Office, Re: Zarya of the Dawn (Registration # VAu001480196), 21 February 2023.
473. Zarya of the Dawn, p. 7.
474. Zarya of the Dawn, p. 8.
475. Zarya of the Dawn, p. 9. Italics added.

protection. For argumentative support, the USCO cited the US Supreme Court case in Burrow-Giles, which establishes the author as the one who 'actually formed the picture' and who thereby has acted as 'the inventive or master mind'. A user of Midjourney will not fulfil these requirements because the textual prompts may only influence the generated images, but do not directly dictate a specific result. Accordingly, users of the system lack sufficient control over the end result, as the prompts 'function *closer to suggestions than orders*, similar to the situation of a client who hires an artist to create an image with general directions as to its contents'.[476] Overall, transcribing the reasoning of the USCO to the terminology used in this dissertation, the crucial weakness of Kashtanova's claim lay in the lack of creative control and originality causation characterising the relationship between her creative choices – the prompts – and the end result. While the effort expended by Kashtanova was readily acknowledged, her endeavours were categorised as non-authorial skill and labour rather than free and creative choices capable of conferring originality on the end result. (In this dissertation, I refer to the latter as *authoring* for brevity.)

The second USCO case warranting mention is that concerning Jason Allen's attempt to register the image *Théâtre D'opéra Spatial* as a copyright-protected work. The case acquired additional notoriety because Allen entered the image into the 2022 Colorado State Fair's annual fine art competition, in which it received first prize. The subsequent revelation of the extent of the AI system's involvement in the creative process sparked controversy among commentators. The whole affair, of course, highlighted deeper-lying notions related to what it means to author a work in the era of high-performance generative AI systems. Like Kashtanova, Allen used the Midjourney system to create the image, and the core issues determining the possibility of registering it as a work were largely the same as in the previous *Zarya* case.

Allen's creative process consisted of three stages: generating the image using Midjourney, making manual adjustments to it using Adobe Photoshop, and upscaling the image using Gigapixel AI. In total, Allen claimed to have spent over 80 hours on the creative process. The process consisted phases such as 'brainstorming how to phrase the written prompt and tweaking it to adjust artistic elements such as lighting and colo[u]r harmony', making approximately 900 drafts of the image, and revising the text prompts 'at least 624 times'.[477] Nonetheless, citing the earlier *Zarya of the Dawn* case, the USCO argued that these endeavours do not give him an authorship claim to the generated image. The issue of creative control is again at the centre of the USCO's reasoning, as it emphasised the unpredictability plaguing the relationship between prompts and generated outputs. Since his 'sole contribution to the Midjourney Image was inputting the text prompt that produced it', Allen did not exercise sufficient 'creative control of the claimed elements of the work'.[478]

Several further points need to be emphasised, not least the USCO's position on the claimant's burden of proof. The USCO noted that the adjustments made in Adobe Photoshop could be copyright-eligible on their own, but the Board had not received

476. Zarya of the Dawn, pp. 9-10. Italics added.
477. Khulman 2023; Théâtre D'opéra Spatial, p. 2.
478. Théâtre D'opéra Spatial, pp. 4-7.

'sufficient information to make that determination'. In effect, the Board appears to think Allen had not presented sufficiently compelling evidence that the visual attributes – or 'claimed elements' – of the image had resulted from his creative efforts. This strikes me as a rather strict take on the prospective author's burden of proof. First, it does not seem unreasonable to suggest that the mere manual editing performed by Allen could suffice to meet the originality threshold, especially considering the notable differences between the 'raw' and edited versions of the image.[479] Furthermore, the multi-stage cumulation of creative endeavours must be considered. Allen's creative efforts combine the formulation of the authorial goal, its execution by, *inter alia*, adjusting the prompt 624 times, and the post-generation editing of the image through a creative process that spanned over 80 hours. Now, even if a considerable portion of the creative endeavours probably are to be categorised as primarily non-authorial in nature (skill and labour, dictated by technical constraints, etc.) and Allen's creative control over the generation of images was far from absolute, it does not appear implausible that the cumulative effect of the creative choices made throughout the process could be sufficient to meet the originality threshold concerning the 'claimed elements' of the image, especially considering that the threshold is generally considered to be low.

Based on these arguments, one might well challenge whether the USCO's ruling applies the criteria for copyright protection in a uniform manner, or whether the technical tools utilised by Allen have not led the USCO to an unduly strict take on the issue.[480] In his complaint, Allen had also argued that a failure to recognise creative endeavours like his will leave a 'void of ownership troubling to creators'.[481] The USCO rejected this suggestion by reiterating their categorisation of the image as produced by a non-human agent. To my mind, Allen's concern is far from unfounded, especially if the line of argumentation applied by the USCO were to persist over the long term. Given the USCO's emphasis on not having received 'sufficient information' to grant protection to the claimed elements, one might ask whether Allen's claim would have been significantly impacted had he given a more detailed explication of the creative choices associated with manually adjusting the image. Allen has filed an appeal at the District Court of Colorado, where he continues to pursue the argument. In the appeal, he also supplies further details on his creative process.[482] It remains to be seen how the court rules on the issue.

Further clarity on the USCO's position on the issue of protecting creations containing AI-generated portions was given in its January 2025 report of the register of

479. The two images are available side by side in Théâtre D'opéra Spatial, p. 6.
480. A similar point is made by Hugenholtz 2024, p. 18, who notes that 'works of art [such as those at issue in Zarya of the Dawn and Théâtre D'opéra Spatial] are the result of a complex creative interplay between creator and machine, involving hundreds of iterative prompts, countless drafts and redrafts, and extensive redaction. They are the product of human creativity at all stages of the creative process, and should in my opinion be treated no differently than works of photography or traditional visual art'.
481. Théâtre D'opéra Spatial, p. 7.
482. *Allen v. Perlmutter*, 1:24-cv-02665, (D. Colorado), filed 26 September 2024.

copyrights.[483] A clear emphasis was put on the distinction between ideas and expression and the degree of control the author exercises over the work's expressive elements. Prompts alone were not deemed to provide sufficient human control over the end result, since they largely function as instructions conveying non-protected ideas: 'While highly detailed prompts could contain the user's desired expressive elements, at present they do not control how the AI system processes them in generating the output.'[484] The USCO proceeds to state that:

> There may come a time when prompts can sufficiently control expressive elements in AI-generated outputs to reflect human authorship. If further advances in technology provide users with increased control over those expressive elements, a different conclusion may be called for.[485]

However, if the human contributor selects, coordinates, and arranges the AI-generated material in a creative way, the requirements for copyright protection can be met. Here, the USCO references its Zarya of the Dawn decision (*see* above), in which it noted that 'the placement and arrangement of the images and text on each of the Work's pages' contained sufficient creativity to meet the requisites for protection.[486] Lastly, the USCO also pointed out that many AI systems offer tools allowing users to 'select, edit, and adapt AI-generated content in an iterative fashion', which might increase the user's control of the expressive elements of the end result.[487] Whether this type of creative process can yield authorship to the end result 'will depend on a case-by-case determination'.[488]

7.2.2 A Contrasting Chinese Perspective

A contrasting approach to the sufficiency of issuing text prompts is provided by two Chinese cases involving AI-generated images: the Beijing Internet Court (BIC) case *Li v. Liu*, and the Changshu People's Court's so-called *Half-Heart* case.[489] The facts of the *Li v. Liu* case were largely similar to the USCO cases in that the copyright claim rested on the input provided by Li through elaborate prompting of a generative system, this time Stable Diffusion, whose functionality is very similar to Midjourney. The underlying copyright regulation contains requirements of 'intellectual achievement', 'originality', and 'expression', which, in practice, amount to a largely similar set of criteria to

483. USCO 2025, Copyright and Artificial Intelligence, Part 2: Copyrightability, Issue No. 1060 – 29 January 2025.
484. USCO 2025, p. 18.
485. USCO 2025, p. 21.
486. USCO 2025, p. 25, citing Zarya of the Dawn, p. 5.
487. USCO 2025, p. 26.
488. USCO 2025, p. 27.
489. A brief analysis of 'Half-Heart' case is available here: https://www.chinaiplawupdate.com/2025/03/chinese-court-again-rules-there-is-copyright-in-ai-generated-images/, accessed 14 June 2025.

those applied in the US or EU.[490] This makes the BIC's drastically different argumentation and ruling more indicative of a different approach to the broader principles and policy rationale. The BIC noted that in issuing the prompts, Li made many creative choices, choosing attributes such as 'ultra photorealistic' and 'colour photo' for art type, 'Japan idol' for subject, detailed character descriptions like 'in locations', 'golden hour', and 'dynamic lighting' for environment, 'cool pose' and 'viewing at camera' for character presentation, and 'film texture' and 'film simulation' for style. Furthermore, after reviewing the initial image, Li adjusted some prompt words and modified the parameters until he obtained the desired outcome.[491] In contrast to Allen's process behind Théâtre D'opéra Spatial, Li did not make post-generation manual adjustments to the image.

Based on the pre-generation creative choices, the BIC considered Li to have met the requirements of originality and intellectual achievement. In its argumentation, the court also reflected on whether the creative process was mechanical in the sense that if the creative input is 'based on a certain order, formula, or structure, different people will get the same result'. As changes to the inputs were demonstrated to produce different outcomes during the court proceedings, the BIC was satisfied that the creative process was not mechanical, thereby pointing towards originality and protection. In granting Li's copyright claim, the BIC also emphasised that the 'core purpose of the copyright system is to encourage creation'. This warrants an interpretative approach favourable to encouraging more people to use the latest tools, as this will allow creativity to prosper in accordance with the underlying policy rationale.[492]

The Changshu People's Court's 'Half-Heart' case was similarly positive in its approach to authorship of AI-generated content. The case featured a copyright claim to an image depicting a half-heart floating on water, with its reflection forming a complete heart. The image was created using Midjourney and further refined in Photoshop.[493] The court held that AI-generated works can qualify for copyright protection if they reflect the creator's original intellectual input, particularly through strategic prompt design, iterative refinement, and post-processing. It found in favour of the plaintiff, ruling that the image met the threshold of originality and had been used without authorisation by the defendant.[494]

490. He 2024, p. 301 notes that it is higher than a 'sweat of the brow' standard and akin to the US Feist standard. Moreover, Lu 2021, pp. 15-16 points out that 'Chinese judicial practice also generally incorporates the criterion of 'a reflection of personality' into the concept of originality'. Similarly, although addressing the concept of originality on a general level without any relation to the BIC case, Gervais 2024, p. 1101 notes that the 'notion of originality is, in fact, a worldwide standard, even though it is not explicitly spelled out in international treaties'.
491. https://english.bjinternetcourt.gov.cn/pdf/BeijingInternetCourtCivilJudgment112792023.pdf, accessed 18 January 2025.
492. https://english.bjinternetcourt.gov.cn/pdf/BeijingInternetCourtCivilJudgment112792023.pdf, accessed 13 May 2024.
493. Chatterton et al. 2025.
494. Chatterton et al. 2025; Wininger 2025.

7.2.3 Concluding Thoughts on the Current Case Law on AI-Generated Outputs

Overall, the USCO and Chinese courts made analogous points in their analysis of the largely similar factual circumstances. The opposing outcomes are ultimately due to the different attitudes to the predictability of the end result and the specificity or genericity of the human creative input that accomplishes it. While the USCO's approach can be deemed on the stricter side, the Li v. Liu judgment appears rather liberal. Where one settles on the spectrum between a strict or liberal approach will be a matter of adjudicative taste, and the accumulation of case law is likely to clarify different jurisdictions' attitudes to where the line between sufficient creative control over the end result is to be drawn.

Several scholars have weighed in on this issue. The perhaps most liberal view is proffered by Lee, who takes the benchmark for sufficient creative control from the US Supreme Court *Feist* case. He describes a creative process where he prompts Midjourney to generate a 'photograph of tall giraffe standing behind one man in his thirties with red hair and a beard, wearing a black suit and sunglasses sitting all alone on a bench in Central Park', whereupon Midjourney generated four different images corresponding to the description. Lee argues that this selection of elements is sufficient to justify copyright protection, noting that the level of creativity is 'at least equivalent to taking a point-and-shoot photograph of a stranger sitting on a bench in Central Park'.[495]

Even while accounting for the jurisdictional differences, this is a rather generous take on applying the copyright requisites in the context of interacting with an AI. A more moderate approach is suggested by Leistner and Jussen. They note that a sufficiently complex series of prompts could warrant copyright protection, if the prompts successively refine the output through an iterative process to gradually correspond to the personal ideas of the AI system user.[496] More broadly, they identify the problem of protection AI-generated outputs as closely related to the idea/expression dichotomy. In an argument similar to the specificity-generality distinction discussed in section 1.5.2, they state that 'the idea/expression dichotomy in fact amounts to a *gliding scale* of increasing individualization of one or more initial ideas, the process of which, at a certain degree of individualization, tips into a sufficiently concrete expression'.[497] They identify the question of where exactly to draw the line as a policy decision, where factors beyond the incentives-costs ratio should be weighed in, such as practical burdens and inefficiencies resulting from how the barrier for protection is set.[498]

Hugenholtz also takes a reasonably positive view towards the possibility of protecting AI-generated creations. He notes that AI system users can influence the

495. Lee 2024, p. 1535.
496. Leistner and Jussen 2025, p. 14.
497. Leistner and Jussen 2025, p. 15. Italics in original.
498. Leistner and Jussen 2025, p. 17.

outputs both through pre-generation choices – such as prompts – and post-generation redaction. While conceding that many of the expressive features contained in the end result may be machine-generated and thus non-protected, he notes the possibility for iterative interaction with and refinement of the creation. Through such a process, the distance between prompts and end result may gradually disappear, allowing the user to 'arrive at a result that it will call his or her own'.[499] Hugenholtz mentions Allen's *Théâtre d'Opéra Spatial* as an example where the interaction between creator and machine meets the necessary criteria. Since it was shaped by human creativity 'at all stages of the creative process ... [it] should be treated no differently than works of photography or traditional visual art'.[500]

The notion of holding the AI-generated and traditional creative processes to the same standard warrants some further reflection on how to measure the requisite degree of creative control in light of the USCO's decision in the *Théâtre d'Opéra Spatial* case. In rejecting Allen's claim to the image, the USCO emphasised the unpredictability of the generative process, likening the user prompts to suggestions rather than orders, akin to commissioning a visual artist to create an image. I am not convinced that this is the most accurate analogy to make in the context of iteratively prompting an AI system. Granted, if someone commissions a visual artist to produce an image of a theatre stage located in space and leaves all creative-expressive details to the artist, then the artist is the only agent with a plausible authorship claim. (This would be analogous to issuing only one prompt and letting the AI model do the rest.) However, if the commissioner were to look over the shoulder of the artist throughout an 80-hour creative process and make 624 specifications as to the desired attributes along the way, then it does not appear as clear-cut that the creative conception of the commissioner is insufficiently reflected in the end result. In fact, it would seem rather unintuitive to think that no part of the painting's expression reflects the creative contribution of the commissioner.

To summarise the discussion on current case law and the notion of 'authorship through prompting', I find it difficult to dispute the arguments for the *possibility* of obtaining an original result through an elaborate series of iterative prompting targeting specific features of the output for further refinement. Accordingly, the USCO's denial of copyright protection to Allen's Théâtre D'opéra Spatial strikes me as unreasonably strict, especially given the high numbers of creative choices required of Allen and their iterative refinement of the end result. Nonetheless, the bar for granting protection in such cases should certainly not be set too low.

In finding the proper balance between the two extremes, I deem the alignment between authorial intent, external realisation, and end result to be helpful for crystallising the core issues. If the AI system user is not sufficiently engaged in the process of externally realising the underlying authorial goal, as is likely to be the case if the prompting session does not contain at least some instances of iterative refinement of

499. Hugenholtz 2025, p. 130. Hugenholtz uses the terms conception, execution, and redaction to describe the different phases of creating an AI-generated work.
500. Hugenholtz 2024, p. 18.

the output, it does not seem plausible that his original expression would become reflected in the end result. Moreover, I find it unintuitive to characterise an image or text resulting from one or two prompts – even if these were to be complex, such as Lee's request of a man and a giraffe at Central Park – as an intellectual creation reflecting the AI user's personality. Accordingly, the likelihood of gaining sufficient creative control grows considerably with each iterative refinement. In many ways, such iterative refinements have a similar effect on the likelihood of obtaining protection as the stringing together of words in traditional textual expression: a sequence of a few words is not particularly likely to be original, but the more words are added to the sequence, the more likely the text is to be an original work.

Yet, even if one concedes the possibility of creating original works through mere prompting – or through a combination of prompting with post-generation redaction – this is much more likely to be realised with AI-generated text and images than with music. The key reason for this is the high level of prompt adherence exhibited by text and image models. Although the user cannot predict the outputs with certainty, the system's ability to respond to complex and detailed commands in the context of continuous iterative refinement should provide the user with sufficient creative control over the end result.[501]

By contrast, AI-generated music tends to exhibit a considerably lower degree of prompt adherence. Admittedly, systems such as AIVA, Suno, or Udio allow users the option to issue prompts either as freely formulated text or through standardised tags or controls. They also permit the type of iterative refinement previously identified as crucial for achieving a sufficient level of creative control over the final output. However, the much lower precision with which AI music outputs adhere to user instructions makes it substantially more difficult to achieve a sufficiently close connection between prompts and end result. As noted in section 2.1.4, music generation models only tend to respond to prompts on the level of genre, style, instrumentation or other similarly broad tags. This limitation is unlikely to grant the user the requisite degree of creative control, even where a considerable amount of iterative refinement is involved. Consequently, while it appears somewhat unlikely that one might issue 624 prompts to a human painter or a high-performance text-to-image model and not get an authorship claim to at least *some* part of the end result, the failure to meet the originality threshold appears significantly more plausible in the context of prompting music generation models.

Due to the limited possibility of controlling the outputs through prompts, the present chapter's analysis of the creative process in the context of AI-generated music will instead examine the pre-generation creative choices as a whole – i.e., not only prompting – with particular emphasis on the process of developing the model, since this could potentially afford human contributors greater possibilities of influencing the outputs.

501. Leistner and Jussen 2025, p. 15 aptly note that such a process may trigger an 'ownership intuition' in the users, if they 'subjectively feel that they in some way personally influenced the result of the AI's process'.

7.2.4 The Question of Evidence: Proving That a Creation Was Authored

Before concluding the discussion on authorship through prompting in the context of current case law, the question of evidence needs to be addressed briefly. This issue concerns the fact that a claimant who has utilised generative AI to create a work may – and often will – need to present evidence that the work was *authored*.[502] Addressing the evidentiary dimension also creates an opportunity to introduce European case law into the discussion. A case involving an AI-generated image was decided by the district court of Prague. The plaintiff claimed copyright protection for an image created by prompting the AI system DALL-E to:

> create a visual representation of two parties signing a business contract in a formal setting, for example, in a conference room or in a law office in Prague. Show only hands.

The court stated that authorship is predicated on a natural person having created the work, noting that the plaintiff had presented no evidence in support of this apart from stating that the image was based on his prompt. The court found this insufficient for meeting the burden of proof and therefore rejected his claim.[503]

If the plaintiff's contribution indeed only consisted in issuing the mentioned prompt without any further creative input, it is easy to agree with the court's assessment. However, the court's emphasis on the plaintiff's burden of proof, reminiscent of the USCO's above-mentioned arguments in the *Zarya of the Dawn* case, has certain important implications. Most notably, the consistently reiterated requirement that the party claiming copyright must present sufficient evidence concerning the creative process clearly suggests that a presumption of authorship does not automatically favour the claimant in the new era of generative AI.[504] At its clearest, this sentiment is expressed in the USCO's AI Registration Guidance, which notes that 'applicants have a duty to disclose the inclusion of AI-generated content in a work submitted for registration and to provide a brief explanation of the human author's contributions to the work'.[505] Given the proficiency of modern generative AI systems and the ease with which their outputs can pass the Turing Test, the copyright assessment of numerous forms or disciplines of creative expression – including music, text, and images – is poised to undergo a paradigm shift. Whereas all published creations traditionally benefited from a presumption of authorship, the advent of high-performance generative AI may warrant presuming a creation unauthored until proven authored. This seems like a reasonable policy, although creators utilising

502. *See* Chapter 4 about the concept of authoring.
503. Judgment (in Czech) available here: https://justice.cz/documents/14569/1865919/10C_13_2023_10/108cad3e-d9e8-454f-bfac-d58e1253c83a, accessed 14 May 2024.
504. For instance, section 7 of both the Finnish and Swedish Copyright Acts establishes the presumption of authorship as a default rule. Axhamn 2021, p. 73 points out the potential for exploiting this rule.
505. AI Registration Guidance 2023, p. 193. Leistner and Jussen 2025, p. 20 also note that the claimant may struggle to show sufficient proof for the AI-generated output constituting his or her objectively identifiable expression.

generative AI tools will need to document their creative process with greater care than was required before.

Overall, it appears that a successful copyright claim based on a multi-stage cumulation of creative choices – from initial training data selection through model architecture, fine-tuning, and prompting to the final outputs – should be possible even within jurisdictions that assess the relationship between pre-generation input and final outputs strictly. However, to justify such claims, it may be necessary to disclose many of the crucial materials, creative decisions, and technical solutions that hold the key to the system's (artistic) performance. As of yet, developers of generative AI models have been reluctant to do so.[506] Of course, no copyright claims based on multi-stage cumulation of creative choices – such as a combination of training data selection, model design, and prompting – have yet been litigated, meaning that AI model developers have thus far had little reason to disclose the crucial creative choices underlying the system's creative functionality. Needless to say, such cases will become a more realistic prospect once the controversy over unauthorised training data usage and other transparency-related issues is resolved. The AI Act's emphasis on transparency might play a role in advancing progress toward this outcome.[507]

7.3 THE INTERACTION BETWEEN HUMAN CONTRIBUTORS AND THE AI MODEL

7.3.1 Initial Remarks on Premise and Structure

As shown by the discussion in the previous section, the prospective author's burden of providing sufficiently compelling evidence of having authored the content at issue is likely to play a crucial role in determining whether AI-generated compositions receive protection. In examining the creative choices that could potentially provide such evidence, two issues stand out as particularly noteworthy. First, the inquiry whether the creative choice can contribute to the originality of the end result. That is, whether the creative endeavour qualifies as an act of authoring. Second, the relationship and originality causation between the creative choices and the musical attributes of the end result. In the following sections, we will delve into these issues in detail by examining the stages of training data selection, preprocessing, model architecture design, fine-tuning, output conditioning, prompting, and iterative refinement. These stages will be discussed both on a general level and by using the MusicLM and MusicRL models as illustrative examples.

506. Note that Meta's research team did release MusicGen on open source, but nonetheless withheld certain materials, *see* Copet et al. 2024, p. 5. Overall, most commercial ventures provide very scant information on the data and model design powering their respective systems. *See* Chapter 2.

507. Especially Article 53 of the AI Act, which requires providers of general-purpose AI models to draw up and keep up-to-date the technical documentation of the model, including its training and testing process and the results of its evaluation.

7.3.2 Overarching Remarks on the Technical Aspects of AI Model Development

Before delving into the aforementioned examination, it is important to first provide an overview of the fundamental workings of AI models. For this purpose, we revisit the discussion of neural networks introduced in Chapter 2. Neural networks, which form the backbone of AI models, fundamentally operate by extracting statistical patterns from their training datasets. These patterns are then utilised to generate new content in a style consistent with the input data. The pattern extraction process is computationally demanding because it involves iteratively adjusting model parameters based on prediction errors to optimise the model's fit to the training data. The inherent complexity of music also demands neural networks of substantial size to extract patterns advanced enough for high-quality music generation. Moreover, achieving satisfactory performance typically requires training on vast datasets. These factors are further compounded by the architecture of neural networks, where increases in dataset size and model parameters result in an exponential escalation of computational demands, since each additional layer or parameter interacts with the entire structure during training. Consequently, training and operating an AI model is a computationally intensive and resource-demanding endeavour, particularly for complex creative tasks such as music generation.

To illustrate the practical implications of these computational demands and their impact on distinguishing between authorial and technically dictated creative choices, it is useful to consider the initial stages of training a model on audio data.[508] After selecting which audio files to include in the training dataset, the raw audio undergoes a preprocessing phase to facilitate efficient learning. Typically, this involves compressing the continuous waveform into a sequence of discrete, structured representations known as tokens. This compression is often achieved through techniques like quantisation or autoencoding, aiming to retain perceptually important characteristics of the audio signal - such as timbre, rhythm, and pitch - while discarding redundant information. These tokens serve as a compact, learnable abstraction of the original data. To further support efficient processing, the tokens are mapped into high-dimensional vector embeddings, capturing relationships between them in a form suitable for model training. This two-step transformation, from waveform to tokens and then to embeddings, greatly reduces the computational burden while preserving the essential content needed for downstream modelling. The progression from raw audio to learned patterns not only reduces the volume and complexity of the dataset but also reorients the information toward structures that a model can efficiently internalise. The table below summarises the main operations at each stage and their respective purposes:

508. As noted in Chapter 2, generative AI models can also be trained on symbolic musical representations; however, the most notable recent models are trained directly on audio data.

Stage	*Main Operation*	*Purpose*
Dataset collection	Raw waveform audio collected and standardised	Provide diverse real-world material for learning
Tokenisation	Convert audio into discrete tokens capturing essential features	Create compact, learnable representations of complex audio
Embedding	Map tokens into high-dimensional vectors	Organise data to facilitate recognition of patterns and structures
Training (pattern extraction)	Learn statistical relationships between embeddings	Build internal models of audio structures for generation tasks

An important aspect of preprocessing the dataset and designing the model architecture involves striking a balance between reducing the size of the data and preserving critical musical information. For instance, smaller-sized embeddings enable the model to process longer *context lengths*, which refers to the span of prior data that the model can consider when identifying patterns and relationships. This is crucial for recognising key features, such as recurring motifs or harmonic progressions, that contribute to musical coherence. However, overly aggressive compression risks discarding essential features, such as the melodic and harmonic structures crucial for generating coherent and high-quality music. Conversely, embeddings that retain too much data can overwhelm computational resources, thereby restricting the context length and the model's ability to extract sophisticated patterns. In music, where understanding and maintaining temporal dependencies is vital for coherence, designing efficient embeddings is a decisive factor that directly impacts the richness and quality of the generated outputs.

To summarise, technical and authorial creative choices are closely intertwined in AI model development. While all stages of AI model development – from training data selection and model architecture design to fine-tuning – include creative decisions that shape the musical attributes of the model's outputs, the quality of the generated music is often significantly influenced by improvements in data representation and computational efficiency. The creative efforts seeking more efficient representations are largely dictated by technical constraints, which are liable to dilute the direct causation between the authorial creative choices and the musical attributes of the output. Nonetheless, this does not automatically preclude sufficient originality causation. Even if several modules or algorithms are contained in the AI model, one might argue that the combination of many such component parts along with the creative choices made in their utilisation could still constitute original expression that is sufficiently reflected in the musical attributes of the model outputs, especially as the process of selection is expressly geared towards producing an artistic-authorial end result. The following sections endeavour to lay the groundwork for forming a nuanced understanding of this issue.

Before proceeding to this investigation, it is necessary to address the commonly stated notion that the functionality of an AI model – both training and generation – is a *black box*, whose workings are impenetrable to human inquiries and reasoning. As discussed in Chapter 2, this is not necessarily an inaccurate characterisation, but it requires significant qualifications to avoid an overly simplistic understanding of the interaction between human and AI. While the data processing performed in the hidden layers of a neural network can indeed be difficult for a human observer to comprehend, the relationship between the input and output layers operates well within the bounds of human reasoning. After all, the whole point of using a neural network specialised in generative tasks is to extract statistical patterns from the input data and use those patterns to generate similar content based on a probabilistic process.[509] Thus, AI-powered content generation cannot be deemed inexplicable or random: generating useful results expressly depends on the humanly comprehensible relationships among input data, model design choices, prompts, and system outputs. The AI model undoubtedly incorporates an element of randomness, but not to a degree that warrants characterising the relationship between human input and AI output as predominantly random.[510] Instead, the outputs reflect the alignment between statistical probabilities derived during training and the structured constraints imposed by the model's design and operation.

7.3.3 Training Data Selection and Preprocessing

In looking for the human contributions to AI-generated compositions from a chronological perspective, one must point out that the contributions farthest upstream usually are those behind the compositions used as training data, since these often have a considerable influence on the model outputs.[511] However, given that the question of licensing the use of protected works for training data purposes falls outside the scope of this dissertation, the first stage of human creative input to be considered in our analysis is the selection of compositions to include in the training datasets. Overall, it is worth pointing out that the process of selecting training data may occur more than once during the production of a generative AI model, as it is not uncommon to use one larger body of training data to enable the general-purpose capabilities of the model and a smaller dataset to fine-tune the model for more specific purposes.

A notable challenge during training data selection concerns the procurement and availability of suitable music samples. When developing music generation models, suitable training datasets of adequate size are not as plentiful or easy to obtain

509. Hedrick 2018, pp. 328-329 presents a similar argument.
510. A similar point is made by Hertzmann 2018, p. 15. Overall, one must note that the degree of randomness is often manually adjusted in generative AI systems, and is often referred to as adjusting the *temperature*. The temperature controls the randomness of the model's output by influencing the probability distribution over possible next tokens during generation. *See, inter alia*, Cooper and Grimmelman 2024, p. 44.
511. Lee, Cooper, and Grimmelman 2024, pp. 33-34 also make a similar point.

compared to image or text models. The first decision that needs to be made is whether to use symbolic or audio representation of music. The availability of training data becomes particularly scarce if one opts for symbolic representation. For instance, datasets of MIDI files may range in the tens of thousands of entries or perhaps hundreds of thousands at best. By comparison, ChatGPT reportedly was trained on 300 billion words.[512] The libraries of other machine-readable symbolic representations, such as MusicXML or ABC Notation, tend to be even smaller.

The availability of traditional sheet music in PDF form is somewhat larger,[513] but it would need to be converted into machine-readable format to be useful for music generation purposes, and converting PDFs to digital sheet music is much more prone to errors and noise than the corresponding operation of running photographed book pages through text recognition software. Accordingly, the use of symbolic representation of music tends to operate at a significant disadvantage concerning the scale of potential training data available. This disadvantage is further compounded by the fact that most of today's high-performance generative AI model architectures expressly rely on using very large datasets for training. Nonetheless, this does not rule out the possibility of reasonably successful generation using models trained on symbolic datasets. For instance, AIVA produces rather handsome music, as evidenced by the samples available on its website, despite being trained on MIDI files rather than waveform audio.[514]

The use of waveform audio as training data will greatly expand the pool of potential training data to select from, and the use of audio input for training has been accelerated by the general trend of developments within the AI space focused on expanding training datasets and model size. Furthermore, the widely used transformer architecture also tends to perform better with larger datasets.[515] Consequently, many of today's prominent music generation systems are trained on audio files. However, using audio input presents unique challenges that persist even if plentiful training data and computational resources were to be available.

To illustrate, let us imagine a developer aiming to create an AI model that generates melodies in the style of R&B, a genre characterised by its rich harmonic progressions, syncopated rhythms, and melismatic vocal figurations. To achieve this, the training data must include tracks that clearly exemplify these compositional elements. However, as noted in Chapter 2, publicly available audio recordings typically combine several musical layers – vocals, instrumental backing, and percussion – into a single audio file. To isolate the melodic features, such as the lead vocal or instrumental lines, the developer would first need to perform source separation, which involves extracting individual components from the mixed audio. The source separation is rarely executed perfectly and may fail to accurately isolate the melodic content, especially if the layers are densely intertwined.

512. https://www.businessinsider.com/google-researchers-openai-chatgpt-to-reveal-its-training-data-study-2023-12, accessed 2 February 2025.
513. imslp.org, accessed 9 August 2025, the largest online repository of public domain sheet music, lists 240,729 works by 28,550 composers as of 22 January 2025.
514. https://www.aiva.ai/, accessed 28 July 2025.
515. *See* Chapter 2 regarding the transformer architecture.

Once the melodies are isolated, the AI model needs to extract patterns such as pitch sequences, rhythmic motifs, and harmonic relationships from the data. R&B melodies might feature syncopated rhythms that create a 'push-and-pull' effect against the underlying beat, or they might include chromatic passing notes that add a soulful, expressive quality to the melodic line. If the source separation process fails to account for these characteristics, the AI might not get sufficient access to these compositional patterns. For instance, it might miss the way certain rhythmic syncopations align with chord changes or the nuanced interplay between the melody and harmony. This challenge is further intensified by the need to substantially compress the dataset during preprocessing, which may inadvertently remove pitch variations, rhythmic patterns, or harmonic transitions that are essential for accurately capturing the stylistic essence of R&B melodies.

This trade-off highlights the tension between scale and specificity in designing AI models for music generation. If the developer opts to train the model on a vast dataset, such as all available R&B recordings, the model gains access to a broad spectrum of stylistic and compositional patterns. This approach can improve the diversity and robustness of the generated melodies, as the model can identify commonalities across a wide range of examples. However, the developer's influence on specific attributes of the melodic output diminishes, as the model's learning priorities will be dictated more by generic patterns in the data than by deliberate design choices.

Conversely, selecting a smaller, manually curated dataset allows the developer to exert greater control over the model's outputs by focusing on specific compositional attributes, such as syncopated rhythms or chromatic passing tones characteristic of R&B melodies. Manual preprocessing can further enhance this influence, enabling the isolation and emphasis of subtle features that might otherwise be lost in a larger, less curated dataset. Such deliberate curation could make the model's outputs align more closely with the developer's creative vision. Still, even when selecting and preprocessing a highly specific training corpus, it is essential to include a sufficiently high number of audio files to maintain robustness and avoid overfitting. Overall, the approach focused on small training datasets resembles an expanded version of David Cope's *Experiments in Musical Intelligence* of 1992, only executed with larger and more 'artistically ambitious' training datasets and modern algorithms for pattern extraction and music generation.[516]

However, even if the creative choices described above certainly can significantly contribute to shaping the eventual system outputs, the relationship between the training data selection and the precise musical attributes of the outputs tends to be rather vague. A possible exception is when the system design allows the model to overfit to or memorise the training corpus, which can lead to so-called regurgitation of the training data.[517] Incidentally, researchers have developed a model that employs

516. *See* Chapter 2 about EMI. By 'creative ambition' I refer to the fact that training a model on a corpus like J.S. Bach's chorale harmonisations, although certainly not without merit, serve a limited practical-artistic purpose in 'the real world' of music production. Simply put, who needs a machine that generates chorale harmonisations in the style of J.S. Bach?.

517. *See* section 2.2.1 above.

advanced data attribution techniques to identify and quantify the extent to which specific parts of the training corpus have influenced different elements of the generated outputs, using methods that estimate the impact of removing individual training samples on the likelihood of generating those outputs.[518] The aim of this model is to facilitate an equitable royalty distribution system by quantifying the influence of specific copyrighted training data on AI-generated music.[519]

7.3.4 The Originality of Training Data Selection and Model Architecture Design

To assess the originality of the choices related to training data selection and model architecture design, as well as the causal link between these creative choices and the musical attributes of the model outputs, we shall examine the creative process behind MusicLM and its successor, MusicRL, in greater detail. These models are particularly suitable for analysis, as their components and creative processes have been extensively documented in published research.[520] As noted above, the architecture of MusicRL – which constitutes a refined version of MusicLM – is both highly complex and relatively accurately described, providing an effective case study for this discussion.[521]

In essence, the analysis seeks to determine whether there is a relationship of *originality causation* between the pre-generation choices and the audio files generated by the AI model. For *the originality causation* requirement to be satisfied, the impact the creative choice will have on the musical attributes of the model output needs to be sufficiently foreseeable at the time of decision-making. To help grasp the data collections being examined, we shall use a concrete example of the AI model's output: a 30-second track generated by MusicRL with the prompt 'wistful, nostalgic indie folk-pop song with a strong bass and a deep male voice'.[522] Henceforth, we will refer to this as the 'folk-pop track'.

In examining the collection of creative process that led to this folk-pop track coming into existence, the first relevant choices concern the selection and preparation of the training corpus. In developing MusicLM, two main datasets were used: the Free Music Archive (FMA) dataset and a corpus of 5 million audio clips, amounting to 280k hours of music at 24 kHz.[523] The finer artistic reasoning underlying this choice of training data were not given, but considering the ready availability of the FMA and the very large size of the latter dataset, it would be fair to assume that the finer compositional nuances contained in the audio clips were considered only on a very

518. Deng et al. 2023, pp. 4, 6.
519. Deng et al. 2023, p. 1.
520. A notable challenge in examining the most proficient contemporary music generation systems is the scarcity of publicly available information concerning both their training datasets and model architectures.
521. The architecture of MusicLM and MusciRL was explained in section 2.2.1.
522. The sample examined can be directly accessed at https://google-research.github.io/seanet/musiclm/rlhf/audio_samples/musicrlhf-ru-0.wav, accessed 22 January 2025.
523. Agostinelli 2023, p. 5. To enable its joint embedding space, MuLan was trained on a dataset of 44 million audio recordings spanning 370K hours. *See* Huang et al. (Mulan: A joint embedding of music audio and natural language), p. 1.

general level, if considered at all. Therefore, while the choice of training dataset impacts any composition the model generates, the musical attributes of these do not reflect the authorial intent of the developers with much precision: the intention seems to have been to compile *a* training corpus, but the notion of *what kind* of training corpus was too imprecise to contribute to the originality causation between training data selection and the end result's musical attributes.[524]

After selecting the training dataset, the second group of potentially significant creative choices relate to producing representations of the training data, as the waveform audio needed to be translated into numerical form through tokenisation and embedding. As explained in the previous section, finding means of reducing the size of the training dataset while preserving its most essential attributes for pattern extraction is one of the key features of designing generative AI models.

In the MusicLM system, three models – SoundStream, w2v-BERT, and MuLan – were selected to represent and process the input data. SoundStream compresses the waveform input into discrete tokens using Residual Vector Quantisation (RVQ),[525] reducing the dataset's size while aiming to preserve essential acoustic details. These tokens form the foundation for further processing. Meanwhile, w2v-BERT, a model designed for self-supervised speech processing, generates semantic tokens that capture long-term dependencies in the audio data. Through Masked Language Modelling (MLM), w2v-BERT predicts missing segments in audio sequences, enabling it to extract temporal and acoustic relationships critical for music coherence. However, the tokens generated by w2v-BERT are not inherently tied to specific textual or stylistic labels. MuLan, a model specialising in joint text-audio embeddings, bridges this gap by aligning audio patterns with textual descriptions. Using two encoders trained on paired audio-text samples, MuLan creates shared embeddings that combine both textual and acoustic attributes. This alignment allows MuLan to label the semantic tokens extracted by w2v-BERT, enriching them with descriptive context. For example, while w2v-BERT identifies acoustic patterns, MuLan can attach labels like 'wistful', 'male voice' or 'indie folk-pop' to them, which contributes towards enabling more precise and prompt-sensitive generation.

Is there, then, a relationship of originality causation between the choices related to representing and processing the data and the musical attributes of the folk-pop track? Arguments both for and against can be found. Perhaps the weightiest argument against originality causation is that the choice of these models was not directly concerned with shaping the attributes of the folk-pop track. Instead, the intention was to find a way of compressing the data for pattern extraction and enabling greater prompt adherence. Therefore, these choices aimed to enable the functionality of the AI model rather than to shape the musical attributes of the folk-pop track. Under this view, one might state

524. Note the similarity to the Monkey Selfie case discussed in Chapter 4, where it was concluded that Slater's authorial intent was aimed at creating a monkey selfie, but he failed to sufficiently control *what kind* of selfie.
525. Zeghidour et al. 2021, pp. 2-3.

that there is a causal relationship between the creative choices and the folk-pop track's attributes, but no originality causation.

In contrast, arguments for originality will need to rely on the notion that the development team's choices form part of a long, cumulative, multi-stage, and multi-collaborator sequence of creative decisions, where the sheer number and interaction of these choices could potentially lead to meeting the originality causation requirement. The logic underlying this line of argument is based on the idea that creating an original musical work typically involves assembling individually non-original building blocks, whose combination can nonetheless produce an original result.

A comparison to the template maker's contribution to Composition X2 will illustrate this.[526] The Taurus chord progression, overarching ABA structure, and AABA repetition scheme for melodic development selected by the template maker undoubtedly constitute non-original building blocks when considered in isolation. Even when taken together, the selection of these three building blocks would not be sufficient to meet the originality threshold. Instead, the template maker's claim to originality lies in the specific design of how the chord progression, ABA structure, and repetition scheme – along with other selected building blocks – were intended to interact.

Could the development team's selection of the SoundStream, w2v-BERT, and MuLan models be considered analogous to the template maker's selection of a chord progression, structure, and repetition scheme, in terms of their role in supporting originality causation between creative process and end result? In theory, the creative contributions could perhaps be viewed as analogous parts of the respective compositions' ontologies. However, it seems rather obvious that the degree to which the model developers could foresee the musical attributes of the folk-pop track when choosing preprocessing models was significantly lower than the extent to which the template maker could predict and shape the musical attributes of Composition X2.

The argument for protecting the folk-pop track will therefore rely on the idea that there is at least some degree of foreseeability between creative choices and end result, and that this foreseeability does not fall below a minimum threshold for originality causation.[527] At this stage, the arguments for the development team's copyright claim to the folk-pop track do not appear particularly convincing. However, the possible argument for protection would be that the creative contributions accumulate throughout the entire creative process, eventually achieving the requisite level of originality causation through the cumulative effect of numerous creative choices. To investigate this possibility, we need to examine the next stages of the track's genesis in order to gain a sufficiently comprehensive grasp of the pre-generation contributions as a whole.

526. Composition X2 was created in collaboration between the template maker (myself) and a template fulfiller (a musician acquaintance).

527. There is, of course, no formal de minimis threshold for originality causation. The point made here is simply that the influence a creative choice exerts on the expressive attributes of the resulting work may be so trivial that it is intuitively implausible to consider the maker of such a choice a co-author of the composition.

7.4 FINE-TUNING A GENERATIVE AI MODEL

7.4.1 General Remarks on Fine-Tuning

In this section, we shall examine how creative choices related to fine-tuning an AI model can influence the musical attributes of the model's outputs. The first part of the section will discuss this issue on a more general level, whereas the second part investigates the relationship between fine-tuning and originality causation by using MusicLM and MusicRL as practical examples.

Fine-tuning is a crucial phase in AI model development across all generative tasks, as it allows developers to adapt a pre-trained, general-purpose model to excel in specific tasks. Fine-tuning involves adapting a pre-trained, general-purpose model by training it further on a smaller, targeted dataset to prioritise specific outcomes. As explained in Chapter 2, this process typically adds a small number of trainable parameters or modifies the weights of certain layers in the underlying foundation model, allowing it to specialise without requiring the entire model to be retrained. Fine-tuning leverages the existing knowledge encoded in the pre-trained model while enabling adjustments to align with the desired tasks or outputs. A smaller but well-fine-tuned model can often outperform a larger, less targeted model because it focuses on features and patterns directly relevant to its specialised task.

In music generation, fine-tuning can significantly enhance the model's ability to generate outputs that adhere closely to stylistic or compositional goals. For instance, a foundation model might be trained on a vast corpus encompassing numerous musical genres, time periods, and instrumentations. Fine-tuning could then refine the model for specific tags or labels offered as user options, such as 'jazz', 'swing', 'mellow', 'upbeat', 'wistful', 'guitar', or 'big band'. This targeted fine-tuning adjusts the model's parameters to prioritise patterns, stylistic features, and compositional elements most relevant to each label, while still retaining the general capabilities learned during the foundational training. The hierarchical approach provides several benefits. First, it reduces the computational cost of creating separate models for every possible tag by leveraging a single, versatile foundation model. Second, it enhances the ability to control the stylistic and compositional attributes of the generated outputs, as the fine-tuning process aligns the model more closely with specific user demands. Lastly, it offers a scalable framework for expanding the model's functionality, as new tags or labels can be fine-tuned iteratively without the need to retrain the entire system.

To accomplish this, one might use supervised fine-tuning, a method where the general-purpose model is adapted using a carefully selected and curated dataset to specialise in specific musical styles or attributes. For instance, to refine the model's ability to generate jazz music, developers might compile a fine-tuning dataset targeted at the stylistic hallmarks of jazz, such as syncopated rhythms and complex harmonic progressions that distinguish it from other genres of music. Through this process, the model can develop a nuanced understanding of the genre's foundational features, enabling it to generate compositions that embody the essence of jazz. One might then fine-tune this model on additional datasets to further enhance the model's ability to accurately generalise stylistic features. Dividing the jazz genre into subcategories such as swing, bebop, cool jazz, and modal jazz allows the model to generate compositions that more accurately reflect the unique characteristics of each style. When assembling such datasets, developers might also aim for coherence in terms of melodic, harmonic, and textural patterns, which can further add to the consistency and stylistic fidelity of the generated music. This targeted approach not only aligns the model's outputs with precise stylistic goals but also enhances its capacity to produce compositions that are both musically coherent and faithful to the intended genre.

However, even if this method can greatly improve model performance, it is also important to ensure that the datasets are sufficiently large and diverse to allow the model to accurately generalise musical patterns and structures. A too-small training dataset often leads to overfitting, where the model also learns irrelevant features of the training data. This reduces the model's generative output, since the model will not be able to generalise to unseen data. Therefore, a balance must be struck between coherence in genre, style, and mood, and the size and diversity of the data to enable the model to generate musically high-quality compositions. Another potential challenge, particularly relevant for the cascading use of several fine-tuning datasets described above, is the risk that the model 'forgets' the general knowledge contained in the underlying foundation model. This phenomenon, known as *catastrophic forgetting*, can undermine the versatility of the model, making it overly specialised in the latest fine-tuned style at the expense of its broader capabilities.[528] In extreme cases, catastrophic forgetting can destabilise the model's overall performance, leading to inconsistent or nonsensical outputs even within the fine-tuned domain. This can result in outputs that lack the coherence, diversity, or quality expected of a high-performing generative model.[529]

7.4.2 Fine-Tuning with RLHF

A widely used fine-tuning method is reinforcement learning from human feedback (RLHF). It should be noted that while RLHF is technically a form of fine-tuning, it is sometimes distinguished under the label of alignment,[530] as its primary goal is not merely to specialise the model for a specific style, but to adjust the model's outputs to better reflect human preferences, particularly with respect to subjective qualities such as musicality or text adherence. In RLHF, the adjustment is achieved by collecting human feedback on generated outputs, which is then used as training data to build a reward model. The reward model teaches the system to favour attributes deemed successful by the evaluators. The premise is similar to the supervised fine-tuning described earlier, in that developers aim to improve the model's performance by focusing on specific musical aspects for fine-tuning. For instance, the stylistic authenticity of bebop music could be enhanced by asking evaluators to score the model's outputs based on how well they incorporate bebop-specific elements, such as bebop

528. Luo et al. 2023, pp. 2-3; Liu et al. 2024, p. 3.
529. Wang et al. 2022, pp. 1-2.
530. For instance, Lee, Cooper, and Grimmelman 2024, pp. 5-6, 36 have separate categories for model fine-tuning and alignment when breaking down the AI supply chain into eight stages.

scales, tritone substitutions, or rapid interval leaps. Alternatively, if the goal is to improve the model's ability to compose melodies, evaluators might be asked to provide feedback on attributes like melodic fluidity, harmonic compatibility, or the naturalness of phrase structure.

RLHF is particularly relevant to examining the creative choices involved in producing the aforementioned folk-pop track, as the core refinements of MusicRL – the model that generated the track – were achieved through RLHF. The key question is what kinds of creative decisions were required during the RLHF process, and whether there is a causal link between those choices and the musical attributes of the resulting track. Before moving on to the examination, it is important to highlight the potential significance of the process's iterative nature: several reward models were developed by experimenting with different methods of combining user feedback, with the resulting variations in musical outputs carefully observed and evaluated.

From a chronological perspective, the first creative choices were made in deciding which aspects of the underlying MusicLM system's output to target. The development team stated that the fine-tuning efforts were focused on improving the semantic and coarse acoustic modelling capabilities,[531] since these are 'the most important contributors to acoustic quality, adherence to the text and overall appeal of the generated music'.[532] The team chose to develop three distinct reward models:[533]

(1) A prompt adherence reward model that measures alignment between generated music and textual prompts using MuLan's bi-modal embeddings (*see* above about the functionality of the MuLan model).
(2) An audio quality reward model, which evaluates how closely the generated music matches professional audio standards, using human ratings to ensure perceptual accuracy.
(3) A user preference reward model, which indicates user preferences based on feedback from 300,000 evaluators who selected their preferred track from pairs of generated music.

Having constructed these reward models, the team proceeded to experiment with three different ways of utilising them:[534]

- *MusicRL-R* fine-tunes the underlying MusicLM model in multiple stages over the course of 20,000 training steps. First, it uses the text adherence model, then the audio quality model, and finally, it combines the two models linearly to enhance both prompt adherence and sound quality. *Training steps* refer to the individual iterations during which the model processes a subset of the training

531. The modelling of the coarse acoustic tokens, as specified in Borsos et al. 2023, pp. 4-5, aims at capturing the high-level features that influence how sounds are perceived, such as the melody's basic structure and rhythm patterns. By contrast, the fine acoustic modelling goes deeper into the details of the audio signal, like vibrato or changes of dynamics.
532. Cideron et al. 2024, p. 5.
533. Cideron et al. 2024, pp. 5-7.
534. Cideron et al. 2024, p. 7.

data (a mini-batch) and updates its parameters using an optimisation algorithm (like gradient descent).

- *MusicRL-U* fine-tunes MusicLM using only the user preference reward model. This involves fewer training steps (5,000) and focuses solely on aligning outputs with user preferences.
- *MusicRL-RU* is the most complex alternative. It starts MusicRL-R, already fine-tuned on text adherence and audio quality. Then it applies an additional fine-tuning step utilising the user preference reward model (1,000 training steps).

The MusicRL-RU model essentially uses a cascaded approach to fine-tuning the MusicLM model by aiming to leverage the strengths of all three reward models to enhance prompt adherence, sound quality and the attributes preferred by the evaluators. Figure 7.1 illustrates the multi-stage nature of the process of developing MusicRL by fine-tuning the underlying MusicLM model.

Figure 7.1 The Multi-Stage Fine-Tuning of MusicRL

As the figure shows, the development team made a considerable number of creative choices. It is noteworthy that while the process of constructing and utilising reward models on the whole has a technical character and can therefore not be considered to belong entirely in the 'free and creative choices' category, many of the creative decisions made by the team were essentially entirely unhindered by technical constraints. For instance, the decision to focus on semantic and coarse acoustic modelling, and the specific design of the reward models around text adherence, audio quality, and user preference, were largely unconstrained by technical necessity. Furthermore, the team's experimental findings – that cascading the different reward models in a multi-stage fine-tuning process produced the best results – can arguably be considered an original sequence of creative choices. This can be illustrated with reference to the double-creation criterion: it is not plausible to suggest that another AI development team tasked with fine-tuning the MusicLM model would have settled on the same means, especially considering the cumulative three-stage nature of utilising the reward models.[535]

535. Incidentally, this line of reasoning bears some similarities to the Finnish Supreme Court judgment KKO 2005:43 discussed in Chapter 3, where the Court noted that, because the authors considered many factors – such as the students' progressively improving ability to comprehend

On this basis, one might argue that the fine-tuning effort whereby MusicLM was refined into MusicRL could be deemed original and thereby quality as a protected work. It is equivalent to the instruction set for Stairway to X 2.0, both regarding the meeting of the originality threshold and allowing for characterisation as a *latent realisation* of musical expression.[536] This is because neither the development team's fine-tuning effort nor the Stairway instruction set constitutes a complete representation of a musical passage's compositional attributes. Instead, they are sequences of instructions inviting subsequent agents to provide creative contributions that turn the latent realisation into an *actual realisation* of its expressive potential.

7.4.3 The Originality Causation Between Fine-Tuning Efforts and Model Outputs

Even if one were to consider the development team's fine-tuning effort an original work, this will not give a copyright claim to the folk-pop track unless there is originality causation between the fine-tuning efforts and the musical attributes conveyed by the track. Could such a claim, then, be made? In other words, is it plausible to think that the development team, at the time of constructing the reward models and experimenting with various ways of sequencing and combining them, could predict the musical attributes of the folk-pop track with sufficient precision? Based on how the development team explained the fine-tuning process and the reasoning behind each step, the notion that they could predict the attributes of the folk-pop track even to a rudimentary degree appears rather unlikely.

Accordingly, it seems reasonable to rule out the development team members being considered authors of the folk-pop track. However, even if we assume the development team could not be considered authors of the folk-pop track, this does not mean that no scenario could exist where the originality causation between the pre-generation choices and the post-generation end result would be sufficiently strong to warrant copyright protection. In particular, the experimentation with various ways of utilising the reward models may hold the key to unlocking a path to sufficient originality causation. To get a more practical understanding of what this might look like, we shall move beyond what actually occurred during the development of the MusicRL model into a hypothetical scenario where the input of the development team was more conducive to justifying a copyright claim to the model outputs.

Let us therefore suppose the development team continued to iteratively refine all stages of the fine-tuning process based on the impact these refinements have on the model's outputs. They may take a specific interest in improving the melodic output of the model and compile an entirely new body of feedback to train the reward models on. Instead of asking evaluators to submit preferences as to text adherence, audio quality and overall quality, they might target short- and long-term melodic coherence, the use of chord progressions, or naturalness of phrase structures. Having trained the model on

words of varying difficulty – when selecting which words to include in the glossaries, it was evident that no one else undertaking a similar task would have arrived at the same result.

536. The instruction set for Stairway to X 2.0 is available in the Appendix, item 16.

reward models derived from these user preferences, they might add a further reward model trained on even more specific user preferences, such as intra-phrase melodic arcs, use of syncopations, or interplay between melody and harmony. If each additional stage of fine-tuning is based on the team's examination of the model's outputs, the argument in favour of sufficient originality causation becomes successively more tenable, as its creative process begins to acquire increasingly analogous creative phases compared to Composition X2. (Since this example will transition into a hypothetical scenario rather than describing what actually transpired in the development of the MusicRL model, I will refer to the prospective authors as the 'fictional development team' in comparison to the template maker's creative contribution.)

First, both the fictional development team and the template maker formulated a distinct yet imprecise authorial goal, which guided what kind of creative choices were made. Second, the creative choices are confined to selecting broadly formulated building blocks that do not individually have a direct influence on the specific musical attributes of the end result. Third, the copyright claims of both rely on the cumulative effect of a high number of creative choices. While these building blocks are too broadly formulated to provide sufficient originality causation either individually or in smaller groups, an increasing number of such choices could eventually justify an originality claim to the end result. In the case of the Stairway to X instruction set, the template maker's copyright claim to Compositions X2-X5 is virtually indisputable. By contrast, the fictional development team's position is weaker due to the inherently lower degree of originality causation characterising the relationship between fine-tuning choices and model outputs. Still, as noted at the beginning of this chapter, the question remains whether the sheer volume of creative choices containing at least some originality causation could be enough to provide the fictional development team with a sufficiently strong claim to the model outputs.

Figure 7.2 Fine-Tuning of Hypothetical ExtraRL System

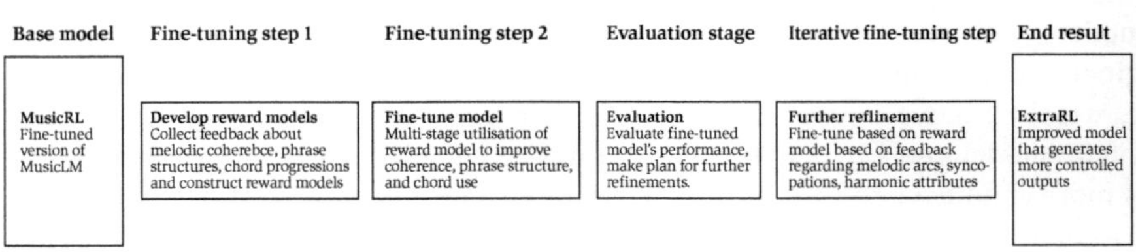

The figure above illustrates the fine-tuning process of a hypothetical ExtraRL model created by the fictional development team. The model is built using MusicRL as a base model with the express intention of gaining greater creative control over its outputs through fine-tuning. Having examined MusicRL's outputs, the team formulates a plan about which elements to target for improvement and proceeds to collect user preferences about short- and long-term melodic coherence, phrase structures, and chord progressions. This feedback is used to create several reward models, which are leveraged to fine-tune the base model in a similar way to how MusicRL was fine-tuned.

Next, the outputs of this fine-tuned version of MusicRL are assessed, whereupon a new plan for desired improvements and targeted elements is formed. The fine-tuning scheme is now repeated by targeting melodic arcs, syncopations, and the interplay between harmony and melody, producing the ExtraRL model. One might also suppose that additional stages of evaluation and iterative fine-tuning are added. (Incidentally, these do not necessarily need to rely on RLHF; one might suppose one stage used supervised fine-tuning on a small, carefully selected dataset instead.)

The significance of iteratively refining the model lies in the progressively strengthening relationship between the system outputs and the fine-tuning endeavours with each iteration. Through this process, the fictional development team acquires a steadily more compelling claim to originality causation between their creative choices and the musical attributes of the system outputs. This is because the fine-tuning measures are expressly aimed at improving targeted features of the outputs. As the number of iterative fine-tuning stages increases, the team's contribution becomes increasingly analogous to the template maker's contribution to Composition X2. (Composition X2 is the composition made jointly by the template maker and fulfiller, which was characterised by the wide melodic leaps introduced by the template fulfiller.) Consequently, the fictional development team could argue for a copyright claim to the model outputs based on the same rationale that supports the template maker's claim to Composition X2.

That said, the originality causation between the template maker's and the fictional development team's contributions - and their respective end results - are unlikely to be on the same level. The template maker's creative control over the outputs is probably considerably greater. Nonetheless, it is not unreasonable to suggest that the fictional development team, by adding a substantial number of iterative refinement stages to the creative process, could establish a plausible authorship claim to the outputs of ExtraRL. This, of course, relies on the fine-tuning endeavours not falling below a minimum threshold for originality causation. That threshold refers to a situation in which the link between the fine-tuning choices and the system outputs, although not entirely absent, is so negligible or trivial that it cannot meaningfully contribute to the accumulation of creative choices necessary to justify copyright protection.

While the notion that the fictional development team indeed could be granted authorship to ExtraRL's outputs does not seem impossible, it is important to note that generative AI models do not necessarily respond to fine-tuning endeavours described above through a linear improvement in both output quality and adherence to the authorial goals of the fictional development team. Accordingly, increasing the extent of human contributors' influence on the generation process does not necessarily correlate with the quality of the system outputs. A comparison to Meta's MusicGen model provides a good illustration of this. It exemplifies a different approach to autonomous music generation, where the focus lies on deriving performance gains from substantial compression of the relevant datasets. The team employed highly sophisticated and innovative techniques, such as cascading codebooks and efficient preprocessing, to compress and tokenise audio data during the preprocessing and training stages. In contrast, the output conditioning and generation were handled using a relatively simple transformer-based architecture with minimal fine-tuning.[537]

The interesting point from a copyright law perspective is that the MusicGen team's creative choices appear to lean more heavily toward the technical optimisation of data processing, whereas the MusicLM and MusicRL teams focused more on elaborate system architectures and iterative fine-tuning endeavours. This suggests that the latter approach – of which the hypothetical ExtraRL provides an extreme example – would be much more likely to provide the developers with a plausible copyright claim, since the more elaborate architecture design and fine-tuning are more susceptible to incorporate human influence on the end result. We shall discuss the potential implications of this at the end of the chapter.

7.5 CONDITIONING SYSTEM OUTPUTS AND PROMPT ENGINEERING

To get a complete view of the pre-generation creative choices, it is necessary to cover how the output signal is conditioned and to what extent this allows the AI model user to influence the model output through prompt engineering. Users familiar with text-to-text models like ChatGPT or text-to-image models like Midjourney will know how extensively the user can influence the generated content through prompting. This has inspired some to envision a prompt-based paradigm for creating content and to reflect on how the copyright framework needs to recalibrate both the copyright eligibility and infringement assessments to accommodate the notion of works authored through prompt engineering.[538]

In contrast to their image and text generation peers, music generation systems typically provide relatively little room for the users to express their creative ideas through text prompts, and the relationship between text prompt and music tends to be rather loose. The folk-pop track discussed above illustrates this issue. While the track certainly shows many similarities to the prompt 'wistful, nostalgic indie folk-pop song with a strong bass and a deep male voice', the similarities are vague and mostly confined to genre-level similarities and very general tags, such as style, instrumentation, or overall vibe. The same applies to the other sample tracks made available by the Google research team, as well as other music generation systems, such as MusicGen, Suno, Mubert, and others. As noted in Chapter 1, this is the core obstacle to authoring musical works through prompting, and it also lies behind the dissertation's expansion towards including other forms of interaction with AI models besides prompting in the examination.

The underwhelming prompt adherence of music generation models also requires some discussion from a technical perspective here. The difficulty of achieving high-level prompt adherence compared to text and image generation models is most likely due to the difficulty of producing high-precision bi-modal embeddings.[539] Granted, the

537. Copet 2024, pp. 1, 3-4.
538. Lemley 2024, pp. 201-203, 208; Vainikka et al. 2024, pp. 6-7.
539. *See* section 2.3.3.

flexibility and precision of the text conditioning is likely to see continuous improvement over the coming years, but whether they can achieve a level that would make text-prompting a viable and efficient tool for professional music production akin to what has already – at least partially – occurred within professional text creation is by no means certain. Overall, it is difficult to imagine a situation where one might 'one-shot' the act of authoring an artistically meaningful piece of music through text prompting. Instead, a substantial succession of specifying or editing prompts is probably needed. This is because compositional contents cannot usually be described with sufficient precision through freely formulated text, unless one also incorporates symbolic representations of music, as was done in the Stairway to X instruction set.

To get a more precise view of how output conditioning and prompt adherence are handled in music generation models, and to gain a comprehensive understanding of the creative choices involved in bringing the folk-pop track into existence,[540] we shall examine how these issues were addressed in the development of the MusicLM and MusicRL models. At the core of MusicLM's process of generating audio outputs based on text commands lies the embedding stage, where MuLan's bi-modal embeddings allow textual information to be integrated with the semantic representations extracted from the training data via the w2v-BERT model. MuLan's embeddings provide the primary mechanism for aligning textual descriptions with audio outputs, serving as the conditioning signal during generation. Meanwhile, w2v-BERT contributes by supplying the semantic tokens that enable the model to maintain long-term coherence across the musical structure.[541]

The actual 'composing' process – i.e., audio synthesis – involves selecting tokens one at a time based on a probability distribution learned from the patterns in the training data. This hierarchical sequence-to-sequence modelling task is the most critical factor shaping the melodic, rhythmic, harmonic, and structural attributes of the output, as it governs in which order the tokens are placed. While prompts provide high-level guidance (e.g., genre, mood, or instrumentation), they cannot dictate intricate compositional details. This limitation arises because MuLan's bi-modal embeddings, while undoubtedly an impressive feat of data processing, cannot track or impose finer-grained compositional structures. Consequently, it is highly unlikely that prompt engineering can meaningfully contribute to the originality of the output.

Two further aspects of the output conditioning in MusicLM warrant special mention here. First, the selection of training data plays a crucial role in influencing the token order, as it dictates the patterns the model learns from. Moreover, the sounds used to synthesise the output tracks – such as vocal and instrumental timbres – are derived from the training corpus, with the acoustic tokens extracted by SoundStream. This means that aspects related to musical texture and instrumentation depend heavily on the recordings included in the training dataset. Second, the semantic modelling stage conducted by w2v-BERT stands out as it extracts features crucial for maintaining long-term coherence in musical output. By impacting the token order, it serves as a key

540. 'Conditioning' refers to the process of guiding or influencing the model's output by providing specific input information (or 'conditions').
541. Agostinelli et al. (MusicLM: Generating Music From Text), pp. 3-5.

process in determining the compositional attributes traditionally considered vital for obtaining copyright protection. Interestingly, w2v-BERT was originally developed for speech recognition, yet it is repurposed here to extract semantic tokens for artistic applications. In addition to demonstrating the adaptability of data-driven models to creative tasks, this also highlights the importance of training data selection in shaping the end result: the semantic patterns critical to the compositional coherence of the generated outputs are derived by a tool designed for entirely different – and comparatively mundane or 'non-artistic' – purposes.

Can the creative decisions related to output conditioning, then, contribute to the originality causation between pre-generation choices and post-generation end results? While the creative decisions related to output conditioning undeniably play a significant role in shaping the generative capabilities of a model like MusicRL, they have a rather limited impact on the originality causation between pre-generation choices and post-generation end results. The combination of MuLan and w2v-BERT primarily serves to enable conditioning by linking textual prompts to audio representations, without directly influencing the specific musical attributes of MusicLM's outputs. Similarly, the bi-modal embeddings generated by MuLan, despite being technically sophisticated, were aimed at facilitating conditioning rather than influencing the specific melodic, harmonic, or rhythmic attributes of MusicLM's outputs. Thus, these choices contribute to the general architecture and functionality of the system rather than to the precise characteristics of its outputs.

The selection of training data has the potentially most significant influence on the semantic ordering of tokens in MusicLM's generation processes. However, the development team's reliance on pre-existing datasets and minimal consideration of the dataset's artistic attributes limits the potential for originality causation. Had the research team exercised greater creativity in curating and assembling the training data, selecting tracks with highly specific stylistic or compositional attributes, they might have strengthened their claim to authorship.

7.6 ORIGINALITY CAUSATION AND COPYRIGHT ELIGIBILITY IN AI-GENERATED COMPOSITIONS

7.6.1 Conclusions of the Previous Sections' Analysis of Originality Causation

The previous sections have explored the interaction between human input and AI model output, both on a general level and through an analysis of the various pre-generation creative choices involved in producing the folk-pop track. It assessed the extent to which these choices influence the musical attributes of the generated outputs. As highlighted at the outset, the inherently low degree of originality causation between pre-generation decisions and post-generation results necessitates the accumulation of a significant number of creative choices across multiple stages to even approach the threshold for copyright protection. While analogies can be made to traditional compositional endeavours – whether in crafting a specific piece of music or developing a more broadly formulated template like Stairway to X – the concept of originality causation remains complex and difficult to substantiate in creative processes involving multi-stage interaction with an AI model.

The key factor determining the degree of this causation is how predictable the end result's musical attributes are at the moment of decision-making. Examining the creative processes behind MusicLM, MusicRL, and the folk-pop track, the arguments for sufficient originality causation appear unconvincing. Even if one were to overlook the need for a minimum level of originality causation for each individual choice,[542] the overall creative control exercised by the development team or other pre-generation contributors over the end result appears much too tenuous to support an authorship claim.

The only stage of the development process that could potentially offer a meaningful claim to originality causation is the fine-tuning stage. However, even here, the creative decisions were not sufficiently targeted at influencing the specific compositional features of the generated outputs. Instead, the fine-tuning endeavours focused on improving broad qualities like prompt adherence and audio fidelity, which, while crucial for the quality of the generated compositions, do not directly shape the melodic, harmonic, or rhythmic elements of the outputs. The hypothetical ExtraRL model illustrated how originality causation could potentially be established, particularly through iterative and elaborate fine-tuning efforts aimed at improving specific musical attributes. While this gives the impression that copyright protection of AI-generated outputs could be possible in at least some scenarios, two important caveats must be noted. First, even with repeated iterative fine-tuning, such efforts may still fall below the minimum threshold of originality causation necessary for copyright protection, as the creative choices' influence over the outputs may remain too abstract and indirect. Second, the iterative fine-tuning method may not represent the most efficient or suitable approach for achieving high-performance music generation. The comparison between MusicRL and MusicGen underscores this point, as MusicGen's reliance on sophisticated preprocessing and architectural simplicity produced outputs of aesthetically similar quality with less reliance on fine-tuning. Still, based on the analysis provided, one cannot rule out scenarios where the copyright protection of AI-generated outputs could be granted. Cases like the hypothetical ExtraRL model, where iterative fine-tuning is used to achieve highly targeted and refined outputs, offer a framework for considering how such protection might be justified.

Overall, achieving a sufficiently convincing link between pre-generation creative choices and post-generation outputs remains difficult, particularly when compared to the more direct and controlled creative processes associated with traditional musical composition. On this basis, liberal, middle, and sceptical approaches to the copyright eligibility of AI-generated compositions can be formulated, which will be the subject of the present section.

542. *See* discussion about a de minimis threshold at the end of section 5.4.3.

7.6.2 Three Approaches to Assessing the Sufficiency of Originality Causation

7.6.2.1 The Liberal and Sceptical Views

The division into liberal, middle, and sceptical approaches to originality causation – which in turn determines granting of copyright protection – hearkens back to the practical aspects of laying copyright claim to AI-generated or AI-assisted creations. As noted in conjunction with Jason Allen's (at least heretofore) unsuccessful attempts to register his *Théâtre D'opéra Spatial* image as a protected work, a potentially very significant aspect of the application of copyright law to AI-generated content lies in how the evidentiary burden is approached. The USCO's approach was to not only place a duty to disclose the utilisation of generative AI in the prospective work's creation but also to require the prospective author to present sufficiently compelling evidence that the 'claimed elements' resulted from the prospective author's creative efforts rather than the AI system's generative process. The combined effect of these requirements points towards an approach where any creation incorporating AI-generated elements will be presumed unauthored unless proven authored. On the whole, I find this to be a perfectly reasonable take on performing copyright assessments in the era of high-performance generative systems. However, the evidentiary burden needs to be calibrated in a way that strikes an appropriate balance between the various involved parties or stakeholders, in the light of both the factual reality of the creative process and the underlying policy rationale of copyright law. To aid this calibration and give the discussion more nuance, liberal, standard, and sceptical approaches to assessing the evidentiary burden will be examined.

The *liberal view* holds that the combination of a high number of free and creative choices expressly aimed at shaping the contents of the end result can suffice for originality causation and copyright protection. Under this, one might think that the fine-tuning process of MusicRL – where the development team selected which elements to target for improvements and how the reward models were to be utilised – could be enough to grant authorship. After all, several creative choices aimed at shaping the outputs were made: the development team selected the semantic and coarse acoustic modelling capabilities because they deemed these to be the 'most important contributors' to, *inter alia*, the 'overall appeal of the generated music',[543] and made an elaborate sequence of free and creative choices in pursuit of this aim in experimenting with the various methods of utilising the reward models to fine-tune the system's compositional outputs. Accordingly, there seems to be a clear intention to compose a piece of music (in the sense of bringing an externally original composition into being in the form of an audio track), and equally clearly, this intention was put to practice by making free and creative choices. Taken together, these considerations suggest that, at least in a *semantic sense* – that is, without considering all the nuances of the relevant legal context – one might consider this to align with the prerequisites for

543. Cideron et al. 2024, p. 5. *See* above.

copyright protection. This argument would gain additional strength if one accepts the tentative suggestion that the creative process bringing the work into being, not just the end result, should be taken into account when deciding on the question of copyright protection.[544]

The liberal view could also be examined by comparing it to the requirement of *general authorial intent*, which has been suggested as relevant for AI-generated outputs. In pondering the problem of the creative contribution having to become 'expressed ... in the final production', it has been noted that the creative process needs to be guided by 'some degree of authorial intent'.[545] Hugenholtz and Quintais have clarified this requirement by noting that the author does not need to have a precise preconception of every original feature of the work. Instead, it is enough for the author to have 'a general conception of the work before it is expressed, while leaving room for unintended expressive features'.[546] They proceed to state that, provided 'the output reflects creative choices by a human being at any stage of the production process, an AI-assisted output is *likely to qualify* for copyright protection'.[547]

Prima facie, this formulation of the requirements on authorial intent could be seen as implying that the creative efforts underlying MusicRL might provide a copyright claim to the folk-pop track. Upon closer reflection, however, this does not appear particularly convincing.[548] While the compositional attributes of the folk-pop track could be seen as the 'unintended expressive features' caused by the creative choices, the development team's general conception of the outputs appears to have been exceedingly broad. After all, their preconception appears to amount to genre-level preconception at best, with even that being slightly doubtful. This makes it rather implausible to think that the folk-pop track sufficiently reflects the development team's creative choices and authorial intent.

Overall, the liberal view can be seen as an ultimately too lenient approach to interpreting the prerequisites for protection. On the one hand, it appears to satisfy the requirements as defined in the Painer ruling. The pre-generation choices – in a creative process such as that of MusicRL – can be deemed both of a 'free and creative' nature and sufficiently numerous to meet the originality threshold, while also being expressly aimed towards bringing a musical composition into existence. On the other hand, the authorial goal that guided the making of the fine-tuning and other decisions typically tend to be much too far removed from the musical attributes of the generated tracks. Simply put, if the authorial goal is defined only on the level of genre and style without making any further specifications as to the musical attributes of the system outputs, the originality causation between the melodic, rhythmic, and harmonic features conveyed by the audio tracks is far from sufficient.

---

544. *See* discussion at the end of section 3.5.2 and about the pending *Mio/konektra* case in section 3.6.
545. Bulayenko et al. 2022, pp. 42-43.
546. Hugenholtz and Quintais 2021, p. 1200. Essentially the same viewpoints are found in Hartmann et al. 2020, p. 75 and Bulayenko et al. 2022, p. 43.
547. Hartmann et al. 2020, p. 76. My italics.
548. It is also highly improbable that the cited researchers meant to express or endorse such a position in making the quoted statement.

At the opposite end of the spectrum is the sceptical view of the claimant's evidentiary burden. In its most extreme form, this perspective holds that any pre-generation creative choices are categorically incapable of contributing to the copyright eligibility of the final output. Given the neutral stance towards the concepts of author and work – where access to authorship and copyright should not be influenced by factors such as aesthetic merit, creative domain, style, or the technological means of creation – these extreme forms of scepticism should be ruled out. However, it is likely that more moderate versions of the sceptical view, such as that exhibited by the USCO in the *Théâtre D'opéra Spatial* case, will be relatively common, particularly in the early years of using generative AI for artistically ambitious creative expression. While this is an understandable position for courts to adopt, it should gradually give way to reduced scepticism as familiarity with and social acceptance of AI-powered creative tools increases.

7.6.2.2 The Middle View: Overarching Analysis

Having covered the liberal and sceptical views of the evidentiary burden concerning originality causation, the *middle view* needs to be examined next. Many core components of the middle view were already noted in discussing the weaknesses of the liberal view. On the whole, the chief challenge in laying copyright claim to AI-assisted creations lies in the indirectness and lack of control associated with the AI model's contributions to the end result. The crucial question therefore is under what conditions one can consider the pre-generation contributors to have exercised sufficient creative control over the end result to lay claim to it. The hypothetical ExtraRL model was introduced to illustrate how the developers of an AI model could increase their creative control over the end result. Its most crucial addition compared to the MusicRL model is that the fine-tuning process is taken further by targeting specific compositional elements of the output. As a result, the creative process becomes largely analogous to a manual template composition such as Stairway to X 2.0.

However, even if the fictional development team's position is similar to the template maker's in the sense that both exercise indirect influence over the end result by issuing broadly formulated instructions, the alignment between creative choices and end result still appears inherently less compelling in the case of the development team. To offset this, the fictional development team would most likely need to introduce several iterative fine-tuning processes targeting the compositional features of the outputs to acquire to sufficient degree of creative control to satisfy the originality causation requirement. The working hypothesis could be that if the development team performs extensive iterative fine-tuning in the manner illustrated in Figure 7.2, its copyright claim to the model outputs should eventually become reasonably plausible.

In examining the copyright eligibility of ExtraRL and its outputs, a potential challenge lies in the creative input – in the form of iterative fine-tuning instructions – being so different from the end result. If we assume the burden of proving the sufficiency of the link between creative process and end result lies on the claimant, as it probably should, the question becomes how the development team can demonstrate that their creative contributions sufficiently predictably control or influence the system outputs. To address this issue, this dissertation has endeavoured to draw an analogy between traditional and AI-assisted creative processes, with manual template compositions constituting the intermediary means of musical composition that can help evaluate creative processes using vastly different technical tools - such as sheet music and fine-tuning endeavours - according to the same standard. The terminology introduced in Chapter 5 was designed to facilitate the examination of these issues. Expressed in this terminology, the copyright assessment centres on comparing the *prospective reproduction* (the generated audio track) to the *source material* (the information or evidence of the fictional development team's fine-tuning endeavours) to determine whether they are similar enough to warrant copyright protection. Essentially, as laid out in research question (7), one needs to determine two things: First, does the source material contain enough specificity to qualify as a work? Second, are its contents reflected in the generated audio tracks with sufficient precision?

The first question will mostly rely on determining whether the development team's iterative targeting of elements such as short- and long-term melodic coherence, phrase structures, chord progressions, intra-phrase melodic arcs, use of syncopations, and interplay between melody and harmony could be considered a musical work akin to the Stairway to X 2.0 instruction set. This hinges on whether the cumulative effect of making many broad references to commonplace building blocks - such as those just enumerated - can offset the instructions' lack of specificity and precision. The crucial component of accomplishing the cumulative effect lies in the extent to which the instructions seek to control the interaction between the individually non-original building blocks. For instance, the template maker's choice of which chord progressions to use through bars 1-41 of the Stairway to X 2.0 instruction set may not have been original in itself. However, when combined with the instructions about melodic development - such as the melodic rhythm and repetition schemes - the instruction set shaped the interplay of several broadly formulated and individually non-protectable features with sufficient specificity to make it into a protected work. As exemplified by the analysis of the template maker's copyright claim to Composition X6, the originality contained in the instruction set was substantial enough to (most likely) withstand the substantial surface-level alterations made by the first improviser and preserve the template maker's copyright claim to Composition X6. In other words, Composition X6 would be within the *implied scope* of the template maker's instruction set, making it a protected reproduction of it.

Overall, I find the analogy between the development team's iterative fine-tuning endeavours and the template maker's broadly formulated instructions regarding the interplay of various musical building blocks to be reasonably plausible. The iterativeness of the process is particularly crucial here, as the claim of sufficiently controlling or foreseeing the musical attributes of the end result appears much less convincing without it. This can be illustrated with reference to two alternative means of producing abstract paintings. In the first scenario, we suppose a prospective author pours 30 different colours into an empty egg tray with as many slots. He does not pay attention to which slots each colour goes in, essentially filling the available slots in a haphazard manner. Following this, he tips the egg tray so that the colours splash onto a canvas placed on the floor. In the second scenario, the prospective author uses a technique resembling that of Jackson Pollock, where the paint splatters are thrown towards the canvas one at a time. The creative process encompasses 30 paint splashes in total, each splash with a different colour. We suppose the two scenarios yield paintings of equal complexity and aesthetic qualities, both of which meet the requirements of seeming originality.[549]

How is the originality causation between creative choices and end result impacted by the differences between the two scenarios? Both creative processes can be said to exhibit a very similar number of creative choices aimed towards creating a painting. The crucial difference between them lies in the alignment between authorial intent, external realisation, and end result, which is much greater in the second scenario. This is due to the gradual nature of forming the colour patterns. As the second painter continuously observes the painting as it is taking shape, she cannot help but let her gradually developing authorial vision guide the area towards which each splatter is aimed and which colour is selected. Consequently, the originality causation between the creative choices and the colour patterns of the resulting painting becomes considerably greater compared to the first scenario.

To my mind, the distinction between iterative and non-iterative fine-tuning processes follows a similar logic. The process of developing MusicRL was more akin to the first scenario in that the creative input was taken to a specific point, after which the control over the specific formulation of compositional attributes was handed over to a non-authorial agent that supplied the precise expression contained in the end result (fortuity in the abstract painting and the AI model in MusicRL). In contrast, by iteratively refining the model, the process of creating ExtraRL was more like the second scenario: while the control over the specific compositional attributes of the model outputs was far from absolute, the continuous engagement with the system and high number of iterative refinements could outweigh the lacking precision with which each creative choice – a fine-tuning effort or splashing paint onto a canvas – is reflected in the end result.

Due to the limited precision with which the fine-tuning choices are reflected in the end result, one or two stages of iterative fine-tuning are unlikely to be enough to meet the prerequisites for protection, just like one or two splatters of paint will not suffice to produce an original painting. However, the higher the number of iterative fine-tuning stages grows, the greater the likelihood of meeting the relevant criteria becomes. While one must acknowledge the technical limitations of fine-tuning an AI model – due to high computational cost, model instability, catastrophic forgetting, etc. – as well as the diminishing returns associated with cascading high numbers of iterative fine-tuning stages, I find that on a middle view, the claimant's evidentiary burden of showing sufficient originality causation could plausibly be met by a creative process such as that of ExtraRL. Whether this type of process is the technically most viable option for developing high-performance music generation models or likely to see

549. About the concept of seeming originality, *see* section 1.8.

widespread adoption is, of course, an entirely different matter. This issue will be revisited in the concluding section of this chapter.

7.6.2.3 Determining the Level of Required Originality Causation on the Middle View

Even if the iterative fine-tuning of a model such as ExtraRL could be deemed sufficient for protection on the grounds described above, whether protection actually should be granted will depend on the circumstances of the particular case. To get some insight into what the required level of originality causation could or should be, we can return to the analogy between ExtraRL and the Stairway to X 2.0 instruction set. In Chapter 6, additions and alterations were gradually introduced to the Stairway to X 2.0 instruction set, enabling an examination of how these changes impacted the authorship claims of upstream contributors. The underlying idea was that analysing the effects of these changes in the context of manual template compositions would provide clearer insights into how the requisites for copyright protection should be assessed in AI-assisted compositional processes. The alterations' impact on the template maker's claims is particularly interesting, since template maker's contribution is the most reminiscent of the fictional development team's.

In examining the template maker's claims and the potential for broadly formulated instructions to establish a copyright claim, Compositions X2, X6, and X7 form a symmetrical collection. The template maker's claim to Composition X2 is hardly in doubt, just as the lack of a claim to Composition X7 is equally evident. Accordingly, Composition X6 – created by the 'first improviser' through additions that filled in the wide melodic leaps found in Composition X2 – is best suited to provide insights into whether the similarities between the source material and the prospective reproduction (i.e., the instruction set and the resulting audio file) sufficiently reflect the template maker's creative choices to warrant copyright protection. The analysis in Chapter 6 emphasised the importance of taking into account both the literally perceivable attributes and the contextual or evolutionary influence exerted by upstream contributors in assessing the degree to which the respective co-creators have contributed to the musical expression of a composition. The reason for this is that only examining who selected the surface-level details of a composition and awarding sole authorship to him may overlook the potentially very significant influence exerted by upstream contributors in designing the contextual framework in which the downstream contributor made his creative choices.

In Chapter 6, the analysis of Composition X6 concluded that the template maker should receive a 40% authorship stake. This was based on the template maker's creative choices being reflected in the end result in two key ways. First, four categories of broad structural patterns attributable to the template maker were identified as directly reflected in the composition. Whether this four-point collection of direct similarities was sufficient to individually give the template maker an authorship claim to Composition X6 was deemed plausible yet uncertain. Second, the template maker's instructions exercised a considerable contextual and evolutionary influence on both the template fulfiller's and improviser's subsequent contributions. Here, too, it seems doubtful whether this indirect influence is sufficient to independently meet the originality threshold. However, when combining the four-point collection of direct similarities with the indirect contextual and evolutionary influence, the degree to which the template maker's creative choices were reflected in Composition X6 was deemed sufficient for giving the aforementioned 40% co-authorship stake.

Given that the purpose of examining the template maker's claim to Composition X6 is to draw an analogy to ExtraRL, this raises the question of how the analogy is drawn and how convincing it is. The chief problem is that while the development team may have made a very high number of broadly formulated instructions – related to short- and long-term melodic coherence, phrase structures, chord progressions, etc. – it does not seem clear that these are reflected in the system outputs in the same way as the template maker's instructions influenced the contents of Composition X6. For the copyright claim to become convincing, the team would need to show that the many broadly formulated instructions they have issued can accumulate in a similar way to the template maker's four-point collection of overarching features and that these become reflected in the system outputs either directly or by exerting contextual and evolutionary influence.

The iterativeness of the fine-tuning process plays a key role in constructing such an argument. To illustrate, let us suppose the team examined MusicRL's outputs and was dissatisfied with the intra-phrase melodic arcs. They then decided to target this element for fine-tuning, proceeding to collect user feedback, selecting several ways in which to leverage this data, and fine-tuning the underlying model on these to produce three new versions of the system. Having examined the outputs of the alternative fine-tuned versions, we suppose the team noticed a moderate improvement in the model. This prompted the team to break down the concept of intra-phrase melodic arcs into the following subsections focused on how naturally ascending and descending melodic movement is juxtaposed, how well the harmonic rhythm supports the melodic arcs, and how natural the relationship between melodic movement and phrase length is. The team then collected new user feedback concerning these elements and leveraged it to construct reward models with which to further refine the system.

Similarly to the difference in originality causation between the egg-carton and Pollock techniques of producing abstract paintings, this type of iterative refinement means that the team can narrow down the very broad instruction like 'we want to improve the output's intra-phrase melodic arcs' to 'we want to control the juxtaposition of ascending and descending melodic movement within phrases, ensure harmonic rhythm provides effective support, and align melodic movement naturally with phrase length'. By breaking down the overarching creative goal into smaller, more specific elements, the team effectively increases the specificity of their fine-tuning process. This allows for a more targeted approach to improving specific aspects of the model's outputs. Through successive iterations, each informed by experimenting with different reward models and evaluating its impact on the system outputs, the creative process becomes increasingly focused. The team not only gains greater control over specific musical attributes but also develops a more refined understanding of how their fine-tuning choices influence the outputs. This, in turn, should strengthen the originality causation between their pre-generation creative choices and the post-generation musical outputs.

Such a process highlights the potential for cumulative creative control in multi-stage refinement. By successively narrowing the scope of feedback collection, reward model construction, and iteration, the team could eventually approach a point where their collective fine-tuning efforts meaningfully impact even subtle compositional details of the generated outputs. This iterative process also exemplifies how creativity in AI-assisted compositions could evolve from abstract, high-level instructions into a deliberate and structured method for realising the underlying authorial goal. Of course, in making this argument, one must keep in mind the caveats issued above related to the practical feasibility of utilising such processes in actual real-world AI model development. Nonetheless, regardless of how widely adopted such processes of AI development are going to become, I find that the hypothetical scenario of developing the intra-phrase melodic arcs through iterative fine-tuning could give an authorship claim to the system outputs that is on par with the template maker's claim to Composition X6.

7.6.3 Multi-contributor AI Development Processes and Joint Works

In contemplating the possibility of granting copyright protection to AI-generated compositions, the impact of a typically multi-contributor, multi-phase nature of the pre-generation creative choices needs to be addressed briefly. Clearly, the most straightforward way of approaching the potential challenges regarding authorship allocation among the potentially very high number of pre-generation contributors is to tie the co-authorship stakes to the originality causation between each contributor and the musical expression of the end result. Examined from the perspective of creative collaboration, the process of the fictional development team described above does not appear much different from the members of a band convening at a studio for a songwriting session, during which a song is written through an iterative process of trying out and gradually refining various musical ideas. Accordingly, the development team's process could arguably be seen as satisfying the requirements of a joint work under FCA section 6.

There are some potential challenges to this. Considering that the originality causation between the development team's creative choices and the system outputs is likely to be on a lower level compared to a more traditional joint work, such as a band convening to write a song together, the situation exemplified by Composition X8 may become realised. That is, the reflection in the end result of each team member's contribution may be so small that none of them individually meet the originality threshold. On a view that requires a co-authorship claim to be based on an individually original contribution, a possible outcome could be that none of the team members can present a sufficient co-authorship claim, whereby the AI-generated composition would not be protected, despite the development team's creative collaboration as a whole satisfying the originality causation requirements. As already noted regarding Composition X8, it appears rather unintuitive to consider an externally original composition ineligible for protection merely because the creative choices that brought it into existence were spread among many different contributors. Instead, if the collaborative effort satisfies the originality causation requirement, the most natural outcome would be to award co-authorship stakes to all collaborators based on how greatly each contribution shaped the original expression contained in the end result, regardless of whether the contributions individually meet the originality threshold.

7.7 SUMMARY

The purpose of this chapter has been to examine the various ways in which human contributors interact with an AI model before the model generates a composition, to determine whether the human contributor(s) could lay claim to the system outputs. A core factor in this evaluation is the notion that in the current era of high-performance generative AI models, essentially any creation must be presumed non-authored unless proven authored. On this view, the party laying copyright claim to a composition incorporating AI-generated content would need to present sufficiently compelling evidence of having authored the 'claimed elements' of the composition. Consequently, one needs to examine the creative process that brought the AI-generated composition into being to investigate what could constitute evidence of it having been authored. All creative choices do not necessarily contribute towards making an AI-generated composition qualify for protection. To identify those creative choices that can, the dissertation has formulated a requirement of originality causation. This means that when the author makes the creative choices that bring the composition into being, there needs to be sufficient alignment between the underlying authorial intent, its external realisation, and the musical attributes of the resulting composition.

The main stages of pre-generation human input – training data selection, model architecture design, output conditioning, fine-tuning, and prompt engineering – were examined to gauge whether they could contribute to meeting the originality causation requirement. One key assumption has been that the originality causation exhibited by each individual choice tends to be much lower in AI-assisted compositions compared to traditional compositional processes. A reasonable assumption is that in most cases, the lower degree of originality causation needs to be outweighed by the sheer quantity of creative choices to justify copyright protection. In turn, this suggests that the pre-generation contributors' copyright claims may become dependent on the creative choices accumulating throughout the multi-stage, multi-contributor creative process.

The creative process of the MusicLM and MusicRL systems was examined from this perspective. The analysis concluded that while many of the decisions could be characterised as 'free and creative' and also directly contributed to shaping the musical attributes of the folk-pop track generated by MusicRL, there was insufficient alignment between the authorial goal and the end result: The authorial goal was too broadly formulated, such as striving for genre-level shaping of the outputs, and the foreseeability of how the creative choice was to impact the end result was too imprecise. Only on a very liberal approach to how the authorship requirements are interpreted could the relationship between pre-generation choices and the folk-pop track be considered sufficient. To illustrate what kind of AI development process might satisfy the relevant requirements on a standard interpretation of authorship, the hypothetical ExtraRL system was examined. The crucial difference between MusicRL and ExtraRL is that the latter incorporates iterative refinement of the system that expressly targets specific musical attributes of the end result. The iterativeness of the fine-tuning process made the analogy between AI-assisted and manually produced template compositions – such as Composition X6 – more plausible. To get a more precise idea of how the originality causation requirement might be met in an iterative fine-tuning process, a detailed comparison between ExtraRL's outputs and Composition X6 was made. The analogy between AI-assisted and manual template compositions was concluded to be reasonably plausible. However, some caveats were made. Most importantly, that incorporating human input into the system outputs through a process of extensive iterative refinement is not necessarily the technically most feasible or efficient way of developing high-performance music generation systems. In the following and final chapter of the book, we shall examine the implications of these conclusions in greater detail.

CHAPTER 8
Conclusions and Final Reflections

8.1 STRUCTURE OF THE CHAPTER

The purpose of this chapter is to summarise and crystallise the answers to the research task set in Chapter 1. The chapter is divided into three sections. The first section defines a technologically neutral definition of a musical work and describes its core elements. The second section discusses the requirement of originality causation and how one should assess the copyright claimant's burden of showing that a composition has been authored in the light of copyright law's policy rationale. The third and final section answers the research questions stated in Chapter 1.

8.2 WHAT IS A TECHNOLOGICALLY NEUTRAL UNDERSTANDING OF A MUSICAL WORK?

8.2.1 General Remarks

Among the core research tasks of this dissertation has been to formulate a technologically neutral definition of what it means to compose a musical work. It has aimed to define what it means to 'author a musical composition' independently from the technological tools – such as musical notation, audio recordings, DAWs, or AI-powered tools – utilised during the compositional process. In Chapter 1, a comparison between traditional and AI-assisted compositional processes prompted the following rhetorical question: since the compilation of a traditional music sheet is routinely deemed to produce a copyright-protected work, should not the same logic apply to the instructions issued in the context of AI-generated compositions? Based on the examination of traditional compositions, template compositions, and AI-generated compositions, some conclusions can be made about how a technologically neutral understanding of what it means to author a musical composition can be drawn.

To address this issue with greater precision, certain idiosyncratic aspects of musical works need to be pointed out. First, although it does not necessarily have a direct legal relevance, a distinction between a 'work' and a 'musical work' can be made. As defined in well-established CJEU case law, a protected work is defined as an intellectual creation resulting from the free and creative choices made by the author, which make the work reflect the author's personality. This means that any sufficiently substantial sequence of creative choices can be considered a work, provided that the choices were not dictated by technical or other constraints. The fine-tuning endeavours that refined MusicLM into MusicRL can therefore undoubtedly be considered a protected work. Yet, due to the limited originality causation between the development team's creative choices and the audio tracks generated by MusicRL, the development team is unlikely to have a copyright claim to the latter. Accordingly, one can characterise the fine-tuning endeavours as a work, but not as a musical work. Here, the distinction between a work and a musical work lies in whether a *musically relevant* data collection can be connected to it through originality causation: Since there is not sufficient originality causation between the folk-pop track and the fine-tuning efforts underlying MusicRL, the latter does not qualify as a musical work.

Another idiosyncrasy characteristic of musical works is that their ontology is often divided into stages of latent and actual expression. The latent stage contains the externalisation of the underlying authorial conception by describing a sequence of musical attributes. The core of distinguishing separate latent stage is that while the author's initial externalisation of the composition may qualify as a protected work, this data collection does not as such fulfil the authorial conception or the underlying reason for creating instruction set. Instead, it requires interpretative input from a subsequent contributor – such as a performer or computer program – to be converted into 'actual' musical expression. It is not unusual that considerable new expressive and compositional attributes are incorporated into the composition upon converting it from latent to actual expression.

Based on the distinction between latent and actual expression, the act of composing music can be defined as issuing instructions that describe musical attributes. This raises the question of what kind of instructions 'count' towards defining the work's contents. Here, a significant challenge is that it may not be possible to get an exhaustive account of the underlying composition's contents by examining the source material created by the author. Even if a prospective reproduction exhibits many discrepancies, alterations, and new additions compared to the source material, it may still be well within the *implied scope* of the underlying composition. No matter how detailed the source material is, it can never exhaustively define all the types of musical expression the underlying composition *can become* when reinterpreted, altered, or expanded upon by subsequent creative agents, whether human or otherwise.[550]

550. A straightforward example of this – which is unproblematic from a copyright and authorship allocation perspective – is Dolly Parton's and Whitney Houston's respective versions of Parton's song 'I Will Always Love You'.

Inspired by philosophically inclined analyses, this warranted characterisation of a musical composition as an abstract entity that exists 'independently of whether anyone performs it, listens to it, or takes any interest in it whatever'.[551] This formulation highlights the legally noteworthy fact that the line-drawing between what should or should not fall within the implied scope of a composition can occasionally become challenging. The most important aspect of this is the notion that a too schematic or literal approach to assessing the similarities between source material and prospective reproduction may need to be complemented by an analysis of the subjectively experienced overall impression elicited by perceiving the composition. Since the determination of whether something 'counts' as a reproduction – or communication to the public – of a work will at least in part depend on the subjective experience of aurally perceiving it, the act of composing music can be characterised as 'setting the parameters' for a certain kind of subjective experience. What does this setting of parameters mean for practical purposes? That the author, guided by her underlying authorial intent, compiles an instruction set describing certain musical attributes, which can be rendered into a certain kind of musical expression.

Whether a prospective reproduction is within the implied scope of the underlying work will be determined by comparing two data collections: the prospective reproduction and the source material. The overall impression of perceiving said data collections will be crucial for this comparison, especially if the similarities between the two data collections are of an indirect or broadly formulated character. Yet, a lack of precision either in the formulation of the source material's description of the musical work or their reflection in the end result will not necessarily rule out the possibility of originality causation. The analysis of Composition X6 illustrated that upstream creative choices can become sufficiently reflected in the end result through the direct duplication of broadly formulated patterns and the contextual and evolutionary influence these patterns exert over the precise melodic, rhythmic, and harmonic attributes of the end result. Among the core research tasks was to examine the degree to which an analogous argument could be made concerning AI-assisted template compositions. In the case of MusicRL, the analogy between the template maker's and pre-generation contributors' claims was not considered convincing due to the low degree of originality causation. However, the hypothetical ExtraRL model provided an example of an AI-assisted template composition that exhibits enough originality causation between the pre-generation contributions and the post-generation end results.

8.2.2 The Meaning of 'Authoring a Musical Work'

To summarise the distinction between the legal concept of 'authoring a musical work' to the actual process of 'composing a piece of music' from a technologically neutral perspective, the following can be stated. Composing is understood as making creative choices with the intention of bringing a certain kind of musical expression into being. Whether a compositional endeavour is to be classified as 'authoring a musical work'

551. Roman Ingarden 1986, p. 2.

depends on the degree of originality causation between the creative choices and end result. The technical tools utilised during the creative process should not impact originality assessment. To help grasp the role played by the technological tools during the creative process, a distinction between two different types of tools or technically dictated creative choices can be distinguished.

On the one hand, technical tools can serve as vehicles for making an author's creative conception externally perceivable and communicable. A music sheet, a digital audio workstation (DAW), or an AI model are all technologies that help translate an underlying composition into a form that others can perceive. Although the degree of predictability and control over how each creative choice shapes the final musical attributes may differ between a music sheet and an AI tool, such differences should not in themselves determine whether the creative process amounts to authoring a musical work rather than merely composing a non-protected piece of music. On the other hand, technical tools and technically dictated creative choices relate primarily to enabling functionality rather than contributing to the end result's originality. For example, using music notation software or particular AI modules – such as MusicLM's use of three separate models to produce bi-modal embeddings of the training corpus – shapes the mechanics of how a composition is externalised, but does not itself add to the originality of the end result. A technologically neutral approach to authorship will influence the assessment of originality only in relation to tools that serve to externalise the creative conception, not those that simply provide enabling functionality.

A further consideration in developing a technologically neutral understanding of musical works concerns the distinction between 'works' and 'musical works'. Chopin's music sheet of the Prelude in E minor, the Stairway to X 2.0 template, and the fine-tuning endeavours behind both MusicRL and ExtraRL all constitute 'works' under copyright law's definition of the concept. However, the fine-tuning – or any other – endeavours behind MusicRL cannot be deemed a 'musical work' because it cannot be tied to any instance of musical expression, such as the system outputs, with sufficient originality causation. By contrast, both the music sheet of the Prelude in E minor and the Stairway to X 2.0 template can be characterised as 'musical works'.

8.3 HOW SHOULD ORIGINALITY CAUSATION BE ASSESSED IN LIGHT OF THE POLICY RATIONALE?

8.3.1 Initial Remarks on Copyright Law's Policy Rationale in the Context of Generative AI

A likely trend in the current era of high-performance generative AI is that compositions containing AI-generated features will be presumed unauthored unless proven otherwise, meaning that parties wishing to lay copyright claim to – wholly or partially – AI-generated compositions need to present sufficiently compelling evidence for having authored them. What needs to be proven is that there is a sufficiently clear link between the creative choices and the composition laid claim to, which has been referred to as the requirement of originality causation. Liberal, middle, and sceptical options for interpreting the originality causation requirements and the claimant's evidentiary burden were presented in the previous chapter. In choosing among these options, one needs to strike an equitable balance between the various involved parties, stakeholders, and society at large in the light of both the factual reality of the creative process and the underlying policy rationale of copyright law. The purpose of this section is to discuss whether the policy rationale might warrant a different interpretation of the copyright eligibility of AI-generated composition from that presented in the previous chapter.

In defining copyright law's policy rationale, the incentivisation of creating new works by rewarding authors for their intellectual endeavours is typically taken as the starting point,[552] which, in turn, needs to be balanced against safeguarding collective cultural or intellectual aims by imposing limitations on the author's exclusive rights.[553] Applying this outlook to AI-generated creations, the question becomes how one ought to balance the personality-based, investment protection, societal, and cultural aspects of the incentivising rationale. If the anthropocentric view of authorship is assumed, as it arguably should, the pre-generation contributors potentially eligible for authorship are the developers and users of the AI system. This means that there are four different alternatives for how to grant authorship to AI-generated outputs: one might award it to the developers, users, both, or neither.

8.3.2 Economic Incentives and AI-Generated Compositions

Based on the analysis of the interaction between human contributors and AI models conducted throughout Chapter 7, the developers – rather than the AI system users – have the best chance of satisfying the originality causation requirements and qualifying as authors of the model outputs. Prima facie, this is a rather counterintuitive outcome, which also seems at odds with the general tenor of the scholarly discussion on how the incentivising effects of copyright law should be applied. Given the veritable investment boom in generative AI applications, there appears to be no shortage of incentives for developing AI models.[554] Granting authorship to the developers is also associated with a double-rewarding problem, where the developers can separately receive compensation for both the distribution of the system and its outputs. Such reasons have led to a trend favouring a cautious approach to granting developers authorship of the outputs, with an emphasis on strong empirical data being needed to justify added incentives

552. For instance, the Infosoc Directive's harmonisation of the Member States' copyright law strived towards enabling 'growth and increased competitiveness of European industry' (recital 4) as well as the maintenance and development of creativity 'in the interests of authors, performers, producers, consumers, culture, industry and the public at large' (recital 9). The CJEU referred to these recitals in its Infopaq I ruling, at para. 36.

553. Haarmann 2014, p. 46; Kivistö 2017, p. 225. *See* section 1.3.1.

554. *See, inter alia,* https://www.mckinsey.com/capabilities/mckinsey-digital/our-insights/the-economic-potential-of-generative-ai-the-next-productivity-frontier#business-value, accessed 31 January 2025. A similar argument is made by the USCO 2025, pp. 34, 36.

towards the development of generative AI models.[555] There is also an intuitively obvious argument that inquires what interest a potential user would have in paying for access to a generative AI model if the model developers become copyright holders of everything the system generates.[556]

The reason for the relative strength of the developers' position lies in the weakness of the system user's claim. As discussed in Chapters 2 and 7, the technical challenges associated with achieving precise output conditioning and prompt adherence within music generation make the notion of producing an original musical work through prompt engineering rather unlikely, at least at the current stage of technological development. This raises the question of whether policy-driven values support lowering the evidentiary requirements placed on certain pre-generation contributors claiming copyright over a given AI-generated composition. Simply put, are there policy-based reasons related to factors such as economic growth, cultural progress, or safeguarding the position of traditional (i.e., non-AI-powered) creative activities that warrant opting for liberal, middle, or sceptical approaches to the copyright eligibility of AI-generated compositions?

As shown by the examination of the MusicLM, MusicRL, and ExtraRL systems, the middle approach to assessing the originality causation between creative choices and end result is such that pre-generation contributors can be granted copyright protection only in rare cases. One such scenario could be constructed through the hypothetical example of ExtraRL. However, there are no indications that such practices for developing music generation systems will become widely adopted, suggesting that awarding (co-)authorship to a pre-generation contributor to a musical composition probably will be a marginal phenomenon in the coming years. Given the unlikelihood of pre-generation contributors – whether developer or user of a system – qualifying for protection on a middle interpretation, one might ask whether the policy rationale gives any reason to opt for a more liberal approach to the originality causation requirements. For instance, do the interests of economic growth or cultural progress warrant granting pre-generation contributors authorship to the outputs of systems such as MusicLM, MusicRL, or MusicGen? This does not seem plausible. The development of music generation systems does not appear to require additional incentives, and it is difficult to see how the interests of economic growth would benefit from a more liberal approach to granting authorship. Regarding arguments based on cultural progress, some arguments could perhaps be found, but at least at the current stage of technical development, these appear more relevant in the context of AI-generated images and text than AI-generated music, due to the technical challenges of accurate output conditioning in this field. On a related note, I also do not think the interests of safeguarding traditional non-AI-powered compositional activities warrants adopting a more sceptical approach to pre-generation originality causation, such as might rule out

555. Craglia et al. 2018, p. 68; Ginsburg and Budiardjo 2019, p. 456; Frosio 2022, p. 169; Sganga 2023, p. 8. However, some viewpoints to the contrary have been put forward, such as by Hristov 2017, pp. 438-439.

556. Many scholars have pointed this out, such as Senftleben and Buijtelaar 2020, p. 807; Hugenholtz and Quintais 2021, p. 1209. Ballardini et al. 2018, p. 12.

the copyright claims of the fictional ExtraRL development team or other instances where pre-generation creative choices might have become plausibly reflected in the system outputs.

Overall, based on the analysis of music generation systems carried out in this dissertation, I find the middle interpretation of originality causation described in Chapter 7 to be reasonably fair and equitable. As a result, pre-generation contributors' access to copyright protection should, at least in theory, strike an appropriate balance in light of the policy rationale. However, this may not necessarily reflect how courts will rule on copyright claims to AI-generated – or AI-assisted – creations. Jason Allen's unsuccessful attempts to register the *Théâtre D'opéra Spatial* image as a protected work provide a good example of this. Considering the substantial number of both pre-generation creative choices and post-generation manual editing, it is evident that Allen's creative input had a much stronger influence on the visual expression of the end result than the fictional development teams' limited impact on the compositional attributes of ExtraRL's outputs.

Given that I suggested the latter might plausibly qualify for copyright protection, Allen's claim, by the same token, should be considered almost certain to succeed. Yet, this was not the case. (The outcome of the appeal is admittedly still pending.) Thus, the USCO's assessment of Allen's claim can be thought to exhibit a scepticism towards the notion of AI-assisted authorship that borders on prejudice. Nonetheless, I do not think the USCO's cautious approach to AI-assisted authorship will come to represent an isolated instance. Rather, I think several similarly sceptical rulings may be given in the coming years. At the same time, the Beijing Internet Court's ruling in the *Lee v. Liu* case provides an example representing the opposite end of the spectrum.

Should the scepticism exhibited by the USCO, then, be considered at least mildly at odds with the policy rationale of rewarding creative endeavours in pursuit of cultural progress? In my estimation, hindsight will point towards answering in the affirmative. Still, one might sympathise with Allen's frustrated attempts in seeking to register his undeniably beautiful image created through a novel and interesting method, but I do not believe the potential long-term harm to the policy rationale of incentivising AI-assisted creativity will be significant.

This is due to two reasons. First, visionary artists will always be drawn to exploring novel means of harnessing emerging opportunities for creative expression afforded by technological developments. An initially sceptical stance regarding the copyright eligibility of such creations is unlikely to significantly deter them from pursuing their innovative artistic visions. Second, the history of copyright law does not lack instances where the artistic avant-garde has challenged paradigmatic notions of what constitutes a work, its reproduction, or worthwhile artistic expression in general. Artistic photography and hip-hop music provide familiar examples from the 19th and 20th centuries, in which new technologies inspired novel forms of creative expression that challenged established views of what it means to author a work, and eventually won recognition among the canon of worthwhile creative expression. In other words, it has historically been common for novel forms of creative expression that challenge prevailing popular sensibilities to undergo a 'trial period' before achieving recognition as equals to their more time-honoured counterparts.

8.3.3 The Cultural and Societal Policy Rationale

As with any potentially or actually disruptive technological development, the advent of high-performance generative AI has raised questions about the need for safeguarding traditional non-AI-powered creative processes. One such concern is that an increased deployment of AI models for creative tasks might come to devalue or marginalise human creativity.[557] Undoubtedly, there are dangers in the prospect of generative AI models flooding society with artificially generated content and thereby impoverishing the diversity of the expression on offer. (The gravest risks related to this, of course, pertain to harnessing generative AI technology for political and societal influencing, but that is not a matter for copyright to regulate.) One might also suppose potential problems of a purely communicative kind might arise. Namely, that genuinely worthwhile content created by human creators through traditional means will experience difficulties in rising above the potentially enormous masses of superficially handsome but ultimately uninteresting AI-generated creative content in vying for the public's attention.

While this is a legitimate concern, I find that an aspiring content creator's quest for finding an audience – which tends to be a considerable challenge even for the most talented content creators early in their careers – is unlikely to be significantly worsened by the impending AI-driven explosion in the sheer quantity of creative content available. This is because the quantity of creative content was already at overwhelming levels before the advent of high-performance generative AI, creating a system where only a fraction of entries actually receive significant attention. To illustrate, data and analytics company Luminate stated that 24% of the 158 million audio tracks on music streaming services it monitored in 2022 attracted zero plays,[558] whereas Spotify reported that 78.4% of their artists had a monthly audience of less than 50 people.[559] Such statistics may not be absolutely representative of the actual state of affairs, but one can reasonably assume that large proportions of the content available for consumption receive either very modest attention or none at all. This also aligns with the winner-takes-all market mechanism characterising the music industry.[560] One might therefore assume that the AI-generated creations relying heavily on automatic data processing mainly will add to the proportion of published content that is largely ignored. The AI Act's obligation to 'enable the detection and disclosure that the outputs of those systems are artificially generated' seems particularly relevant here.[561] At least in theory, it should make it possible to opt out from getting AI-generated results when

557. Bonadio and McDonagh 2020, p. 134; Iaia 2022, p. 25.
558. https://www.musicbusinessworldwide.com/38-million-tracks-on-music-streaming-service-were-played-zero-times-in-2022-elon-musks-book/, accessed 1 February 2025.
559. https://www.musicbusinessworldwide.com/over-75-of-artists-on-spotify-have-fewer-than-50-monthly-listeners/, retrieved accessed 1 February 2025.
560. Rick Everts (15 September 2023): Making it big in live music: a multilevel analysis of careers in live music, Cultural Trends, pp. 1-2, available at https://doi.org/10.1080/09548963.2023.2255849, accessed 1 February 2025.
561. AI Act, recital 120.

searching for music, although the definition of what should count as AI-generated in this context may pose occasional challenges of definition.

On the whole, I do not think that withholding copyright protection from AI-generated works genuinely deserving of copyright protection – as I personally find both the *Théâtre D'opéra Spatial* image and ExtraRL's outputs to be – will do much in the way of safeguarding the material and moral interests of authors that utilise traditional means of composing music.[562] Simply put, the eventual co-existence of high-quality AI-generated and traditionally composed music appears both likely and unavoidable. Attempts to hinder this development through a strict application of copyright protection prerequisites to creative processes that utilise AI-powered tools are unlikely to yield significant benefits.

Another commonly voiced concern is that an increased deployment of generative AI may lead to cost-cutting in the creative industries, jeopardising both career trajectories and the long-term quality of creative output in the field. In the context of the music industry, the danger of AI-powered tools replacing entry-level jobs in recording studios and small media companies has been frequently raised.[563] While the potential disappearance of entry-level jobs and its adverse effect on traditional career trajectories is certainly a concerning prospect, the notion of disincentivising the development and deployment of generative AI models on such grounds seems like a rather extreme measure with Luddite undertones. If ever-improving music generation systems are poised to increasingly challenge and replace human creators of stock and space-filler music, the likely outcome is that human expertise is reallocated towards more artistically ambitious and demanding tasks. In this regard, one might draw a parallel to cars displacing horses, coaches, and coachmen as well as mechanisation replacing human labour – developments that ultimately 'proved to be good for society'.[564]

8.3.4 Final Reflections on the Current State and Future Developments

How do things, then, currently stand regarding the utilisation of AI models for composing music, and what types of future development are most likely? As shown by the examination of several music generation systems – such as MusicLM, MusicRL, MusicGen, and the hypothetical ExtraRL – the autonomous generation of passable background music is already a reality today and is clearly set to further improve in the coming years. Other systems, like the Udio system mentioned in the introductory chapter of the book, have not only attracted considerable attention and popularity but also produced reasonably handsome compositions. This might give the impression that the workflow of tomorrow's composers will increasingly incorporate AI-powered tools and music generation into their workflows. However, a crucial obstacle to this is the

562. To clarify, this statement expressly refers to the copyright treatment of AI outputs. In the issue of unlicenced training data input, which is outside the scope of this dissertation, the situation may be different.
563. Sturm et al. 2019, p. 11.
564. Frosio 2024, p. 13.

lacklustre prompt adherence exhibited by even the most impressive of today's music generation systems, which may significantly counteract a more widespread incorporation of AI-powered tools into the more ambitious aspects of professional compositional workflows. This is associated with a lower likelihood of AI-powered tools replacing manual input as the primary compositional means through which copyright-protected musical expression is created.

Here, we find potentially noteworthy differences between autonomous music and text – or image – generation. In the latter, the notion of authoring an original work through mere prompt engineering does not appear particularly far-fetched in scenarios where an output is created by subjecting an initial prompt to several stages of iterative refinement. The crucial difference between high-performance text models and state-of-the-art music generation systems lies in the former's superior prompt adherence and better capability of allowing the user to gradually create the work by making iterative additions. The examination of the technical aspects of developing music generation systems has also indicated that significant improvements in prompt adherence and iterative refinement, while certainly not impossible, are not a foregone conclusion.

One way in which the limitations of text-to-music conditioning can come to be mitigated is through a combination of text and sound prompting. The idea is that since textual descriptions of music have inherent shortcomings, the user could provide audio samples as prompts to further specify the desired compositional features. For instance, terms such as 'expansive', 'repetitive', or 'mellow' might not be easily translated into particular types of musical expression. However, if the user can play an excerpt on their instrument that exemplifies the kind of expansive or repetitive melodic development they envision, the interaction between pre-generation contributions and system outputs could take a more artistically interesting turn. However, for such a compositional method to plausibly produce musical expression that reflects the system user's creative choices – and thereby unlocks access to both viability and a copyright claim to the result – the capabilities of music generation systems to allow for iterative refinement through prompting would likely need to see significant advancement.

The example of ExtraRL and the extensive fine-tuning of pre-existing foundation models aligns with another possibility: the increasing capabilities and availability of high-performance, open-source music generation systems may inspire a new compositional method that occupies a middle ground between traditional composing and AI model development. In this context, one might draw parallels to the emergence of sound sampling and DAW-based composition, where electronic devices came to replace traditional musical instruments in conveying musical expression.

Regardless of whether these methods gain traction and popularity, it appears almost inevitable that new, continuously evolving AI-powered tools will inspire the creative minds of the future to develop innovative and unforeseen means of musical expression. Drawing upon the lessons of history, one might also predict that these novel forms of creative expression will elicit a wide array of reactions, ranging from enthusiastic adoption to intense scepticism. Similarly, it seems inevitable that a new equilibrium will eventually be achieved, where various genres incorporating AI-generated input secure their places in the cultural landscape.

8.4 RESULTS AND CONCLUSIONS: ANSWERS TO THE RESEARCH QUESTIONS

To present the results of the dissertation, we shall provide answers to the research questions stated at the beginning of Chapter 1. To illustrate the research task, the example of Model A being prompted by User A to produce Composition A was introduced. This example served as the basis for stating the following seven research questions, of which the first two state the main focus of the research task, and the rest address various sub-components of the inquiry:

(1) Can Composition A and similar AI-generated compositions constitute musical works under copyright law?
(2) If they can, which party or parties can claim an exclusive right to them and on what grounds?
(3) What are the requirements on the creative process of Composition A for it to qualify as a protected musical work?
(4) How should one determine whether the relationship between pre-generation creative contributions and the post-generation end result is to be considered sufficient to make the latter into a copyright-protected work?
(5) How does a musical work come into being and how should one define its contents?
(6) How can one define the component parts of a musical work and the compositional process in a way that accurately accounts for the utilisation of AI-powered creative tools?
(7) Under what conditions can one consider a sequence of instructions describing musical attributes (i) to be sufficiently precise and (ii) to have become reflected in the relevant data collection with enough accuracy to warrant copyright protection?

The first can be answered in the affirmative. Composition A and similar AI-generated compositions can indeed constitute musical works under copyright law. To address the specific circumstances which determine whether Composition A can be considered a musical work and the second research question's query regarding the allocation of authorship, questions (3)-(7) need to be discussed. Research question (3) concerns the requirements placed on the creative process, which were examined in Chapter 3. It stated that the requirements are satisfied if the melodic, rhythmic, harmonic, and other attributes of Composition A resulted from a series of free and creative choices that reflect the author's personality. In essence, this means that the copyright eligibility of Composition A hinges on the relationship or link between the creative process and its end result, leading to question (4), which asks how one is to determine whether said link between creative choices and end result is sufficient.

As stated in Chapter 1, this suggests a two-phase analysis where one first identifies all the free and creative choices that contributed to bringing Composition A into existence. Next, one examines how much each choice contributed to shaping the musical attributes of Composition A. In theory, this suffices to address the core research task expressed in questions (1) and (2): If the free and creative choices – related to training data selection, model architecture design, fine-tuning, or prompt engineering – made during the creative process influenced the musical attributes of Composition A with sufficient precision, copyright protection is possible. It will be allocated to the contributors whose creative choices are meaningfully reflected in the composition's musical attributes.

The challenge of implementing this approach lies in that the legal order, due to the novelty of this compositional method, may struggle to assess the relationship between the creative choices and the end result. While there is a rich tradition of assessing the link between a composer's choice of notes on a music sheet and a singer's performance of it, the relationship between choices such as the selection of an embedding model or an iterative fine-tuning sequence and the musical attributes of an AI-generated audio track is far less straightforward. This challenge led to the formulation of questions (5)-(7), which explore what it means to compose a musical work and how the creative process behind a music generation system aligns with this concept.

Chapter 5 deconstructs the ontology of a musical work, dividing it into three stages: underlying composition, source material, and prospective reproduction. Research question (6) touches upon features discussed in Chapters 4 and 6. Chapter 4 introduces, defines, and justifies the concept of originality causation, which measures the extent of creative control the author exercised over the end result. The degree of originality causation correlates with the copyright eligibility of the end result: If there is originality causation between a creative choice and the musical attributes of Composition A, the maker of the choice should have a valid (co-)authorship claim to it.

A defining aspect of the creative choices that accomplish an AI-generated composition is that they typically do not determine the musical attributes of the end result with the same precision as a composer inserting notes into a music sheet. Even if this means that Developers A and User A's authorship claims to Composition A may be inherently weaker than those based on compiling a traditional music sheet, it does not necessarily follow that the originality causation requirement could not be met.

Ultimately, determining the degree of originality causation involves assessing the circumstances under which a sequence of creative choices – consisting solely of broadly formulated descriptions of musical building blocks – can acquire sufficient specificity to meet the originality causation requirement. This closely aligns with the idea/expression dichotomy, which states that commonplace musical building blocks are classified as ideas and cannot be protected, whereas their specific utilisation through the author's creative input can become protected expression.

Chapter 6 addresses this issue from the perspective of traditional musical composition by introducing a template composition consisting of broadly formulated instructions that subsequent contributors can render into an 'actual' piece of musical expression. The template composition allows for an analogy to be drawn between existing case law on distinguishing between ideas and expression in music copyright and the specificity-generality distinction central to determining whether sufficient originality causation exists between pre-generation creative choices and the post-generation end result. This constitutes the answer to research question (6), which inquires how one might define the component parts of a musical work in a way that accounts for the utilisation of AI-powered creative tools. Accordingly, the analysis conducted throughout Chapters 4-6, which addresses research questions (5) and (6), provided the requisite tools for answering research question (7).

To answer research question (7), which concerns the conditions under which a sequence of instructions describing musical attributes can be considered both sufficiently specific and sufficiently reflected in the end result, Chapter 7 examined various features of how human contributors interact with an AI model and how significantly this interaction can influence the musical attributes of the output. It concluded that the creative process of the MusicRL system did not exhibit a degree of originality causation sufficient to grant access to copyright protection. By contrast, the hypothetical ExtraRL system could plausibly support an authorship claim for the fictional development team. The crucial difference lay in the fictional development team making numerous iterative refinements to the system, specifically targeting the musical attributes of the final output. However, even if the fictional development team's authorship claim was reasonably plausible, the likelihood of such practices for developing music generation systems becoming commonplace was deemed relatively low.

Consequently, research questions (1) and (2) can be answered in greater detail. Composition A can qualify as a musical work if the creative choices of Developers A or User A are sufficiently specific and sufficiently reflected in its musical attributes. User A's contribution meets neither criterion. Developers A may meet the criteria if the development of Model A involved multiple stages of iterative refinement targeting specific elements of the model's output.

Appendix

Item 1

Stairway to X 1.1

Composition 1

Item 2

Stairway to X 1.1

Composition 2

Item 3

Stairway to X 1.1

Composition 3

Item 4

Stairway to X 1.2

Composition 4

Item 5

Stairway to X 1.2

Composition 5

Item 6

Stairway to X 1.2

Composition 6

Item 7

Stairway to X 1.1

Composition 7

Item 8

Stairway to X 1.1

Mock performance 1 (Composition 1)

Item 9

Stairway to X 1.1

Mock performance 2 (composition 1)

Item 10

Stairway to X 1.1

Mock performance 3 (Composition 7)

Item 11

Stairway to X 2.0

Composition X1

2

Item 12

Stairway to X 2.0

Composition X2

2

Item 13

Stairway to X 2.0

Composition X3

2

Item 14

Stairway to X 2.0

Composition X4

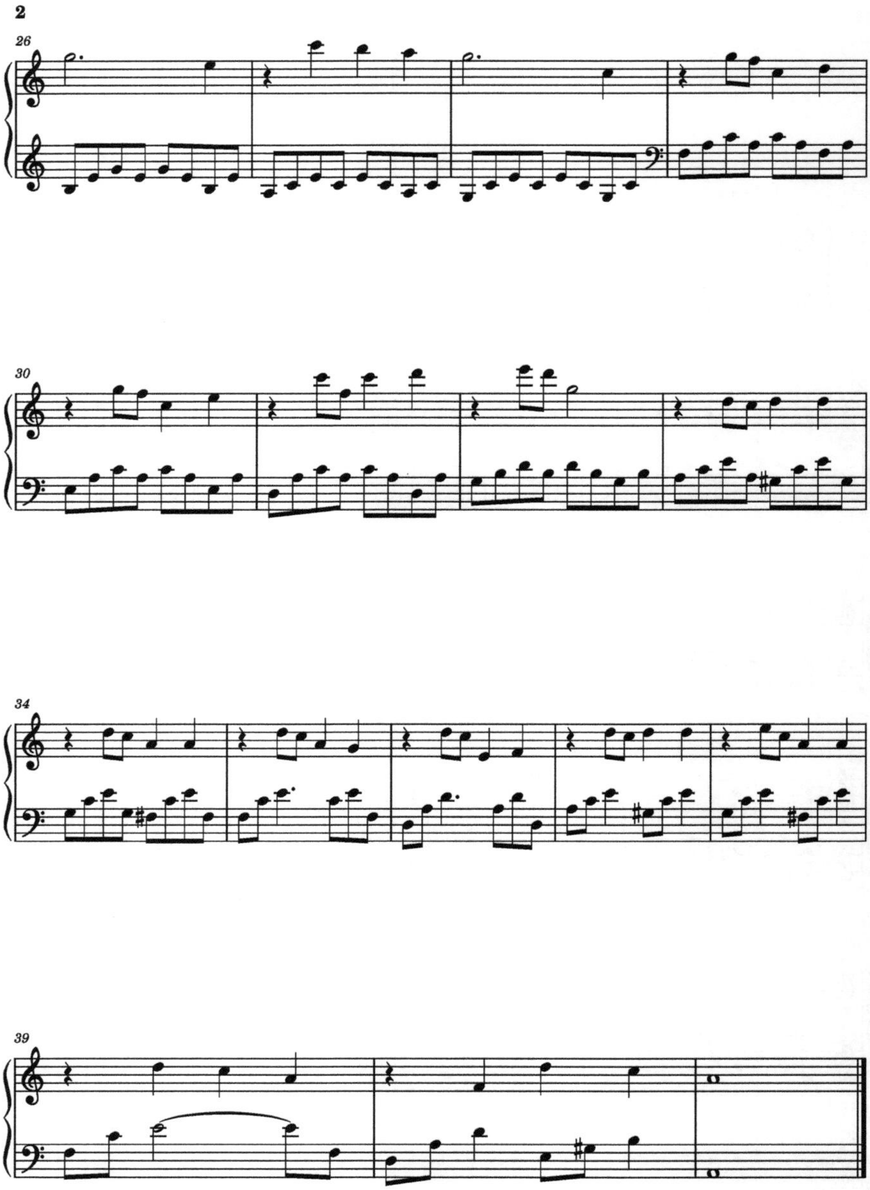
2
26
30
34
39

Item 15

Stairway to X 2.0

Composition X5

Item 16

Instructions for Stairway to X version 2.0

Provide the attached file with melodic content. The accompaniment is written into the lower staff of the piano part, and is not to be changed. The prescribed rhythm of the melody is given on the uppermost staff. The melodic content is to be written into the right hand staff of the piano part. Please adhere to the instructions below.

1. The piece is in ABA form
   a. A-section: Bars 1-16
   b. B-section: Bars 17-32
   c. Recapitulation: Bars 33-41
2. The A section (bars 1-16) consists of two features
   a. The Taurus-progression.
   b. The so-called 'Theme X', *see* picture i. b.

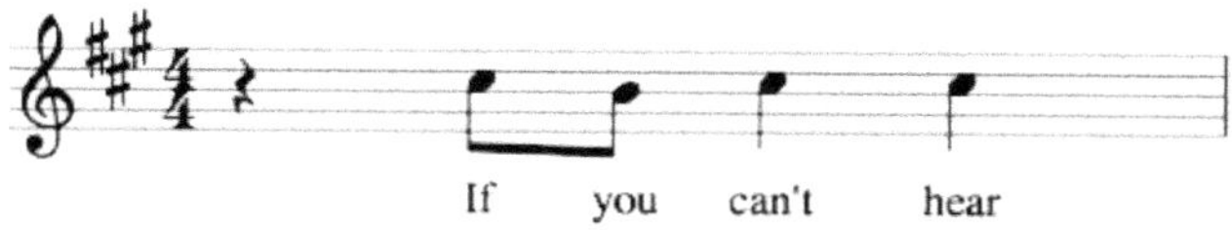

Theme X in "Blurred Lines"

   c. The starting pitch of Theme X can be chosen freely, but the rules of harmonic compatibility narrow the range of realistic options
3. Precise instructions for the A section
   a. Bars 1-2. Repeat Theme X two times.
   b. Bars 3-4. The rhythm of Theme X is to be repeated, otherwise the melodic notes can be chosen freely.
   c. Bars 5-8. Repeat the contents of bars 1-4. Small variations are allowed in bars 6-8.
   d. Bars 9-12. Add new melodic material. Bar 11 is to be identical to bar 9.
   e. Bars 13-16. Repeat the contents of bars 1-4. Bar 16 will contain a modulation to the key of the B-section.
4. Precise instructions for the B section
   a. In C major. A new chord progression in the left hand.
   b. The section is 8 + 8 = 16 bars long, consisting of a 8-bar passage that is repeated.
   c. The melodic rhythm is identical to bars 9-12. It is possible, though not mandated, to use the same or similar melodic material for both.
   d. Bar 19 is to be identical to bar 17.
   e. Bars 25-32 repeat the preceding 8 bars, but small variations are allowed, especially in bars 27-32. The variations are to be modeled on the analogous passage of bars 19-24. It is allowed to change the rhythm so that a pair of consecutive crotchets are replaced by a minim.
5. Precise instructions for the recapitulation
   a. Repeat bars 1-8 with small variations.
   b. Bar 33 can begin with a rest (as indicated) or with a crotchet note.
   c. To prepare the fast approaching conclusion of the piece, the accompaniment will gradually move slower. A similar deceleration of note values is recommended in the melody as well. One may also use fragments of motifs from various parts of the composition in a heretofore unprecedented order.

As at the end of the B-section, it is allowed to change the rhythm so that a pair of consecutive crotchets are replaced by a minim.

Item 17

2

20
Rhythm
Pno.
24
Rhythm
Repeat bars 17-24
Small variations allowed
Pno.
28
Rhythm
Pno.
32
Rhythm
Repeat bars 1-8. Variations allowed, see instructions.
Pno.
36
Rhythm
Pno.

3
40
Rhythm
Pno.

Bibliography

Sources

Aarnio, Aulis, Essays on the Doctrinal Study of Law, Springer, 2011.

Aarnio, Aulis, Oikeussäännösten systematisointi ja tulkinta, in Häyhä, J. (ed.) Minun metodini, WSOY 1997, pp. 35-56.

Aarnio, Aulis, The Rational as Reasonable, D. Reidel Publishing Company, 1987.

Agostinelli, Andrea et al., MusicLM: Generating Music from Text, 2023, available at https://arxiv.org/abs/2301.11325, accessed 12 February 2025.

Alén-Savikko, Anette et al. (eds), Muuttuva tekijä 2020.

Alter, Karen J., The European Union's Legal System and Domestic Policy: Spillover or Backlash? International Organization, Vol. 54, No. 3, Legalization and World Politics, Summer, 2000, pp. 489-518.

Aplin, Tanya F., Subject Matter (Book Chapter), in Research Handbook on the Future of EU Copyright, 2009, p. 3, available at SSRN: https://ssrn.com/abstract=2437006, accessed 12 February 2025.

Arewa, Olufunmilayo B., A Musical Work Is a Set of Instructions, 52 Hous. L. Rev. (2014), pp. 467-535.

Axhamn, Johan, Copyright and Artificial Intelligence: With a Focus on the Area of Music, in Rosenmeier, M. (eds), Festskrift til Jørgen Blomqvist, 2021, available at https://lucris.lub.lu.se/ws/portalfiles/portal/97631996/Slutlig_version_03_0041_0_Festskrift_210505_adj.pdf, accessed 13 February 2025.

Badhan, Maithili, Comprehensive Guide to Chain-of-Thought Prompting, https://www.mercity.ai/blog-post/guide-to-chain-of-thought-prompting, accessed 11 February 2025.

Ballardini, Rosa, He, Kan and Roos, Teemu, AI-Generated Content: Authorship and Inventorship in the Age of Artificial Intelligence, in Pihlajarinne, T., Vesala, J. and Honkkila, O. (eds), Online Distribution of Content in the EU, Edward Elgar 2018, available at https://www.cs.helsinki.fi/u/ttonteri/pub/aicontent2018.pdf, accessed 13 February 2025.

Bathaee, Yavar, The Artificial Intelligence Black Box and the Failure of Intent and Causation, 31(2) Harv. J.L.& Tech., Spring 2018.

Bennet, Joe, We Can Work It Out: Methods in Forensic Musicology, in Bonadio, E. and Wei, C. (eds), ZhuMusic Borrowing and Copyright Law: A Genre-by-Genre Analysis, Hart Publishing 2023.

Bently, Lionel, Authorship of Popular Music in UK Copyright Law, 12(2) Information, Communication & Society (2009), pp. 179-204, available at https://doi.org/10.1080/13691180802459948, accessed 15 March 2025.

Bergström, Svante, Uteslutande rätt att förfoga över verket, Lundequist 1954, available at https://www.juridikbok.se/book/466587, accessed 12 February 2025.

Bischoff, Susan, The Next Chapter in the 'Metall auf Metall' Saga: Pastiche to Be Clarified by the CJEU, 21 September 2023, https://copyrightblog.kluweriplaw.com/2023/09/21/the-next-chapter-in-the-metall-auf-metall-saga-pastiche-to-be-clarified-by-the-cjeu/, accessed 12 February 2025.

Blazek, Paul J., Why We Will Never Open Deep Learning's Black Box, https://towardsdatascience.com/why-we-will-never-open-deep-learnings-black-box-4c27cd335118, accessed 2 February 2025.

Bonadio, Enrico and McDonagh, Luke, Artificial Intelligence as Producer and Consumer of Copyright Works: Evaluating the Consequences of Algorithmic Creativity, 2 Int. Prop. Q. (2020), pp. 112-137.

Boorman, Stanley, The Musical Text, in Cook, N. and Everist, M. (eds) Rethinking Music, Oxford University Press, 2001.

Borsos, Zalán et al., AudioLM: A Language Modeling Approach to Audio Generation, 2023, available at https://arxiv.org/abs/2209.03143, accessed 12 February 2025.

Bosher, Hayleigh, Music Copyright Infringement Cases in US and UK: Building a House Upon the Sand or the Rock?, in Bosher, H. and Rosati, E. (eds) Developments and Directions in Intellectual Property Law: 20 Years of the IPKat, Oxford, Oxford University Press, pp. 276-292.

Bowen, José A., Finding the Music in Musicology: Performance History and Musical Works, in Cook, N. and Everist, M. (eds), Rethinking Music, Oxford, Oxford University Press, 2001.

Briot, Jean-Pierre, Hadjeres, Gaëtan and Pachet, Francois-David, Deep Learning Techniques for Music Generation, available at https://arxiv.org/abs/1709.01620, accessed 11 February 2025.

Brown, Tom B. et al., Language Models are Few-Shot Learners, 2020, available at https://arxiv.org/abs/2005.14165, accessed 11 February 2025.

Bulayenko, Oleksandr, AI Music Outputs: Challenges to the Copyright Legal Framework, 28 February 2022, available at SSRN: https://ssrn.com/abstract=4072806, accessed 12 February 2025.

Burk, Dan L., Thirty-Six Views of Copyright Authorship, by Jackson Pollock, 58 Hous. L. Rev. (2020), 263, pp. 263-326.

Butler, Mark J., Playing with Something That Runs: Technology, Improvisation, and Composition in DJ and Laptop Performance, Oxford University Press, 2014.

Carey, Teresa L., Beethoven's Unfinished 10th Symphony Brought to Life by Artificial Intelligence, available at https://www.scientificamerican.com/podcast/episode/beethovens-unfinished-10th-symphony-brought-to-life-by-artificial-intelligence/, accessed 12 February 2025.

Carnovalini, Filippo, Open Challenges in Musical Metacreation, 2022, available at https://arxiv.org/abs/2208.14734, accessed 11 February 2025.

Casas Vallés, Ramón, The Requirement of Originality, in Derclaye, E. (ed.), Research Handbook on the Future of EU Copyright, Edward Elgar Publishing 2009.

Chatterton, Edward, Zhang, Joanne and Blackford, Liam, Another Chinese Court Finds That AI-Generated Images Can Be Protected by Copyright: The Changshu People's Court and the 'Half Heart' Case, 2025, available at https://www.lexology.com/library/detail.aspx?g=4a4f2ad0-3d9e-41ee-b6b9-cc9341542699, accessed 14 June 2025.

Cheong, Yew Choong, Decoding Idiosyncratic Hairpins: Dynamic Changes or 'Notated' Rubato?, 2(1) MMJ (2019), pp. 4-20, available at https://so04.tci-thaijo.org/index.php/mmj/article/view/189241, accessed 12 February 2025.

Cideron, Geoffrey et al., MusicRL: Aligning Music Generation to Human Preferences, 2024, available at https://arxiv.org/abs/2402.04229, accessed 12 February 2025.

Cohen Jehoram, Herman, The Dutch Supreme Court Recognises Copyright in the Scent of a Perfume, 28(12) E.I.P.R. (2006), pp. 629-631.

Cole, Toby and Chinoy, Helen Krich (eds), Directors on Directing: A Source Book of the Modern Theatre, Macmillan 1976.

Collet, Pierre, Stochastic Optimization Algorithms, 2006, available https://arxiv.org/ftp/arxiv/papers/0704/0704.3780.pdf, accessed 2 February 2025.

Cook, Nicholas, Music, Imagination and Culture, Oxford University Press, 1992.

Cooper, Feder A. and Grimmelman, James, The Files are in the Computer: On Copyright, Memorization, and Generative AI, 2024, available at https://arxiv.org/abs/2404.12590, accessed 11 February 2025.

Copet, Jade et al., Simple and Controllable Music Generation, 2024, available at https://arxiv.org/abs/2306.05284, accessed 12 February 2025.

Copland, Aaron, How We Listen To Music, 1988, https://springmuse.hunter.cuny.edu/wp-content/uploads/2019/01/Copland-How-We-Listen-To-Music.pdf, accessed 19 October 2024.

Craglia, Max (ed.), Artificial Intelligence: A European Perspective, European Commission 2018.

Craig, Carys and Laroche, Guillaume, Out of Tune: Why Copyright Law Needs Music Lessons, in Doagoo, B.C. (eds), Intellectual Property for the 21st Century: Interdisciplinary Approaches, Toronto, Irwin Publishing 2014, pp. 43-71.

Davies, Stephen, The Ontology of Musical Works and the Authenticity of Their Performances, 25(1) Nous (March 1991), p. 21 https://doi.org/10.2307/2216091, accessed 9 August 2025.

Davis, Elizabeth, Schubert's 'Unfinished' Symphony Completed by Artificial Intelligence, available at https://www.classicfm.com/composers/schubert/unfinished-symphony-completed-by-ai/, accessed 12 February 2025.

Défossez, Alexandre et al., High Fidelity Neural Audio Compression, 2022, available at https://arxiv.org/abs/2210.13438, accessed 12 February 2025.

Deng, Junwei, Zhang, Shiyuan and Ma, Jiaqi, Computational Copyright: Towards a Royalty Model for Music Generative AI, 2023, available at https://arxiv.org/abs/2312.06646, accessed 13 February 2025.

Derclaye, Estelle, AG Szpunar's Opinion in Mio/konektra: A Welcome Clarification of the CJEU's Case Law on Works of Applied Art, Kluwer Copyright Blog, 2 June 2025, available at https://legalblogs.wolterskluwer.com/copyright-blog/ag-szpunars-opinion-in-miokonektra-a-welcome-clarification-of-the-cjeus-case-law-on-works-of-applied-art/, accessed 9 September 2025.

DeVlieger, Dana, Promoting Creativity: How the Use of Music Analysis Affects Value Judgments in Copyright Litigation, 2020, available at https://conservancy.umn.edu/items/1125bb67-1fc4-4fc7-90e5-9544885e9aff, accessed 12 February 2025.

DeVlieger, Dana, Searching for Similarity: Confirmation Bias in Forensic Analyses of Popular Music, 34(2) JPMS (2022), pp. 91-111, https://doi.org/10.1525/jpms.2022.34.2.91, accessed 13 February 2025.

Dhariwal, Prafulla et al., Jukebox: A Generative Model for Music, 2020, available at https://arxiv.org/abs/2005.00341, accessed 12 February 2025.

Dreier, Thomas and Karnell, Gunnar, Originality of the Copyrighted Work: A European Perspective, 39 J. Copyright Soc'y U.S.A. 289 (1992).

Eidsvold-Tøien, Irina and Stenvik, Are, Copyright for Performers: An Obligation under International Law, 18(10) JIPLP (2023) https://doi.org/10.1093/jiplp/jpad073, accessed 9 August 2025.

Emanuilov, Ivo and Margoni, Thomas, Forget Me Not: Memorisation in Generative Sequence Models Trained on Open Source Licensed Code, 7 February 2024, available at https://ssrn.com/abstract=4720990, accessed 23 March 2025.

Epperson, Gordon, Article on Music in Encyclopedia Britannica, available at https://www.britannica.com/art/music, accessed 15 March 2025.

European Copyright Society, Opinion on the Pending Reference Before the CJEU in Case 310/17 (Copyright Protection of Tastes), available at https://europeancopyrightsociety.org/wp-content/uploads/2018/03/ecs-opinion-on-protection-for-tastes-final1.pdf, accessed 12 February 2025.

European Copyright Society, Opinion of the European Copyright Society in Relation to the Pending Reference Before the CJEU in Cofemel v G-Star, C-683/17, available at https://europeancopyrightsociety.org/wp-content/uploads/2018/11/ecs-opinion-cofemel_final_signed.pdf, accessed 12 February 2025.

European Copyright Society, The Protection of Works of Applied Art under EU Copyright Law, Opinion of the European Copyright Society in MIO/Konektra (Cases C-580/23 and C-795/23), 3 December 2024, available https://europeancopyrightsociety.org/wp-content/uploads/2024/12/ecs-opinion-mio-konektra.pdf, accessed 24 March 2025.

Everts, Rick, Making It Big in Live Music: A Multilevel Analysis of Careers in Live Music, 22(5) Cultural Trends (2024) https://doi.org/10.1080/09548963.2023.2255849, accessed 9 August 2025, available at https://www.tandfonline.com/doi/full/10.1080/09548963.2023.2255849#abstract, accessed 13 February 2025.

Falstrom, Carl A., Thou Shalt Not Steal: Grand Upright Music Ltd. v. Warner Bros. Records, Inc. and the Future of Digital Sound Sampling in Popular Music, 45 Hastings L.J. 359 (1994), available at https://repository.uchastings.edu/hastings_law_journal/vol45/iss2/4, accessed 14 March 2025.

Fernández, Jose David and Vico, Francisco, AI Methods in Algorithmic Composition: A Comprehensive Survey, 48 JAIR (2013), pp. 513-582 https://doi.org/10.1613/jair.3908, accessed 9 August 2025.

Fishman, Joseph P. and Garcia, Kristelia, Authoring Prior Art, 75 Vand. L. Rev. 1159 (2023) pp. 1159-1210.

Frosio, Giancarlo, Four Theories in Search of an A(I)uthor, in Abbott, R. (ed.), Handbook of Artificial Intelligence and Intellectual Property, Edward Elgar, 2022, pp. 155-177.

Frosio, Giancarlo, The Artificial Creatives: The Rise of Combinatorial Creativity from Dall-E to ChatGPT, 7 February 2023, Garcia-Murillo, M., MacInnes, I. and Renda, A. (eds), Handbook of Artificial Intelligence at Work: Interconnections and Policy Implications, Edward Elgar, 2024, pp. 225-249, Queen's University Belfast Law Research Paper, available at https://ssrn.com/abstract=4350802 or http://dx.doi.org/10.2139/ssrn.4350802, accessed 13 February 2025.

Geiger, Christophe, Intellectual Property and Investment Protection: A Misleading Equation, 14 November 2021, in Fischer, V. et al. (eds), Gestaltung der Informationsrechtsordnung: Festschrift für Thomas Dreier zum 65. Geburtstag, Munich, Beck, 2022, pp. 7-19., available at https://ssrn.com/abstract=3958320, accessed 5 March 2025.

Gervais, Daniel, The Machine as Author, 105 Iowa L. Rev. (2020), p. 2053.

Gervais, Daniel, Second-Degree Intellectual Property, 39(3) Berkeley Tech. L.J. (30 September 2024), pp. 1091-1116, available at https://doi.org/10.15779/Z38W66995Q, accessed 19 February 2025.

Gervais, Daniel J. and Judge, Elizabeth F., Of Silos and Constellations: Comparing Notions of Originality in Copyright Law, 27 Cardozo Arts & Ent. L.J. (2009), p. 375.

Ginsburg, Jane C. and Budiardjo, Luke A., Authors and Machines, 34 Berkeley Tech. L. J. (2019), p. 343.

Gonzalez Cerrillo, Adrian and Hakim, Sana, 'Levitating' Lawsuits: Understanding Dua Lipa's Copyright Infringement Troubles, available at https://www.iplawwatch.com/2022/03/21/levitating-lawsuits-understanding-dua-lipas-copyright-infringement-troubles/, accessed 5 March 2025.

Griffiths, Jonathan, The Role of the Court of Justice in the Development of European Union Copyright Law, in Stamatoudi, E. and Torremans, P. (eds), EU Copyright Law, A Commentary, Edward Elgar Publishing 2014.

Guadamuz, Andres, The Monkey Selfie: Copyright Lessons for Originality in Photographs and Internet Jurisdiction, 5(1) Internet Policy Rev. (2016) https://doi.org/10.14763/2016.1.398, accessed 9 August 2025, available at https://ssrn.com/abstract=2752461, accessed 12 February 2025.

Haarmann, Pirkko-Liisa, Immateriaalioikeus, Talentum Media, 5th ed., 2014.

Hadjeres, Gaëtan, Pachet, François and Nielsen, Frank, DeepBach: A Steerable Model for Bach Chorales Generation, 2017, available at https://arxiv.org/abs/1612.01010, accessed 12 February 2025.

Harenko, Kristiina et al., Tekijänoikeus, Alma, 3rd ed., 2024.

Hartmann, Christian et al., Trends and Developments in Artificial Intelligence Challenges to the Intellectual Property Rights Framework, European Commission 2020, available at https://digital-strategy.ec.europa.eu/en/library/trends-and-developments-artificial-intelligence-challenges-intellectual-property-rights-framework, accessed 24 March 2025.

He, Tianxiang, AI Originality Revisited: Can We Prompt Copyright over AI-Generated Pictures?, 73(4) GRUR Int. (April 2024), pp. 299-307, https://doi.org/10.1093/grurint/ikae024, accessed 13 February 2025.

Hedrick, Samantha F., I 'Think', Therefore I Create: Claiming Copyright in the Outputs of Algorithms (2018), 8(2) NYU JIPEL (2019), available at https://jipel.law.nyu.edu/vol-8-no-2-1-hedrick/, accessed 13 February 2025.

Heiniö, Mikko, Näkymätön tekijä, Lakimies 7-8/2013, pp. 1172-1183.

Hertzmann, Aaron, 'Can Computers Create Art?', 7 Arts (2018) available at https://arxiv.org/abs/1801.04486, accessed 13 February 2025.

Hiller, Lejaren, Encyclopedia Britannica Article on Computer Music, last updated 8 February 2025, available at https://www.britannica.com/art/electronic-music/Computer-music#ref395219, accessed 13 March 2025.

Hilsdorf, Max, 3 Music AI Breakthroughs to Expect in 2024, 30 December 2023, available at https://medium.com/towards-data-science/3-music-ai-breakthroughs-to-expect-in-2024-2d945ae6b5fd, accessed 12 February 2025.

Hinton, Stephen, The Emancipation of Dissonance: Schoenberg's Two Practices of Composition, 91(4) Music & Letters (November 2010), pp. 568-579 https://doi.org/10.1093/ml/gcq092, accessed 9 August 2025.

Hirvonen, Ari, Mitkä metodit: Opas oikeustieteen metodologiaan, Helsinki 2011.

Hirvonen, Ari, Konkreettinen oikeuslähdeoppi: normimateriasta rakenteisiin ja ratkaisutoimintaan, Lakimies 7-8/2020, pp. 954-971.

Hoikka, Mikko, TN 2024:3: Hiekkapaperia vai sorkkarautaa teoskynnykselle?, Lakimies 5/2024, pp. 731–737.

Hristov, Kalin, Artificial Intelligence and the Copyright Dilemma (September 1, 2016), 57(3) IDEA: The IP Law Review (2017), available https://ssrn.com/abstract=2976428, accessed 13 February 2025.

Hu, Edward J. et al., Low-Rank Adaptation of Large Language Models, 2021, available at https://arxiv.org/abs/2106.09685, accessed 2 February 2025.

Huang, Qingqing; et al., MuLan: A Joint Embedding of Music Audio and Natural Language, 2022, available at https://arxiv.org/abs/2208.12415, accessed 12 February 2025.

Hugenholtz, P. Bernt, Copyright and the Expression Engine: Idea and Expression in AI-Assisted Creations, 27 February 2024, available at http://dx.doi.org/10.2139/ssrn.4982516, accessed 3 April 2025.

Hugenholtz, P. Bernt., Prompts Between Idea and Expression. Generative AI and the Work of Authorship, Nordiskt Immateriellt Rättsskydd nr 1 2025, pp. 125-132.

Hugenholtz, P. Bernt and Quintais, João P., Copyright and Artificial Creation: Does EU Copyright Law Protect AI-Assisted Output?, 52 IIC (2021), pp. 1190-1216 https://doi.org/10.1007/s40319-021-01115-0, accessed 9 August 2025.

Husa, Jaakko, The Traditional Methods of Comparative Law, Siems & Jen Yap (eds), The Cambridge Handbook of Comparative Law, Forthcoming, 1 January 2023, available at https://ssrn.com/abstract=4418563, accessed 6 March 2025.

Härkönen, Heidi, A Narrative Approach to the Standard of Originality in EU Copyright Law: The Story of a Dress, 56 IIC (2025) pp. 289-319 https://doi.org/10.1007/s40319-025-01562-z, accessed 9 August 2025. Härkönen 2025a.

Härkönen, Heidi, AG's Opinion in Cases Mio and Konektra Clarifies Criteria for Assessing Copyright Infringement, IPR Info Publication 3/2025, available at https://iprinfo.fi/artikkeli/ags-opinion-in-cases-mio-and-konektra-clarifies-criteria-for-assessing-copyright-infringement/, accessed 9 September 2025. Härkönen 2025b.

Härkönen, Heidi, Onko teoskynnyksellä tulevaisuutta?, IPR Info Publication 2/2024, available at https://iprinfo.fi/artikkeli/onko-teoskynnyksella-tulevaisuutta/, accessed 2 December 2025.

Iaia, Vincenzo, To Be, or Not to Be … Original Under Copyright Law, That Is (One of) the Main Questions Concerning AI-Produced Works, 71(9) GRUR Int. (11 August 2022), pp. 793-892 https://doi.org/10.1093/grurint/ikac087, accessed 9 August 2025, available at https://ssrn.com/abstract=4528143, accessed 17 February 2025.

Ingarden, Roman, The Work of Music and the Problem of Its Identity, Berkeley, University of California Press, 1986.

Ingham, Tim, The Train Has Left the Station: AI Music Platform Udio Is Already Spitting Out 10 Songs a Second, 13 May 2024, available at https://www.musicbusinessworldwide.com/the-train-has-left-the-station-ai-music-platform-udio-is-already-spitting/, accessed 27 August 2024.

Ingham, Tim, 38 Million Tracks on Music Streaming Services Were Played ZERO Times in 2022. (Or: Why Spotify Should Take a Leaf Out of Elon Musk's Book.), available at https://www.musicbusinessworldwide.com/38-million-tracks-on-music-streaming-service-were-played-zero-times-in-2022-elon-musks-book/, accessed 13 February 2025.

Jacobs, Jo Ellen, Identifying Musical Works of Art, 24(4) JAE (1990) https://doi.org/10.2307/3333108, accessed 9 August 2025.

Jackson, Roland, Performance Practice: A Dictionary-Guide for Musicians, Psychology Press, 2005.

Johnson, George, Undiscovered Bach? No, a Computer Wrote It, 11 November 1997, available at https://www.nytimes.com/1997/11/11/science/undiscovered-bach-no-a-computer-wrote-it.html, accessed 13 March 2025.

Jones, Jonathan, The Digital Rembrandt: A New Way to Mock Art, Made by Fools, available at https://www.theguardian.com/artanddesign/jonathanjonesblog/2016/apr/06/digital-rembrandt-mock-art-fools, accessed 12 February 2025.

Kalegasi, Bartu, A New AI Can Write Music as Well as a Human Composer, 3 September 2017, available at https://futurism.com/a-new-ai-can-write-music-as-well-as-a-human-composer, accessed 12 February 2025.

Karhu, Juha, Kohti 2000-luvun oikeuslähdeoppia, Lakimies 7-8/2020, pp. 1017-1034.

Karnell, Gunnar, European Originality: A Copyright Chimera, in Intellectual Property and Information Law: Essays in Honour of Herman Cohen Jehoram.Edited by G.J.H. Mom & J.J.C. Kabel, The Hague, Kluwer Law International, 1998, available at https://www.scandinavianlaw.se/pdf/42-5.pdf, accessed 12 February 2025.

Karnell, Gunnar, Rätten till programinnehållet i TV, Jurist- och samhällsvetareförbundet 1970, available at https://www.juridikbok.se/book/10945, accessed 12 February 2025.

Karnell, Gunnar, Verksbegrepp och upphovsrätt TfR 1968, pp. 401-441.

Keyes, Michael J., Musical Musings: The Case for Rethinking Music Copyright Protection, 10 Mich. Telecomm. & Tech. L. Rev. (2004), p. 407.

Khulman, Abigail, The Death of Art(ificial)istry, 2023, https://arizonastatelawjournal.org/2023/10/24/the-death-of-artificialistry/, accessed 13 February 2025.

Kim, David Hyun-Su, The Brahmsian Hairpin, 19th-Century Music, Vol. 36, No. 1, Summer 2012, pp. 46-57.

Kivistö, Martti, Tekijänoikeus omaisuutena: näkökulmia tekijänoikeuden yleisiin oppeihin, Lakimies 2/2017, pp. 222-229.

Kivy, Peter, On the Concept of the 'Historically Authentic' Performance, 71(2) The Monist, Aesthetics and the Histories of the Arts (April 1988), pp. 278-290 https://doi.org/10.5840/monist198871220, accessed 9 August 2025.

Kohler, Josef, Das literarische und artistische Kunstwerk und sein Autorschutz, 1892, available at https://books.google.fi/books/about/Das_literarische_und_artistisc he_Kunstwe.html?id=YXJclJ67grwC&redir_esc=y, accessed 12 February 2025.

Koktvedgaard, Mogens, Immaterialretspositioner, Juristforbundets forlag, 1965.

Kummer, Max, Das urheberrechtlich schützbare Werk, Bern, 1968.

Lahdelma, Imre and Eerola, Tuomas, Cultural Familiarity and Musical Expertise Impact the Pleasantness of Consonance/Dissonance But Not Its Perceived Tension, 10 Sci Rep (2020), p. 8693, https://doi.org/10.1038/s41598-020-65615-8, accessed 12 February 2025.

Lee, Edward, Prompting Progress: Authorship in the Age of AI, 76 Fla. L. Rev. (2024), p. 1445, available at https://www.floridalawreview.com/article/126449-promp ting-progress-authorship-in-the-age-of-ai, accessed 15 June 2025.

Lee, Edward and Moshirnia, Andrew, Do Experts Matter? A Study of the Effect of Musicologist Testimony in Music Cases, 2022(2) U. Ill. L. Rev. (2022), pp. 707-804.

Lee, Katherine, Cooper, Feder A. and Grimmelman, James, Talkin' 'Bout AI Generation': Copyright and the Generative-AI Supply Chain, J. Copyr. Soc. U.S.A. (Forthcoming 2024), available at https://arxiv.org/abs/2309.08133, accessed 25 March 2025.

Leistner, Matthias and Jussen, Rebecca, The Flattening of Creative Industries? A Closer Look at Copyright Protection of AI-Based Subject Matter, 2 January 2025, available at http://dx.doi.org/10.2139/ssrn.5080250, accessed 16 June 2025.

Lemley, Mark A., How Generative AI Turns Copyright Law Upside Down, 25 Colum. Sci. & Tech. L. Rev. (2024), p. 190 https://doi.org/10.52214/stlr.v25i2.12761, accessed 9 August 2025.

Lenemark, Richard, Högsta domstolen tar sig ton rörande musikplagiat: Kommentar till NJA 2002 s. 178, in Ur svensk rättspraxis, NIR 2022.

Levin, Marianne, Lärobok i immaterialrätt: upphovsrätt, patenträtt, mönsterrätt, känneteckensrätt, 13th ed., 2023.

Levinson, Jerrold, Music, Art, and Metaphysics, Ithaca, Cornell University Press 1990.

Lippman, Edward A., A Humanistic Philosophy of Music, New York, New York University Press, 2006.

Liu, Chengyuan et al., More Than Catastrophic Forgetting: Integrating General Capabilities for Domain-Specific LLMs, 2024, available at https://arxiv.org/abs/2405.17830, accessed 20 March 2025.

Liu, Xubo et al., Separate Anything You Describe, 2023, available at abs/2308.05037? > https://arxiv.org/abs/2308.05037, accessed 12 February 2025.

Lowe, Steven T. and Burroughs, Scott A., Consider the Grecian Urn: Why Prior Art Has No Place in Analyzing Substantial Similarity under the Copyright Act, 23 Chi.-Kent J. Intell. Prop. (2024), p. 110, available at: https://scholarship.kentlaw.iit.edu/ckjip/vol23/iss2/7, accessed 5 March 2025.

Lu, Bingbin A., Theory of 'Authorship Transfer' and Its Application to the Context of Artificial Intelligence Creations, 11 Queen Mary J. Intell. Prop. (February 2021), p. 2 https://doi.org/10.4337/qmjip.2021.01.01, accessed 9 August 2025.

Lund, Jamie, An Empirical Examination of the Lay Listener Test in Music Composition Copyright Infringement, 29 March 2012, available at https://ssrn.com/abstract=2030509, accessed 12 February 2025.

Luo, Yun et al., An Empirical Study of Catastrophic Forgetting in Large Language Models During Continual Fine-Tuning, 2023, available at https://arxiv.org/abs/2308.08747, accessed 13 February 2025.

Makkonen, Kaarle, Luentoja yleisestä oikeustieteestä. Helsingin yliopiston Yleisen oikeustieteen laitoksen julkaisuja 1998.

Machuron, Charles-Louis, AIVA: The Artificial Intelligence Composing Classical Music, October 2016, available at https://www.siliconluxembourg.lu/aiva-the-artificial-intelligence-composing-classical-music/, accessed 12 February 2025.

Mattila, Tuomas, Yhteistyö tekijänoikeudessa 2022.

Mezei, Péter, From Leonardo to the Next Rembrandt: The Need for AI-Pessimism in the Age of Algorithm, 2020, available at https://ssrn.com/abstract=3592187 or http://dx.doi.org/10.2139/ssrn.3592187, accessed 22 April 2025.

Mezei, Péter, From Strategy to Extremism: Greenwashing Generative AI, 2025, available at https://papers.ssrn.com/sol3/papers.cfm?abstract_id=5054033, accessed 22 April 2025.

Minkkinen, Panu, Oikeus- ja yhteiskuntatieteellinen tutkimus: suuntaus, tarkastelutapa, menetelmä?, Lakimies 7-8/2017, pp. 908-923.

Minsker, Evan, 'Blurred Lines' Appeal Gets Support From More Than 200 Musicians, available at https://pitchfork.com/news/67932-blurred-lines-appeal-gets-support-from-more-than-200-musicians/, accessed 12 February 2025.

Mylly, Ulla-Maija, Tekijänoikeuden omaperäisyyden harmonisointi Euroopan unionissa, Lakimies 6/2016, pp. 907-930.

Nierhaus, Gerhard, Algorithmic Composition: Paradigms of Automated Music Generation, Springer 1st ed., 2009.

Nolan, Beatrice, Google Researchers Say They Got OpenAI's ChatGPT to Reveal Some of Its Training Data with Just One Word, available at https://www.businessinsider.com/google-researchers-openai-chatgpt-to-reveal-its-training-data-study-2023-12, accessed 13 February 2025.

Nordell, Per J., Dubbelskapande i teori och praktik, NIR 4/1995.

Nordell, Per J., Rätten till det visuella, Stockholm, 1997, available at http://urn.kb.se/resolve?urn=urn:nbn:se:juridikbokse-f430e, accessed 14 March 2025.

Nordell, Per J., Upphovsrätten som ett jämförelseobjekt. Kommentar till Högsta domstolens dom NJA 2017, s. 75 (Svenska syndabockar), NIR 2017/3, pp. 303-313.

Norrgård, Marcus, Interimistiska förbud i immaterialrätten, Kauppakaari 2002.

Ouyang, Long et al., Training Language Models to Follow Instructions with Human Feedback, 35 Advances in Neural Information Processing Systems (2022), pp. 27730-27744, available at https://arxiv.org/abs/2203.02155, accessed 2 February 2025.

Palmer, Caroline, Music Performance, 48(1) Annu. Rev. Psychol. (1997), pp. 115-138 https://doi.org/10.1146/annurev.psych.48.1.115, accessed 9 August 2025.

Pasquier, Philippe et al., An Introduction to Musical Metacreation, 14(2) CIE (2017), Article No. 2, pp. 1-14 https://doi.org/10.1145/2930672, accessed 9 August 2025.

Peczenik, Aleksander, Vad är rätt? Fritzes 1995.

Phillips, Fiona and Rotstein, Fiona (eds), Intellectual Property Forum Issue 123, March 2021, available at https://www.wilmerhale.com/-/media/files/shared_content/editorial/publications/documents/20210316-ipsanz-intellectual-property-forum-issue-123-march-2021.pdf, accessed 12 February 2025.

Pickett-Groen, Nicole, The Next Rembrandt: Bringing the Old Master Back to Life, 24 January 2018, available at https://medium.com/@DutchDigital/the-next-rembrandt-bringing-the-old-master-back-to-life-35dfb1653597, accessed 13 March 2025.

Pihlajarinne, Taina, Teoskappaleen valmistus: tekijänoikeuden yleisten oppien koetinkivi? Lakimies 7–8/2013, pp. 1217–1233.

Pihlajarinne, Taina, Eurooppalaisen tuomioistuinkäytännön hyödyntäminen immateriaalioikeuden tutkimuksessa, Lakimies 4/2012, pp. 547–558.

Plaugic, Lizzie, Musician Taryn Southern on Composing Her New Album Entirely with AI, 27 August 2017 available at https://www.theverge.com/2017/8/27/16197196/taryn-southern-album-artificial-intelligence-interview, accessed 12 February 2025.

Quintais, João P., Generative AI, Copyright and the AI Act, 56 CLSR (April 2025), p. 106107, available at https://doi.org/10.1016/j.clsr.2025.106107, accessed 13.3.2025.

Rafaeli, J.S., I'm a Human Man Being Sued by a Monkey, available at https://www.vice.com/en/article/3knmnv/im-a-human-man-being-sued-by-a-monkey, accessed 12 February 2025.

Rahmatian, Andreas, Concepts of Music and Copyright: How Music Perceives Itself and How Copyright Perceives Music, Edward Elgar 2015.

Rahmatian, Andreas, European Copyright Inside or Outside the European Union: Pluralism of Copyright Laws and the 'Herderian paradox', 47(8) International Review of Intellectual Property and Competition Law (2016), pp. 912-940 https://doi:10.1007/s40319-016-0531-4, accessed 9 August 2025.

Rahmatian, Andreas, The Musical Work in Copyright Law, 73(1) GRUR Int. (2024), pp. 18-33 https://doi.org/10.1093/grurint/ikad105, accessed 9 August 2025.

Rahmatian, Andreas, Originality in UK Copyright Law: The Old 'Skill and Labour' Doctrine Under Pressure, 44 IIC (2013), pp. 4–34 available at https://doi.org/10.1007/s40319-012-0003-4, accessed 16 March 2025.

Ramalho, Ana, Intellectual Property Protection for AI-generated Creations: Europe, United States, Australia and Japan, Routledge, 2021.

Ramponi, Marco, What AI Music Generators Can Do (And How They Do It), 2023, available at https://www.assemblyai.com/blog/what-ai-music-generators-can-do-and-how-they-do-it/, accessed 11 February 2025.

Reybrouck, Mark, Podlipniak, Piotr and Welch, David, Music and Noise: Same or Different? What Our Body Tells Us, 10 Front. Psychol. (2019), p. 1153.

Richter, Goetz, Composers Are under No Threat from AI, If Huawei's Finished Schubert Symphony Is a guide, available at https://theconversation.com/composers-are-under-no-threat-from-ai-if-huaweis-finished-schubert-symphony-is-a-guide-111630, accessed 12 February 2025.

Richman, Bruce, 'How Music Fixed 'Nonsense' into Significant Formulas' in Wallin, N.L., Merker, B. and Brown, S. (eds) The Origins of Music, The MIT Press, 2000.

Ricketson, Sam, The 1992 Horace S. Manges Lecture: People or Machines: The Bern Convention and the Changing Concept of Authorship, 16 Colum.-VLA J.L. & Arts (1991), p. 1.

Rink, John, The Line of Argument in Chopin's E Minor Prelude, 29(3) Early Music (3 August 2001) https://doi.org/10.1093/em/29.3.435, accessed 9 August 2025.

Ritchie, Stanley, Authentic Reconstruction of Musical Performance: History and Influence, 28(3) TDR (Autumn 1984) https://doi.org/10.2307/1145627, accessed 9 August 2025.

Roederer, Juan G., The Physics and Psychophysics of Music, Springer, 4th ed. 2008.

Rognstad, Ole-Andreas, Creations Caused by Humans (or Robots)? Artificial Intelligence and Causation Requirements for Copyright Protection in EU Law, in Pihlajarinne, T.A. and Alén-Savikko, A. (eds), Artificial Intelligence and the Media, Edward Elgar, 2022.

Rognstad, Ole-Andreas, Copyright Protection for Output Resulting from Use of Generative AI Systems: Some Reflections, Nordiskt Immateriellt Rättsskydd, 2025/1, pp. 134-144.

Rosati, Eleonora, Copyright at the CJEU: Back to the Start (of Copyright Protection), in Bosher, R. (ed.), Developments and Directions in Intellectual Property Law: 20 Years of The IPKat, Oxford University Press, 2023.

Rosati, Eleonora, The Levola Hengelo CJEU Decision: Ambiguities, Uncertainties ... and More Questions, 2018, available at https://ipkitten.blogspot.com/2018/11/the-levola-hengelo-cjeu-decision.html, accessed 12 February 2025.

Rosati, Eleonora, The Monkey Selfie case and the Concept of Authorship: An EU Perspective, 12(12) JIPLP (December 2017), pp. 973-977 https://doi.org/10.1093/jiplp/jpx199, accessed 9 August 2025.

Rosati, Eleonora, Infringing AI: Liability for AI-Generated Outputs under International, EU, and UK Copyright Law, 16(2) Eur. J. Risk Regul. (June 2025), pp. 603-627.

Rosenmeier, Morten, Værkslæren i ophavsretten, Jurist- og Økonomforbundets Forlag, 2001.

Ross, Alf, Ophavsrettens Grundbegreber, TfR 1945, pp. 321–353.

Rouard, Simon, Massa, Francisco and Défossez, Alexandre, Hybrid Transformers for Music Source Separation, 2022, available at https://arxiv.org/abs/2211.08553, accessed 12 February 2025.

Russell, Stuart J. and Norvig, Peter, Artificial Intelligence: A Modern Approach, Pearson Education, 3rd ed. 2010.

Sag, Matthew, Copyright Safety for Generative AI, 61(2) Hous. L. Rev. (2023), pp. 295-348.

Samuelson, Pamela, Allocating Ownership Rights in Computer-Generated Works, 47 U. Pitt. L. Rev. (1985) pp. 1185-1228, available at https://lawcat.berkeley.edu/record/1112407?v=pdf, accessed 19 February 2025.

San Roman, Robin et al., From Discrete Tokens to High-Fidelity Audio Using Multi-Band Diffusion, 2023, available at https://arxiv.org/abs/2308.02560, accessed 12 February 2025.

Schovsbo, Jens, Copyright and Design Law: What Is Left after All and Cofemel? – Or: Design Law in a 'Double Whammy', 14 January 2020, available at http://dx.doi.org/10.2139/ssrn.3519156, accessed 12 February 2025.

Schovsbo, Jens, Rosenmeier, Morten and Petersen, Clement Salung, Immaterialret, 7th ed., 2024.

Seaver, Nick, Knowing Algorithms, in Vertesi, J. and Ribes, D. (eds), digitalSTS: A Field Guide for Science & Technology Studies, Princeton University Press, 2019.

Selznick, Philip, 'Law in Context' Revisited, 30(2) J. Law Soc. (June 2003) https://doi.org/10.1111/1467-6478.00252, accessed 9 August 2025.

Senftleben, Martin, Generative AI and Author Remuneration, 54 IIC (2023), pp. 1535–1560 https://doi.org/10.1007/s40319-023-01399-4, accessed 9 August 2025.

Senftleben, Martin and Buijtelaar, Laurens, Robot Creativity: An Incentive-Based Neighbouring Rights Approach, 42(12) E.I.P.R. (2020), pp. 797-812.

Senn, Olivier, Kilchenmann, Lorenz and Camp, Marc-Antoine, Expressive Timing: Martha Argerich Plays Chopin's Prelude Op. 28/4 in E minor, International Symposium on Performance Science 2009, available at https://www.researchgate.net/publication/268214618_Expressive_timing_Martha_Argerich_plays_Chopin's_Prelude_op_284_in_E_minor, accessed 12 February 2025.

Sganga, Caterina, The Notion of 'Work' in EU Copyright Law after Levola Hengelo: One Answer Given, Three Question Marks Ahead, Eur. Intell. Prop. Rev., Forthcoming, 15 December 2018, available at https://ssrn.com/abstract=3323011, accessed 12 February 2025.

Sganga, Caterina, Say Nay to a Tastier Copyright: Why the CJEU Should Deny Copyright Protection for Taste (and Smells), 14(3) JIPLP (March 2019), pp. 187–196 https://doi.org/10.1093/jiplp/jpy161, accessed 9 August 2025.

Sganga, Caterina, Is There Still a Policy Agenda for EU Copyright Law?, IIC – online first on 1 August 2023, Forthcoming, available https://ssrn.com/abstract=4579413, accessed 13 February 2025.

Siltala, Raimo, Oikeustieteen tieteenteoria, Suomalainen Lakimiesyhdistys 2003.

Smits, Jan M., What Is Legal Doctrine? On the Aims and Methods of Legal-Dogmatic Research, in van Gestel, R., Micklitz, H.-W. and Rubin, E.L. (eds), Rethinking Legal Scholarship: A Transatlantic Dialogue, New York, Cambridge University Press, 2017.

Snyder, Francis, Law in Context: A Personal Roadmap, Cahiers de méthodologie juridique, No. 38, 2024.

Sobel, Benjamin, A Taxonomy of Training Data in Artificial Intelligence and Intellectual Property, Lee, J.-A., Hilty, R.M. and Liu, K. (eds), Oxford University Press, 2021.

Sobel, Benjamin, Elements of Style: Copyright, Similarity, and Generative AI, 38 Harv. J.L. & Tech., Forthcoming (18 May 2024) Cornell Legal Studies Research Paper Forthcoming, available at https://ssrn.com/abstract=4832872, accessed 4 March 2025.

Sorvari, Katariina, Vastuu tekijänoikeuden loukkauksesta: erityisesti tietoverkkoympäristössä, Alma verkkokirjahylly 2005.

Sousa e Silva, Nuno, The Boundaries of EU Copyright Law: Cheese, Jeans and a Military Report in the Court of Justice, iii(1) M&CLR (April 2019).

Stamatoudi, Irini A., Originality under EU Copyright, in Torremans, P. (ed.), Research Handbook on Copyright Law, Edward Elgar, 2nd ed. 2017.

Steel, Emma, Original Sin: Reconciling Originality in Copyright with Music as an Evolutionary Art Form, 37(2) E.I.P.R. (2015), pp. 66-80.

Strömholm, Stig, Upphovsrättens verksbegrepp, Norstedt 1970, available at https://www.juridikbok.se/book/400617, accessed 12 February 2025.

Strömholm, Stig, Rätt, rättskällor och rättstillämpning: en lärobok i allmän rättslära, Norstedt 1981.

Strömholm, Stig, Användning av utländskt material i juridiska monografier, SvJT 1971, pp. 251-263.

Sturm, Bob L.T. et al., Artificial Intelligence and Music: Open Questions of Copyright Law and Engineering Praxis, 8(3) Arts (2019), p. 115, available at https://doi.org/10.3390/arts8030115, accessed 13 February 2025.

Synodinou, Tatiana-Eleni, The Foundations of the Concept of Work in European Copyright Law in Synodinou, T. (ed.), 'Codification of European Copyright, Challenges and Perspectives', The Hague, Kluwer Law International, 30 January

2012, pp. 93-113, 2012, available at https://ssrn.com/abstract=3589121, accessed 12 February 2025.

Synodinou, Tatiana-Eleni, The Desirability of Unification of European Copyright Law, in Rosati (ed.), The Routledge Handbook of EU Copyright Law, 2021.

Thesleff, Alexander, Teoskynnyksen ylittyminen vai teoksena pitäminen?, IPR Info Publication 3/2024, available at https://iprinfo.fi/artikkeli/teoskynnyksen-ylittyminen-vai-teoksena-pitaminen/, accessed 12 February 2025.

Tickle, Glen, Daddy's Car, a Song Composed by Artificial Intelligence Created to Sound Like the Beatles, available at https://laughingsquid.com/daddys-car-a-song-composed-by-artificial-intelligence-created-to-sound-like-the-beatles/, accessed 12 February 2025.

Tolonen, Hannu, Oikeuslähdeoppi, WSOY, 2003.

Tuori, Kaarlo, Kriittinen oikeuspositivismi. WSOY, Helsinki, 2000.

Tuori, Kaarlo, Oikeusjärjestys ja oikeudelliset käytännöt, Helsinki, Forum Iuris, 2013.

van Eechoud, Mireille et al., Harmonizing European Copyright Law, Kluwer Law International 2009.

van Eechoud, Mireille, Along the Road to Uniformity: Diverse Readings of the Court of Justice Judgments on Copyright Works, 2012, available at https://dare.uva.nl/search?identifier=535b93e3-cbfd-4747-85ea-de0a326a3ffd, accessed 12 February 2025.

Vainikka, Eliisa, Soronen, Anne and Kallio, Saara-Maija, Is Prompt Engineering the Future of Screenwriting? Views of Professional Screenwriters and Commissioners About the Impact of AI Technologies on Their Profession, 0(0) CST: The International Journal of Television Studies (2024), pp. 1-19 https://doi.org/10.1177/17496020241269277, accessed 9 August 2025.

van Hoecke, Mark, Deep Level Comparative Law, EUI Working Paper Law No. 2002/13, available at https://cadmus.eui.eu/bitstream/handle/1814/191/law02-13.pdf, accessed 6 March 2025.

van Gompel, Stef, Creativity, Autonomy and Personal Touch: A Critical Appraisal of the CJEU's Originality Test for Copyright, in van Eechoud, M. (ed.), The Work of Authorship, Amsterdam University Press, 2014, pp. 95-143.

van Gompel, Stef and Lavik, Erlend, Quality, Merit, Aesthetics and Purpose: An Inquiry into EU Copyright Law's Eschewal of Other Criteria than Originality (September 16, 2013), Revue Internationale du Droit d'Auteur (RIDA), No. 236 (April 2013), pp. 100-295, available at SSRN: https://ssrn.com/abstract=2326425, accessed 2 February 2025.

Vaswani, Ashish et al., Attention Is All You Need, available at https://arxiv.org/abs/1706.03762, accessed 11 February 2025.

Vaver, David, Principles of Copyright Law, WIPO Publication No. 844(A/E/F), 2002.

Veltman, Chloe, Google's Latest AI Music Tool Creates Tracks Using Famous Singers' Voice Clones, 17 November 2023, available at https://www.npr.org/2023/11/17/1213551049/googles-latest-ai-music-tool-creates-tracks-using-famous-singers-voice-clones, accessed 12 February 2025.

Walker, Stephen M.II, Supervised Fine-Tuning (SFT), available at https://klu.ai/glossary/supervised-fine-tuning, accessed 11 February 2025.

Wang, Yihan et al., Two-Stage LLM Fine-Tuning with Less Specialization and More Generalization, 2022, https://arxiv.org/abs/2211.00635, accessed 13 February 2025.

Weckström, Katja, A Contextual Approach to Limits in EU Trade Mark Law, Oy Nord Print Ab, 2011.

Wilhelmsson, Thomas, Siviilioikeuden hiipivä eurooppalaistuminen ja Suomen oikeuslähdeoppi, Lakimies 7-8/2020, pp. 1172-1196.

Wilhelmsson, Thomas, Den nordiska rättsvetenskapens metoder och fri digital rörlighet av rättsliga idéer inom EU, Juiridisk Tidskrift Nr 1 2019/20, pp. 112-136.

Wilson, Conrad, Notes on Bach: 20 Crucial Works, Eerdmans Pub Co 2005.

Wininger, Aaron, Chinese Court Again Rules AI-Generated Images Are Eligible for Copyright Protection, 2025, available at https://www.chinaiplawupdate.com/2025/03/chinese-court-again-rules-there-is-copyright-in-ai-generated-images/, accessed 14 June 2025.

Ylikallio, Anton, Musikalisk sampling som användarrätt enligt EU-rätten, Nordiskt Immateriellt Rättsskydd, 3/2021, pp. 249-273.

Zeghidour, Neil et al., SoundStream: An End-to-End Neural Audio Codec, 2021, available at https://arxiv.org/abs/2107.03312, accessed 12 February 2025.

Web Resources Without Credited Authors

An A.I. Hit of Fake 'Drake' and 'The Weeknd' Rattles the Music World, available at https://www.nytimes.com/2023/04/19/arts/music/ai-drake-the-weeknd-fake.html, accessed 12 February 2025.

Amici Brief Katy Perry, available at https://www.digitalmusicnews.com/wp-content/uploads/2020/01/Katy_Perry_Flame_514_Amici_Brief_Filed.pdf, accessed 12 February 2025.

Beethoven's 10th Symphony Completed by AI. This Is How It Sounds, available at https://www.telekom.com/en/media/media-information/archive/beethoven-s-10th-symphony-completed-by-ai-633060, accessed 12 February 2025.

CISAC, Global Economic Study Shows Human Creators' Future at Risk from Generative AI, available at https://www.cisac.org/Newsroom/news-releases/global-economic-study-shows-human-creators-future-risk-generative-ai, accessed 4 March 2025.

David Slater's Webpage, available at http://www.djsphotography.co.uk/original_story.html, accessed 12 February 2025.

DeepBach Uses 'Deep Learning' to Create Music in the Style of Bach, available at https://www.synthtopia.com/content/2016/12/22/deepbach-uses-deep-learning-to-create-music-in-the-style-of-bach/, accessed 12 February 2025.

Ed Sheeran Statement in Response to His Victory in the UK High Court, available at https://www.instagram.com/p/CcANzfhjaHL/, accessed 12 February 2025.

Encyclopedia Britannica, available at https://www.britannica.com/art/music, accessed 29 September 2024.

'Few-Shot Prompting', available at https://www.promptingguide.ai/techniques/fewshot, accessed 11 February 2025.

Folk-Pop Track Direct Link, available at https://google-research.github.io/seanet/musiclm/rlhf/audio_samples/musicrlhf-ru-0.wav, accessed 13 February 2025.
McKinsey Assessment of the Economic Potential of Generative AI, available at https://www.mckinsey.com/capabilities/mckinsey-digital/our-insights/the-economic-potential-of-generative-ai-the-next-productivity-frontier#business-value, accessed 13 February 2025.
Nearly 80% of Artists on Spotify Have Fewer Than 50 Monthly Listeners, available at https://www.musicbusinessworldwide.com/over-75-of-artists-on-spotify-have-fewer-than-50-monthly-listeners/, accessed 13 February 2025.
Petrucci Music Library, available at https://imslp.org/, accessed 12 February 2025.
Samsung Unveils New AI-Powered Smartphone in Fight Against Apple, available at https://www.ft.com/content/e8a403b0-0bdb-455b-b083-ef3ef50bc473, accessed 12 February 2025.
The 'Blurred Lines' Case Scared Songwriters. But Its Time May Be Up, available at https://www.nytimes.com/2020/03/24/arts/music/blurred-lines-led-zeppelin-copyright.html, accessed 12 February 2025.
The Sibelius Academy's Teaching Materials on Music Analysis, available at https://web.uniarts.fi/aleatori/indexcc6d.html?id = 302&la = fi, accessed 13 February 2025.
TikTok Owner Bytedance Buys AI Music Company Jukedeck, available at https://www.musicbusinessworldwide.com/tiktok-parent-bytedance-buys-ai-music-company-jukedeck/, accessed 12 February 2025.
Transforming the Future of Music Creation, available at https://deepmind.google/discover/blog/transforming-the-future-of-music-creation/, accessed 12 February 2025.
Web Resource (Dark Sanctuary v. Bushido), available at https://blogs.law.gwu.edu/mcir/case/dark-sanctuary-v-bushido/, accessed 12 February 2025.
https://aws.amazon.com/deepcomposer/, accessed 12 February 2025.
https://dictionary.cambridge.org/dictionary/english/music, accessed 12 February 2025.
https://en.wikipedia.org/wiki/Fountain_(Duchamp), accessed 12 February 2025.
https://www.flow-machines.com/, accessed 12 February 2025.
https://github.com/magenta/magenta, accessed 12 February 2025.
https://google-research.github.io/seanet/audiolm/examples/, accessed 12 February 2025.
https://google-research.github.io/seanet/musiclm/examples/, accessed 12 February 2025.
https://www.ibm.com/blogs/think/nl-en/2017/06/06/intro-watson-music/, accessed 12 February 2025.
https://investor.shutterstock.com/news-releases/news-release-details/shutterstock-announces-acquisition-amper-music, accessed 12 February 2025.
https://www.merriam-webster.com/dictionary/music, accessed 12 February 2025.
https://openai.com/index/jukebox/, accessed 12 February 2025.
https://openai.com/index/musenet/, accessed 12 February 2025.
https://suno.com/home, accessed 12 February 2025.

https://wikisource.org/wiki/Prelude_in_E_minor,_Op._28,_No._4_%28Chopin %29, accessed 12 February 2025.

https://x.com/udiomusic/status/1805694761891778783?s = 46&t = R5LBnDmluUM1q 9hD0liYVg&mx = 2, accessed 2 February 2025.

YouTube Links

Bach Style Chorale Emmy David Cope: https://www.youtube.com/watch?v = PczDLl 92vlc, accessed 11 February 2025.

Can You Tell the Difference Between AI and Human Composers?: https://www.yout ube.com/watch?v = PmL31mVx0XA&t = 331s, accessed 12 February 2025.

Jukedeck Demo: Create Unique Music for Your Videos in Seconds, https://www.you tube.com/watch?v = jfs1k7krXt8&t = 51s, accessed 12 February 2025.

The Bach Effect: What the GREATS Hear That You Don't: https://www.youtube.com /watch?v = UNgrH8u-IIc, accessed 12 February 2025.

DeepBach: Harmonization in the Style of Bach Generated Using Deep Learning: https://www.youtube.com/watch?v = QiBM7-5hA6o, accessed 12 February 2025.

Franz Schubert: Symphony No. 8 in B minor, D.759 ('Unfinished') Finalized by Artificial intelligence: https://www.youtube.com/watch?v = _6OUGRsslJY, accessed 12 February 2025.

Beethoven X: The AI Project: Complete (Bonn Orchestra): https://www.youtube.com /watch?v = Rvj3Oblscqw&t = 158s, accessed 12 February 2025.

Break Free: The First AI-Composed Pop Song | Lyrics by Taryn Southern: https:// www.youtube.com/watch?v = XUs6CznN8pw, accessed 12 February 2025.

MusicLM Generates Music from Text [Paper Breakdown]: https://www.youtube.com /watch?v = eaqO5uT0G9Q&t = 1209s, accessed 12 February 2025.

Introducing Music AI Tools: Louis Bell, Producer/Songwriter, Builds a Track with Just a Hum: https://www.youtube.com/watch?v = aeYU3_7IKCM&t = 19s, accessed 12 February 2025.

The Emerging AI Revolution in Music | Jesse Josefsson: https://www.youtube.com/ watch?v = v4m_A8JxUZs&t = 1895s, accessed 12 February 2025.

Transformers Explained Easily: Part 2 – Generative Music AI: https://www.youtube. com/watch?v = ctbvMnbylsA&list = PL-wATfeyAMNqAPjwGT3ikEz3gMo23pl-D &index = 19, accessed 12 February 2025.

The Transformative Power of Classical Music | Benjamin Zander | TED: https://www .youtube.com/watch?v = r9LCwI5iErE, accessed 12 February 2025.

Dolly Parton – I Will Always Love You (Audio): https://www.youtube.com/watch?v = lKsQR72HY0s, accessed 12 February 2025.

Whitney Houston – I Will Always Love You (Official 4K Video): https://www.youtub e.com/watch?v = 3JWTaaS7LdU&list = RD3JWTaaS7LdU&start_radio = 1, accessed 12 February 2025.

4 Chords | Music Videos | The Axis of Awesome: https://www.youtube.com/watch? v = oOlDewpCfZQ, accessed 12 February 2025.

Why the Katy Perry/Flame Lawsuit Makes No Sense: https://www.youtube.com/wa tch?v = 0ytoUuO-qvg, accessed 12 February 2025.

Les Mémoires Blessées: https://www.youtube.com/watch?v=O8lo9S55wSI, accessed 12 February 2025.
Fan Made:Tala Om Vart Du Ska Resa – Landslaget: https://www.youtube.com/watch?v=8XS1Fb0wPLI, accessed 12 February 2025.
Vill du bli min fru Drängarna: https://www.youtube.com/watch?v=OTZxtUxdoSc, accessed 9 August 2025.
This Midjourney Technique Will Put You in the Top 1%: https://www.youtube.com/watch?v=DjXx694Ddxw, accessed 13 February 2025.

Index

www.ingramcontent.com/pod-product-compliance
Ingram Content Group UK Ltd.
Pitfield, Milton Keynes, MK11 3LW, UK
UKHW020245290926
15470UKWH00002B/757